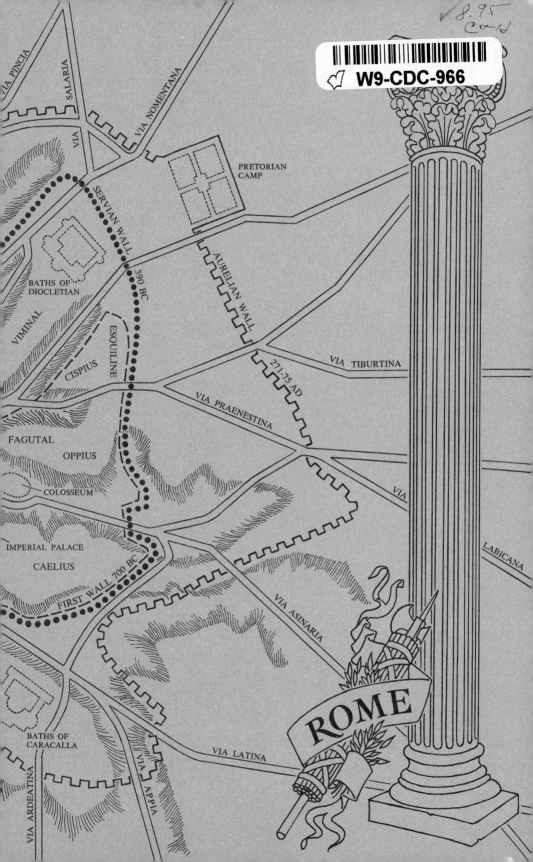

ROME

ROME

MAURICE ANDRIEUX

ROME

Translated by Charles Lam Markmann

FUNK & WAGNALLS, NEW YORK

TO MY FRIEND

Noël Pinelli,

WHO KNOWS AND LOVES

OLD ROME

"The only city common to all and universal! It is the capital of all the Christian nations; there every man is at home."

—MONTAIGNE

CONTENTS

FOREWORD

All roads, it is said, lead to Rome, and, in the end, they lead almost everyone there; no city in the world or in history has held more fascination for men's minds or stirred more emotion in their hearts. For the history of civilization was acted out in the hollows among its hills. Rome is the summit "whence all has come, whence all has gone." It is the mother and the inspiration of all peoples, but none more than the French has been nourished and enriched by this heritage. It is the key to our history. It was Rome that sketched the first outline of France; it is the composite of the ideas and the institutions with which Rome endowed us that has saved us from succumbing to the agonies of invasions. Our customs and our tastes, our way of living, our ways of thinking and feeling were fashioned in the school of Romanness and in the breath of its spirit. It is to Rome that we owe our religion, our language, and the best of our laws. The Roman spirit is infused in us in such a manner that it has been possible to say that, if we were deprived of the moral tendencies that flow from it, there would be virtually nothing French left to us.

The history of Rome is therefore a family history for us. Unfortunately it is to be found only distributed in a great number of books. There have been thousands of them on the antiquities, the conquests, the annals of Rome. Many scholars have measured the ruins of Rome, described the palaces and the churches. Every pope has had his biographer. There is not an episode in the thirty centuries of Rome's history that has not been examined in detail a hundred times. But the traveler who sets out "in the direction of Rome," as Stendhal said, cannot burden himself with so many books on art, on literature, and on history. Yet Rome is not one of those cities that strike the traveler at first sight. Its antiquity has been given back to us only in installments; in the course of the centuries its churches have been rebuilt, restored, rejuvenated; the topography of the city has been altered. In order to understand Rome an introduction is essential; without it there is the danger of "seeing a beautiful fresco as only a fragment of blackened wall." And how can the need be satisfied by "guides" that offer only a very dry erudition? After one has consulted them, one knows the need for other conversation.

It is this desire of the mind that we have sought to fulfill. This book was born of the regret that we so often felt, when in Rome, because it had not been written. Its purpose is to tell the story of the Eternal City without turning up our noses at its legends, but in such a way that the structure of events should emerge as clearly as possible. It is our ambition to give curious minds a means of situating in time the ruins, the monuments, and the works of art in such fashion that without further research they can be utilized as milestones or reference marks of history. We have borne in mind the advice of Thiers: "In history one must always say: 'The scene takes place . . .'"

No one could remain an indifferent spectator before the monuments of Rome and its great ruins. In a city where everything that occurred has acquired a universal echo there is not a stone that does not offer precious information and that cannot be used in the building of history. But one must know how to question it. When and how were these monuments built or destroyed or mutilated? What events, what manners, what customs suggested their construction, compelled their alteration or caused their ruin? And what was the life of the men who erected these walls, reared these domes into the air, built these churches and these palaces, painted or carved the works of art that adorn them? These are all questions to which we hope that the answers will be found in the course of a narrative that we shall dedicate ourselves to keeping close to Roman life in order to make for better understanding of the works that arose out of that life.

In other words, we intend to restrict this study of Rome to its metropolitan and, in a way, intimate history. Rome has always been great within its walls. It is there that we wish to see the genius of a people live and endure. We shall not follow the conquerors along the world's roads that they marked with their feats and their efforts. We shall wait for the tide of war to carry invaders or subject peoples to the foot of the Capitol. All the races of the world in their turn arrived there, just as almost all the great men of history, superb or shamed, have made their appearance there. It is within the circle of the immortal hills that we shall watch the succession of the eras and the traces that they have left.

We have no illusion that, considered from this point of view, the history of Rome will shine in a new light. We have no ambition other than to make it accessible and familiar. It is our hope, too, to offer the nourishment of recollection to the general and tender nostalgia with which everyone who has ever truly breathed its perfume leaves Rome.

It will be immediately clear to the reader that we could not have relied on our own resources alone for all that makes up this book and that we have had to labor in the illumination of many authors. Like Montaigne we are obliged to say: "All that I have done here was to make a collection of foreign flowers, having added nothing of mine save the cord to bind them." The bibliographical sources of this book are so many that we have been obliged to sacrifice the idea of listing in their totality the works that have been of help. It is possible that certain borrowings from them have not been precisely identified. We hope that such involuntary omissions may be graciously forgiven.

PART ONE

ANCIENT ROME

CHAPTER 1

THE ERA OF THE KINGS

THE ORIGINS

Once upon a time. . . . Why should a history of Rome begin differently from a fairy tale? Is it not one? A man—a simple shepherd or a king's son—took his plowshare and traced on a barren hillside the outline of a city, and that city became the master of the world. It is understandable that so prodigious an adventure should have given rise to a world of fables and legends. These caprices of popular imagination, put into the form of heroic tales by the ancient authors, represent the whole of our information on the origin of the Eternal City and the early ages of its life. It is in vain that modern science has subjected the tales and the myths to the crucible of its disciplines: the childhood of Rome remains the domain of hypothesis and fiction.

This does not mean that efforts should be abandoned to understand the foundation and development of those puny villages that were to build the most powerful empire that the world has known. It would be an act of genuine desperation to reject *in toto* everything that has been handed down to us by a tradition so well established over the centuries that it has become almost a national epic. This is all the more the case because, rid of its divagations, that tradition has some possibility of representing, as it were, a simplified and schematized truth.

Whether the date of the foundation of Rome is set in 753 B.C., as

3

tradition would indicate, or two centuries earlier, to accord with the opinion of archeologists, it is certain that in those distant days the region that the city occupies today was not entirely deserted. The Palatine has yielded traces of a village that antedates the time of Romulus, and there is ground to believe that each of the hills along the Tiber had a rudimentary history of its own before the story of Rome began. But, if a race of shepherds sought shelter for its flocks on those summits, these could have been only primitive settlements where men had to fight wolves for possession. Pulled back into their citadel in the Alban Hills, the Latins had not yet attempted permanent colonization in an area whose physical character made it so inhospitable.

The Latin bank of the Tiber was in fact a maze of swamps and forests. The river often flooded it, in a fashion that is easy to picture when one sees the records of its crest levels etched in the façade of the Minerva church.* As late as the nineteenth century, they often turned the Pantheon square into a lake, and Pietro Bernini's *Barcaccia* recalls the greatest of the floods, which made it possible to cross the Piazza di Spagna by boat. The Tiber has never had that charming aspect that the Latin poets have ascribed to it with an amazing flattery. And even today it has nothing of the *"caeruleus Thybris"* of which Virgil sang. Its swift, swirling current, its roiled, muddied waters give it the stern appearance that fits its destiny. Little imagination is needed to picture the fierce aspect that it must have had when, still an untamed stream rushing out of the forests, it poured its waters over the deserted banks.

When it fell back within its bed, the vast Velabrian marshes from the Palatine to the Quirinal and the Capitoline retained a moisture that made the soil spongy and fostered the growth of a disordered vegetation of willows and reeds. The mists that rose from it covered the whole area with a veil (Velarium) that furnished the name for the swamp on which Rome was built, thus fulfilling the legendary prophecy that predicted the erection of the world's magnificent capital out of a slough. The area has long since been drained, but the waters that supplied it can still be seen welling up out of a dark, moss-carpeted tunnel near the Church of St. George, itself full of dampness and mildew. No more is needed, in these relatively unfrequented parts, to evoke the smell of the ancient marsh and the time when the region was only the solitude of which Livy speaks and where the early life of Rome's first king was situated.

* Santa Maria sopra Minerva. Italian names of persons and places are used only when they are better known abroad under these names than under translated names.

This savage wilderness was dominated by wooded hills whose appearance and number have been altered by time.* Their slopes were once sharper; the valleys that surrounded them were deeper. It was on one of these hills that the miraculous adventure of Rome was to begin. It was the smallest of them, but the best in terms of strategic advantages; its position appointed its destiny. The foundation of a city on this precipitous site was indeed no random phenomenon: it satisfied an imperative concern with safety. Originating in the Orient, the Etruscans, who had already subdued Tuscany and Umbria, had just appeared at the Tiber, facing Latium with the tragic threat of invasion. In order to meet this danger, the Latin Confederation, which had been led by Alba for three hundred years, undertook the defense of its natural boundary by establishing an outpost for observation and resistance at the point that was easiest to reach—that is, where an island in the Tiber made the crossing less difficult. There was a string of heights that could make an invaluable first line of defense. One of them, the Palatine, directly dominated the river at its most vulnerable point. This hill was therefore assigned to serve as the advance outpost of the Latin world. At its summit, where the flocks grazed, there was already the embryo of a village. It was essential to populate it with men who could subsist there by their own labors and act as its garrison. Those who had been banished from their tribes for their crimes or through family quarrels were recruited for the task. Fugitives were assured of asylum there and were guaranteed religious protection by the erection of a wall that it was sacrilege to scale.

THE REMNANTS OF ROME'S FIRST ERA

Was this wall the work of Romulus? Was Romulus a simple shepherd for the Alban kings, or was he the grandson of one of them, assigned by them to construct an outpost for defense? Roman pride enveloped him in the glories of legend, even to the point of imputing divine ancestry to him. Tradition links his name to the primitive compound of which many very

---

* Today there are eleven hills on the perimeter of Rome, eight of them on the right bank (Pincio, Quirinal, Esquiline, Viminal, Caelius, Palatine, Aventine, and Capitoline) and three on the left bank (Janiculum, Monte Mario, and Vatican). Within the city there are hillocks that have been created by the accumulation of ruins and other matter of all kinds; each is called a *monte* even though their modest elevations hardly justify the word: Monte Giordano, Monte Cinto, Monte Citorio, Testaccio.

damaged fragments were discovered by the nineteenth-century excavations (the most important is behind the round church of St. Theodore and the best preserved is at the southwest corner of the Palatine). But here archeology gives the lie to legend: the wall called Romulus' is closer to the end of the Etruscan kingdom than to the beginnings of Rome. This proof is no bar to the possibility that the first boundary of Palatine Rome was drawn by Romulus in the form of a single fortified trench or a rustic wall that the Etruscan kings replaced with a less primitive defense. This was the compound of Roma Quadrata: its shape was that whose broad outline was perpetuated by the prescribed plan of the Roman military camp.

But it is not possible to connect with Romulus that black stone (*lapis Niger*) found in 1899 in the Forum at the edge of the Comitium, which some have tried to portray as the divine shepherd's cenotaph or even his tomb. Aside from the fact that the black paving that has given its name to the whole does not go back beyond the sixth century A.D., the much more antique monument that it covers does not appear to have been of funeral intent. The ancient relics that have been found there (offerings, bits of pottery, and small statues) were not lying in chronological layers, a fact that leads to the supposition that, brought from other areas, they were tossed down here as fill. In short, this mysterious construction cannot be considered the tomb of the Eternal City's founder without conflict with Roman tradition, which says that its first hero vanished from the Field of Mars in the black clouds of a tempest in order to join the ranks of the gods. Nor does any of the old texts speak of any recollection of a grave of Romulus. If they had even thought that it might exist, Romans of every age would have continued to venerate it and it would not have been left for so many centuries in oblivion.

In sum, no remains, even in ruins, have been found that can be called authentic evidences of the life of Romulus. There is no trace of the hut in which he is supposed to have lived, that Casa Romuli that was revered until the fourth century A.D. The cave of Lupercal, in which the wolf was supposed to have given suck to the divine twins, was also honored as if it were a temple: it is still being looked for in the neighborhood of the church of St. Anastasia.

On the Palatine, however, there is no lack of ancient remnants going back to the earliest period of Rome: a strange conical tank near Livia's House, graves that might have been those of the first companions of Romulus. A circular room found beneath the *tablinium* of the Flavian palace might have been the *mundus* of Roma Quadrata, the sacred trench filled with offerings. Not far from the temple of Magna Mater—the Great Mother—below the terrace of the palace of Tiberius, excavations have revealed a whole village of huts dating back to the first Iron Age—that is, the very period of the legendary founding of Rome. Although none of these remains can be linked to a specific person or event, they are no less valuable as a whole in bringing us closer to a past that had seemed most remote and highly dubious. Granted, they do not corroborate the tales of which Romulus and his immediate successors were the heroes, but they make it impossible to refuse all credence to the traditions that have arisen on lost memories and to the sight of monuments that are ruins today. The fact that popular imagination has remedied these losses by the invention of fables and the further fact that the gaps of history have been filled with fictions do not prevent us from sensing, under the stories of tradition, the core of probability that they conceal.

THE SABINE KINGS

If we are left in ignorance as to the circumstances of the life of Romulus, we are equally ill informed on the parts played by the three Sabine kings whom tradition lists as his successors—Numa Pompilius, Tullus Hostilius, and Ancus Martius. One is inclined to think that they were monarchs of a most primitive kind, kings of scattered villages whose only common bond was their attempts to contain the threat of the Etruscans, which was constantly growing.

The Latin village of Romulus did not long remain isolated. Other villages grew on the hills near the Tiber. Toward the end of the seventh century B.C., seven of them were to consolidate in order to assure the defense of the river, forming what was called the Line of the Seven Hills; it survived until the Etruscan conquest. These villages accepted a single king, a joint military leader, but that was the limit of the ties that they formed. There is no trace of any centralized organization; the league was only a conglomeration of independent villages. Rome had not yet been born.

The villages from whose unification the city was to arise experienced nonetheless a parallel evolution. Their dwellings, which were still reed huts supported by frames of stakes covered with clay, lost their circular or elliptical shape and adopted the rectangle that was to be the form of the Roman house; the use of iron spread; the technique of pottery was developed. Finally a society was formed and gradually became organized on bases that were common to the Seven Hills. Within the families, or *gentes,* which were kept unbroken, the leaders or masters formed a hereditary nobility, the patricians. Favorites or "clients" who sought their assistance provided the lower class of the *gens;* between masters and clients—dependents—a system of reciprocal rights and duties evolved. Along with the *gentes* there grew up an inferior population, composed of the conquered and of voluntary immigrants. This was the *plebs,* that *plebs* that was later to strive to wrest political rights from the patricians in a long struggle that would dominate Rome's internal history.

In Roman tradition the Sabine kings appear endowed with qualities that history cannot accord them. In contrast to their legend, they did not create a Roman state, which did not emerge until later; they did not found Ostia, the creation of which grew out of conceptions that were beyond them; they did not destroy Alba, whose fall was the result of rivalries to which they were strangers.

Their reputation as town planners is equally unwarranted. It is they who are fallaciously called the builders of some of the earliest monuments in the Forum: the Curia, the Regia, the temples of Janus and Vesta. The swampy valley from which the Forum was only slowly to emerge was merely a wilderness in the time of the Sabine kings, at best used as a burial ground. The Curia, the erection of which was ascribed to Tullus Hostilius, was built long after his reign. Then, it was still the time of wood and straw huts. It was in some structure of this sort that the council of rustic patricians, still dressed in the skins of beasts, must have met: this council, which assisted the king, was the ancestor of the Senate.

For similar reasons, the temple of Janus Bifrons, which endured until the end of the empire—and which was of bronze—could not have been built in an age when construction methods were still quite primitive. As for the temple of Vesta, the house of the Vestals, which adjoined it, and the Regia, the residence of the kings, which is adjacent to the Vestals' house, it would be impossible to ascribe their creation to King Numa unless it is assumed that in the beginning these were only rudimentary buildings that were replaced by stone structures at some later period. The circular shape of the temple of Vesta, which reproduces that of the Roman peasant's original hut, might support this hypothesis. Nevertheless, the ritual objects that have been found in a nearby pit go back at most to the third century B.C., and this makes it impossible to assert that priestesses of Vesta lived there earlier.

The physical civilization of the period was still very primitive and far behind that of the neighboring regions. To lift out of their swamps those villages that the Sabine kings ruled with difficulty there was first needed that tremendous and decisive event in the history of Rome, the Etruscan conquest.

THE ETRUSCANS

It was in the middle of the seventh century B.C. that the Etruscans crossed the Tiber and invaded Latium. In actual fact they could have done so far earlier; the puny barrier of the Roman hills would have been quite inadequate to resist them. If they had for so long done nothing, it was because no urgency had caused them to extend their dominion to new lands. After two centuries of holding back, they felt the desire for this move and they found no difficulty in satisfying it. Does this mean that they then unleashed a warrior mass on Latium for purely military conquest? That was not their way. In the areas that they already occupied, the Etruscans represented only an infinitesimal minority in relation to the subject populations. It was always their method to send bands of immigrants ahead under resolute leaders and to implant their influence in a peacefully conquered country. They were not to act otherwise with respect to Rome, where their acquisition of power would be so subtle that it could be attributed to the natural operation of local institutions.

The Etruscans' rule was a wise one: they did not try to suppress indigenous races and they were satisfied to superimpose themselves on them. This was effective: their dominance was the forge of Rome's greatness. It must be added that they contributed a civilization far superior to that of the wretched villages on Roman soil, from which they would bring to birth a glorious city and a puissant state.

THE CLOACA MAXIMA

Physically, progress was tremendous; stone houses supplanted the huts of clay and straw, public buildings were erected, works of art were begun, roads were laid out. The vast morass that made the Roman valleys an uncultivated wilderness was drained. The Etruscans were past masters in the art of regulating the flow of waters; while the improvement of the banks of the Po was to stand as their masterpiece, they gave the foot of the Seven Hills an outstanding proof of their skill by transforming the Roman mudhole into a fertile plain through a skillful drainage project. A huge network of underground pipes carried off the stagnant Velabrian waters to the Cloaca Maxima, which emptied them into the Tiber. This elder of Rome's engineering achievements still exists; and it still serves as a central collection artery for the sewers that carry off to the river the waste of the area of which the Forum is the center. The Cloaca Maxima is the monument "that best testifies to the power of the Etruscan kings, the monument that has best survived them." Its masterfully designed tunnels and its great full concave arch that empties into the Tiber abreast of the Ponte Rotto have withstood twenty-five centuries of pressure by soil and water. All the other edifices of this period have disappeared, destroyed by fires, by earthquakes, by the erosion of time or by the wickedness of men; the work of the Tarquins remains just as Pliny the Elder once described it: "impregnable."

THE REAL FOUNDING OF ROME

The draining of the marshes, complemented by the improvements in the banks of the Tiber and the destruction of the neighboring forests, led the tribes to abandon the pastoral for the agricultural life; a race of peasants put out roots in a soil that had become generous. Another result of these vast undertakings was the elimination of the barriers that isolated the hills of Rome from one another. The communication lines that were established among them made it possible for them progressively to come together, to be concentrated and to assume the political form of towns. These towns were not slow in achieving an urban unity soon endowed with the appropriate organisms and with very advanced administrative institutions, such as the registry office established by Servius Tullius, which was to fall into disuse under the Republic and not to be restored until Augustus. It was indeed the Etruscans who brought to Roman soil and there established, as they had already done elsewhere, that concept of the *urbs*—city—that had not existed before they came. In spite of legend, then, the founding of Rome was an Etruscan achievement.

This urban unity that they accomplished was reinforced by the Etruscan kings with a suitable political organization. The individualism of the old Roman villages vanished in a centralized administration; the three component elements of the population (Latins, Sabines, and Etruscans) were given common structures and organized into thirty *curiae,* which were city districts comparable to the *arrondissements* of modern Paris, or the postal zones of New York City.

Having turned this amalgam of villages into a city, the Etruscans were to give it a name: they called it Roma because of a phonetic distortion of the very ancient name of its river, which was Rumon. Modern scholars all agree in accepting the belated appearance of the name of Rome. This correction brought to an end the discussions over which ancient historians lingered so long: whether Romulus had given his name to the city that he was supposed to have founded or whether the city gave him its name. It must now be conceded that the legendary founder of Rome is known by a name that was conferred on him only after the event, by a tradition in which epochs were confused.

THE SERVIAN WALL

It was long believed that, in order to provide a symbol of the close union of the Tiber villages quite as much as to give them protection, the Etruscan kings built a wall to surround the territory that they ruled. It was Servius Tullius who received the credit for having erected the wall that still bears his name and whose traces can still be followed through the city, for large fragments of it are still visible. This wall is the first view of antiquity afforded to the traveler who arrives at Rome's central railroad station: he sees a piece of it that has been left standing among the tracks; proceeding to the new sections of the city by way of the Quirinal, he finds other fragments of it, the most important of which is in Piazza Magnana-poli, half hidden in the greenery of a little square.

But archeology does not corroborate this legend any more than that of Romulus' wall. In its greater part, the wall ascribed to Servius Tullius does not date back to the Etruscan period; its peperino blocks show quarry marks of the fourth century B.C., and it was indeed at that time that the censors discussed the question of constructing a stone rampart. It is possible only that the builders here and there incorporated parts of the Etruscan wall, whose characteristic features have been found integrated into the more scientific construction of the fourth century.

Were the archaic wall that flanks the Stairs of Caius on the Palatine and the peperino cliff that, at the Capitol, rears its primitive ruggedness above the little Piazza Tor de' Specchi part of the Etruscan kings' line of defense? The same question can be raised for the fragments discovered near the theater of Marcellus and the Capitol in the neighboring garden of the Ara Coeli. If so, they and the Cloaca Maxima would be the sole Roman traces of the building activities of the Etruscans, who peopled the city with many structures all vanished today or hidden beneath the ruins of later monuments.

THE BIRTH OF THE FORUM AND THE CIRCUS MAXIMUS

It was also to the Tarquin dynasty that Rome owed the conversion of the Forum into a center of city life. The origins of the Roman Forum, like those of the city itself, are more legendary than historical; in this context there have been even allusions to the memories of the golden age brought by Saturn. In actuality, the condition of the area before the Etruscan invasion, as confirmed by the deep excavations made in the search for prehistoric deposits, precludes any thought that the Forum could have been utilized earlier as a regular meeting place or a permanent market. It was situated in a swampy, wooded valley, always flooded by the waters of the Tiber, Velabrian seepages, and the rainfall that washed down from the surrounding heights. It was the great enterprises of the Etruscan kings that, by draining the area, made possible its use as a center of trade. The Forum became a vast square soon surrounded by shops and porticoes and adorned with temples—in other words, already furnished with the traditional attributes that were to make it, as it were, the brain from which the whole life of the city flowed—and, later, the whole life of the civilized world.

The Etruscans made another decisive contribution to the development of collective urban life with the introduction of games. *Circenses!*—it was the Etruscans who gave the Romans the taste, and the means of gratifying it, for this magic entertainment that one day they would find as indispensable as bread. This period was the time of the Circus Maximus, whose huge arena (uncovered during the Fascist period) lies at the foot of the Palatine, at the end of that long, narrow Murcia Valley that separates the Palatine from the Aventine. It was to become that sumptuous circus adorned with obelisks and statues that dazzled the ancient world. Three hundred thousand spectators could be accommodated in comfort on its tiers. Its successive beautifications, of which archeologists have discovered only the ruins, were to mark the growth of the Roman people's passion for the spectacles that were staged there. In the days of the Tarquins the circus was still only a modest race course, but spectators already flocked to it in large numbers and sat or stood in masses on the lower levels of the hills to watch the maneuvers of the chariots. The original populations of the federated villages, in fact, had been enlarged with many elements from all parts of Latium, who had established themselves in the lowlands that the vast engineering projects had opened to colonization.

THE VULCANAL / THE TEMPLE OF JUPITER / THE TARPEIAN ROCK

The Etruscans had founded a Roman city, created a Roman state. They completed their work of colonization by endowing that city and that state with "that principle of unity without which the ancients never conceived a national life: a common worship." The Vulcanal, carved in the same bedrock that formed the Capitoline at the foot of which it stood, behind the arch of Septimius Severus, was perhaps the first effort at the establishment of one of those cults, new to Rome, dedicated to the forces of nature (in this instance, fire).

But it was on the Capitoline that the Etruscans set up the center of the city's religious life, inaugurating the prodigious destiny of this little height that was to become the symbol of Roman grandeur. The Capitoline was composed of two separate summits. On one the Arx already stood—the citadel of Rome and its supreme rampart from the dawn of its history; the church and what remains of the convent of Ara Coeli are on the site today. It was on the southern crest that Tarquin the Elder laid the foundations of the temple dedicated to the trinity of Jupiter, Juno, and Mercury, which was to be completed by the last of his successors only a short time before his downfall.

The temple of Jupiter has not left "much more trace than the passage of Saturn" on the Capitoline. A few inchoate remains of its foundations, a piece of wall are all that remain of it, if indeed these vestiges—like the fragment of fluted column and the Corinthian capital in marble from Mount Pentelicus that have been found there—did not come from one of the restorations that were successively ordered by Sulla, Vespasian, Titus, and Domitian. For this temple of the Capitoline trinity was four times destroyed by fire before it disappeared so completely during the Middle Ages that for centuries even the memory of its site was lost.

It is barely a hundred years since archeological investigation made it possible to discover its site and reconstruct its plan, as it was shown in a bas-relief placed beside the stairs in the Palace of the Conservators and always faithfully followed in the successive reconstructions. According to the testimony of Tacitus, in fact, it was the will of the gods that the original appearance be always religiously preserved. A coin of the republican period that portrayed the exterior of the temple had already given a very accurate idea of its appearance. It was a much modified imitation of the Doric temples of Greece. It rested on a high base, the huge substructures of which were still admired by the Romans of the Empire.

Above the pediment there was a *quadriga* in terra cotta, the erection of which had been preceded by miraculous incidents that were taken as omens of Rome's high fortune. The temple was embellished with ancient statues that have vanished without leaving any trace. In the end, fascinating and rich as it is, Etruscan art was represented in Rome only by works that came from other sources. Only the Capitoline wolf, which was to be made the symbol of Rome and of Italy, seems to have been cast there. It was the only animal sacred to Mars, and the suckling twins were not added to it until the Renaissance.

For more than a thousand years the Capitoline temple was to remain the concrete symbol of Roman power. It was there that the pomps of the triumphs concluded, it was to this shrine that prayers, acts of grace, and tributes of all kinds were directed; it was at its base that all the peoples brought under the law of Rome came to prostrate themselves. From the site that is dominated now by the Palazzo Caffarelli, it overlooked the Forum and the whole Roman universe. The memory of it remains so dominant in Roman history that, standing on this hill where no sign of it remains, one cannot help "reconstructing it in the mind and contemplating it in spirit." But we know that it was there. . . .

"The Tarpeian Rock is near the Capitoline." Become a proverb to teach the presumptuous that disaster is often the neighbor of triumph, this sentence tells us little of the place where speedy execution awaited heinous criminals. This rock, whose reputation was as sinister as its appearance and which the visitor seeks out in a spirit of schoolboy duty, should no doubt be situated on the cliff that dominates Via della Consolazione. Between the Capitoline, which symbolized triumph, and the Tarpeian

Rock, where enemies of the state expiated their ambitious errors, there is indeed only a short distance. From the very place of execution the doomed could see for the last time what had generated their crimes, and the terrible antithesis embodied in this juxtaposition was a lesson of awful eloquence in the danger that lay in violation of the Roman law.

The reign of the Etruscan kings—Tarquin the Elder, Servius Tullius, and Tarquin the Proud—lasted one hundred fifty years. Their achievements marked a decisive stage in the history of Rome. Out of the dust of villages that seemed to have no future they created not only a city and a state but a military power and also the capital of the Latin world. For, to the advantage of Rome, the Etruscans restored the Latin federation that had been destroyed by the fall of Alba. They were to be poorly thanked for so great an achievement. The revolution of 509 B.C. was brutally to drive them out of a land that they had led into the light and enriched beyond calculation.

CHAPTER 2

THE REPUBLIC

THE FIGHT FOR LIFE

Roman tradition, always intent on enhancing national virtues, has invested the revolution of 509 with the character of a liberation movement. In fact, the events that led to the fall of the last Tarquin king far transcended the framework of the Tiber's hills: they were the consequence of the recession of the Etruscan world under the double pressure of the Gauls, who had appeared in northern Italy, and of the Greeks, who had founded already powerful colonies in the south. The Etruscans had made Latium the keystone of their empire: it was there that they were attacked and vanquished, near Aricia. The rising of the Latin villages completed their defeat. The Romans—who had taken no part in this action—rushed to the aid of the victors and proclaimed the end of the Tarquin dynasty. Plebeians and patricians had joined together in this belated revolt for completely opposing reasons.

The misfortune for Rome was that this so-called liberation dragged it down from its place as the capital of Latium to the condition of an isolated city, threatened by the appetites of its neighbors; since all had suddenly become its enemies, Rome had to defend itself against a world of hostility.

The first and perhaps the greatest miracle of Rome was the fact that it managed at that time not only to break the ring that was closing on it and to re-establish its hegemony over Latium, but also to extend it far beyond, as far as southern Italy. But this conquest lasted only a hundred years, and it exhausted Rome's resources. So, having triumphed over its nearest enemies, it found itself incapable of resisting the distant enemy who arose to devastate in a few days the magnificent fruits of a century of heroic efforts. It was in 390 B.C. that the Gauls, who had progressively routed the Etruscans from the Po Valley, crossed the Apennines, cut the Roman army to pieces on the banks of the Allia, and entered Rome, which had been abandoned by its population at the news of the military disaster. As an illustration of that exodus, let us point out that in that throng of fugitives there were Vestal Virgins, on foot and without servants, laboriously carrying their sacred objects and the holy vessels of their worship. The Gauls could sack the city at their leisure, destroy the temples, burn the houses. Only the Capitol was spared—saved, according to the legend, by the vigilance of its sacred geese.

Once again ruined, once again isolated—for its former enemies had raised their heads again—once more threatened with death, Rome did not flinch before the ordeal. Having redeemed the freedom of its territory for two thousand pounds in gold, it rebuilt its ruins and itself behind that wall, inaccurately called Servian, whose traces we have already encountered. But speed had been essential and money had been short; the new city wore the signs of that haste and that poverty. The broad avenues that had been laid out by the Etruscans were succeeded by narrow, winding streets; the populace had to huddle together in barren houses that were too few, unhealthy, and unsafe. Misery was king in the hovels.

Once the city had been rebuilt as well as circumstances permitted, the stubborn resolve of its people brought it back to its former power. Forty years of courage and forceful policy were enough for this resurrection. Victorious wars and well-timed treaties assured Rome's hegemony over the whole of central Italy and prepared it for that colossal undertaking of world dominion that was the work of future centuries. On the threshold of this fabulous conquest, Rome, which had already given so many proofs of its ability to survive and to dominate, had become a cohesive citadel, an active city, a strong state, despite the burdens imposed on it by constant wars and the incessant rivalry between plebeians and patricians that racked it.

INTERNAL CRISIS / THE TEMPLE OF CONCORD

The principal artisans of the fall of the Etruscan kings, the patricians set up the Republic to their own exclusive advantage. The Senate and the Consulate were its cornerstones: three hundred Conscript Fathers constituted a supreme council, while two consuls, elected for a year, jointly held the executive power. The *plebs* had no share in the government. This class was growing larger and larger, however, and the demands of the times were burdening it with increasing obligations in the double guise of taxes and military service. Soon it had to be admitted to political responsibilities; the principle of the proportionality of rights and duties, which was the foundation of the ancient societies, compelled the establishment of the *comitia centuriata,* which united all citizens in the armed forces without regard to birth.

Actually, for a long period the people's participation in these assemblies was only a mockery. Nevertheless, as it grew in numbers, the *plebs* was progressively to make its influence effective during a two-hundred-year struggle that was extremely complex and that was marked by many violent episodes, the most curious of which was certainly the withdrawal of the *plebs* to Monte Sacro. This is a very low hill, now covered with great modern apartment houses, that is visible when one has crossed the little Anio River on the old Ponte Nomentano. Democracy won its first victory with a weapon that it has never given up since: the strike. The memory of those troubled times still pulses today, too, on the Aventine, now hushed among its many cloisters where the only voice is that of bells. Yet it was in these ambiences that now turn the mind only to serenity and peaceful prayer that words of fire rang out that incited the people to extremes of violence.

In 370 the *plebs* won the right to furnish one of the consuls from its own ranks. This was a major event, which was to be determining in Rome's greatness; it was celebrated by the erection of the temple of Concord, whose platform still dominates the Forum from the last slopes of the Capitoline, opposite the arch of Septimius Severus. The frieze of the temple and some very remarkable architectural fragments are displayed in the Tabularium; the bases found in the *cella** are in the Capitoline Museum. The Republic was to make the temple of Concord a kind of museum, the first in which Rome could take pride. It contained a number

---

* The room in a temple that houses the statue of the divinity to whom it is dedicated.—Translator.

of masterpieces, the loot of distant conquests and the offerings of precious objects that the Romans became habituated to consecrating to the goddess of peace, Concordia, in order to win her favor. This temple played a major part in the history of the Republic. The Senate met there often. It was there that Cicero delivered his fourth oration against Catiline, which led to the condemnation of Catiline's confederates.

Civil strife continued long after the construction of the temple, on a wall of which a sour wit wrote one night: "This temple to Concord was built by Discord." It was not until 300 B.C. that the Hortensian law eliminated the last distinctions between patricians and plebeians. The equality of the two orders was established on the religious, political, and legal levels. Priests were chosen without any considerations as to their birth; the plebeians had access to the Senate and to all public offices under the Republic, including the Consulate. A statute applicable to both orders was enacted: this was the Law of the Twelve Tables. The domestic crisis was resolved. Strong in the close union of its sons, Rome was ready to embark on the conquest of the world.

THE TOOL OF CONQUEST

The tremendous power of expansion that Rome developed over five centuries is one of the most interesting phenomena in political history. Indeed, the reasons that drove the city on the Tiber to overflow its boundaries to the ends of the then known world elude analysis and remain a secret that will leave the field indefinitely open to historical investigation. Rome's imperialism cannot be explained in any satisfactory fashion by spiritual, economic, or biological necessity. Rome experienced no social or population pressure that would have caused it to look to conquest for solutions to problems—which indeed could only be created by that conquest. One can find so few reasonable explanations for the bewildering Roman conquests that one is tempted to ascribe them to sheer luck, as the Greeks did in order to salve their own pride when they were defeated. In any event, if this theory is discarded as too simplistic, it is impossible to find another to take its place and there is nothing on which to fall back except the mysterious predestination to which all Rome's old historians and poets refer. *Tu regere imperio populos, Romane, memento* (Remember, Roman, that to govern peoples is your destiny)—Rome had made this maxim its own long before Virgil wrote it.

While the structure of Roman society provides no clue to its history, it does make it possible to understand how and why the conquest was successful. Rome and Latium were populated by a race of stubborn, strong, and courageous peasants. In the many alterations that it has undergone since its foundation and in the organization of its urban life, Rome had never repudiated its pastoral origins. It remained the village of farmers symbolized in history by Cincinnatus. Its household religion, like its national religion, clung to its roots in the soil. Work on the land was the only manual labor that did not dirty the hands of the warrior. Social life was organized around farm life. Even in the city there were great gardens, orchards, vineyards (those of the Vatican were said to produce the worst wine in the area). A mere step outside the city walls, the plain was rich in pasturage and crop land. The countrymen went to Rome to sell their products and buy all kinds of wares. They were not greeted with the slightly contemptuous condescension that is the rule in French cities. Far from considering himself more intelligent than the peasant, the city man regarded him with real admiration. All sorts of qualities were attributed to him. "When our ancestors wished to praise a good citizen," Cato was to say, "they used such terms as good tiller of the soil, good farmer." An aura of undeniable prestige surrounded agricultural occupations: rich Romans considered it an honor to own land and they were proud to be able to list themselves among the rural tribes.

While this peasant race supplied the soldiers, it was the aristocracy that provided the leaders. It furnished them in great number and of the highest quality because its very structure fostered their development. In the family the father was absolute chief and master ("he alone commands, he alone owns, he alone judges"). In the *gens,* "that larger-structured family," the chief exercised the same prerogatives of command on a broader scale. And the duties of public office gave to those who attained it (and they did so by merit) an unparalleled training. A race of soldiers, a race of leaders—that was the secret of Rome's good luck. Let us add to these things a natural taste for greatness and power that Roman aristocracy, loyal to its remote origins, was never to renounce.

THE GREAT CONQUEST

During the fourth century Rome established dominance over central Italy and extended it as far as the Adriatic. It was only at the cost of bitter battles that Rome achieved this. It subdued the fierce mountaineers of the

Apennines, the Samnites, only by virtue of tenacity and courage and after many ordeals, occasionally aggravated by humiliating reverses. One such forced its defeated troops to parade with bowed heads through the Caudine Forks. But the reverses could not undermine Roman tenacity. Out of these ordeals its sword would emerge "so tempered that it could never break again."

The Samnites having been crushed, Rome attacked the Hellenic colonies in southern Italy, that Magna Graecia that had hired the famous Pyrrhus, king of Epirus, with his thirty-five thousand mercenaries and his celebrated elephants, to resist the legions. After a few initial successes at excessive cost ("One more such victory," he said after the battle of Asculum, "and I shall go back alone to Epirus"), Pyrrhus was vanquished at Beneventum in 275 and the Romans became the masters of the entire Italian peninsula.

When they began to covet the riches of Sicily, they collided with the formidable strength of Carthage. The awful hand-to-hand wars between Rome and Carthage lasted more than a century. These were the famous and cruel Punic Wars that shook the earth in a dramatic alternation of successes and reverses in which for many months Rome's fate and the Empire's survival hung in the balance. Hannibal, having invaded Italy, overwhelmed the Roman army under Flaminius, a consul, near Lake Trasimeno in 217 and smashed Varro's army a year later at Cannae (Cannes). He might have taken Rome, for he had reached its walls, but he allowed his troops to grow slack among the delights of Capua. Once again Roman obstinacy regained the lost ground, carried the war into Africa and won conclusive victory in 146 over the rival city, whose empire became the Roman province of Africa.

Earlier Rome had conquered Macedonia (148) and then all of Greece (146). The fall of Carthage facilitated the conquest of Spain, completed by the capture of Numantia in 133. Egypt and Asia Minor voluntarily placed themselves under Rome's jurisdiction and became the province of Asia in 129. In order to effect better communications with Spain and the Pyrenees, Rome conquered all the Gauls' territories between the Alps and the Pyrenees and, in 125, made them the province of Narbonensis, where Romans founded the cities of Aix and Narbonne.

As the result of all these annexations, Rome dominated all the shores of the Mediterranean, which henceforth it could call *mare nostrum.* The greatest empire that the world had ever known was born.

ROME DURING THE CONQUEST

If we have catalogued Rome's conquests so cursorily, that is because they range so far beyond that city horizon to which we mean to restrict ourselves. While its legions were carrying their eagles ever farther abroad, Rome was experiencing the repercussions of the military achievements that made it the capital of a constantly enlarging world. The news that came from increasingly remote theaters of operations roused excited emotions in a mass already fired by the lack of detailed certainties. There was feverish speculation on the signs and wonders that came from the gods: the statue of Mars at the Capenian Gate perspired, lightning struck the temple of Spes (Hope). There were constant religious ceremonials, attended by vast, anxious throngs.

Rome had many occasions for pride; often too it trembled for its freedom and its life; but the humiliation of a defeat always sired the bitter determination to erase it. When, during the Samnite wars, the people learned of the shameful sequels to the defeat in the Caudine Forks, a multitude invaded the Forum, whose shops were closed as a token of mourning. Curses were shouted on the beaten army, oaths were taken never to open the city's gates to the disgraced troops. But, as soon as they appeared, ashamed and skulking along the walls, pity triumphed and they were given solace. Then the crowd streamed to the Field of Mars to enlist in the legions that were to renew the fierce struggle and carry it to a victorious conclusion. That was Rome. It bowed its head under the ordeal, but raised it again at once, and its patriotism burst out in heroic resolutions.

When it was released from its agonies and the triumphal time of its arms began, fantastic accounts "came out of every stone in the forum." Chroniclers and politicians stood at the base of the speakers' platform, dispensing honest reports or spreading false rumors, sparing, Gaston Boissier said in his *Promenades Archéologiques,* "neither statesmen who did not have the luck to be popular nor generals who failed to gain victory at the first encounter." The populace ran to hear the news as it crowded the porticoes and the temples to see the loot seized from the enemy. Victorious commanders did not hesitate to display narrative paintings exalting their exploits. One of them, Manlius, the *praetor,* was so self-intoxicated that he stood beside the picture that showed his feats of arms in order to provide any elaborations that might be requested. This publicity earned him election as consul a year later.

As always occurs after a bloody war, each new conquest ignited a frenzy of pleasure seeking. Festivals were many. Above all the people delighted in the spectacle of the conquering generals and the enchained enemies. Great military ceremonies marked the end of each victorious campaign. The commander who had led it was taken to the Capitol in a golden chariot drawn by four white horses. Painted to the eyes, his face dyed red, he was clothed in a robe of purple and crowned with laurel. A great troop of musicians and dancers preceded him; behind him marched the eminent prisoners whom he had taken; then came his troops in battle order, decked "with the tokens with which their valor had been rewarded." They sang their own praises and their general's, but they spiced them with jests, occasionally cruel ones, that the victor had to endure as atonement for his success. (It was during his triumph that Caesar was compelled to listen to bitter reproaches for his love for Cleopatra.) The parade was concluded with consuls, senators, and chariots, often in great number, piled high with the booty seized from the enemy.

The ceremony of the triumph introduced in Rome that great element of representative government, popular opinion. The route led through streets decked with flowers and crowded with an excited throng, from the city gates to the Capitoline by way of the Circus Maximus, the Via Sacra, and the Forum. Along the way there were arches of triumph, embellished with bas-reliefs showing the losers' cities, rivers, and ships. It was to become the custom to build these arches of stone and marble in order to perpetuate the memory of the great deeds of generals and emperors. The triumphal procession ascended the steep rise of Clivus Capitolinus to the temple of Jupiter, where the ritual sacrifices were performed. Today's stroller walks on the same stones as the greatest men of history.

THE MAMERTINE PRISON AND THE GEMONIAN STAIRS

It was at the place where the climb began that the conquered leader, who had been exposed all day to the insults of the crowd, was taken out of the procession; he was removed to the Tullianum to be slaughtered by having his throat cut. This was the fate of Vercingetorix and Jugurtha, among so many others.

The *carcer,* which was not given the name of "Mamertine Prison" until the Middle Ages, is the oldest prison in Rome, and for a long time it was the only one. "Rome," Juvenal said, "is content to have a single prison." The Tullianum owed its name not to Servius Tullius, the Etruscan king, but rather to the presence of a spring (*tullius,* in the ancient tongue), the same spring whose origin is attributed to St. Peter: he is supposed to have miraculously brought it into being in order to baptize his jailers. The only access to the jail was through a round opening cut into its roof; on the ground floor there was a quite large hall, of more recent construction, which has now been transformed into a chapel. The Mamertine Prison is actually under the church of St. Joseph of the Carpenters.

Alongside the *carcer,* almost on the site of the steps that lead to the Capitol, stood the Gemonian Stairs, where the corpses of executed criminals were displayed before they were thrown into the Tiber. All that remains of those stairs of shame is "a memory of which our [French] language has preserved a vestige."

CITY PLANNING UNDER THE CONQUEST / THE ORGANIZATION OF THE FORUM / THE FIRST AQUEDUCTS AND THE FIRST ROMAN ROADS

The conquests had brought about a complete transformation of the city. Its growing renown attracted a number of immigrants from nearby regions to live inside its walls. The defeated countries, on their side, had furnished the elements of a new population: slaves taken by force and free men who had voluntarily gone to Rome in the hope of profit. This multiplication of the population, like the matching growth of its needs, had made Rome a large city equipped with the essential facilities that made a sojourn there, if not comfortable and alluring, at least almost free of serious problems and dangers.

Progressively the city had developed improvements that assured a relatively high level of health. True, it was often necessary to be on guard against those "solstitial" diseases of which the ancient writers speak and that were called plagues when their toll rose higher. The extremely numerous shrines dedicated to Hygeia and to fevers of every description are as many monuments to the fears of the ancient Romans.

Nevertheless, in this city that was always overpopulated, the republican era shows only one instance of those spectacular epidemics that in antiquity raged through so many other large centers. And it dates back to the remote epoch of the Samnite wars. To put an end to it, the Sibylline Books declared, Aesculapius, son of Apollo and god of health, must be fetched from Epidaurus in the guise of the sacred serpent. When the galley in which the serpent was being transported stood off Rome, the serpent escaped and sought refuge on the island in the Tiber. So a temple to the god was erected there, and some traces of it survive near the church of St. Bartholomew. The worship of Aesculapius was still so rigorously protected in the fourth century A.D. that four officers of the Palatine suffered martyrdom for their refusal to adore him. The church of the Four Crowned Saints (destroyed by the Normans and rebuilt by Paschal II) still rears its powerful buttresses on the site of their execution, their reddish stone shapes looking like those of a medieval fortress. The church has added to the adoration of the four saints that of five sculptors put to death at the same time for having refused to make a statue of Aesculapius. The dedication of the Tiber island to health was to outlast paganism, too; as the site of a number of health institutions and the Great Hospital of St. John of God, it carries on a tradition that has never been broken.

While special honors were paid to the god of medicine, the health of Rome was assured by more directly efficacious practical measures. Thus, as the city progressively grew larger, the authorities had the wisdom to surround it, by protecting the original forest, with that precious belt of green of which Rome is so proud still. The streets were so solidly paved that in some places the same stones are there today. The Forum, which had always been the heart of political life at the same time that it was a great market place, was gradually stripped of the numerous decrepit and unsanitary shops that surrounded it. The oldest (*tabernae veteres*) had been replaced as early as 210 B.C. by practical, well-equipped premises (*tabernae novae*). Soon destroyed by fire, they were rebuilt on a new site that also became a great market place, the Macellum. It occupied the whole of the ground on which the Forums of Caesar and Augustus were later to be built. Other, specialized markets were also established: for cattle, for vegetables, for fish. These various arrangements succeeded in releasing the Forum from its original mercantile purpose and reserving it for the functions of religious and political life.

A fundamental health factor for an overpopulated city was the construction of aqueducts that reached out to great distances in order to supply water chosen especially for its purity. The first of these was built at the time of the Samnite wars. Laid underground, it followed the route that was later to be taken by Nero's aqueduct. In those days the sole aim was utilitarian. It was only later that the utilitarian was joined by the grandiose and the fashion arose that would erect great aerial aqueducts that, as Chateaubriand said, would bring water to Rome "on arches of triumph."

Even Rome's second aqueduct, built after the defeat of Pyrrhus (it entered the city through the Esquiline gate) showed a certain tendency to esthetic desires. Before the end of the Republic, four new aqueducts were to carry water to Rome from the eastern hills (Aqua Appia, Aqua Annia, Aqua Marcia, and Aqua Tepula). By the fourth century A.D. their number had risen to nineteen. The majestic ruins of their arches still endow the Roman countryside with its stirring grandeur. The aqueducts were to constitute so essential an element of urban life that, in the medieval period, Rome was to survive all pillage as long as its aqueducts were preserved; the day when they were cut (by Vitiges in 537) was to mark the beginning of a period of decline that would last almost ten centuries.

It was also at the time of the Samnite wars that the first Roman road was opened, that Via Appia that is still the queen of Roman roads. Appius Claudius, the censor, paved it with stones brought from great distances and so skillfully joined to one another, though without mortar, that they seemed to form a natural whole.

Just before his departure for Trasimeno, where he was to be defeated and killed by Hannibal, Consul Flaminius opened the Via Flaminia, which led to Umbria; the Romans who throng Corso Vittorio Emanuele today pay no attention to the fact that this ancient road is the greatest achievement of its kind that the ancient Romans have left us.

It was also during the period of conquest that Rome began to create amusement places for itself. It already had the Circus Maximus; this was subjected to major improvements. In 221 Flaminius gave the city another circus almost as large; he had it built near the Columna Bellica, from the top of which the consuls shot an arrow in the direction of the country on which they were declaring war. Nothing of this great edifice remains. Only the neighboring street, Via delle Botteghe Oscure, preserves the memory of the shops set up in the arcades of the circus. It was on the actual ruins of the circus that in the twelfth century the church of Santa Catarina de'Funari was erected: she was the patroness of the ropemakers who had set up their businesses in the huge arena.

THE TABULARIUM AND THE AEMILIAN BRIDGE

The most beautiful example of secular architecture that the Republic has handed down to us is certainly the Tabularium, which it erected on the Capitoline in its last century (78 B.C.) as the central depository for its archives. All that has survived to us is the part of the building that dominates the Forum; on the side facing the Capitol square everything has disappeared except the foundations, on which the Senator's Palace rests. The Tabularium was built of great blocks of peperino, that volcanic stone that was used by all the old Roman architects and that derived its name from its resemblance to "molded pepper." Huge substructures supported two stories, only one of which has been partly preserved; it serves as a repository for numerous architectural and sculptural fragments from neighboring buildings. The great gallery that ran the length of the side facing the Forum was illuminated by high arcades that have since been walled up. The upper story was also adorned with a line of arcades and topped by a platform decorated with statues.

This vast façade of the Tabularium gave the Forum the backdrop that until then it had lacked. It shows that the Romans of the Republic strove for an effect of perspective that the imperial architects were to carry to the extreme of *trompe-l'oeil*. But it should be noted that, well before Caesar and Augustus, Roman architects had sacrificed purely utilitarian concerns to an esthetic vision which it has too often been said belonged only to their descendants.

Many other improvements were also the work of the Republic, notably the construction of the Aemilian Bridge, the oldest of the stone bridges across the Tiber, in the second century B.C. Completed by Scipio, the conqueror of Carthage, and restored by ten popes, it was half ruined under Clement VII and is known today as the Ponte Rotto. It still retains some of the volcanic-stone bases of its original construction. They provide our first example of the specifically Roman vault. The vault had been well known to the Etruscans, but for centuries the secret of it had been lost. It was unknown to Greece, where the columns of temples were connected by beams.

Conquest, which had created needs, had at the same time supplied examples, brought financial resources, contributed materials and techniques. But the development of the city had taken place without method. Badly built, overpopulated, hampered by an inadequate system of public thoroughfares, Rome still looked like Vetus Roma (old Rome), poor in charm, whose age-old flaws were to be rectified only by the city planning of the emperors.

THE TEMPLES OF THE REPUBLICAN ERA

The custom of raising altars to the gods in order to win their favor or to thank them for their help was as old in Rome as the city itself. Romulus himself, according to tradition, had inaugurated it by erecting a shrine to Jupiter in gratitude for the god's help, which had halted his soldiers' ignominious rout before the Sabines. Undoubtedly it was only a sacred wall, and it had vanished, like all the creations of the same character that might have been built in the earliest era, which was ignorant of the use of durable materials. The first stone temples date from the Etruscans; and even they long remained few. It is reasonable to believe that there were only four in the Forum at the time of the sack of Rome by the Gauls. A century later, sacred edifices had become so numerous and the Forum was so well supplied with them that, after the first war against Tarentum, when Cineas went to offer Pyrrhus' conditions to the Senate, he reported to his master that Rome had "looked like a temple" to him. The remark exemplifies the monumental aspect that the city presented as early as the third century B.C.; it made a sharp contrast with the appearance of private dwellings, still shabby and built of wood. When the dictator Camillus rebuilt Rome after the passage of the Gauls, he created a scandal by endowing his own house with a gate of bronze: this luxury was to be reserved to sacred edifices until the time of Augustus.

The increase in temples during the period of conquests is to be explained by the religious spirit and the gravity of the dangers. In a critical moment a leader or a body of soldiers would make a vow to erect a monument to the god whose help was being asked. Not all the temples that were built in this period were of military origin, however, since at least three were dedicated to Venus.

Juno, the goddess of marriage, had had her temple on the Aventine since the beginning of the conquest period, for it had been built to honor the statue of the goddess that Camillus had brought back from Veii and, so tradition had it, the statue itself had ratified the transfer "with a miraculous movement of its head." It was long believed that the twenty-four Corinthian columns of the church of St. Sabina had come from this temple; scholars have decided that there is nothing to the belief. The only vestige of it that remains to us is the marble mask that pours water into a sarcophagus in front of the Dominican monastery.

Out of all this burgeoning of sacred edifices, only two temples have managed to survive almost intact into our own time. Both are near the Tiber in the ancient Forum Boarium (now the Piazza della Bocca della Verità). They are invaluable examples of Greek-Italian architecture; their precise proportions and their elegant simplicity have earned them such appreciation from the most sophisticated visitors to Rome that it has been argued by at least one traveler that they alone are enough to warrant the journey to Rome. The shrine inaccurately called the temple of Fortuna Virile is a reconstruction, dating back to the last centuries of the Republic, of an older building dedicated to an ancient Italian goddess, Mater Matuta, the goddess of morning. Before it became the church of St. Mary the Egyptian, it was the recipient of offerings from women who sought to hide physical imperfections from their husbands. If the architecture of this temple seems somewhat rude, as if to match the rather rugged piety of Cato's contemporaries, the round shrine that is its neighbor is nothing but delicacy. It was a charming little structure open all round, composed only of a domed hemisphere borne on a Corinthian series of twenty fluted columns in white marble. It is known as the temple of Vesta, although archeologists deny it this name; but they cannot agree on another for it. This shrine to an unknown goddess was to become a Christian church in the Middle Ages under the delightful name of Santa Maria del Sole, as the result of the discovery of a miraculous image of the Virgin in a box from which a bright ray of light shone when the lid was opened. In order to turn this temple into an enclosed church it was necessary to brick up the intervals between its columns, and consequently it lost much of its lightness.

A few steps farther, the remains of three other temples of the republican period are integrated into the structure of the church of San Nicola in Carcere, near the theater of Marcellus. It is assumed that these were the temples of Juno Liberatrix, Spes, and Janus. A few columns are recognizable but, in order to imagine the rest, one must descend into the basements "with the sacristan," as J.-J. Ampère, the historian, advised. On the other hand, before the theater of Marcellus, there are two columns erected on a high podium, the remains of the temple of Apollo Sosianus.

Near the Largo Argentina, below the square, recent excavations (1926–30) have uncovered four republican temples, one of them round in shape, that form a group quite evocative of the period that gave them birth. The one to the right of the round temple, during the Middle Ages, was made into a church dedicated to St. Nicholas, and its two apses are still to be seen.

Also on the Palatine, behind the so-called Cabina zone and crowned by a picturesque group of ilex, there is the high podium of the temple of Cybele, Magna Mater, consecrated in 204 at one of the most critical periods in the Second Punic War. The many architectural fragments found there date from a reconstruction by Augustus. Similarly, it is to a restoration by Tiberius that we are indebted for the three high Corinthian columns of the temple of Castor and Pollux, the most magnificent columns that have ever soared up from earth and that are one of the most impressive elements in the panorama of the Forum. This temple, of which imposing ruins remain, commemorates the Republic's first victory, at Lake Regillus in 496 B.C. The news of this victory was brought to Rome by the two Dioscuri, in the shape of two young men of great beauty and superhuman stature, who reached the city at nightfall after a stop to water their foaming horses at the fountain of Juturna, the goddess of healing waters. The fountain still stands beside the temple, in the sacred enclosure created during the Empire, and the waters that feed it still come from the same spring as in the days of Castor.

As for the temple of Saturn that dominates the center of the Forum from the height of its monumental stairway above the Via Sacra, it would still be unknown to us if first Augustus and then Diocletian had not uncovered it. It is only from the time of Diocletian that we can date the eight granite columns carried on white marble bases and surmounted by Corinthian capitals to form a great lyre singing the glory of the days of fable. Begun, according to tradition, by the last Etruscan king, this temple was the most venerated shrine of republican Rome, which placed in it the city treasury that was to be stolen by Caesar in a shameless burglary.

The other relics of the republican era in the Forum are almost shapeless; all that is left of the temple of Vesta is a base in heavy blocks of tufa; of the Regia, where the Pontifex Maximus lived, there are only the bottoms of thick walls; and even less is left of the Vestals' residence. All that has survived in these high places is of imperial restoration.

THE STRATIFICATION OF ROMAN MONUMENTS

In all honesty, it must be admitted that it is only because of the emperors' work of reconstruction that any of the great edifices of the Republic have come down to us. It is useless to seek any trace of the many other monuments of the period though it is known that they stood for centuries in the Forum. The Forum that we see today, set apart and put in order by tremendous archeological efforts, is not that of the Republic but that of the Empire. It offers only the memory of the twelve Caesars and above all of the last emperors. If the sites occupied by the temples of the Republic are known almost with certainty today, it is because the traces of most of them were found beneath the monuments of another age. It is indeed this superimposition of buildings of various periods that explains the remarkably rich harvest of the excavations carried out in Rome. When it was decided to build a temple, a site was chosen as the best precisely because it was the busiest; for that very reason it was already occupied by another temple, which was therefore doomed to destruction. But, in contrast to what was and is done everywhere else, the old structure was not demolished: the new one was simply built on top of it. Whereas in a modern city the ground is always being dug out, in Rome it was constantly growing higher as a better vista was sought through the creation of artificial eminences. The method was no different when it was a question of building a whole new section of the city: the old section was buried and the new one was built on top of it. That is why it is always a certainty in Rome that beneath any given monument the remains of several superimposed earlier structures will be found before the original soil is reached, occasionally at a great depth.

Stendhal was hardly exaggerating when he said that there was not a fathom of land in the center of Rome that had not successively been the site of five or six equally famous monuments. The story of the church of St. Clement as Gaston Boissier tells it is a splendid example of the marvelous discoveries that can be made by digging into the soil of Rome:

St. Clement is an admirable basilica of the twelfth century that contains beautiful frescoes by Masaccio. During the course of repairs that were being made, it happened that an older church was found beneath the existing basilica, with curious paintings and columns of marble and granite; it dated from the time of Constantine and had been used for seven centuries until the sack of Rome by Robert Guiscard. Encouraged by this discovery, the excavators dug more deeply and soon, under the older church, they found a shrine to Mithra and fragments of a Roman house built at the beginning of the Empire. Then, going still deeper, they uncovered tufa structures that were certainly from the first years of the Republic and perhaps even from the period of the kings. Thus it was a succession of monuments of every epoch and it was enough to descend a few stairs in order to contemplate the spectacle of the whole history of Rome from its foundation to the Renaissance.

THE CONSEQUENCES OF THE CONQUESTS

The conquest of the Mediterranean world was to have consequences of great importance for Rome; it brought about the complete transformation of the social structure, of private and public morals, of popular mentality and even of the functioning of institutions. All these changes derived from the Hellenic influence, which showed itself first with the conquest of Magna Graecia and achieved dominance after the defeat of Perseus, which made Macedonia a Roman province in 168 B.C. The triumph of Lucius Aemilius Paulus, its conqueror, marked a date of tremendous importance in Roman history. Rome had just discovered—and would at once adopt—a new mode of life and thought.

Until then the Romans had clung to that species of rural asceticism that they owed to their origins. Their manners were simple and their customs somewhat uncouth. To till the soil and defend it, to offer the Republic the contribution of one's labor, one's endurance, and one's bravery, to honor the familiar deities—these were virtually the unbroken horizon of the Roman citizen. The mercantile spirit had not yet arrived. Concerns of an intellectual or artistic nature were alien to him. But the soldiers who had taken part in the Macedonian expedition came home dazzled. Behind their general's triumphal chariot, 250 other chariots loaded with Greek statues and pictures made their laborious way up the Capitoline. In this procession Greek art entered Rome and incited an irresistible infatuation. Every civilian or military official whom the Republic assigned to Greece was thenceforth to return with his own personal collection. The peaceful conquests of the enthusiasts were also accompanied by violence, sacrilege, and all the wicked practices of a Verres. This methodical looting was to continue for two centuries, and that is why, though Rome itself has been despoiled on many occasions, its monuments, its museums, and its private collections still possess the richest accumulation of Greek antiquities in the world.

It was not only the sculptures that poured into Rome; it was also men steeped in Hellenic civilization, whether brought back as slaves or arrived of their own choice in the hope of a better life. They included a great number of artists, men of letters, workers trained in sophisticated skills. They were to serve the Romans as secretaries, physicians, and magicians, tutors for their children, decorators for their houses. Their influence established a new taste. Everything was to change its form. Rome was to shed its overgrown-village ways and assume the bearing of a metropolis. The primitive little shrines would become great temples. The Curia was to be resplendent with marble, the tribune with statues. The gods themselves, who were only names, for lack of an art that could make it possible to represent them plastically, were to acquire personalities with their new incarnations in the superb bodies of the dwellers on Olympus.

Much has been said to the effect that, in consequence of this rapid enrichment of Latium, the Roman people's acquisition of the finest expressions of beauty from the shores of Greece put an end to any attempt to create their own; Rome, it has been argued, was too overpowered by the "ancient kiss" to produce an art of its own. In order to bolster this theory, its advocates cite the very many imitations of Greek models that Roman antiquity has handed down to us. It is true that the museums of Rome are filled with imitation as well as authentic Grecian works. Nevertheless it would be unjust to view the Romans as mere imitators. Their sculpture is enough to prove that to the undeniable Greek and Asian influences they added enough in personal invention and new conceptions to sire from this mixture a form of art that, without any pretensions to basic originality, is no less typically Roman. The statues and the busts of famous men that stand in so many rows in the museums of the Capitoline and the Vatican are the proof of that. Whereas the Greeks were predominantly concerned with the body's beauty, the Romans obviously took the study of faces as their theme. This direction flowed naturally from their realistic disposition: they did not intend to leave abstract images of themselves.

André Suarès has said that Roman antiquity was no more than "the baroque of the Greeks"; even if the statement is accepted as truth, it could be applied only to the realm of the plastic arts. In architecture Roman creativity produced important works, surpassing, occasionally by a great deal, its models. This was not only because of the adaptations imposed by soil and climate. It is above all because the sagacious race of *quirites* (knights), which borrowed from its neighbors and its subjects whatever might be of use to it, also knew how to adapt what it imitated and to accommodate to its own genius the inventions of others. More and more the Romans impressed their own character on the alien arts that they began by imitating. And, when they applied that character to works that required majesty and grandeur, such as amphitheaters, aqueducts, and arches of triumph, they made it produce masterpieces.

These observations are made without any underestimation of the Greek influence that introduced Rome to the light of the arts and radically transformed its life. For manners and morals were to become quite as steeped in Hellenism as the arts. The customs of the Greeks were taken up, and little by little they supplanted the traditional customs. The Romans learned their language, studied their religion, copied their way of living. In a word, Hellenic civilization took root in Rome.

Unhappily that civilization, as brilliant as it still was, was nonetheless enervated and already decadent; and the more so in that it arrived in Rome by way of the Hellenic kingdoms of Asia, where the excess of sophistication had already initiated the corruption of morals. It was to be difficult for plain Roman minds, brutally confronted with exciting temptations, to escape the counsels of a philosophy that did not put forward political honesty and devotion to the state as the ultimate ends of man. Although the "ancestral custom" found zealous defenders, such as Cato the Elder, it was overwhelmed by a new spirit. The old Roman type disappeared gradually, and Juvenal summed up the accounts of the change in a few words when he wrote: "The vanquished world has revenged itself on us by giving us its vices."

In fact, more and more germs of corruption had been implanted. Not the least was the quick enrichment of the Roman aristocracy during the conquests. It was to this class that all the profit went, because it was the source of the generals, the proconsuls, the governors, the tax collectors, all the tyrants, all the pillagers who exploited the conquered lands, while the Senate, to which as a rule they belonged, did not exercise the slightest supervision over them. In such a climate of immorality it was inevitable that the stern virtues that had been the strength of the Roman aristocracy should disappear. Long suppressed, the desire to enjoy overflowed into a life of luxury. Houses were no longer limited to the all-purpose room that the old *atrium* had been; now it was merely a vestibule from which many rooms opened, all adorned with statues and decked with paintings and mosaics. Food had become sophisticated; the old meals of bread rubbed with garlic and vegetables cooked in water were ridiculed; the plates were now of silver, the wines were often from Greece. There was competitive bidding for the services of Greek cooks. Dinners of the rarest delicacies lasted all night. The Hellenic custom of reclining on a couch at meals had been adopted. Oriental furniture inlaid with gold and ivory, Babylonian carpets, perfumes were bought at outrageous prices. Everywhere there was "that ostentation of costly objects and that profusion of riches practiced only to demonstrate the fact of possession, the absurd and vulgar luxury of the upstart" (Guglielmo Ferrero).

The enrichment of the Roman aristocracy had had even more damaging effects on the social structure. The small rural landowners—an honest, industrious class that had been the foundation of Roman power—had disappeared, decimated by the wars, ruined by their creditors, or forced to give up their lands to them. Great estates had been created, which were cheaply worked for their owners by slaves, the number of whom had been considerably augmented by the conquests (it was customary among all ancient peoples to sell prisoners of war as slaves). The former owners had no other choice than to go to Rome and swell the ranks of that vast proletarian class that, unable to find work there (trade was in the hands of the equestrian class,* and artisanry was performed by slaves), lived on the charity of the rich in a state of dependency. Above all, the poor sold their votes to the rich. For they were still citizens: they wore the toga and they voted. Since the masters of the Senate and of public office used power for self-enrichment, the desire to attain it encouraged them to financial sacrifices that provided the livelihood of a whole class of idlers. This class, enlarged by the freedmen, former slaves of foreign origin, had lost its exclusively Roman character. Rome had become a cosmopolitan city; men of all races and all colors mingled there. As a necessary consequence of this mingling, patriotism had dwindled.

The corrupt aristocracy, the debased proletariat, the morals, the thinking, the social structure had been so profoundly altered and perverted that after the defeat of the Gracchi's attempt to re-establish the middle class—a defeat caused as much by the lack of effort among the proletarians as by the resistance of the nobility—Romans found themselves divided into two opposing camps: aristocracy and proletariat. A hundred years of civil wars were to follow, and to end in the downfall of the Republic.

THE TIME OF THE CIVIL WARS

Throughout the first century B.C. there was a three-sided drama among the democratic party, the senatorial oligarchy, and the military leaders, whose victories were gradually to give them the ascendancy over the two parties, which they would support or oppose in turn until they could harness them beneath their own yoke. For there were many wars in those

---

* Originally a military category (cavalry), the equestrians relatively quickly became a social class corresponding to the modern upper-middle-class finance capitalists.—Translator.

days: against Jugurtha, king of the Numidians, whom Marius was to vanquish; against the Teutons and the Cimbrians, against the Italians themselves, weary of supplying Rome with soldiers and money without obtaining citizenship; against Mithridates, who had succeeded in raising the province of Asia and whom Sulla was to defeat for the first time in Greece; against rebellious Spain, which Pompey forced back into the Roman domain; against the southern slaves whom Spartacus had raised; and against Gaul, whose conquest and Romanization were achieved by Caesar.

While the legions maintained Roman order far away, social and political disintegration increased in Rome itself, where in the end anarchy took over. The constitutional machinery had stopped functioning; elections were won by corruption, conspiracy, and occasionally force. The number of Romans living on nothing but the sale of their votes was rising daily. Since election was no longer determined by merit, the magistrates were losing their authority. The Senate itself violated its own dignity with indecent brawls. Justice was held in contempt because it was openly for sale. All kinds of crimes were absolved; the only thing that was still prohibited, Cicero was to say, was "to go and kill the head of a family in his own house." At a sufficient price, a court could be persuaded to convict anyone. The scale of payments was known: according to Calidius, there was a minimum of thirty thousand *sestertii* for getting rid of anyone of pretorian rank.

It was not enough to bribe assemblies and buy votes; the favor of the mass was solicited with feasts that in the end became almost continuous. Flora, the rich courtesan who was Pompey's friend, reinstituted the games, fallen into disuse, that had been held in the early days of the Republic in honor of the goddess of agriculture. She bequeathed all her property for this purpose. It was then that the flower games began to be held in the Campo dei Fiori, and they turned out so badly that they became the festival of the courtesans. The feasts hallowed by tradition, the Saturnalia and the Lupercalia, were supplemented by a huge number of votive celebrations that provided the occasion for showing unimagined luxury. All Rome turned out for them, and not only the mass of the people but also the magistrates and the Senators themselves, the matrons and even the Vestals. The number of theaters multiplied. In that of Scaurus, which was to be the model for the Colosseum, there was room for eighty thousand persons. Most of these theaters were built of wood and have disappeared. Pompey's was the first to be built entirely of stone for permanent use. Let us say of it only that, while it was of comparatively modest size (it had only thirty thousand seats), it included a remarkable innovation: forced drafts of air "mitigated the heat in it," thus achieving what is today called air-conditioning. While it was used for Greek dramas with amazing stage effects, it was also the site of animal combats, where five hundred lions appeared in five days. Elephants were put to death in Rome for the first time; their groans so aroused the pity of the spectators that Pompey was cursed by the crowd that he was striving to please.

As sensitive as this crowd was, it had no pity for slaves torn to pieces by beasts or for vanquished gladiators. We despise, Cicero said, "gladiators who try to save their lives by every possible means." These bloodletting performances, however, had not yet achieved the popularity that they were to have two centuries later, when the savage games of the Colosseum enchanted frenzied crowds. A distant inheritance from the Etruscans, they had been brought back into usage at the time of the Samnite wars as a means of arousing warrior virtues; the fashion for them, which was to grow constantly, was deeply rooted in Rome in the last days of the Republic.

These circuses were expensive, but the ambitious men who competed with one another for the honor of paying for them expected profitable compensation for their generosity. They impoverished themselves for the public only in the hope of recouping their losses in some province to which popular backing would win them an appointment. Once established there, they trafficked in everything, even promotions to the rank of centurion, and looted the countries entrusted to their rule. Whole populations were bled dry by their exactions. An infinite mesh of conspiracies kept all the pillagers immune to prosecution. The laws themselves concealed the scandals.

Yet in all this laxity there were public men who remained honorable. One would like to think that such was the case of that plebeian edile named C. Publicius Bibulus, whom the Senate rewarded with a tomb in blocks of travertine, which stands on the right of the monument to Victor Emmanuel—the illustrious neighbor to which this tomb owes its prominence. It has the added interest of serving as a topographical landmark: it stands on the exact spot where the Via Flaminia began.

Another great official who was faithful to his duty in a time of depravity has left a more useful reminder in Rome: the Bridge of Fabricius, which leads to the island in the Tiber. Of all the seventeen Roman bridges, it is the only one that can be called ancient, for it has remained virtually the same as it was in the year 62 B.C., when Fabricius had it built. It was not the work of a demagogue looking for popularity: it was the honest job of an official whose function it was to build bridges and roads. There is a tendency to forget the name of this honorable technician, for his bridge is now called the Ponte Quattro Capi because of the two four-headed statues of Hermes that adorn its entrance.

MORAL AND POLITICAL DETERIORATION

If public morals had become deplorable by the end of the Republic, private morals were no better. Luxury made an insolent ostentation of itself; the hills were covered with rich private houses. The remains of some of them from the time of Sulla, found on the Palatine, can give some idea of the richness of their marble and their decorations. Such indulgences were the more suspect because public buildings preserved their character of strict austerity. All the riches of Greece and Asia abounded in these ostentatious palaces, sometimes with ridiculous caprice. Lucullus set up his dining room in an aviary; Sergius Orata installed a swimming pool on the roof of his house. Everyone tried to dazzle Rome with his insensate expenditures. These were supported by speculation; this was easy, and the constant changes in interest rates made lending a kind of sport. Everyone was engaged in it, with the assistance of a horde of moneychangers, brokers, usurers, and traders. Bankers became kings and were to reach the point at which they could outweigh the influence of the Senate.

Every passion had free rein, without restraint, and social ties came to have no more validity than political ties. Marriages were made and unmade for profit, at the whim of whatever wind was blowing through the Forum. Becoming the inspiration for all kinds of immoral schemes, women, once the symbols and custodians of family virtues, now abandoned their homes. A temple could be built for Venus with the fines imposed on dissolute matrons.

Kept out of public affairs by the laws, wives often managed to play indirect parts in them through their husbands; this was absolutely new in Roman customs. It is no small surprise to learn that so many of those proud Romans who at a distance convey so strong an impression of authority were ruled by their wives, quite as much as any middle-class husband today. "We give orders to all other men," old Cato said, "and we take them from our wives." It was public knowledge that Sulla, who had the soul of a despot, meekly followed the political views of his wife, Matella Fulvia; Cicero was completely in the hands of his wife, Terentia. None of this had any effect on the dangerous rise in the number of courtesans, and the precepts of religion were neglected and derided. Roman life had become "a bacchanal."

Arrived at its height, this moral and political deterioration began to have its natural results: conspiracies arose, the most notorious of which was Catiline's. The jousts of oratory were deserted for blood battles. Riot became an almost permanent state. "There is no longer a Republic," Cicero cried in those days; "there is no longer a Senate; there is no dignity left in any of us. We have lost not only all our sap and all our blood, but even the color and the old look of the city." "Order and justice were dead in these days," Tacitus wrote later. In other words, the rule of the Republic had ended.

But the country (the real country, as we say) remained, as it wanted to live. It was the military authorities who made that possible. Since Marius had opened its ranks to the proletarians, the army had become a professional army, dedicated more to the fortunes of its leaders than to legality. And every now and then, between two campaigns, its leaders, sometimes joined by common interests and sometimes rivals, would undertake the reconstruction of the state, under various forms and relying indiscriminately for support, in accord with political fluctuations, on parties whose conflict was the root cause of the anarchy. Marius, Sulla, Crassus, and Pompey were to carry out a series of *coups d'état* that, without making them unchallenged masters, were to implant military dictatorship in the corpse of the republican constitution. In the end it was Julius Caesar who assured himself of supremacy by eliminating Pompey, his most dangerous rival, with whom he had briefly shared power in the first triumvirate (Crassus, Pompey, and Caesar). In January, 49 B.C., having left Gaul and crossed the Rubicon with the historic remark *"Alea iacta est,"* he marched on Rome, resolved to battle his way to power. He pursued Pompey into Thessaly and defeated him at Pharsalia. Then he had himself made dictator for life with the title of Imperator and extremely broad powers that gave him supreme authority over the army, the state, and even religion. In theory, all the machinery of government continued to exist, but Caesar reigned as a sovereign, without accountability and without check or balance. All that was left of the Republic was its name.

CHAPTER 3

CAESAR

THE THEATER OF POMPEY

Caesar's ambition was monarchy; he wore the dress of the ancient kings, he had a golden throne in the Forum, he gave his name to the month of July. But the kingly title was hated in Rome, which accepted the fact of servitude but not the name that some wanted to give it. Caesar was assassinated in the midst of the Senate on March 15, 44 B.C. by a group of conspirators at whose head he was amazed to find Brutus, who was believed to be his son and who had always enjoyed his protection. Stabbed twenty-three times by daggers, he died at the foot of Pompey's statue, which was spattered with his blood. If this statue is really the same one that is displayed in the Palazzo Spada, where the Council of State meets today, there is hardly a single monument in Rome more imbued with history.

In any event, what is left of the theater of Pompey enables us to establish the setting of one of the greatest events in antiquity. The picturesque Campo dei Fiori quarter is curiously gashed by streets with sudden corners or apparently illogical turnings (notably Via de' Chiavari, Via del Sudario, Via dei Barbieri). That is because these streets have outlived the building that blocked their courses, and that was the theater of Pompey. Its ruins are there, beneath the Palazzo Righetti (now the Palazzo Pio), and the houses round Sant' Andrea della Valle still mark its outlines. If one dug deeply enough, one would uncover not only the foundations of the theater but also the huge Greek statues that embellished it and that Cicero had undertaken to supply. One of them, *Hercules Mastaï,* which is now in the Vatican Museum, was discovered in 1864 during a new project for shoring up the foundations of the *palazzo.* The eleven others still lie buried with the precious materials that, for the first time in Rome, were used for the construction of a place of entertainment in violation of law and custom alike. Still, in order to avoid action by the censors, Pompey was obliged to put a temple at the top of his theater so that the marble steps and benches intended for the spectators could be considered the stairway to a religious edifice. It was in the hall opening onto the large portico that the dramatic scene of Caesar's murder took place. The Curia having been destroyed by fire shortly before, the senators were using this hall, from which, when their business had been completed, they could watch the day's theater offering.

Pompey's theater was the first large building to be erected by a private individual for the pleasure of the public. For monuments were beginning to play an important part in the clashes of forces that were contesting for popular favor. Even shrines were used for propaganda purposes. Pompey had dedicated the temple above his theater to victorious Venus, a rather extreme way of celebrating his own merits. He had also had a dramatic catalogue of his military successes put on display in another temple, dedicated to Minerva; its site is occupied today by the church of Santa Maria sopra Minerva, or the Minerva, where Lacordaire* was ordained.

THE TEMPLE OF VENUS GENITRIX AND CAESAR'S FORUM

Caesar, who was a member of the highest nobility of Rome, was no more retiring than his rival, whose ancestry, at least, was modest. Although Caesar, demagogically parading a false modesty, had taken up residence in the popular Suburra quarter, once he had become imperator he had no qualms about erecting, in the center of the Forum that bore his name, a temple to Venus Genitrix in order to overwhelm the people with his proud claim of direct descent from the mother of Aeneas. The three magnificent marble columns, the capitals, the friezes, and the cornices that still rise there are the remains of a restoration by Trajan. Caesar's temple,

---

* Jean-Baptiste Henri Lacordaire was a nineteenth-century French Dominican reformer and writer.—Translator.

no doubt, like all the monuments of that period, had simply columns of travertine, but on the walls there were an Ajax and a Medea by the painter Timomachus; on the threshold stood a statue of Venus carved by the Greek Arcesilaus; a golden Cleopatra testified to the dictator's "impassioned homage" to Ptolemy's daughter. The open court in front was embellished with a statue of Caesar "mounted on a splendid steed with almost human feet and toenails half the length of the toes." Later there was also a marble statue of the conqueror of Gaul, which is preserved in the Capitoline Museum and a replica of which stands on the Via dei Fori Imperiali.

The temple of Venus Genitrix was the major adornment of the Forum that Caesar had created as his retort to Pompey's ventures in self-advertisement. It was an arrogant notion, but also a useful action, since the old Roman Forum was no longer adequate to the needs of the larger city. The action was to be emulated by Augustus, Vespasian, Nerva, and Trajan under the pressure of mounting necessities. But Caesar's Forum would remain the model for all: each would include a temple dedicated to a particular deity in a large rectangular area bounded by porches. Caesar's Forum, which included a long row of fine *tabernae* (shops), was always the largest, with its almost sixty-five thousand square feet, and the busiest. It extended far beyond the portion that was cleared during the Fascist period, running along the great artery that joins the Piazza Venezia and the Colosseum.

THE CURIA / BASILICA JULIA AND BASILICA AEMILIA / THE SAEPTA JULIA

Once he was the all-powerful master of Rome, Caesar evolved great projects for the improvement and beautification of his city, but he did not have time to bring them to fruition. Many of the monuments that were completed—or even initiated—only after his death were the direct product of his thinking. Such was the case of the Curia. The traditional meeting place for the Senate since the beginning of the Republic, it had suffered many vicissitudes, the last of which had led to its total destruction during the troubles of 52 B.C. Caesar rebuilt it from the foundations up, but he died too soon to dedicate it himself. Although it is still called the Curia Julia, the building that we see today is not the one that was begun by Caesar and destroyed by the great fire that occurred under Nero. The present Curia was the work of Diocletian. At least this is true of what has survived a series of various mutilations; the portico has vanished, like the outer marble facings; the bronze gates are only copies, the originals having been carried off to the church of St. John Lateran during the papacy of Alexander VII.

Nor did Caesar live to see the completion of the Basilica Julia. This is the large structure, more than a hundred yards long and more than fifty yards wide, whose considerable remains can be seen at the lower part of the Forum. Only the bases of the columns are ancient; the columns themselves were restored with materials taken out of the foundations and used for the reconstruction.

The creation of the Basilica Julia was a reaction to new exigencies. It had very long been the custom for the courts to sit in the Forum, in the open air; it was only about 180 B.C. that a movement began to take the courts indoors, into buildings exclusively for their use. This was the origin of the basilicas. Those that had been built, one after another, in the Forum (the Porcian, the Fulvian, the Aemilian, the Sempronian) had become inadequate by the time of Caesar; this offers some idea of the rapid increase in the population and the development of its legal procedures. It must be noted also that the citizen of the dying Republic was becoming more and more interested in courtroom matters. He paid little attention to his family and even less to his wife. The basilica was the recognized meeting place for all the idle and the curious; everything arrived there sooner or later, from the pettiest thefts to the consuls' breaches of trust. Besides, the crowd thronged the basilicas even when the courts were not sitting, sometimes to escape the heat or the rain, sometimes simply to play dice or checkers. The fanciers of these tranquil pleasures have left their traces, which time has been unable to erase from the Basilica Julia, in the form of game-board patterns cut into the marble of its pavements.

Another basilica is connected with Caesar's memory because indirectly he paid for its construction. In the course of the devious politicking by which he was preparing his rise to power, the aspiring dictator had appropriated fifteen hundred talents out of Gaul's gold in order to buy a rival, whom a shred of scruple persuaded to apply the price of his betrayal to some contribution to the public interest. He belonged to the Aemilia *gens,* one of whose ancestors, a consul in 179 B.C., had ordered the construction of a basilica appointed to commercial uses, especially those of the moneychangers. It was this building, by now greatly run down, that Lucius Aemilius Paulus replaced with a monument that Cicero described as "at once pleasing to the people and a tribute to him who caused it to be erected." In fact, the ruins of the Basilica Aemilia, which extend from the

Curia to the temple of Antoninus and Faustina, attest to the richness of its marbles and the elegance of its decorations. In contrast to so many Roman monuments whose crumbled ruins were used for anonymous reconstructions, the marbles of this basilica, of which large remains survived into the Renaissance, are known to have been employed in the construction of Cardinal Corneto's palace in 1503 by the great architect Donato Bramante, with whom such practices were only too common. As for the magnificent columns of Phrygian marble, they were taken to the Basilica of St. Paul, where they were ruined by the great fire of 1825.

At the time of his death Caesar's mind was filled with a host of plans for the beautification of Rome. He wanted a theater that would have dwarfed Pompey's; he did not have time to finish it. Augustus assumed this charge: the result was the theater of Marcellus. Caesar had also dreamed of presenting the city with a huge circus, and it was he who first had the idea for the Colosseum, which was not put into execution until the time of the Flavian emperors. He also wanted to improve the port of Ostia and even to change the Tiber's course in order to acquire a large area that was to be used for military maneuvers, so that the Field of Mars would be available for further building. Caesar had already begun to erect a huge portica there with many aisles, the ruins of which are buried beneath the church of Santa Maria in Via Lata, the Doria and Bonaparte palaces and part of the Piazza Venezia. It was to be Agrippa who would complete this great project, and Augustus who would give it the name of Saepta Julia. It was obvious that the enlargement of Rome was the great objective of the divine Julius. Cicero was highly critical of the plan, accusing the dictator of considering the city too small to hold him.

The enormous sums that Caesar poured into his vast projects without reckoning costs came in large part from the booty that he had piled up in Gaul and from the sale of the slaves whom he had brought back from there. In the market that functioned at the foot of the temple of Castor and Pollux he retailed many of the ancestors of my compatriots, a fact that, though he does not trumpet it in his *Commentaries,* has been reported for us by Strabo.

THE FORUM OF THE REPUBLIC

The political period of the Forum ended with Caesar. Henceforth public business would be put into the hands of officials chosen by the monarch. The people would be kept entirely out of it. They would go to the Forum only to stroll or to take part in decorative ceremonials or in that singular procession (*pompa circensis*) that took the images of the gods to the circus so that they might be entertained by watching the games. The area that had heretofore been so zealously kept open was gradually to be taken up by great honorific monuments that would wipe out the memory of the Rome of austerity and heroism as well as that of the city inflamed by quarrels in which the Republic had perished. There would no longer be the triumphal statues of conquering generals, or the shrines of the virtues that protected the city. No trace of the Scipios, of the Gracchi, of Cato, of Marius, of Sulla, of Pompey would survive there. And yet, though the centuries have jumbled the stage setting, it was indeed there that a universe of ideas and forces was created by which we still live.

Let us not leave this holy place, which pulsed with a people in the golden age of its genius, without at least forming some idea of its topography. While restricting our objective to an over-all, synthesizing view, we should picture the Forum of the Republic in our minds as a succession of terraces on which, so to speak, we can observe the political constitution of Rome, each level of difference representing another step in the hierarchy of power. In the lower part, which is the true Forum, the *plebs* gathered; a few steps higher there was the Comitium, on the slope that leads to the place where the church of St. Martin stands today. This square esplanade was the meeting place of the nobles—that is, the influential citizens who governed Rome: it was there that the *comices curiates* convened and that all the problems of the day were debated in the open air. From the Comitium one went on to the Curia, where the Senate held its sessions. Above this was the Graecostasium, a broad platform where foreign envoys waited to be escorted into the Senate. The whole was dominated by the temple of Concord, erected in honor of the peace concluded between patricians and plebeians, the lesson of which was not always heeded.

In this very strictly governed state everything was subject to words; that meant that the orators' tribune (the *rostra*) was pre-eminent in it: it was considered a sacred place. It had been installed on the Comitium, below the Curia, from which the Senate could observe it. "The Senate," Cicero said, "has its eye on the tribune and holds it in the hollow of its hand in order to prevent it from being rash and to hold it to its duties." The wall that supported it was decorated with the iron rams of the ships captured at Antium (now Anzio). A sundial told the time until, 159 years before

Christ, the first water clock was installed. It was from the height of this tribune that the great men of the Republic poured the floods of their eloquence over the people. One after another, the Scipios and the Gracchi, Antony and Caesar appeared there. It is still a matter of astonishment that the words of these orators, however impressive they might have been, could have subdued open-air throngs that were almost always stormy, if we are to believe the ancient writers who likened them to "the waves of an angry sea." It was commonplace, in the crowd of listeners, to exchange insults, threats, and even blows; bloody clashes were not infrequent. We know that, in order to make themselves heard, the speakers adopted a technique suited to the environmental difficulties: they cadenced and, so to speak, chanted their speeches, at the same time accompanying them with expressive mimetics. Nevertheless it is hard to believe that they could have dominated the tumult—all the more so when one reflects that the citizens who took no interest in the subject went on busying themselves noisily with other matters. Astonishingly, the funeral processions of important persons traversed the Forum even when it was filled by a meeting, and the audience would be deafened by the sound of trumpets and the cries of mourning women, hired for the occasion. Then confusion was combined with uproar; nevertheless, it was the rule that the orator of the day continue to shout out his lungs from the tribune without a thought to wind or tide. But—as was observed later, and as we can still observe today—it was not always the speeches that determined the votes.

These *rostra* of the Comitium are known to us today only through a coin that has provided us with a conventional portrayal of them. Those that can be seen in front of the arch of Septimius Severus were completed only after Caesar's death and were used for nothing but speeches by the emperors and funeral orations over them. The only unimpeachable evidence of the republican period that survives in the Forum is that Via Sacra that ran its length and that still contains numerous blocks of its original paving. From the Arch of Titus to the Capitoline we can follow its traces, which have given rise to so many quarrels among the learned. It is no longer marked by statues and arches of honor, but we know that all the conquerors of the world, hailed by the throng, rode in triumph the length of this road that was the most glorious in Rome and whose every stone calls forth the great memories of the city's history.

CHAPTER 4

AUGUSTUS

THE ESTABLISHMENT OF THE EMPIRE

Caesar's slayers believed that they were saving the Republic; the dictator's death launched Rome into a new era of highly confused troubles, out of which emerged the triumvirate of Antony, Lepidus, and Octavian, a sort of cartel of rival leaders who merged their forces for the immediate task. What they conceived this to be was a savage purge of their opponents, in which three hundred senators and two hundred equestrians were killed. Cicero was among the victims, even though he had always striven "to keep to the middle of the road." The abominations of Sulla's time returned: the manhunts, the severed heads impaled on the speakers' tribune. The triumvirs had explained that, "enlightened by the fate that his own clemency had earned for Caesar, they would leave no enemies behind them." They adhered rigorously to this charming program. Thereafter all that they had to do was to settle the question of supremacy among themselves. It was finally resolved in favor of the youngest of them, Octavian, Caesar's adopted son.

Sickly and timorous, he had not at first seemed capable of claiming his paternal heritage: it did not take long to learn that, beneath these semblances of weakness, there were a profound political intelligence and a stubborn ambition. It was through the use of these qualities that he got rid of his rivals: Lepidus by persuasion, Antony by making him appear to be

47

an enemy of Rome by reason of his love for Cleopatra, queen of Egypt. Antony having been beaten at Actium and Cleopatra having committed suicide by offering her breast to an asp, Octavian made Egypt a Roman province and emerged as the champion of the nation's cause. He had no difficulty in establishing an absolute monarchy under the cloak of republican institutions, ostensibly preserved with great cleverness but revised in such a way as to operate only to his own exclusive benefit. Thus he acquired the whole of public power and was, as it pleased him, consul, tribune, prince of the Senate, chief justice, Pontifex Maximus, and supreme military commander. Army, administration, legislation, religion all came together in his hands.

The political system that he inaugurated is called the Empire, the Latin *imperator* being translated as *emperor*. But the many-faceted men who, beginning with Octavian, were to rule the Roman world for five centuries would not be emperors in the modern understanding of the word: there was no automatic inheritance of power. Their government was to be only a form of rule that owed its power, as it did its name, to its military strength: "an absolute, if precarious, power that condemned him who held it to the constant solicitation of support from the soldiery and the populace." The Roman emperors would see only flatterers, not subjects, at their feet.

This did not prevent the Roman world under Octavian, soon renamed Caesar Augustus by the addition of a *cognomen* that indicated he was a sacred personage, from reverting to the one-man rule that had guided its first steps and laid the foundations for its greatness. This return to monarchy was to arrest the descent that was rapidly leading it to ruin. Augustus employed his power not for his personal gratification but for the restoration and the renewal of the state in every sphere. Thanks to him, throughout that long era that historians have called the Principate, Rome regained prosperity and power. It was an end of anarchy, of civil war, of rebellion of any kind both in Rome and in the Empire. *Pax romana*—the peace of Rome—was to reign and to bear those precious fruits of every peace: well-being and progress.

AN ANIMATED CAPITAL

The city of Rome, quite naturally, was the first beneficiary. "The Age of Augustus" was to change its appearance, its structure, and its way of living.

Now the master of a vast empire, Rome had grown to the dimensions of a great capital. According to some historians, its population had by this time reached two million. The suburbs had begun to march up the slopes of the Aventine, the Caelius, and the Esquiline; across the river there was now a new quarter, the Trastevere, as it is known today, which was populated by Orientals and Jews and was linked to the city by four bridges.

Even more than in area the city had grown in height. Private houses were now to be found almost exclusively on the hills. Each was built round an *atrium,* which was connected with rooms whose number and opulence depended on the occupant's wealth. Except for the Forum and the little valley occupied by the Circus Maximus, all the lowlands that separated the hills were covered with tenements four to six stories high; these belonged to rich owners and were occupied by tenants. "The inhabitants of Rome," Cicero said, "are perched one on top of another as if they were trying to climb into the sky." There had never been a flight to the suburbs from Rome; the uncertainty of communications would never have permitted it. But it was as much out of choice as out of necessity that the population huddled on itself in the central areas.

The blocks of houses were pressed tightly together, separated only by narrow, winding, and often hilly streets, sometimes so steep that stairs had to be cut. Nowhere were there those regular patterns and symmetrical harmonies that were the beauty of the Greek cities in the Orient. The faulty growth of the city dated from its rebuilding after the sack by the Gauls: since that time no one had ever made a serious effort at city planning. The confusion was aggravated by the very many chance fires that had occasionally razed whole quarters. The residents' manner of living made such disasters inevitable. After each of them, narrow streets would be laid out at random and lined with higher and higher houses bristling at every story with cantilevered balconies. The streets of Rome were like the corridors of an underground city, or mountain passes. The sun never reached them. The Romans of those days had a very high esteem for the coolness that prevailed in them, which, no doubt wrongly, they considered "good for the health."

These streets were very animated, full of itinerant merchants who offered, in loud voices, all kinds of wares from sulphur matches to caged birds and trained animals, including "small foodstuffs," the sale of which outside the markets was permitted. Thus pedestrians risked the distasteful experience of being jostled by an offal vendor who wore on his head a ring from which bleeding tripes or lungs were dangling. The idle crowds that wandered along the major avenues found other sources of entertainment there. There were street performers in abundance: magicians, snake charmers, and even bare-knuckle boxers, all competing for popular attention and the few coins that might be thrown.

Movement was difficult in all this conglomeration. Vehicles of every description tried to make a passage, from private litters to heavy chariots drawn sometimes by eight or ten oxen. Bottlenecks were constant and led to the rousing discussions that are the most honored tradition of such phenomena. The noise was deafening: there was never so loud a city as the Rome of those days. Every kind of sound mingled with every other in such a cacophony that, according to Seneca, the dead themselves could have heard it. Everyone racked his brain for a means of making noise, even the moneychangers with their coins. A thousand excitements added to the din—here someone was chasing a mad dog, there a goatherd was trying to recover his animals that had wandered off among the crowd, somewhere else a troop of young pigs was squealing. In those streets that were absolutely impossible for vehicles, pedestrian movement was hardly any easier: children played loudly in the thoroughfare and tradesmen worked outside their shops at occupations that were occasionally extremely intrusive, like the ropemakers who were forever blocking all passage.

Such was Rome at the end of the first century B.C. Caesar had dreamed of remedying the confusion of the city, but his premature death had made it impossible for him to achieve or even to perfect his plans.

THE RELIGIOUS REVIVAL

It was Augustus who was to turn Rome into a new city and a splendid capital. The age lent itself to the accomplishment of a program of buildings and monuments. The civil wars were over; foreign wars were so rare that the temple of Janus, whose gates were open only when the legions were campaigning, had been closed. The authority of Augustus was unchallenged and sovereign. As Tacitus put it, Rome had "peace and a sovereign." These were favorable conditions for the domestic tasks that Augustus, as a matter of taste, preferred. When he said: "I found a city of brick; I want to leave a city of marble," he had given the remark a very broad meaning, whose aspiration certainly transcended the realm of architecture. He was to dedicate himself to a huge project of reconstruction, and for this purpose he was to enlist administrators, poets, and historians, as well as architects and artists. He wanted to give back to Rome all its power and all its luster.

To this lofty end, he turned first to the revival of religion. Roman religion was a state religion; in the troubled period of the great political struggles, it had lost its rigor and the traditional observances had been neglected. It had given way to a kind of atheism, or eclectic deism like Cicero's. With Augustus the city was to be led back to the observance of the most ancient rites, which the greatest poets of the time—Virgil, Ovid, Propertius—would be instructed to restore to prominence. And, in order for piety to find asylum in sacred edifices that might inspire and sustain it, the sovereign occupied himself first of all with the restoration and reconstruction of all the temples that had fallen to ruin during the civil wars. In the single year of 28, he restored more than fifty of them.

But this was not the limit of his ambition. Employing new materials, he applied wholly unprecedented conceptions to the art of building. In due course we shall discuss the progress of the arts in his time. They were totally to alter the appearance of Rome, where the richness of colonnades and capitals was to spread with astonishing volume. The three columns of the temple of Castor and Pollux that still stand in the middle of the Forum testify to the architectural magnificence of this epoch.

THE FORUM OF AUGUSTUS

The proclaimed desire of Augustus to "put religion on the side of the Empire" was to lead him to build a number of new temples. He listed them with some self-satisfaction in his *Res Gestae*. The most famous are the temples of Iulius Divinus and Mars the Avenger (Ultor), which were supposed to perpetuate Caesar's memory but also to celebrate the vengeance exacted by Augustus from his father's enemies. For he never forgot that it was by professing to avenge Caesar that he had managed to succeed him.

The temple of the deified Caesar stood at the eastern end of the Forum, at the same spot where the people had burned the dictator's body on an improvised pyre after Antony's inflammatory speech. All that remains of it is the podium that thrust out over the area of the Forum in order to form a kind of tribune decorated with the rams from Cleopatra's ships, burned at Actium.

As for the temple of Mars Ultor, it was the center and the jewel of the

Forum, to the construction of which Augustus devoted one-third of a century and which he dedicated two years before the Christian era with sumptuous festivities enhanced by a roundup of 260 lions in the Circus Maximus, a crocodile hunt in the Circus Flaminius, a naval battle between Persians and Athenians, and a complete re-enactment of the capture of Troy. The acquisition of land by expropriation had been slow and expensive, but the whole quarter was transformed into a monumental area worthy of Rome's majesty, astounding in its size, and staggering in its richness. The rarest materials had been used in building the temple of Mars: the most precious marbles had been brought from Africa, great blocks of stone from Gabies, timber from Rhaetia.* The building was lavishly adorned with Greek masterpieces: two bronze statues and two pictures of Apelles, in particular, had been stolen from the palace of Alexander the Great; Caesar's sword, which the people were supposed to venerate, was one of the few ornaments of the temple that had not been acquired through pillage or as booty of the victory of Philippi. The privileges that Augustus accorded to this rich shrine made it the equal of the temple of Jupiter: it was the meeting place of the Senate when matters of war or peace were to be decided; the public treasury was placed there under the guardianship of the god, who did not deter daring thieves from stealing it, as Juvenal reported with great amusement.

The whole base of this temple, a solemn flight of stairs, and three splendid columns are still standing. These are enough to enable us to reconstruct it visually, just as we can the whole Forum of which it was only a part. The temple opened onto two broad streets, flanked by great enclosed halls joined to two large hemicycles: one can still see some of the niches that held bronze statues of the great captains who, from Romulus to Caesar, had given Rome its greatness. There was a gigantic statue of Augustus himself at the end of the square hall, paved in an ancient yellow marble, that was uncovered in recent excavations; there are two stones supporting the feet of a figure eight times life size: Mars or Augustus himself. A tremendous wall, a hundred feet high, formed a boundary for the new Forum on the east side and protected it at the same time from fire and from the insulting proximity of the miserable working-class homes of Suburra. It marked the limit of the vast gap that Augustus must have had to open in the quarter, where whole rows of five-story houses were torn down.

* This Roman province included what is today the Swiss Grisons and much of the Austrian Tyrol and the Italian Alto Adige and Lombardy.—Translator's note.

Let us also mention, because of its unusual purpose and even though no trace of it remains, a temple erected by Augustus to Jupiter the Thunderer, which looked out on the Area Capitolina. The *imperator* was morbidly afraid of lightning, which had once brushed his litter and killed a slave standing next to him; in order to protect himself against it, he always carried a sea-calf skin and, whenever a storm broke, he had no shame about running to hide in the nearest cave that he could find.

Let us observe finally that, with the propaganda motives that governed most of what he did, Augustus had no objections to the presentation of the heroic actions of members of his *gens* as his own feats. The best evidence of this propensity would be the arch of triumph of Drusus, which bestrides the Via Appia and forms a kind of second city gate behind that of St. Sebastian—unless the arch of Drusus was completely destroyed and the one that stands there today is one of the arches of the aqueduct that Caracalla used to fetch water from the Aqua Marcia for his baths. The fact remains that there is often some uncertainty as to the actual origin of ancient monuments.

CITY PLANNING IN THE TIME OF AUGUSTUS / THE PANTHEON AND THE BATHS OF AGRIPPA

From the time of the kings Rome had been divided into four quarters, to which the new settlements established outside the Servian Wall had been joined as well as possible. This arrangement, which had been outgrown by the changes in society, was replaced by Augustus with the creation of fourteen new districts identified in numerical order like the *arrondissements* of Paris or the postal zones of American cities. These districts, themselves subdivided into quarters, enjoyed autonomous administrations; each had its own corps of watchmen for night patrols, charged with preventing fires or promptly giving notice of them. For there could be no thought of extinguishing them, once they had started: there were only the most primitive pumps, which were totally ineffectual. Much more reliance was placed on hooks, axes, and hammers, which were the only useful equipment available. Fires were fought by creating open areas in their paths: this is the reason for the great demolitions that generally came with fires.

The administrative system instituted by Augustus was complemented by a city-planning project: he wanted to replace the anarchic confusion of winding streets with a systematized building scheme that would preserve open spaces and provide adequate room for traffic. Many new buildings were constructed in the old quarters, and new quarters were opened for residence and recreation. The nearest comparison to this endeavor in city planning is that of Napoleon III to create a new Paris. For the first Roman emperor as for the second French emperor, architecture, it has been said, was an "instrument of government." It is unquestionable that the sight of rebuilt temples and a beautified city had much to do with the popularity enjoyed by Augustus. He had his Haussmann* in the person of Agrippa, whose serious, thoughtful face survives in a splendid bust in the Capitoline Museum. This great public servant won the daughter of Augustus in marriage because Maecenas had said to the emperor: "You have made Agrippa so great that you have to make him your son-in-law . . . or kill him." The ancient red marble sarcophagus in which his body was placed is now, in the basilica of St. John Lateran, the tomb of Pope Clement XII.

Among the great achievements with which Agrippa's name is linked the greatest glory to his memory is certainly the Pantheon, which is the most original creation of all Roman art and the work that most symbolizes the everlastingness of Rome. It is considered the best-preserved monument of Roman antiquity, but it has not come down to us in its original appearance and construction. Hadrian made changes in it in the second century A.D. and Septimius Severus made others in the fourth century, though it is impossible to identify the character and importance of these alterations. Abandoned under the first Christian emperors, stripped of its bronze tiles by Constans II, emperor of Byzantium, dedicated as a church in 609 under the name of St. Mary of the Martyrs, used as a fortress in the Middle Ages, in the seventeenth century it lost its last bronzes to Pope Urban VII Barberini, who wanted them to be melted down for the wreathed columns of the canopy of St. Peter's.

But, though the Pantheon has been looted of what made it rich, it has been left, as Stendhal said, with "what made it great." The great portico that serves it as a monumental porch does indeed date from the time of Agrippa, in spite of the dedicatory inscription that adorns its pediment; in the original *cella* one can still see the two great recesses that held the huge statues of Augustus and Agrippa. The daring of the dome will always be admired, rising more than one hundred and thirty feet above the ground

---

* Baron Georges Haussmann, prefect of the Seine under the Second Empire, directed the operations that transformed Paris under Napoleon III.—Translator.

and pouring light down through a great opening to the pink porphyry that paves the center of the temple. It was this cupola that was to give Bramante the idea for the dome of St. Peter's. It was to be repeated by Michelangelo, who liked to say: "You marvel at the Pantheon and you wonder that the earth can support it: I will put it up in the air."

This Pantheon, dedicated "to all the gods," was placed on a site already sanctified by an ancient apotheosis, on that Goat Marsh from which Romulus was supposed to have been swept into heaven by a tempest. Agrippa's selection of it was influenced also by a practical consideration: the morass was unoccupied. It had only to be drained, and an immense area would be available without his having to buy or expropriate land.

Even so, the temple occupied only a very small portion of the area, the greater part being reserved for a great establishment of a kind still unknown in Rome: *thermae,* public baths. The custom of the hot bath, which did not reach Rome from Greece until the third century B.C., had now become general in the city. Villas had baths even for slaves; many city buildings included facilities where, as Horace said, one could be "bathed for a farthing." Public facilities had been opened, some of them run for profit, others subsidized by wealthy private citizens. But these *balneae* had only a hygienic purpose. Agrippa's baths went beyond utilitarian ends; they were intended to offer the people a place for daily relaxation. The great novelty of them was the combination of luxurious bathing facilities with rooms for physical exercise, galleries for strollers, and pleasant gardens. At the same time a new means was made available by which Roman emperors were more and more to profit, augmenting the pleasures that they provided for nothing to the people by adding to the number, the size, the splendor, and the variety of the baths.

The ruins of Agrippa's baths are still visible at the back of the Pantheon, in Via della Palombella. Farther away, in Via Arco della Ciambella, there are other traces of them; hence one can imagine how great an area they covered. It was in order to supply them that Agrippa built the Aqua Virgo aqueduct, whose water, which still issues from the charming Trevi fountain, is believed even today to be able to cure a dozen diseases.

Enriched by the Pantheon and the baths, the Goat Marsh was embellished still further with porticoes and luxurious private houses. It was for the convenience of this new quarter that Via Lata, a straight avenue, was built as the city branch of the Via Flaminia (today's Corso); it became one of the most elegant parts of Rome.

THE THEATER OF MARCELLUS

It had been Caesar's dream to build a new city on the Field of Mars. Augustus accomplished this plan, though he did not confine himself to the area reclaimed by Agrippa from the marsh. The green plain of the Field of Mars ran as far as the turn in the Tiber. Not only was it used as the place for military displays and the training of the legions; it was also the customary place for Romans to stroll. Emerging from the labyrinth of their shadowed streets, they went there in great numbers to enjoy physical exercise or simply to saunter in the clean air and sunlight. This was the area that Augustus intended for leisure and amusement, as much for the nobility as for the people, since at that time both classes were almost equally idle.

Through his efforts the Field of Mars was equipped with porches, baths, theaters, and temples. In order to protect this luxurious new district against floods, major undertakings were launched to regulate the course of the river; it was at this time that the island in the Tiber was given the strange configuration of its shores that made it look like a huge ship that had cast anchor in front of Rome; an obelisk served as the mast and the temple of Aesculapius could be the stern structure. The travertine edging that marked its contour is still partly to be seen at the southern end, under the Morgue stairs, bearing the sacred serpent and the remains of a bust of Aesculapius.

It was not far from Pompey's theater that the new monuments dedicated to spectacles were erected. Of the theater of Balbus, which could hold almost ten thousand spectators, only two Doric columns and a large architrave are still to be seen in Via Santa Maria de' Calderari. The two gigantic statues of Castor and Pollux that adorn the Capitoline stairway were discovered, at the time of Pius IV, in the only accessible part of the ruins of this theater, the heart of which is forever sealed away: they are beneath the little elevation on which stands the Palazzo Cenci in testimony of the wealth, the sufferings, and the crimes of a family that, even after five centuries, has not exhausted the curiosity of historians and playwrights.

As for the theater of Marcellus, it is one of the most beautiful remains of Roman antiquity and the masterpiece of its finest period. Every architect in the world knows its slightest detail. That is not because it has come down to us intact. Its solidity was to be its undoing: used as a fortress during the Middle Ages, it was many times captured and recaptured, a game in which it lost forty of the fifty-two arcades that had adorned its outer wall; but the twelve that survive are enough to show the dignified form and elegant proportions of the building. The construction of this theater, where thirty thousand persons could sit in comfort, had been begun by Caesar. Augustus completed it and dedicated the monument to his nephew, Marcellus, who died at the age of twenty and was made immortal by the sorrowful lines of Virgil: *Tu Marcellus eris.* . . . To mark the dedication, six hundred wild beasts were put to death, a fact that inspired Stendhal to the disenchanted observation: "Today a cantata would be sung for the academic celebration of the sovereign's virtues."

Some parts of the theater are still inhabited, chiefly by poor families whose laundry can be seen drying at the windows. The simplest of lives are lived against this majestic background. This fatherly blend of pomp and poverty is everywhere in Rome: here is a cabbage market at the base of an ancient pillar, there a peddler shelters under a red umbrella against the façade of a ruined temple: wretched shops elbow luxurious *palazzi,* and at the end of an imposing *cortile* clothes are hung to dry on the arms of Greek statues. This constant contrast of the historic and the everyday is one of the charms of this city of contrasts, where, as they say, "pomp resides in the stones and simplicity in the manners."

OCTAVIA'S PORCH AND THE ARA PACIS

Not far from the theater of Marcellus was the porch of Octavia, sister of Augustus and bereaved mother of Marcellus. This portico was not the first construction of its kind in Rome; these had been known since the beginning of the second century B.C. Pompey had built one near his theater, and Caesar's Saepta Julia was simply a very large one. But the novelty in Octavia's was the fact that it was not merely a covered passage for pedestrians but an architectural complex with many uses, designed to attract.

This new concept was to be so much imitated that there would one day be twenty-five porches or porticoes in Rome, fifteen of them on the Field of Mars alone. The portico represented the Roman Empire's most remarkable creation in the field of city planning. Surrounding a great court or a garden, generally rectangular in shape, it was embellished with objects of art and equipped with luxury shops. It was at once a museum, a commercial center, a place in which to walk, to relax, to be amused. Octavia's portico had three hundred columns, some of which still exist. Its interior included the temple of Jupiter, the remains of which are hidden beneath the church of Santa Maria in Campitelli, and the temple of Juno, which was adorned with statues by Praxiteles and of which three fluted columns can still be seen in Via Sant'Angelo in Peschiera. Two *propylaea* of eight columns* served as entrances to the portico. One still survives; within it now there is the church of Sant'Angelo in Peschiera (Holy Angel of Fishermen), in which the Jews (whose quarter this was) were compelled, from 1584 to the time of Pius IX, to listen every Saturday to a Catholic sermon. But the *propylaeum* of Augustus is so majestic that one is inclined to overlook the intrusive church built of the same materials within it.

This central part of Octavia's portico was preserved from the devastation that ravaged this whole quarter because of the practical uses to which it was put during the Middle Ages. It was first made the fish market, and it served as such until the eighteenth century. To the right of the great stone arch that forms the entrance to the church there is still a Latin inscription ordering that any fish longer than the stone on which the inscription is written must be put aside for the *conservatores* of the Capitoline "in gastronomic tribute to the municipal authorities."

It was also the Field of Mars that was the site of the Ara Pacis (Altar of Peace), erected in 13 B.C. to honor the peace that Augustus had established in the Roman world. This monument, one of the most famous of antiquity, was so thoroughly lost during the Middle Ages that for centuries nothing, even its site, was known of it. Opinions were so wide of the mark that, when fragments of it were discovered in 1568, during the excavations for the foundations of the Palazzo Peretti in Via Lucina, the archeologists of the time refused to recognize them. Other architectural relics and statues brought to light in the same place, about 1780, encountered the same rejection and were abandoned to the museums of Florence, Vienna, and the Louvre. When reconstruction of the Palazzo Fiano, at the corner of the Corso and Via Lucina, was required in 1859, workmen encountered an obstacle at a depth of about sixteen feet: a number of fragments of it were recovered and these were finally recognized as parts of the Ara Pacis.

---

* A *propylaeum* (the concept was of Greek origin) was a gatehouse consisting of a small pillared porch.—Translator.

The excavations ordered by the Italian government in 1903 made it possible to identify the monument with assurance, but not to dig it out. It was only in 1937 that the decision was reached—and executed—to extract the Ara Pacis: a difficult task that required the use of all the resources of modern technology. Finally removed from the foundations of the Palazzo Fiano, the Ara Pacis Augustae was set up (temporarily, it was assumed) on a platform facing the tomb of Augustus on the bank of the Tiber. It is still there, absolutely complete: all the various fragments dispersed among the museums of Europe have been faithfully reproduced. On the supporting wall of the platform facing Via di Ripetta, which was finished in 1938 there is a reproduction of the inscription found in Ankara (the Ancyra of the ancients), in which Augustus preserved for posterity the record of his remarkable career.

This kind of review of the monuments that adorned the Field of Mars in the time of Augustus omits all those of which no important remains have come down to us. The ancient authors have left us enthusiastic descriptions of this new quarter as it had become by the end of the reign. It is certain that the gathering of so many and such diversified attractions in one place made the Field of Mars an ideal combination. The magnificent system of porticoes supported on a forest of columns and ornamented with a whole population of statues made it possible for Romans to relax there at any time, safe from rain or sun. It was a place not only for being entertained but also for being seen: it was a place of business for the man intent on constantly increasing his influence. There he could carry on a kind of perpetual candidacy "at large" among the idlers and the useless, "an important class in this population," a contemporary writer observed, "without whom no success is possible."

GARDENS, PARKS, AND FOUNTAINS

Strabo's descriptions help us to appreciate the tremendous efforts made by Augustus to create gardens and pleasances in the city without green that was Rome. These innovations answered the needs of the people, who, cooped up in uncomfortable apartments, had acquired the habit of living outside them. Public gardens had been unknown in republican Rome: this function was certainly not fulfilled by the "sacred woods," few in number and small in size, which did not lend themselves to walking. It was not until Caesar's time that Rome knew the *nemus,* the woods "artificially beautified by art." Augustus was to fashion two gardens on the banks of the Tiber, without damage to the great public part that was to be made out of Caesar's gardens in the area across the river, or Agrippa's in the Field of Mars. In addition, the porches and baths were to give the green areas an extremely important decorative function. This was the origin of the fashion of surrounding buildings with foliage and lawns and turning the spaces between them into gardens. It was to continue progressing; under the Empire, green areas would account for more than one-fourth of the city.

On the Pincio, whose ancient rustic aspect had been kept unimpaired, the rich began to create opulent parks and gardens for themselves. Those of Pompey were on the site of the Villa Medici. The church of Trinità dei Monti was built on the gardens of Lucullus. Those of Sallust covered the eastern part of the Pincio and the whole valley that separated it from the Quirinal. This was the most luxurious park in Rome, on which the historian of Jugurtha had lavished much of the dubious fortune with which he had returned from his proconsulate in Numidia. "Absorbed in his studies in the midst of this splendid greenery, from which one could see the whole of Rome, he wrote magnificent pages aflame with indignation against luxury and the love of riches" (Ugo Enrico Paoli in *Vita romana*). All the hills were covered with more parks, giving Rome that magnificent green girdle that little by little was to become the property of the emperors through purchase, inheritance, or confiscation. In the open spaces the owners built princely mansions surrounded by gardens, "laid out straight as arrows and administered and governed like conquered provinces," in exact exemplification of the Roman spirit. Extensions of the houses, they were themselves veritable outdoor dwellings, well equipped with sections as suitable for company as others were for solitude, and fitted out for the amusements appropriate to every hour of the day. Romans were of one mind in their enjoyment of what Saint-Simon called "the superb pleasure of forcing nature." They exerted all their ingenuity to enhance their gardens with a thousand effects: brooks were diverted, artificial pools were made, shrubs were trimmed in strange fashions to look like urns, pyramids, animals. All that is left of these gardens is the descriptions of them by Pliny. The centuries have destroyed the gardens as they have scattered the bronzes and the Greek marbles, the porches and the nymph shrines that were the jewels of their paths and that made the gardens into splendid open-air museums.

Overflowing the boundaries of their congested city, the more fortunate Romans extended their taste for country homes higher and higher on the slopes of the Alban Hills and the Sabines. The most sumptuous summer resort was Tivoli, which stands cool and smiling today above the white ruins of Tibur, proud of its Sibyl and its little cascades. Sallust, Cicero, and Marius had houses there; illustrious captives such as Syphax, king of Numidia, had the good luck to be sent there, instead of to the Mamertine Prison, to wait for the execution that was inevitable for vanquished leaders. Later, emperors like Trajan and Hadrian would go there to relax from the burdens of office, and Zenobia, queen of Palmyra, lived there, in Villa Adriana, in enforced if luxurious isolation. In the days of Augustus, the outstanding Romans chose Frascati for their villas and their terraced gardens embellished with statues and grottoes and arbors.

The poets of the period, reticent as they were about their city residences, were unrestrained in their praises of their country homes and the charms of life in the shadow of the temples of Vesta and the Sibyl that looked down on the gorge where the Anio flows. Not one of the splendid houses of that age has left any notable traces at Tivoli (the so-called villa of Maecenas is a temple dedicated to victorious Hercules), but it is easy to imagine them quite like the delightful houses that rise today like stairs on that lovely hillside.

To the setting that Augustus provided for contemporary life the abundance of water added a picturesque aspect. Water houses and nymph shrines increased through the work of Agrippa, who, having added three aqueducts to the system established by the republic, introduced and furthered the fashion for the decorative use of running water. "The whole city was filled with the gentle murmur of the waters," Propertius was to sing. Agrippa built at least one hundred and five fountains in the single year of 33 B.C. Under the Empire Rome was to have one thousand three hundred and fifty-two, all decorated with marble basins or granite bowls and many ornamented with sculptures of very great value. In our days too the sound of leaping water is one of the musics of Rome.

THE ARTS IN THE AGE OF AUGUSTUS

The delicate ornamentation proper to small creations appeared at the same time when in larger forms Roman city planning was demonstrating its dual tendency to create vistas and to produce mass effects. Thus esthetic concerns emerged in all spheres to give a framework of pleasure and beauty to city life. Munificence had become "a political institution and a means of ruling the world."

The new impulse was fostered by a double revolution in the art of building. Until this period, Roman monuments had been constructed with huge blocks of stone placed one on another without mortar. This technique, which gave their structures a look of power and grandeur, was never to be abandoned by the Romans. But they began as well to use—and this was new for them—irregular, smaller stones that they joined with a mortar whose strength has become a legend. This method of construction was to be used throughout the imperial epoch, without change and also without progress. It would permit the rapid erection of huge vaults and large edifices. A concomitant discovery had just made it possible to use marble as a facing for walls made of harsher materials. This hitherto unknown technique had been brought to Rome by one Mamurra, who had been in command of Caesar's engineers in Gaul. But this pioneer's name would still be unknown if Catullus had not felt obliged to drown it in the undeserved insults of his eloquent verse.

The wealth of materials was to give the buildings an unprecedented attractiveness; marble supplanted porous travertine in the Republic's constructions. For it was indeed a city of marble that Augustus was to leave, as he had promised; the iridescent materials that he employed everywhere made gratifying contrasts with the older monuments. Even if Rome had no other claim to the world's admiration, it would still be the most amazing museum of marble to be seen anywhere. The columns of its temples and its porticoes afforded an infinite variety of marble: transparent or veined in color like a peacock's tail, green from Egypt, black from Ethiopia, red from Numidia, not to mention what Italy herself still produces: Siena's yellow, Carrara's milk-white, grayish speckled with cherry red. This richness of color opened the way for a new architecture, Oriental in inspiration, for a civilization of marble and porphyry, of the solid and the precious.

It was the love for beautiful stone that gave Augustus the idea of bringing to Rome the great red granite obelisk that had been built in Heliopolis by Ramses III and of dedicating it to the sun. It was the first obelisk that Romans were to see soaring above their city from the Circus Maximus. Fifteen centuries later, Sixtus V was to find it lying broken into three sections, to have it restored by Domenico Fontana, and to erect it at the center of the Piazza del Popolo.

In the artistic renewal of the Augustan "age," architecture was decidedly in first place. It was profoundly affected by the concern with adapting the masses and forms of buildings to the needs created by a new social and political state and to the new customs that it had engendered. One cannot say that a wholly original art came into being; Roman architecture, however, did evolve in the direction of a personal style permeated by the atavistic traits of power and nobility. The early Empire had adopted the Corinthian order, the most ornate, the most opulent, and this order was to penetrate into all the structures that imperial Rome was to build in profusion until its final agony. Greece had originated the Corinthian but made little use of it, preferring the serene virility of the Doric and the feminine grace of the Ionic. But Rome was enchanted by splendor rather than by harmony. It needed, as one author said, "the acanthus on its capitals and the laurel on its triumphant heroes."

Another tendency in the architecture of this period was total concentration on usefulness and efficiency that would afford concrete solutions to everyday problems. Thenceforth this was to be almost a Roman vocation, growing stronger from reign to reign.

Sculpture too was given a new life, which is illustrated in what has been preserved in the museums of the baths and the Vatican, as well as in the bas-reliefs set in the interior walls of the Villa Medici. Previously the only Roman subjects had been stiffly posed busts and figures of men in togas. Under Augustus a historical sculpture came into being and worked through allusion or allegory: a man personified a city, a whole population lived in a frieze. The gods were portrayed in allegorical scenes; crowded processions merged in marble; the friezes of the Ara Pacis depicted an entire day of Roman life. The whole panoply of office was unrolled with a delicacy and at the same time a grandeur that earlier ages had not sought to attain.

At the same time, the use of painting for the decoration of residences became widespread. The frescoes of Livia's House on the Palatine, like those of her country home at Prima Posta, which have very recently been reproduced in the Roman Museum, are excellent examples. These, moreover, are the only ancient paintings that have come down to us, except for those that were found in the ruins and are in a collection, whose center is the "Aldobrandini Wedding," the most famous of all, in a room of the

Vatican library. Greek paintings were no less sought after by collectors than sculptures; out of imitation, a number of Roman paintings were executed for the decoration of homes and baths. They fell with the walls that bore them, without being saved, like those of Pompeii, by centuries of burial.

The reign of Augustus was equally notable for its flowering of literature. In pursuance of his reforms, the emperor personally gave to writers and poets the same encouragement that he lavished on sculptors and architects. In this task he was ably assisted by Maecenas, whose name has become the synonym of the enlightened patron of intellectual endeavor. Augustus had saved Horace and Virgil from proscription; Livy, Ovid, and Propertius were his friends. Circumstances favored this literary burgeoning; the Greek spirit had inspired Roman severity, which, though it was never very inventive, was at least always apt at imitation. Calm having been restored and eloquence having been banished from the tribune, minds had quite naturally turned toward pleasant tasks that were facilitated by the use of papyrus, which had become common. In those days Rome had many bookshops, as well as handsomely stocked libraries. Augustus had established several in the porticoes of Apollo, Livia, and Octavia. The idlers of Rome were seized with a kind of literary fever, "a couplet on yesterday's games was an event"; an epigram became a proverb. The announcement of a new book sent customers rushing to the bookshops.

The circumstances that favored this burst of literature were accompanied by a curious turn of the Roman mind. Artistic occupations were regarded as servile; the work of the artist was considered unworthy of Roman majesty. But literature did not share in this derogation. Oratory, history, and literature in general were practiced by the elite, and highly honored as contributions to Rome's greatness: it could be said that Julius Caesar was quite as proud of his *Commentaries* as of his victories. Augustus' tastes turned him more in the direction of scientific endeavor. He had given much study to the problem of measuring the earth, and it was to commemorate the discoveries that he thought he had made that at one end of the speakers' tribune in the Forum he erected the Milliarium Aureum, that pillar of gilded bronze on which the name of every city in the Empire was inscribed, with its distance from Rome as calculated by the new rules. This Milliarium balanced the Umbilicus Romae at the other end of the tribune, a cylindrical structure in brick that represented the center of Rome and the Empire.

MANNERS AND MORALS

Caesar had attempted in his day, though without success, a reform in customs: as too often happens, bad customs had overcome good laws. Augustus was to succeed, at least in part, in introducing a certain modesty and decency into Roman life. He put an end to racial mixtures by establishing harsh rules for the acquisition of emancipation and citizenship; he strove actively to rehabilitate marital fidelity; he made laws against celibacy; he set up obstacles to divorce. He barred women from attendance at gladiatorial fights.

Men tended to dress too foppishly: there were new kinds of clothing that Caesar had denounced without effect. Augustus re-established the wearing of the toga and preached a return to the customs of old. Hoping to see his example adopted, he boasted that he was dressed entirely in cloth woven by his wife. At his behest the matrons—even those who owned many slaves—resumed spinning and weaving wool. The *imperator* was markedly less successful when he attacked the luxurious tastes of women, who rebelled at using home-made products for themselves. They insisted on wearing softer fabrics, with richer colors. Their vanity and their natural frivolity led them to give excessive attention to their looks. Their education had weaned them away from serious matters, for they had learned chiefly to sing, to play the lyre, and to dance. They continued to be interested only in festivals, pleasant trips, and public holidays, in all of which they found a thousand opportunities to start flirtations that kept gossip alive.

In spite of his good intentions, Augustus had no greater success in elevating the standards of the *plebs,* who remained devoted to the theater and the circus. While attempting at the same time to restore decency to these spectacles, the emperor had to offer a great many of them and invest them with a splendor unknown before his time. The circus itself—the structure—was considerably improved: the last wooden sections disappeared, and a special box for the emperor and his court was installed. The arena was enlarged, and surrounded with a ditch to allow for animal fights. In a word, Augustus did in this respect what many others have always done: he made all kinds of concessions to tendencies of which he disapproved. He had to pay his soldiers, feed the *plebs,* make great donations, and give spectacles: that was the price of his power. The people had given him power only in return for bread and games. Until its death, the Empire would endure the "servitude of the crown."

THE PALACE OF AUGUSTUS AND LIVIA'S HOUSE

Now that he was the master of the Roman world, Augustus established his residence on the Palatine, which, in the last centuries of the Republic, had become "the *faubourg St.-Germain* of Roman aristocracy." He had been born there and his childhood memories gave him a fondness for it. But chiefly he deemed it wise to associate the new system with the oldest Roman traditions. It was his plan to create, in what had been in ages past the cradle of Rome, an imperial citadel that would become the center of government. Giving up the Forum, where his eminence as Pontifex Maximus and the rule of tradition made the Regia his residence, he built on the Palatine, dominating the Circus Maximus, the house that would be gradually, after him, transformed into that imposing imperial palace that was called Domus Augustana, in the ruins of which his residence can be found only with much difficulty. It was a house without ostentation—if Suetonius is to be believed—with columns of ordinary peperino, retaining an appearance of republican simplicity. It would be hardly surprising that, as a matter of political expediency, Augustus should have refused to make a display of luxury that could easily be taken as a sign of tyranny. Nevertheless excavation has uncovered a larger house than was expected, built of infinitely costlier materials than those described by Suetonius. The whole Empire had wanted to take part in the construction of this house, so eagerly that contributions had to be limited to one gold piece per city and one silver *denarius* per citizen. Such a collection certainly produced more than the price of a simple dwelling. In fact, Augustus' house was equipped with a large temple to Apollo, of which the bottom and a great stairway still remain, and with a temple to Vesta that was the twin of that in the Forum. Next to the imperial residence there was also a library, the site of which is now occupied by the monastery of St. Bartholomew, where scholars went to study in the company of the ruler of the world. The legend of the austerity of Augustus' palace undoubtedly owes its origin to the fact that the emperor prided himself on living *"ut unus a populo,"* like everyone else among his fellow citizens, and that for twenty years he used only one of the rooms in the palace, eating cucumbers and lettuce, as much out of concern for appearances as because he had a bad liver and edgy nerves.

Livia's House, in which she lived after his death, was no doubt better adapted to her habits. A priceless example of domestic elegance in the first century B.C., it too stood on the Palatine and it affords us an excellently preserved illustration of a Roman house. There is only one other such left in Rome: that is the patrician's house under the crypt of the church of Santa Maria in Domenica (or della Navicella). One can still see its exquisitely decorated *triclinium,* its bathroom—lacking neither bathtub nor washstand—its cellars with the rows of jars in which wine was left to age. In actuality, it is principally the excavations of Pompeii that have given us our knowledge of the Roman house, designed for fresh air and sleep. For private life was extremely scanty: the men were always off elsewhere on business of their own, and the women did their needlework in the *gynaeceum,* the women's common room.

THE TOMB OF AUGUSTUS

It has been said that there is nothing more dignified and more chaste than Livia's House. These adjectives could not possibly be applied to the grandiose mausoleum that Augustus prepared for his and his family's ashes. It still stands today in the center of the large square that bears the emperor's name, flanked by modern buildings of no style whatever. Its ancient shape was that of the Etruscan *tumuli;* out of a circular base faced in white marble a mound rose some one hundred and thirty feet and was crowned with cypresses, above which towered a gigantic statue of the occupant. The monumental entrance was preceded by a porch, which was flanked by two obelisks, of which one is now in the Piazza Quirinale and the other is in the Piazza Esquilina (in front of Santa Maria Maggiore). Two bronze columns on the two sides of the door were engraved with the *"Res gestae divi Augusti,"* the text of which, as we have remarked, appeared also on the platform of the Ara Pacis.

Perhaps Augustus had chosen as the model for his mausoleum that of Cecilia Metella, erected on the Via Appia in the last years of the Republic. By then it was the fashion to construct huge funeral monuments, the traces of which are still to be seen on the outskirts of Rome. The caprices of the new rich indulged themselves to the full in these. Near St. Paul's Gate, dominating the Protestant cemetery where Keats and Shelley are buried, there is a Pharaonic tomb more than 120 feet high and entirely faced in marble: this is the mausoleum of Caius Cestius. That of the baker Eurysaces, near the Porta Maggiore, was shaped like an oven with many openings, and its bas-reliefs showed the successive steps in the processing of flour; it is the triumphal monument of the craft. Like more than one of those who came after them, the rich men of Augustus' time certainly contemplated with horror the oblivion by which they felt threatened. They made every effort to escape it by making their tombs magnificent monuments. "Those people succeeded," Stendhal wrote, "for I, an Allo-brogian from the north, write their names and you read them so many centuries later." It is true that, if they had not taken it upon themselves to perpetuate their names, we should know nothing of Eurysaces, an obscure baker, or Cestius, who swindled his way to a fortune in the not too interesting career of an *epulon*.* And no doubt we should be equally ignorant of Cecilia Metella, who, for all that she was the wife of Crassus, had nothing to recommend her to posterity even though it was she who taught Cleopatra the best way of dissolving pearls in vingear to be fed to her lovers.

If there are so many sepulchers along the Roman roads, it is because the suburbs were the usual burial grounds, interment within the city limits having been forbidden by law. The Via Appia in particular is an avenue of tombs. One follows another, most of them anonymous, announcing themselves to the traveler only by some scattered ruins: broken columns, empty urns, mutilated inscriptions, busts fallen to the ground, shattered sarcophagi. These devastated tombs have been called the museum of the Roman soul: the nameless faces barely distinguishable in the blurred bas-reliefs are those of the dedicated, disciplined Romans whose modest, unsung work created the greatness of Rome. With the arches of the aqueducts that extend "their poor great wandering bodies" along the horizon, they join in giving a religious solemnity to this land formed, as Chateaubriand said, "out of the dust of the dead and the ruins of empires."

Caesar was made a god by the vote of the Senate. Augustus would accept only apotheosis through the people. That was enough to establish the custom of associating Divus Augustus with the spirits of the familiar deities. Worship of Augustus went from the home to the streets: he had his altars at crossroads. When he died in A.D. 14 at the age of sixty-six, the Senate, in homage to his accomplishments, made him a god on an equal footing with the others, with his own temples and his own priests.

* A priest whose sole activity was the preparation of the banquets offered to the gods when some catastrophe threatened the Republic.—Translator.

CHAPTER 5

THE CAESARS [14-68]

THE HOUSE OF TIBERIUS AND THE PRETORIAN CAMP

The child of Livia's first marriage and the stepson of Augustus, Tiberius had no difficulty in succeeding him. He was a good administrator and a skillful financier. A proverb is credited to him: a good shepherd shears his lambs but he does not skin them. Under his reign the golden age that had been established by the *Pax romana* was to continue. The Empire had reached its greatest growth and perfect balance. From the Euphrates to the Rhine, Rome ruled "all the habitable world." Its rule was pacific, orderly, honest. Just as the most diverse peoples submitted effortlessly to its law, so all classes in its population seemed united in enjoying the benefits of peace. The Empire's treasures flowed into Rome: every province sent its harvests, its fabrics, its gold, "as an inexhaustible fountain pours out its water." "Everything was so in accord with their wishes," Philo, the Jewish philosopher, wrote, "that the Romans thought that they had achieved the utter perfection of all bliss." All that could be seen in the city was gatherings and feasts, horse races, pleasurable amusements. It was as if the age of Saturn had come to life as the poets pictured it, so great were the abundance of goods and the joy of the people.

Tiberius interfered little with Rome's joy, spending the better part of his time on the island of Capri, that jewel of the Bay of Naples. He also lived in his villa in Tusculum, which some have taken as Cicero's house.

Although he spent little time in Rome, he had a palace there, that Domus Tiberiana that he caused to be built behind the temple of the Magna Mater, one side facing the Velabrum. All that has been discovered of it, hollowed into the tufa of the hill, is a few rather confused corridors and some vaulted rooms that must have been service facilities. It is believed that the building was square in shape and that its sections were arranged on the four sides of a large central court bordered with a colonnade. The Domus Tiberiana was in the area that in the Renaissance would be occupied by the Farnese gardens, and the subsoil has been very little excavated. It is thought that this imperial palace was not especially luxurious. Like Augustus, Tiberius too affected simplicity.

The real monument of his reign was the pretorian cohorts' camp, *Castro Praetorio,* whose rebuilt ruins are still used as a garrison, not far from Porta Pia. Tiberius built the camp in order to keep the city in hand: the pretorians, who were to become the Empire's masters, were still only its servants. In spite of all the centuries, the walls of the *Castro Praetorio* still recall the greedy mercenaries who were its first occupants. It is the best-preserved Roman camp that survives to us. It forms a corner bastion in the Aurelian enclosure, and a large part of its wall is merged with the Aurelian Wall.

CALIGULA'S PALACE

It was Caligula who brought the usages of the Asian courts to the Palatine. Although his father was the great and wise Germanicus and he himself was brought up by the first, the virtuous, Agrippina, this grand-nephew of Tiberius was to abandon himself to every excess of vanity and cruelty. In reality he was mad, and his eccentricities defy cataloguing; he ordered triumphs celebrated for victories that were imaginary, and his favorite horse was made a consul. The circus was his chief pleasure; he had his own favorites among the chariot drivers and he forbade the populace to cheer for any others, though it often did so for the pleasure of opposing him. Now that the people had no outlet for their feelings in the Forum, the circus became in effect the scene of demonstrations against the new order.

It could not be expected that Caligula would furnish Rome with any lasting monuments; on the contrary, he destroyed many arches of Agrippa's aqueduct in order to build a wooden amphitheater in what is now the

Vatican. Similarly, he mutilated the vistas of the Forum by building a wooden bridge between the Capitoline and the temple of Castor and Pollux, above the Basilica Julia. Its purpose was to make it easier for him to pay visits to "his brother, Jupiter," for a friendly chat, and even to advise him and occasionally to act for him. In fact, he disguised himself as Jupiter, as Neptune, or as Mercury, and even as Venus, for he believed himself a god and demanded to be honored as such; a god of many shapes who could change his character by changing his dress.

This epileptic maniac required a house in the image of what he thought he was; he built it with the utmost indulgence of his taste for the extravagant and the gigantic. Standing behind the house of Tiberius, at the place where there was a large rose garden from which the vista of the Forum could be seen, it had a wall two hundred feet high. The northern side of this palace rested on a huge artificial platform supported by colossal foundations. All that remains of it is stories of deep archways full of shadows, making an impressive background. A well-timed assassination put an end to the tyrant's extravagances.

CLAUDIUS AND MESSALINA / THE EMERGENCE OF CHRISTIANITY

The Senate was contemplating the restoration of the Republic when some soldiers discovered a man's feet protruding from under a hanging in the palace. Caligula's uncle, Claudius, was hiding there. This upstart, whom everyone thought of as an idiot, was made an emperor. Trembling as he was hauled to the pretorian camp, Claudius was bewildered at his own investiture, at the price of his own fear, so to speak, with a power that Caesar had conquered for the sake of glory and that Augustus had preserved with a kind of genius.

This accidental emperor was to win exceptional popularity among the Romans; an illustration of its extent was the fact that, when he was ill, his palace was besieged by people who "made solemn vows to give their own lives in order to save his." As a matter of fact he was responsible for some wise measures. He concentrated on effacing the memory of Caligula; he pardoned his assassins, removed his statues from the temples, and repaired the Aqua Virgo aqueduct, which Caligula had damaged. He restored the dangerously impaired dignity of government. An expedition into Britain won for him, as for Sulla and Augustus, the glory of enlarging the sacred enclosure of the Pomerium, an act that was reserved for those who had enlarged the dominion of Rome. A triumphal arch in his honor was erected on the Via Flaminia; it would bestride the Corso today at the site of the Palazzo Sciara if the level of that road had not been substantially raised. The arch still exists, buried extremely deep below the roadway. It was brought to light by excavations ordered by Urban VIII in 1641. Fragments of friezes were removed from it, with an inscription and a medallion portraying Claudius; but rain interrupted the digging and it was never resumed. The hole in the ground was filled in and no one gave any further thought to the arch of Claudius. The inscription was sent to the Palazzo Barberini, the medallion to the Vatican. The bas-reliefs are in the peristyle of the Casino Borghese, where English visitors can see the resistance that their ancestors put up against the Romans.

One ground on which Claudius has a claim to glory is his success in a venture that neither Caesar nor Augustus had been able to carry out successfully: the improvement of the port of Ostia. He was also responsible for the longest and best preserved of the Roman aqueducts (Aqua Claudia), which deploys the long line of its arches toward the mountains and endows the Roman countryside with its matchless nobility. It is the monumental arcades of this aqueduct that form the Porta Maggiore in Aurelian's enclosure.

The most important event of the reign of Claudius was the emergence of Christianity within the Jewish colony that had established itself in Rome as a result of Pompey's brilliant Oriental exploits. Although the earliest origins of the church in Rome are still rather blurred, it is legitimate to believe that it was in 42 that Peter, the chief of the Apostles, arrived in the city that was to become the capital of Christendom. He remained there for seven years, during which the new religion made marked progress. Hardly had he gone when Paul arrived in his turn to give the Gospel a broader audience. Official circles took absolutely no notice of the matter.

In spite of his good government and the enthusiasm that he aroused among his contemporaries, Claudius has bequeathed to history only the memory of a ridiculous husband. He was the most deceived husband of all antiquity, and apparently he was barely aware of it—a fine proof of blindness, because his wife was that Messalina whose excesses were the legend of Rome. Juvenal has described her running furtively through the dark corridors of the palace on her way to the brothels of Suburra. Another part of Rome is also associated with the memory of Messalina

—the old gardens of Lucullus, where the Villa Medici stands today. She loved this charming spot and coveted it to such a degree that she arranged a death sentence for its owner because he refused to sell it to her. This stiff-necked fellow was a man of such delicate sensibilities that he ordered the stake at which he was to be burned to be moved "so that the smoke of the fire that would consume his body should not damage his beautiful trees." It was in this garden of delight that Messalina herself, when her husband finally knew the truth and pronounced her doom, was to undergo the punishment that was to end her impure life.

Claudius was not fortunate in his choice of wives. When Messalina died, he married Agrippina, who was hardly better, though she was not unfaithful. She acquired a grim mastery over the gluttonous, alcoholic old man, for that was what the emperor had become, and she took advantage of it to poison him after having prepared the accession of Nero in place of Britannicus. Thereupon she built a temple for him—a very large temple, surrounded by a tremendous portico. Its powerful foundations, which can be seen in Via Claudia on the way toward the Colosseum, provided the stone blocks that were used in the Middle Ages to build the beautiful belfry of the church of St. John and St. Paul.

THE CRYPTO-PORCH OF THE PALATINE AND THE GREAT FIRE OF ROME

Two portraits of Nero, while they are no better likenesses than many others, nevertheless show us the subject's real tastes. One is a statue that clothes him in the attributes of Apollo; the other is a bust in the Vatican that shows him wearing the crown of laurel bestowed on singers in public competitions. It was indeed Nero's ambition to be considered an artist, although he was only a third-rate actor, what would be called today a "ham." But his life was ruled by an insensate lust for applause and a criminal jealousy of those who did not appreciate his talent, and above all of those who had more. His susceptibility to flattery was such that he set Greece free and erased her name from the list of Roman provinces in return for the praises and the wreaths that were lavished on him at Olympia. He maintained a troop of five thousand men whose sole duty was to pay conspicuous homage to his talents as an actor and a musician.

The appalling catalogue of Nero's debaucheries and crimes is a commonplace. We know that he had his brother, Britannicus, and his mother, Agrippina, poisoned. He repudiated and put to death his first wife, Octavia, replacing her with Poppaea, whom he was to kill with a kick in the belly soon afterward because she had made fun of him (a double crime, it was said, because she was pregnant). Each of these murders was celebrated by acts of grace. There was no end to the Roman games, and the imperial orgy went on for ten years. Nero enjoyed abundance in everything: he never wore the same robe twice; he used golden thread for his fishing lines; his mules were shod with silver; the parties that he gave for his friends lasted twelve hours—a single one of them, it was said, cost four million *sestertii* for rose perfume alone.

Although he had sworn to model himself on Augustus, in the early years of his reign Nero felt closed in in the imperial palace: he added to it that *domus transitoria* of which some of the remains have been found in the *triclinium* of the Flavian palace. He had the various imperial buildings joined by the great crypto-porch that is one of the most characteristic monuments of the Palatine. It is typical of those cool galleries where Romans liked to walk or to relax in summer heat. This strange underground corridor, 425 feet long, has come down to us almost intact: the arches of the first section, near Livia's House, are decorated with the little figures of Amor that are indeed of Nero's time.

In A.D. 64 a tremendous fire started in the lowlands of the Circus Maximus and soon spread to all the quarters that led into it. By the time it was finally extinguished by dint of knocking down a vast number of buildings, it had charred two-thirds of the city; only the Field of Mars, the Via Lata quarter, Trastevere, and part of the Quirinal had escaped the disaster. It was the most terrible catastrophe known to Rome since the sack by the Gauls. Nero was accused of having ignited this monstrous pyre. At the very least, he watched its progress with the interest of an "artist," playing his lyre at the top of a tower—which certainly was not, as popular tradition declares, the Army Tower, for it was not until the thirteenth century that its massive square silhouette rose above Trajan's markets.

If it gave him pleasure to watch his capital burn, it gave Nero even more to rebuild it. It had always been his dream to create a new Rome. He fulfilled it by adopting the examples that he had observed during his recent triumphal tour of the great cities of the Orient. His instructions were amazingly sound. He prohibited reconstruction based on individual whim; he laid out plans for the various quarters, the placement of streets, the height of buildings, the area of squares. Nostalgic spirits mourned the old tangled alleys and the houses with too many stories: the city was more unhealthy, they said, now that it had more light. But this was not the general opinion that Seneca summed up in one of his letters: "Rome was burned, but to rise more beautiful from its ashes."

Nero filled the rebuilt quarters with arches of triumph and commemorative trophies. He replaced the temples destroyed in the fire, notably that of Vesta, which was to burn down again soon afterward. Nor did he overlook places of amusement for the multitude whose cheers he needed. He restored the Circus Maximus and at the Vatican he built an amphitheater that was to become the place of execution for Christians, close to what was to be the site of the basilica of St. Peter. Everything that he touched bore the stamp of his megalomania. The splendor of the baths that he erected on the present site of the church of St. Louis of the French inspired Martial to an epigram: "What is worse than Nero? What is finer than Nero's baths?"

Baths and amphitheater have vanished, but the ancient church of San Stefano Rotondo recalls the memory of the Macellum Magnum that he had established in order to assure the food supply of the population, which had increased considerably since Augustus. This was a large building of two stories, in the center of which there was a circular, domed monument, adorned with two concentric colonnades. Rebuilt in the fourth century, it was transformed into the round church of San Stefano, which still retains eight of the pilasters of Nero's colonnade.

NERO'S HOUSE OF GOLD

In replacement of his Palatine palace Nero wanted a house that would be worthy of him and that would bear witness to his omnipotence. This was the famous House of Gold; it covered the whole plain that separated the Palatine from the Caelius and the Esquiline. "Nero's new house," Martial tells us, "bordered on every part of the city." Its entrance was near the Forum, where today there are the ruins of the temple of Venus and Rome, and it extended beyond the present church of Santa Maria Maggiore. In *L'histoire romaine à Rome* (*Roman History in Rome*), Ampère says that it was as if, in Paris, it had covered Mont Ste.-Geneviève and continued as far as the Invalides. This vast expanse contained gardens and parks, woods populated by all kinds of animals, and ponds, the largest of which—on whose drained site the Colosseum would later be built—was, we are told, "as broad as a sea." In order to supply these bodies of water, Nero had built a branch onto the aqueduct of Claudius; its handsome arches can still be seen along Via Statilia near Porta Maggiore and as far as the British embassy's garden (Villa Wolkovsky).

The Domus Aurea was not a single structure, but a harmonious group of buildings of all kinds, joined by long porticoes, that could have made a city. When Nero took possession of this gigantic residence, he said: "At last I can begin to be housed like a man." As for the buildings themselves, "in decorative richness and in the abundance of precious materials, they surpassed the most sumptuous edifices of Oriental despotism." Gold, ivory, precious stones glistened in every panel. In the great circular banquet hall an ingenious mechanism imitated the constant movement of the sky. From the ceiling, made of slabs of ivory, flowers and perfume could be showered on the guests, whose number usually exceeded a hundred.

Of these splendors nothing remains but traces mingled with the ruins of the structures that were later superimposed on them, according to the old Roman fashion (the baths of Titus, then those of Trajan). Access is given by a road at the entrance of the Parco Oppio. An alcove of the imperial bedchamber is recognizable; there are paintings in the Pompeian style in the well-preserved long crypto-portico, and several rooms have traces of their ancient decoration. What is called the hall *della volta dorata* (of the golden dome)" contains admirable specimens of gilding. In a second crypto-portico the walls bear the signatures of Renaissance artists who came here to study the so-called "grotesque" murals that provided the inspiration for the decoration of Raphael's Vatican loggie. The Vatican was to acquire the gigantic porphyry basin that enhanced the little interior garden, as well as the *Laocoön* group.

A huge statue of Nero adorned the entrance porch. It was about 110 feet tall. Later hauled by a team of twenty-four elephants, harnessed in pairs, to a site before the Flavian amphitheater, this stupendous sculpture was to give the amphitheater its name of Colosseo (Colosseum), and then to vanish altogether. Nor has it been possible to find any trace of the huge statue of Augustus that stood in his Forum; nor of the equestrian statue of Domitian that was to be erected later and that is known to have risen higher than the roofs of the Forum's temples. Such colossal effigies were much favored in ancient Rome. In the courtyard of the Conservators'

Museum there are heads and feet from statues whose dimensions must have been prodigious: one enormous marble foot stands on a pedestal at the corner of Via Piè di Marmo in the Field of Mars, and there is a giant toe in the stairway of the Palazzo Alfieri. These huge images were intended to impress the people, to persuade them that the models were above mankind. To the sculptors of these gigantic bulks, who certainly thought that they were creating immortal works, time has quietly given the lie.

THE FIRST PERSECUTIONS OF THE CHRISTIANS / THE CHAPEL OF QUO VADIS DOMINE? AND THE ABBEY OF THE THREE FOUNTAINS

Nero held the Christians responsible for the burning of Rome. This launched the first of the great attacks that were to mark their history. They were an easy target: Christians were not liked, their religion was regarded as a dangerous superstition, and they were accused of all kinds of aberrations and even of crimes. Tacitus has described the persecution of A.D. 64 that gave full rein to Nero's sadism. Even if "the enormous multitude" whose sufferings Tacitus recounts is reduced to a few hundred men and women, the fact remains that the persecution was atrocious and spectacular. In his capacity as leader of the Roman church, the Apostle Peter was its first victim. He had returned to Rome in 59 in order to pursue his apostolate there. A rich senator, Pudens, gave him asylum in a house on whose site the church of St. Pudenziana stands today (at the head of Via Urbana)—one of the oldest churches in Rome, which still contains the table that, according to tradition, St. Peter used as an altar. Imprisoned in the Tullianum (later to be the Mamertine Prison), where he is supposed to have brought a miraculous spring to life, the apostle was crucified head down (as, out of humility, he had requested) in Nero's circus, near the Vatican area. It is believed that he had expected the persecution and tried to flee from Rome. But he had barely turned into the Via Appia when he met Jesus, carrying his cross. "Lord, whither goest thou?" Peter cried, and the Son of Man is supposed to have replied: "I am returning to Calvary to be crucified anew." Grasping at once his divine master's meaning, Peter resolutely faced round and went back to his martyrdom. There is a little chapel at the site of this legendary encounter, not far from Porta San Sabastian; it is known as Quo Vadis Domine?. The only interest in this apocryphal tale is its support of the tradition that links the Via Appia to the earliest memories of Christian belief.

Another victim of note—though somewhat later—was the Apostle Paul, who, having been arrested in Spain, was sent to Rome to be executed. Since he held Roman citizenship, he was spared the ignominy of crucifixion; he was beheaded in a little valley near the road to Ostia, about three miles outside Rome. The authorities chose this lonely site in fear lest the public sight of his martyrdom incite a mass fervor among the Christians. Bounding three times over the ground, Paul's head is supposed to have made three springs pour forth, a miracle honored by the three churches of the Abbey of Three Fountains, built in the eleventh century on the exact site of the execution and later rebuilt or restored. The shrine of the three springs, which have since been walled in, contains three rounded cenotaphs in black marble; a large pagan mosaic pavement from Ostia is its floor; in a corner, behind a barred grill, is the stump of the little post on which, before he struck, the executioner positioned Paul's head.

These modest shrines are more appropriate to the adoration of the apostle of the afflicted and the disinherited than is the vast and cold basilica of St. Paul Beyond the Walls, which consecrates the ground in which his body supposedly lies. His memory is linked to another Roman sanctuary, the church of Santa Maria in Via Lata on the Corso (next to the Palazzo Doria), which was built on the site of the guardhouse of troops of the Saepta Julia in which Paul was reported to have been held after his arrest and where, tradition says, he wrote his famous Epistle to the Hebrews. This church, rebuilt in the seventeenth century and endowed by Pietro Berrettini da Cortona, painter and architect, with an elegant façade, was the Bonapartes' parish, and the bodies of a number of members of the family are buried there.

Nero's colossal constructions for himself and his numerous great public works drained the public treasury; Italy and her provinces were looted for the reinforcement of the imperial finances. The emperor's extravagances and crimes finally roused the people; the legions mutinied and the Senate proclaimed him an enemy of the people. Betrayed by all, driven to suicide, Nero plunged his sword into his throat, but only after having declaimed a few appropriate Greek verses and asserted his talent one last time: "Then he must die . . . so great an artist" (June 11, 68). That night the citizens of Rome ran through the streets wearing the special caps of freedmen.

CHAPTER 6

THE FLAVIANS [68-96]

THE FORUM OF PEACE AND THE ARCH OF TITUS

The house of Augustus died with Nero. The Flavian family that came to power after the brief and stormy reigns of Galba, Otho, and Vitellius was to afford the first example of a real dynasty in Rome. It governed for only thirty years, but it left profound imprints that are still visible in the city.

With the Flavians the middle class came into power. The first of these emperors, Vespasian, was also the first emperor who made no claims whatever of eminent ancestry. His major thought was to undermine the posthumous popularity of Nero, whom, by some curious whim, the people began to admire as soon as they had got rid of him. Vespasian could think of no better means of obliterating Nero's memory than to destroy everything that was a reminder of Nero. He had Nero's statue re-erected on the Via Sacra, where, transformed into an image of Apollo by the addition of rays round the head, it was now no more than a decorative figure. He would have liked to destroy the House of Gold: but he contented himself with removing its masterpieces of Greek art, draining the artificial lake that was its jewel, and making this the site of the Colosseum. It was with the same intention that he rebuilt the temple of Claudius, which Nero had destroyed out of hatred for his stepfather.

For Vespasian was not concerned only to destroy; on the contrary, his

79

was the vocation of the builder, to such a degree that he joined in the work with his own hands. When he launched the reconstruction of the temple of Jupiter, he himself participated as an unskilled laborer. He devoted a most particular fervor to the construction of a little forum, at some distance from that of Augustus, to celebrate the victories of his Oriental campaign. This Forum "of Peace," whose site is now bisected by the Via dei Fori Imperiali, included a library into which, in the sixth century, the church of Saints Cosmas and Damian was incorporated; it also contained a temple that was said to be one of the finest monuments in Rome. In any case it was the most richly decked. All the relics brought back from Judea were piled up in it, beginning with those of Solomon's temple. Barely a trace of this temple of Peace remains. The base of one of its columns is in the Palazzo Farnese; another lies in a flower bed on Via dei Fori Imperiali.

The writers of the Empire seem to have spent a great deal of time in this Forum of Peace, no doubt because of its library but even more certainly because there were so many bookshops nearby. Martial, who had his own there, gave a friend various details that would enable him to recognize it among all the others. The remarks of the authors of those days demonstrate that bookshops were very numerous and prosperous in Rome, for copyists (who were slaves) were so industrious that many works circulated in editions of more than a thousand copies. Pliny the Younger and Seneca tell us that authors' rights were not unrecognized and that their work brought them considerable sums. But legal battles between authors and publishers were already a known phenomenon. "Do Cicero's works belong to Cicero, who wrote them," Seneca wondered, "or to Dorus, who bought them?"

Though Vespasian was a valorous soldier and a man of taste, his name has been prosaically linked by history with certain little booths that he established in the cities for the convenience of the passer-by. The emperor who was responsible for so many practical amenities equipped the streets of Rome with urinals made of large terra-cotta jars, rather like barrels without covers.* These were supplied, maintained, and replaced by the municipal authorities, who imposed a tax to pay for this work. His son, Titus, was opposed to the tax, and Vespasian answered him with a remark that has become a proverb: "*Pecunia non olet* (money has no

---

* In France their improved successors are still called *vespasiennes;* they are known as *vespasiani* in Italy, where they are dwindling (perhaps under the influence of Americanization?).—Translator.

odor)." For that matter, he was a prolific coiner of terse maxims. When he felt that death was at hand, he rose from his couch and said: "An emperor ought to die on his feet."

Suetonius says that Titus, who succeeded Vespasian, was "the love and the light" of the human race, even though he had been brought up in Nero's court among mountebanks and sycophants. His memory is perpetuated by the lovely triumphal arch that was dedicated to him in homage for his capture of Jerusalem in 70, one of the bloodiest events in all antiquity. The Arch of Titus stands on that hog's-back ridge (the Velia) that separates the valley of the Forum from the lowlands of the Colosseum. In antiquity it was called Arcus in Sacra Via Summa: so it was on the Via Sacra at the highest point in its course. Its excellent state of preservation must be credited to the architect Giuseppe Valadier, who restored it under Pius VII in such fashion that it was said that it was no longer the Arch of Titus, it was the Arch of Pius. The extent of Valadier's restorations was justified by the deplorable condition of the monument, which had been incorporated into the Frangipani fortress in the Middle Ages and no better treated in later eras: in the eighteenth century monks had even occupied the interior and cut windows into one side of it. Only the central part of the arch is ancient, but its interior bas-reliefs would be enough in themselves to make it an invaluable relic: with marvelous mastery they portray the triumph of Titus, the vanquished leaders in chains at his feet, the relics of the temple of Jerusalem (the holy altar, the silver trumpets, and the seven-branched candelabrum), and the city itself, whose fire-ruined walls seem on the point of crumbling. Figures are distributed on several planes with such felicity that, though they are not very many, they seem to constitute a throng; the progression of scenes on a concave line creates a perfect illusion of depth and space.

The triumphal entry of Titus into Rome, which these bas-reliefs recall, was one of the most remarkable ever witnessed. The procession included chariots four stories high that depicted cities taken by storm, ravaged provinces, praying crowds being put to the sword. For so great an occasion the prisoners had even been clothed in beautiful costumes, so that, as one observer remarked, "one did not see the sorrow imprinted on their faces."

The great event that Rome was celebrating on that glorious day was to have a consequence that neither Vespasian nor Titus could anticipate. The destruction of Jerusalem had devastated the original center of Christianity, and it was Rome on which the succession would fall. The Roman church had won its patent of nobility through the executions of the Apostles Peter and Paul. The number of its faithful was increased by the arrival of Christians from Palestine, and it was then that the city of the Caesars became that metropolis of Christianity that it was to remain.

THE FLAVIAN PALACE

During his short reign Titus had built only baths, of which little trace remains (between the Colosseum and the modern church of St. Peter in Chains). His brother, Domitian, was to leave his name associated with more grandiose architectural achievements than any other emperor except Augustus. For he wanted his middle-class origin to be obliterated, he wanted to be worshiped as a god and to reside in a shrine. He was the first actually to sit on a throne. This was the origin of that Flavian palace whose ruins fill all the central part of the Palatine. As there was a shortage of space, it was decided to fill in the depression between the hill's two peaks, and the palace was built on this artificial site. All that is left of the buildings is broken marble, shattered columns, pavements, fragments of tumbled walls. Ivy and green vines have invaded the ruins; clumps of bushes have made themselves at home in Domitian's drawing rooms. Nevertheless the ground still shows the outlines of this Roman house built on a gigantic scale: it measured 492 by 295 feet! The peristyle alone had an area of 32,300 square feet, and the rest was in keeping.

The walls were faced in marble, the floors were paved in porphyry, old yellow marble columns and colossal statues in red and green porphyry adorned the rooms. In this splendid residence, Domitian—"that half-Nero," as Tertullian called him—maintained the theatrical ceremonial of Oriental courts. He dispensed justice in the solemnity of a hall, shaped like a basilica, that was 180 feet long and 131 feet wide. The imperial throne was separated from the public by a marble balustrade of which some fragments have been found.

The tremendous excavations that uncovered the whole site of the palace in the nineteenth century were not the first. In fact, excavations undertaken 150 years earlier by Francis I, Duke of Parma, had uncovered the public rooms, which at that time were in very good condition. Immediately the most valuable contents were removed for the benefit of the Farnese Museum and everything salable was sold. Thereafter the imperial residence was once again entombed.

Today the area is clear, but not bare. Stripped of their marble facings, the walls have been ornamented with little designs, the columns have been re-erected and the heads have been restored to the statues. All this affords a certain animation to the setting and gives the visitor a pleasant welcome. On this hill of desiccated grandeurs, only the ruins of the Flavian palace afford a place that can recall the tremendous power of the emperors without at the same time arousing a feeling of awe. It is a melancholy, moving garden.

At the same time that he was building his palace, Domitian had a stadium built on the other side of the Domus Augustana and somewhat below it. This was perhaps a race course and more probably a drill ground for his bodyguards. Later Hadrian was to use the site for the great two-story exhedra and the imperial loggia that were Bramante's models for the Belvedere recess in the Vatican.

THE COLOSSEUM

Domitian is still involved when the Colosseum is under discussion, for it was he who completed it. Before it gained its name from the colossal statue of Nero that Hadrian put at its entrance, it was called the Flavian Arena. It was indeed the work of that dynasty, which, lacking the authority that the Caesars derived from ancient traditions, had to rely more on public opinion.

Imperial Rome has left no monument more revealing of the passions that moved the capital. It is sad that this monument should be a monument to savagery, but so it is: it symbolizes a basic trait of the Roman people, who have never had a soft heart. They have always despised sorrow and have never taken pity on death. Cutting the throats of the conquered was in the tradition of Rome: a fratricide had launched its career, every stage of which was landmarked by murder. The conquest of the universe had so intoxicated Roman sentiment that it no longer brooked the limitations of humanity: "this people could be entertained only with blood."

Combat of man against beast and later against other men was certainly of long standing. Caesar and Augustus had exploited it abundantly in order to win popular favor. But it was the Flavians who gave these bloody sports their definitive frame and a magnitude that disturbs us. Previously they had been held only twice a year. In the Colosseum the schedule grew until it was on a daily basis. Soon there was a shortage of professional gladiators and recourse was had to prisoners of war. The Colosseum has seen the deaths of Bretons, Dacians, Ethiopians, Germans, Gauls. What baffles the imagination is not that for five centuries generations of men savored the sadistic joy of seeing their fellows kill one another without mercy but that these men whose deaths were offered as a spectacle never tried to save their lives or at the very least to sell them dearly by turning on the crowd.

Is it necessary, when one speaks of the Colosseum, to give any reminder of the Christians who were martyred there? It has been said that the religion of the world was determined in the arena of the Flavian amphitheater, that it was there that Christianity triumphed. It would be a bizarre irony of fate if the shameful pleasures of the Colosseum had assured the salvation of mankind and the ruins were the monument at once of Roman cruelty and of Christian honor. Nevertheless, one must not take at face value the legendary tales of the huge number of Christians killed in the Colosseum. Many names have been mentioned without evidence, many figures have been lightly arrived at. There can be no doubt that men and women have paid for the crime of refusing to light incense at the feet of idols. "It was the custom to throw to the beasts those condemned for the crime of offense to majesty or offense to divinity. Christians were more than once included among such heinous criminals." But we know that the official place for their execution was Nero's circus. When the king of Poland asked Pius V for a precious relic, he was given a handful of its dust. Furthermore, it was only in the seventeenth century that the adoration of the martyrs of the Colosseum began and that Stations of the Cross were instituted round the arena.

Although the real interest of the Colosseum lies in its spiritual significance more than in its architecture, from the latter point of view it remains the most monumental creation of Rome and the most representative architectural testimonial to its genius. It stands as the great epilogue, the rough, strong fruit of that ancient civilization of which Greece had been the exquisite flower. The three orders that were always separated in Greek architecture were brought together here on an ascending scale. "Arcade on arcade," Byron said, "Rome would seem to have been trying, by assembling all the trophies of its history in a single monument, to merge all its cries of triumph into one." It is easy to forget the imperfection of a few details, the lack of logic in certain decorations included only out of an excessive concern with ornamentation. If the Colosseum is viewed in its total mass, its harmony, its magnitude, and its strength are overwhelming. The whole beauty of the structure lies in its simplicity. It is supported by itself alone, unshakable, and thus, as Taine remarked, how much superior to the Gothic cathedrals with their buttresses that seem like a crab's claws. And how forcefully it speaks, how well it conveys its meaning, all alone and without rhetoric, like certain Latin inscriptions in their dramatic brevity.

Sixty thousand spectators were comfortably accommodated on its steps, which rose almost 150 feet above the arena. They were not exposed to bad weather: a system of movable awnings, worked by an ingenious arrangement of ropes, made it possible to cover or uncover all or some of the steps. Now and then an emperor would order, as fancy moved him, "the sun to shine" on some section of the spectators, who always felt flattered. The brilliant arrangements of corridors and stairs demonstrate the degree of technical perfection to which Roman architects had attained. Their mastery showed its brilliance in the extreme skill with which they utilized disparate materials and in the solidity of the wholes. The Romans used only the least possible amount of mortar to join the stones of their structures. They employed quite heavy blocks so that they would be held firm by their own mass. But, in order to make them still more stable, they cut a small square mortice into the lower blocks and set in it a bronze pin whose exposed portion was buried in the block above. Thus these stones, which were called male and female, were joined, as "President" Charles de Brosses* put it, "in unending *coitus.*" It might have been supposed that, since they were invisible from without, these bronze pins were safe inside the huge blocks. All, however, have been ripped out, and the holes that disfigure all ancient walls are the signs of these innumerable extractions. When one thinks of the enormous labor of recovering them and the size of the scaffolds that it must have required, especially in the case of the Colosseum, one wonders whether the Barbarians, who were chiefly responsible for this vandalism, did not think these bronze pins were gold. Otherwise there is no explanation for so much labor at so little gain.

Though it was strong enough to withstand the cataclysms of twenty centuries, the Colosseum has not been preserved from the evil deeds of

---

* An eighteenth-century French writer, president of the first Burgundian parliament, known for his translations from the Latin and his descriptions of Italy.— Translator.

men; it has served in turn as a fortress for the Roman barons, as a quarry for the building of churches and palaces, as a lime factory in Renaissance times, as a gunpowder mill under Napoleon, and as a storage place for corpses when Rome was devastated by cholera in 1836. The vandalism that ruined the Flavian amphitheater stone by stone came to an end only when the church sanctified the remains and covered them with indulgences: it was Benedict XIV (1740–58) who consecrated it to the Passion of Jesus Christ in memory of the martyrs. But the most effective safeguard of the Colosseum has been the intellectual and spiritual movement that compelled the recognition of the nobility of the mutilated ruins, enforced the respect that is their due, revived curiosity about them, and inspired the learned research of which they have ever since been the subject. "President" de Brosses was the last visitor of any standing to be unmoved by this new sentiment. He would have preferred that half the Colosseum be demolished in order to be used for the restoration of the other half; better half an amphitheater in good condition, he argued, than a whole amphitheater in ruins. Twenty-five years later the poetry of these ruins entered into literature, where it was to inspire the lyric rhapsodies of Goethe, Byron, Chateaubriand, and so many others. No relic of Rome has a greater faculty than the Colosseum for engendering a certain philosophic reverie; for such large parts of it have remained intact that the mind can reconstruct it in its entirety and people it with its ghosts. How easily thought can restore to it its rich decorations, the gold of its porches, the mosaics of its steps. And yet it seems even more imposing in its mutilation. "It was only a theater," Stendhal said, "and it is the finest relic of the Roman people."

THE CIRCUS AGONALIS / DOMITIAN'S VILLA / THE JANUSES

For those too delicate of spirit to savor the bloody spectacles of the Colosseum, Domitian arranged other, more sophisticated pleasures. The charming Piazza Navone in the Field of Mars, rectangular at one end and rounded at the other, was built on top of a circus constructed by Domitian, the Circus Agonalis, whose shape it retained. Its houses mark the peripheries of the circus and their foundations are the ancient steps of the stadium, which have survived here and there and can be seen, in particular, in Via Zanardelli. In Mussolini's time there was talk of digging them out, but this would have required the demolition of the whole quarter.

Wisely, the project was abandoned. Beneath the tiers of the stadium there were vaulted cubicles that were used by prostitutes. One such *fornix* was the scene of the miracle that preserved the virtue of St. Agnes. The church that bears her name and rears its fine baroque façade beside the square was built on the very spot where the saint's hair shielded her from the eyes of her assailants.

Was the circus in Piazza Navone fitted out from the start for nautical displays? That might be inferred from Martial's remark to Domitian: "You have shown us chariots racing in the midst of the waters." What is certain is that in the eighteenth century the square was often flooded on summer Sundays, to the great delight of the populace, which flocked there to watch the maneuvers of the great lords' splendid boats.

It has been said that Domitian was a romanticist of spectacle. Martial has catalogued the strange hunts that he organized in the circus, transformed into a forest full of ostriches and deer. He was also adept at spicing the most barbarous amusements with literature: his country house was flanked by an amphitheater where orators, poets, and gladiators contended for the applause of the public. Statius, the Neapolitan poet, was the victor there one day, with a German who had succeeded in strangling a huge bear. The amphitheater was part of the sumptuous villa that Domitian had had built on the site of Alba Longa, the legendary city founded by Ascanius, the son of Aeneas. This villa was almost as large as Hadrian's in Tivoli. Its remains can be seen in the gardens of Villa Barberini, which were annexed in 1929 by the Lateran Concordat to the papal estate of Castel Gandolfo, that "Versailles of the Popes" where the supreme pontiffs spend the summer.

A relentless builder, Domitian was always on the alert for an excuse to indulge his passion. At the height of the fire in 64, there was a flood of vows to erect altars to the gods in order to prevent a recurrence. Once the danger was over, no one gave the vows another thought. Domitian undertook to remedy this breach of faith: this was the origin of a series of shabby and unesthetic monuments (columns and little arches in the "Janus" style) that for a time cluttered the Forum and the city's intersections. Only one of these altars was found in the nineteenth century on the Quirinal, near Sant'Andrea: its inscription cited the reason for its construction and initiated the annual sacrifice of a red calf and a pig. All these altars have vanished from the Forum, like the colossal equestrian statue that Domitian erected there: "You embrace the Forum," Statius wrote. "Your brow gleams above the neighboring temples."

Let us not leave Domitian without pointing out that he completed the temple of Vespasian, which Titus had pledged to his father's memory. This temple was close to the temple of Concord, in front of the gate of the Tabularium; it was reached from the Clivus Capitolinus by a monumental flight of stairs, part of which, as well as three of the tall fluted columns of the great portico, is still visible.

CHAPTER 7

THE ANTONINES [96-192]

NERVA'S FORUM

In the beginning of the second century A.D. virtue mounted the imperial throne in the person of Nerva, who, however, reigned little more than a year. This brief interval was enough for him to overturn the habits of the earlier reigns and to set examples that were followed. His statue stands in the Vatican: it is that of an ailing old man with a grave expression. He was humane and charitable: he ordered the demolition of Domitian's absurd triumphal arches, condemned informers to death, and sold his own possessions in order to help the poor. He suppressed the games and imposed order on the spectacles, and even on religious ceremonials. He abandoned the luxurious residences on the Palatine for a home in Sallust's gardens, which had become imperial property under Tiberius. A great palace, backed up against the cliff of the Quirinal, housed the emperor and his court; it was adorned with sculptures, some of which are preserved today in the Museum of the Baths (a head of Aphrodite, a bas-relief of the birth of Venus) and in the Capitoline Museum (*The Dying Gaul*). The obelisk that stands before the church of Trinità dei Monti came from Sallust's gardens, like the yellow marble columns of the balustrade of San Pietro in Montorio.

Nerva lacked both the time and the desire for much building. The forum that bears his name and that links those of Vespasian and Augustus was built by Domitian, and its attribution to Nerva rather than to the execrable Domitian has been called an equitable injustice. All that remains of this forum, which has been called Palladian because it was dedicated to Minerva (Pallas Athene), is part of its surrounding wall, a statue of the goddess, and two columns. In the eighteenth century there were still seven others; Pope Paul V used their marble for the decoration of his fountain on the Janiculum—another example of the vandalism of civilized ages that has inflicted far more damage than the barbarous epoch on Rome's monuments.

TRAJAN'S FORUM

The greatest service that Nerva performed for the Empire was to assure the succession of Trajan by adopting him. Trajan was the model of an emperor: he was deemed worthy to bear the name of "most good," which until then had been bestowed only on Jupiter. After his time, when the highest praise was to be paid to an emperor, it was said that he was "happier than Augustus, better than Trajan." The Christians of the Middle Ages refused to concede that so good an emperor could be damned. Hence there arose the legend that Pope St. Gregory, moved by Trajan's virtues, had asked God—and received assent—that he be saved. An echo of this merciful tradition survives in the ritual of the Greek church: "O God, forgive him as thou hast pardoned Trajan through the intercession of St. Jerome." And we know that Dante did not hesitate to admit Trajan to his Paradise.

Of all the great edifices built by Trajan, it is only his famous column that has come down to us, if not intact, at least perfectly preserved. There was all of Trajan in this monument: its summit bore his statue, later replaced by St. Peter's, and its base housed his ashes, sealed in a golden urn. Trajan's Column was the outstanding example and the best executed of the triumphal columns; it was the model for Antoninus' column and for that in the Place Vendôme in Paris. The continuous spiral formed by its bas-reliefs rises toward the victorious emperor like the homage of the world. Two thousand persons form his guard of honor "in a great clash of arms, a veritable poem in stone." But the poetry of Rome is never more than rhymed prose. Most certainly Greece made marble sing hymns of quite a different beauty. The Roman epoch did not soar: it left its record at ground level, majestic and hard. Trajan's Column is nothing else but a campaign report, the sculptured report of Trajan's expeditions, as a result of which the Danube was made Roman. Every detail of the armament and equipment of an army on the march is reproduced on it. Viewed from the ground, these narrative bas-reliefs can hardly be appreciated in their details, but plaster molds of them have been made for reproduction; several of these, and some of the most beautiful, are in the hall of the Vatican, where there is a fresco of the battle of Constantine by Giulio Romano (Giulio Pippi). Under the portico of the church of the Holy Apostles there is an eagle surrounded by a crown; this is a reproduction of a Roman insigne on Trajan's Column.

This column was only one component of the Forum that the emperor built where there was room—that is, north of the Forum of Augustus. Trajan's Forum was embellished with four large groups of buildings: the Greek and Latin libraries, on either side of the column, extended as far as Piazza Venezia; a temple is still buried beneath the prefecture; the huge Basilica Ulpia was five hundred and twenty-five feet long; two of its columns were re-erected by the French in 1812. The Forum properly so called was a vast square flanked by two enclosed halls: in the center stood a gilded bronze equestrian statue of the emperor. A majestic arch of triumph with three openings adorned the main entrance to the forum, which was joined to the other imperial forums to form a magnificent procession of esplanades, porticoes, and temples parallel to the old Forum. Thus there arose a whole quarter of sumptuous monuments and, as Pliny called it, "a labyrinth of marvels" in which the stroller could indulge himself in "the illusion of leading a triumphal celebration." Nothing in the world had ever attained to such a degree of magnificence.

Trajan's Forum was the jewel of this unique complex: it eclipsed all the others in its greater size and its more majestic elegance. And also in a delicacy, a balance of proportion and line and, in sum, a harmony whose secret Rome was soon to lose. Two and a half centuries later, Emperor Constans, who came to Rome in 356, said that he had never seen a more beautiful monument. "Nothing like it could ever be built again," he told Ormisdas, a Persian prince accompanying him. "At the very most, this could be done again," he added, pointing to the equestrian statue of the emperor. "But why bother with the horse," the Persian retorted, "if one cannot have the stable?"

Trajan's Forum was dominated by the impressive hemicycle of the markets that scaled and concealed the slopes of the Quirinal. In order to give the Forum the space that it required, the architect, Apollodorus, eliminated the artificially constructed landfill that joined the Capitoline and the Quirinal. He even cut into the Quirinal, and it was no doubt in order to provide it with a solid stone retaining wall against landslides that he built that great three-story edifice in which 150 shops and vast trading halls recreated the atmosphere of the Oriental *souks*. A construction worthy of a Pharaoh, it required the removal of more than thirty-five million cubic feet of soil, carried cartload by carload to a site behind the Pincio. This gigantic bazaar of imperial Rome has survived eighteen centuries of history almost intact because of its sturdiness. It was a fortress for the Colonna family, then a retreat for monks, who turned its shops into cells, and finally a garrison. The Fascist government cleared it of its medieval additions: the sections that had fallen were rebuilt and the whole was restored to its original appearance. Its upper platform, towering almost two hundred feet above the level of the imperial forums, has become, like the summit of the Palatine and the terrace of the Pincio, one of those incomparable places that seem to have been created for "the delight of the eyes, the mind, and the imagination." The combination of Trajan's Forum and markets is assuredly the most original specimen of imperial city planning; it rivals the most ambitious creations of modern architects, to whom it can still offer lessons and models. In the form in which the imagination can restore it to its original perfection, it reflects the face of Rome at its greatest.

OTHER RELICS OF TRAJAN

There are many portraits of Trajan in Rome. The love that the people bore him gave rise to a host of these. To us they are disappointing: the low forehead, the ordinary features, the soft expression of the face in no way evoke the man's outstanding qualities: intelligence, firmness, rectitude, kindness.

His rectitude shone in everything that he did. While he punished Christians who insisted on clinging to their faith, he refused to persecute them, and prosecuted them only because of the independent association that they formed and that was contrary to the principle of absolute centralization that was basic to the Empire. Artisans' organizations were repressed quite as harshly as Christian communities.

Trajan was open and straightforward. Augustus had had the imperial box in the Circus Maximus altered so that he could watch the spectacles without being seen: Trajan had these improvements removed so that he was completely visible to the crowd, thus increasing the seating capacity to more than three hundred thousand.

The rise in the Roman population had necessitated this enlargement. It was also because of unceasingly growing needs that Trajan made substantial changes in Caesar's Forum, notably by the addition of the porticoes known as the Basilica Argentaria at the southwest end. The traders in silver whom it housed were in no sense the peaceable practitioners of a modest artistic trade. They were bankers and moneychangers who carried on their trading and financing operations in a chaos of bids and offers. The Basilica Argentaria was as noisy as any modern stock exchange.

The most inventive change that Trajan made in Caesar's Forum was the construction of the *forica,* a luxurious public (but not free) toilet, above the shops. Undoubtedly it was of the same period as the facilities in Largo Argentina, discovered with the republican temples. It was certainly of the same category: that is, equipped with distracting comfort, endowed with unbelievable luxuries, decorated with a prodigality that it has never occurred to us to lavish on establishments of this nature. This luxury in public toilets seems all the more paradoxical to us in view of the fact that private houses (which had no water at all and therefore could not be connected with the sewer system that carried waste into the Tiber) had absolutely no sanitary facilities. The residents had to go downstairs in order to empty their chamberpots into the nearest receptacle. Some of them saved themselves the climb back by simply emptying the pots out the windows, a tradition that has not entirely died out of the southern cities.

It was not only utilitarian improvements that Trajan contributed to Caesar's Forum; he had the temple of Venus Genitrix rebuilt in rich materials. The travertine columns of Caesar's time were replaced by the magnificent marble columns whose fragments and capitals are still to be seen there. Splendid bas-reliefs adorned the temple's *cella:* most of them are now in the Villa Medici. In the Roman Forum Trajan decorated the white marble balustrade of the tribune with extraordinary bas-reliefs that depicted his life. One of them portrays the burning of the register of unpaid debts before a delighted throng of debtors.

Trajan had built extremely luxurious baths on one of the peaks of the Esquiline, the Oppius. The ruins are still there, mingled with those of Nero's House of Gold and often superimposed on them, for they formed the foundations of the baths. Nero's luxurious apartments were in fact filled in and buried without a thought and, indeed, without even any attempt to salvage the masterpieces with which they were adorned. The determination to erase Nero's memory that was characteristic of the Flavians was even more marked in Trajan.

THE TEMPLE OF VENUS AND ROME / HADRIAN'S TOMB (CASTELLO SANT'ANGELO)

Trajan was succeeded by Hadrian, a Spaniard like himself, whose only resemblance to him was his liking for huge building projects. Hadrian was well versed in architecture and he himself drew the plans for the temple of Venus and Rome. It was the largest in the city: it was almost as long as St. Sophia in Constantinople and half as long as St. Peter's in Rome. The whole was composed of two temples coupled back to back, their two *cellae* joining in opposite directions; it was surrounded by a portico supported by eighty granite columns. Each of the temples was embellished with ten columns at the façade and twenty on each side, all of them Parian marble. Some have been discovered and re-erected. The exact area occupied by the temple, with its irregularly curved contours, was ascertained by marking the sites of the missing columns with privet, of the walls with laurel, and of the stairs with box trees. The apses have survived. That of the temple of Rome turns toward the Forum; it can easily be seen from the convent of Santa Francesca Romana.

When Hadrian's thoughts moved to the subject of his tomb, he determined to surpass the work that Augustus had undertaken to the same end. Having lived long in Egypt, he wanted a tomb that would be the equal of the Pyramids. His mausoleum is that enormous round tower beside the Tiber (now Castello Sant'Angelo) that constantly comes into view wherever one walks in the city. Its color is an exquisite gray-pink. Even though the Renaissance superimposed itself on it with magnificent insolence, and in spite of the changes that the centuries have made in it, it still looks not very different from what it was in Hadrian's time. It is still an emperor's tomb. All that is missing is the ornaments that relieved its massive severity. It has lost its girdle of columns and the circular ledge that bore the splendid statues that the Greek soldiers hurled at the attacking Goths in the fourth century. The altar has been replaced by a terrace dominated by an angel whose legend we will recount presently. The inscriptions listing the persons whose remains were laid in the mausoleum still existed in the sixteenth century. It was Pope Gregory

XIII who removed them in order to use the marble for the decoration of St. Peter's. This provoked J.-J. Ampère to the amply justified complaint: "To destroy inscriptions in order to acquire a few more pieces of marble is truly one of the greatest barbarities that anyone can perpetrate, especially in the view of a member of the Academy of Inscriptions." Many other parts of the mausoleum have disappeared. Twenty-four columns made from a single block of purple marble formed the portico of the temple that crowned the structure: they were later used to support the cedar ceiling of St. Paul's Beyond the Walls and they collapsed in the fire that ruined the old basilica in 1823. As for the colossal fir cone that rose above the highest point of the tomb, it was carried off to the Vatican and gave its name to one of the courtyards there. Next to it strutted bronze peacocks, the birds of Jupiter, which were also removed from the mausoleum, where they symbolized the apotheoses of the empresses. The ashes of many of these ladies were placed beside Hadrian's funeral urn, whose red porphyry lid, according to some archeologists, is now the basin of the baptismal fonts in the basilica of St. Peter's.

Above the massive cylindrical tower of the tomb rose a *tumulus* planted with cypresses. The monument was topped by a square altar bearing a bronze *quadriga* showing Hadrian ruling the world. For fifteen centuries this gigantic tomb was Rome's fortress, the popes' protecting redoubt, and occasionally their prison. It is so intimately merged in the city's history that the story that we propose to tell of it will often cause us to recall its hours of glory and woe.

Just beside the mausoleum a bridge, the Triumphal Bridge, crossed the Tiber and led to the Via Aurelia. Hadrian wanted a bridge that would lead only to his tomb. That is the bridge that one crosses today on the way to St. Peter's (Ponte Sant'Angelo). Except for one arch, nothing of it has been changed, aside from the replacement of the statues that decorated its parapets by angels designed by Bernini and executed by his pupils—and this, from the artistic point of view, may not represent progress.

HADRIAN'S VILLA

Some twenty miles outside Rome, on the road to Tivoli, Hadrian had built a tremendous villa intended for his relaxation from the burdens of exercising sovereign power. There he had artificially collected all the memories of his official life by reproducing the monuments that he had admired in his travels through the Empire. There were very accurate imitations of the Lyceum, the Academy, the Prytanaeum, and the Poecile of Athens, Egypt's Canopus, the Elysian Fields. Hadrian had added an artificial lake, a water theater isolated on an island, and strange underground constructions representing Hades, where he retired for meditation. In order to try to picture this hodge-podge, imagine a rich modern American bedecking his estate in Ohio with Constantinople's St. Sophia, the Cathedral of Burgos, the Parthenon, the temple of Angkor, the Louvre, and the Auteuil racetrack.

In the midst of so many buildings stood the imperial palace with its baths, its gardens, and its barracks. The whole group of these structures was so vast that for a long time its ruins were believed to be those of a city. Today almost all that is to be seen there is huge blocks strewn among the brambles, broken columns, fragments of walls invaded by ivy. The Barbarians passed that way; but it was chiefly the Renaissance that populated Europe's museums with the statues, the paintings, and the mosaics that were still there in the sixteenth century. This was the source, in particular, of the Capitoline Museum's old red marble faun and gray marble centaurs, the Vatican's Muses and Flora, the Villa Albani's bas-relief of Antinoüs, and the marvelous dove mosaic that has so often been copied in modern art (in the Capitoline Museum's Hall of Doves).

Hadrian himself drew the plans for the villa and all the buildings on the grounds. He had a real talent for architecture and would allow no one to cast aspersions on it. Apollodorus, the architect of Trajan's Forum, said one day of a building that his emperor had created: "If the goddesses sitting in that temple stood up, they would crack their heads on the dome." He paid for that with his head.

THE TEMPLE OF ANTONINUS AND FAUSTINA / THE ANTONINE PILLAR / THE TEMPLE OF HADRIAN DEIFIED

For the French it is a source of pride that the wisest and most virtuous of the Roman emperors was of Gallic stock. This accomplished sovereign was Antoninus Pius; to his wife, Faustina, out of a courtesy of which she was not worthy, he accorded the honors of divinity. The temple that he built in the Forum in her honor was later, for reasons of frugality, reconsecrated to the emperor after his death. It was one of the most remarkable temples of the imperial epoch. It alone of all the buildings in the Forum is still represented by all the columns of its façade, at the top of a majestic flight of twenty steps. The *cella,* which has preserved the greater part of its marble facing and its frieze adorned with vultures, houses one of the finest specimens of Roman decorative art. In the eleventh century it was transformed into the church of San Lorenzo in Miranda, a name that is believed to have been inspired by the awe induced in the erudite by the noble ruins that cover the Forum.

The "Antonine Pillar," in spite of the inscription that Pope Sixtus V felt obliged to have carved into its base, was never dedicated to Antoninus Pius. Frenchmen looking for some memory of their compatriot in the Field of Mars must turn to the obelisk of Monte Citorio, in the repairs of which a funeral column dedicated to Antoninus and Faustina was used. The pedestal of this column, preserved in the Vatican gardens, is ornamented with a bas-relief that shows the emperor and his wife being carried off to Olympus by a winged spirit. Many times since then painters have depicted saints borne into heaven by angels who looked like the genius that carries Antoninus and Faustina through the air. Christian art, obviously, has never been afraid to take its models among the heathen.

Although they have taken away his column, Antoninus Pius has no ground for complaint against the archeologists. They have accorded him the credit, falsely ascribed to Augustus and Agrippa, for having honored his father in 145, in spite of the Senate's opposition, with the construction of the temple of Hadrian Deified, which was long taken to be a temple to Neptune and which is still incorrectly given the name of the sea god. Today it is the stock exchange, having previously been the customs house (Piazza di Pietra). What remains of it to offer us an example of imperial luxury at its apogee is chiefly the eleven fluted Corinthian columns in the wall of the modern building. The temple stood on a high podium adorned with trophies symbolizing the Empire's provinces; some of these are now in the Vatican Museum and others are in the courtyard of the Conservators' Palace. It is their subjects quite as much as the style itself of the temple that make it possible to establish the exact date of its construction.

THE PILLAR AND THE EQUESTRIAN STATUE OF MARCUS AURELIUS

The triumphal column in Piazza Colonna, inaccurately called the Antonine Pillar, celebrates the victories of Marcus Aurelius. The friezes in superimposed spirals that recount his campaigns have a historical interest as great as those of Trajan's Column, but they are far from having the same artistic merit. The design is coarser, the projection of the cordon that separates them destroys the effect of the whole. The structure was infected by the decadence that was setting in at the time of its construction. A statue of Marcus Aurelius used to dominate the column; it was replaced in the eighteenth century by one of St. Paul.

There are still very many portraits of Marcus Aurelius in Rome's museums. His popularity was so great that it was a point of honor for every house to have a portrait of him. The most remarkable surviving image of him is the equestrian statue in gilded bronze that stands in the center of the Capitoline Square. His whole character comes through, and it is as if one could hear him addressing his troops.

It was a mistake in identification that saved this statue from the destruction that was the usual fate of the bronzes of antiquity: in the Middle Ages it was believed to be a statue of Constantine, the first Christian emperor. If the bearded warrior had been recognized for the fierce persecutor of Christians that Marcus Aurelius was (St. Cecilia was one of his victims) in spite of all his philosophy, there can be no doubt that, duly melted down, the statue would have gone to adorn some tabernacle. Protected by this mistake, Marcus Aurelius stayed where he was in front of the Lateran Palace until Michelangelo suggested moving him to the Capitoline. There is a stubborn legend to the effect that, far from fading with time, the gilding of the bronze spreads from century to century and that the day when it covers the whole statue will be that of the end of the world. Here again, in a ridiculous guise, one encounters the old Roman notion that the destiny and the existence of Rome are bound with the world's.

Another triumphal monument was dedicated to Marcus Aurelius: one of the four arches that decked the Via Flaminia. It still existed in the middle of the seventeenth century, having escaped the furies of the Middle Ages and the vandalism of the Renaissance. It was Pope Alexander VII who tore it down, on the incredible pretext of facilitating vehicular traffic in the street that is now the Corso. This destruction is celebrated in an inscription that glorifies the Chigi pope for it quite as if it had been a matter of "removing a shanty or an obscenity." But the arch was ornamented with bas-reliefs of inestimable worth and it perpetuated the memory of the most justly popular and the wisest of the emperors.

His son, Commodus, found all his ambitions gratified whenever he entered the arena of the circus to prove his right to the appellation that he had conferred on himself: Hercules. His artistic endeavor can be summed up in an act that showed his presumptuousness. He had the colossal statue of Nero at the entrance of the Colosseum beheaded so that his own image could be placed on its shoulders. With this popinjay Rome's decadence began.

ROME IN ITS GOLDEN AGE

Let us not leave this brilliant era of the Empire without a glance at what had become in its golden age the sovereign city of the world.

Jérôme Carcopino has masterfully emphasized the basic contrast that marked its physical appearance:

On the one hand, the high figure of its population, like the architectural grandeur and the marble beauty of its public buildings, made it kin to the great metropolises of the modern west. On the other hand, the overcrowding to which it condemned its multitudes, on rolling land limited in its area by nature and man alike, the strangulation of its tangled streets, the wretchedness of its municipal administration, the dangerous congestion of its traffic brought it close to those medieval cities described in old chronicles, whose alternately seductive and sordid picturesqueness, whose careless deformities and anarchic swarms have been preserved into our own day by certain Mussulman cities.

Many famous observations by Juvenal instruct us in the inconveniences of a city that was the most magnificent in the world.

A poet's caprices? Indeed not. It seems certain that almost one million and eight hundred thousand persons were packed inside that narrow perimeter. The existence of the enormous imperial park that surrounded the city prevented the growth of the suburbs that should have been built at a considerable distance from the center of the city. It had been compelled to grow upward, and speculation in rental properties had led to the construction of excessively high buildings (often of five and six stories, as we have seen) built of inadequately stable materials. Collapses were daily occurrences: fire and collapse recur obsessively in all the writers of the Empire.

Most Roman houses were quite similar to those civilian barracks that we have today. Two fragments of apartment houses of this kind can still be seen in Rome: the large façade incorporated in the Aurelian Wall near

Porta San Lorenzo and the one that has become the lateral wall of the church of Saints John and Paul on the Caelius. The mosaic of Santa Pudenziana has preserved pictures of smaller apartment buildings, but they are still quite high. The excavations in Ostia, in particular, have given us a very complete knowledge of the large Roman house by showing its general plan as well as its interior layout: wretched hovels elbowed apartments whose comforts exceeded our modern refinements.

The appearance of the city afforded disturbing contrasts: while certain official quarters enjoyed a spacious beauty, others were like Oriental labyrinths. What is more, the narrow, twisting streets were by far the most numerous. Crowded by noisy, motley swarms, they were always deafening even though daytime vehicular traffic in them was forbidden. Rome was the first capital to adopt this method of solving the urban traffic problem. This regulation, which was adopted only very belatedly, reduced the blocking of streets without making any difference in the number of pedestrians or the confusion of the most used arteries. On the other hand, it made night even louder than day. "Anyone who could count the number of hours lost from sleep," Martial said, "could tell how many hands struck against pans to bewitch the moon." And he added: "Whenever I want to sleep, I run to the country."

It is true that the tumult and the congestion in the streets made residents long for the peace of the countryside. No other people of antiquity accustomed like the Romans to living in a huge metropolis had so keen an appreciation of the poetry of nature and the delights of country life. In the days of imperial splendor the city overflowed extensively into the country. Beyond the parks of the emperors and the nobility, there was a multitude of villas and country houses in which prosperous Romans spent their leisure. These houses extended as far as the Tusculan hills and Tivoli. It was only during the centuries of decadence that the Roman countryside became that vast expanse of marshy underbrush abandoned to malaria that made so deep an impression on the romantics.

It is not our intention to describe the private lives or the collective existence of the Romans of this period. This task has been fulfilled in learned works despite the difficulties created by the fact that Latin literature, for all its great wealth and the prodigious diversity of its subjects, has only rarely given us glimpses of the life of every day. Ugo Enrico Paoli (*Vita romana—Roman Life*) and Jérôme Carcopino (*La vie quotidienne à Rome à l'apogée de l'Empire—Daily Life in Rome at the Height of the Empire*) have succeeded in recreating a vanished world on the basis of fragmentary testimony and often obscure allusions. Their remarkable works afford us a perfect introduction to the life of the city and answer the host of questions raised by our curiosity. Those answers are occasionally disconcerting; thus we learn that in spite of its great size Rome rarely gave names to its streets and never put numbers on its houses: an address was given in terms of some nearby landmark supposedly known to everyone.

On the other hand, many Roman customs were sufficiently close to our own to make us aware how little the lapse of twenty centuries means in certain respects. In 1959 the Louvre held an exhibition dealing with private life in Greece and Rome, a kind of retrospective exhibition of the household arts of two thousand years ago. Everyone was impressed with the modernity of the things on display: many could have been transplanted into our modern homes without any alteration.

Let us conclude this very incomplete picture with some brief glimpses at the condition of slaves, for the increase in their number in imperial Rome was one of the strangest social phenomena of antiquity. The rich patricians supported an amazing number of them; the slaves divided the household tasks according to rules of such minute specialization that each slave had only a very restricted field of activity. Those who were charged with greeting a visitor at the street door of the house left the task of introducing him for their colleagues. Others had as their sole function daily morning visits to present their master's greetings to his friends; still others carried invitations. The serving of meals was divided among an army of specialists. Even the slaves who performed confidential duties had only narrowly defined tasks: the secretaries were assisted by letter writers, the booksellers by copyists. The ephemeridian did nothing but tell his owner the date. Very wealthy houses, some of which, the ancient authors tell us, had as many as ten thousand slaves, were weighed down with uncountable armies of servitors whose sole function was to be there. It might as well be said that they did nothing; certainly it is legitimate to suppose that their work exacted only a minimum of exertion on their part. It was definitely preferable to be a rich man's slave rather than an impoverished freeman. No doubt in poorer houses the slave's position was less enviable. But the slave always had the possibility of freedom through emancipation, which was in no way unusual.

THE TESTACCIO

It is not only temples, aqueducts, and arches of triumph that the Empire has bequeathed to us. Rome owes it a mountain, or at any rate a hill, that rises near the Tiber in the neighborhood of Porta San Paolo. Higher than Monte Sacro, it is only a very little lower than the Capitoline. From its summit the view of Rome is very broad—it was Poussin's favorite.

As its name indicates, the Testaccio was composed of the remains of broken pots. The Romans made extensive use of terra-cotta objects: *amphorae* for wine, jars for oil, water pots in all sizes. They made even some of their barrels of ceramics, similar to the one in which Diogenes is portrayed in a bas-relief of Villa Albani. In addition, all kinds of goods were carried in clay vases, not in baskets, bags, or boxes, as is the practice today. There was unquestionably a great quantity of pottery. Nevertheless the accumulation of so vast a collection of its fragments in a single place has long been a mystery. The Middle Ages resolved it in their own fashion, by surrounding it with legends: it was believed that the Testaccio was composed of urns that had contained the offerings of subject peoples, so exalted was the medieval mind's idea of the antique greatness of Rome.

Rejecting this explanation, the ages known as enlightened replaced it with others that were hardly more reasonable. Was it mandatory for Romans to take their no longer wanted pottery to the Testaccio? That would have been a most unusual law, given the size of the city; in any event, there has been no evidence of any municipal ordinance to that effect. According to another hypothesis, the hill was created out of rejects from neighboring pottery workshops. But how could these artisans have produced so much defective merchandise, unless that was their specialty? Besides, we know that this quarter was never favored by potters.

Theories had reached this point when, in 1867, on the left bank of the Tiber, where now the Ponte Testaccio stands, mooring rings for ships were discovered, as well as steps for dock workers. These facilities obviously belonged to the Emporium, that great port of Rome that was so well equipped with quays and warehouses that, except in the area of the Field of Mars, the river could not be seen and formed no part of the urban setting. The military port, the *statio marmorum,* the *statio annona,* the warehouses of Galba and Germanicus, Agrippa's *horrea* were all known already.* But the discovery of a whole loading and unloading area near the Testaccio dissolved the mystery that had surrounded the little mountain; it was part of the Emporium's harbor system and was used for disposing of the containers that had been employed for water-borne shipments of supplies (oil, wine, etc.) to Rome. Machinery adapted to the purpose was employed to pile the pottery extremely high.

* The *statio marmorum* was the marble dock and warehouse, the *statio annona* was the foodstuff dock and warehouse, and the *horrea* were the granaries.— Translator.

CHAPTER 8

THE DECLINE

THE PALACE AND THE ARCH OF TRIUMPH OF SEPTIMIUS SEVERUS

Momentarily arrested by a few good emperors, the decay of Rome was resumed, to encounter no other obstacle than the reign of Septimius Severus (197–211). This passing restorer of the Empire was a man of mixed blood, a severe, hard African whose watchword was "Let us labor." The history of Rome's monuments owes a great deal to this tower of industry. When he undertook to repair the damage inflicted by the great fire that had raged through the Palatine in 191, under Commodus, he did not stop with the restoration of the buildings that had suffered; he extended the imperial palace southward. Room for this project was lacking; he resolved the problem as Caligula had done on the side that overlooked the Forum: he ordered the erection of a gigantic artificial platform that dominated the valley of the Circus Maximus, and on it he built a new wing of the imperial palace, the Domus Severiana, which looked out over the broad panorama of the Aventine, the Via Appia, the Janiculum, the Vatican height, and Monte Mario.

Below the panoramic terrace of the Domus Severiana stood the Septizonium, which, based on the floor of the valley, rose as high as the structures on the Palatine. It was not the chief entrance to the palace but a magnificent decoration whose only purpose was a display of pomp and circumstance. It faced the road that brought travelers from Africa into Rome, and it was said that Severus had built it in order to excite the admiration of his arriving compatriots.

All that remains of the Septizonium is the drawings of it made by Renaissance artists. In their time its three stories (not seven, as erroneous legend had it: the building owed its name to the number of the planets) were still standing, each adorned with rich columns in its forepart, cornices with ornamental moldings, and niches filled with statues. It was Pope Sixtus V who destroyed this luxurious building at the end of the sixteenth century in order to utilize its valuable materials in his own building projects. But we can still admire the row of arcades supported by high pilasters that served to enlarge the hill's area and to create an artificial elevation for the buildings that they supported. Roman architecture had rarely achieved such an effect of solemnity and grandeur by such simple means. The palace and its approaches were brightened with waterfalls and fountains; it had its own hot baths in an annex. It was to meet the needs of this complex that the route of the aqueduct of Claudius was altered so that it crossed the valley and scaled the Palatine, where the ruins of several of its arches survive.

The Domus Severiana concluded the cycle of imperial construction on the Palatine. In all, five palaces were built there in random order, ill assorted, each period having contributed its own without any thought of harmonizing it with its predecessors. In spite of that unconcern with the harmony of the whole, a dramatic impression of force surges out of the mass of broken walls and fallen archways. As for the substructures, which have been explored methodically, they have made it possible to reconstruct the accessories of the imperial courts. The discoveries have included prisons, guards' barracks, and even, in front of the Domus Augustana, the Paedagogium, which was the boarding school for pages. The *graffiti* that cover its walls, some of them satirical, are those of a rather critical generation. This was where the famous caricature was found that showed a worshiper praying to a crucified figure with the head of a donkey.

Other finds have brought to light curious similarities between Roman courtiers and those of Louis XIV, who abandoned their own houses and castles to crowd together in the unsanitary quarters of Versailles. The clearing of the lightless rooms on the Palatine revealed beautiful paintings and mosaics of very great elegance. No doubt these were the property of an aristocracy among the imperial household, composed of freedmen whose good graces were solicited by everyone because these men dominated the emperor and often governed the Empire. Grown important and rich, they resigned themselves, in order to remain near their master, to living in servants' quarters hardly brighter than caves: but they beautified the walls with works of art that were almost invisible.

Though time and the malice of men have not spared the palace of Septimius Severus, the arch of triumph with its three archways (like that in the Place du Carrousel in Paris) that was dedicated to the emperor on the sixth anniversary of his accession to the throne still stands at the foot of the Capitoline, below the Forum. It is one of the best-preserved monuments of ancient Rome. It has lost only the decorations of its platform, which depicted the emperor and his two sons seated in a bronze chariot drawn by four horses.

Though it has come down to us in such excellent condition, this beautiful creation has nevertheless had its share of experiences, which, in contrast to those of so many other Roman monuments, were more comic than tragic. The strangest was that of which an eighteenth-century magistrate was the hero. Ordered in 1714 to get rid of the hawkers who had established themselves under its arches, he simply set himself up in their quarters and even appropriated all the rooms above the archways. Living in some and renting out the rest, he maintained this unlawful occupancy for forty years. His battles with the municipal authorities, who tried in vain to evict him, could be the inspiration for a comic-heroic poem that would have no lack of color.

The arch of Septimius Severus was on the route of all the great Roman public celebrations.

The beauty of its proportions and the mediocrity of its bas-reliefs show that architecture was declining less quickly than sculpture; the whole is harmonious, but the decorations are dull. "It is not a poet who speaks in these statues," someone has said, "not even a good reporter; it is a vulgar old soldier boasting of his exploits every night in a tavern." In the long inscription on the coping that was supposed to convey the fame of the deeds of Septimius Severus to the most remote posterity, one name has been erased, and the void recalls the tragedy that stained the emperor's home with blood: one of his sons, Caracalla, stabbed another, Geta, in their mother's arms in order to be the sole heir to power.

The frenzy with which the murderer pursued every memory of his victim is still evidenced by the little arch set in the outer wall of the church of St. George in the Velabrum, from which, this time, not only Geta's name but his portrait was removed. This little arch was built by the cattle dealers in thanks to the emperor and his family for having given them their nearby forum of Janus Quadrifons, whose indomitable solidity has withstood men and ages. It is one of the rare remaining examples of structures of its kind (though they were plentiful in Rome), with which at one time Domitian compulsively filled the Forum. The Roman ediles thought of everything, and particularly of providing shelter from sun and rain for those of their fellow citizens whose work kept them out of doors. This circumstance was the origin of the Januses, arches with four façades and four archways. The one in the Forum Boarium is interesting only as it shows the care that was taken in Rome with buildings of secondary importance: it is constructed of white marble blocks so huge that their mass discouraged the demolition teams of the Renaissance and the arch could be used as a fortress during the civil wars of the Middle Ages without suffering any appreciable damage.

Septimius Severus left other relics in the Forum. Behind the *rostra* he placed that round structure that is the Umbilicus Urbis Romae (the navel of the city of Rome), the symbolic center of the Empire, which forms a pendant to the Golden Milestone.

THE REGIA AND THE HOUSE OF THE VESTALS

It was also Septimius Severus who was responsible for the last rebuilding of the temple of Vesta and the structures connected with it: the residence—or, as some prefer to call it, the cloister—of the Vestals and the house of the Pontifex Maximus, which was called the Regia and in which Caesar lived. It was from there that, ignoring the sinister omens, he went out on his last day to be murdered. This religious aggregate, the foundation of which was supposed to date back to King Numa, had undergone many ordeals in the course of the centuries, including the fires of 64 and 191, each of which had destroyed it from top to bottom.

Septimius Severus (and his wife, Julia Domna) preserved the circular shape of the temple of Vesta, which reproduced the original hut, but they gave the priestesses' house a new splendor in keeping with the great honors that were paid to them. They had numerous servitors; even the consul's chariot made way for them; any offense against them was punishable by death. Their worship went back to the earliest days of Rome. The care of the sacred fire and the guardianship of the Palladium, the holy pledge of the Empire's continuity, were not their only tasks; they were often called on as arbiters of disputes, and they accepted custody of wills and all other valuable documents that required absolute safekeeping. In addition, it was believed that they had no difficulty in obtaining miracles from the goddess whose altar they served.

The ruins that survive attest to the richness of their house, on which marble was lavished. The Vestals have occasionally been compared with Catholic nuns, with whom, however, they had very little in common. Aside from the fact that the Vestals' vows were not lifelong, the purity that was demanded of them was only physical. They knew neither the "state of recollection" nor mortification. Still less were they bound to poverty, for they lived in luxury at the expense of the public treasury. In strict proportion to the honors that were paid to them, their defections were punished without mercy: they were buried alive in the Campus Sceleratus, near Porta Salaria, if they permitted the fire of love to ignite in their hearts.

Round the *atrium,* and reflected in the antique pool whose periphery was girdled with a garland of roses, there were statues of eminent Vestals who were celebrated for their modesty and their meticulous devotion to their sacred duties. The sculptures show the details of their rich but severe dress, their short hair, the cord that caught their tunics at the waist, and the round *bulla* that they wore on their bosoms as nuns wear crosses. This gallery of the Vestals has been much looted: many of the statues have vanished (the most beautiful and valuable is in the Museum of the Baths), but the pedestals remain with their inscriptions. From one of them a name has been scratched out: it was that of a priestess who scandalized the pagan world by becoming a convert to Christianity.

Though the Vestals' bedrooms have disappeared, their reception hall and their six private drawing rooms are still discernible. But it is above all the *atrium* that recreates the poetic setting of their life; it is the purest flower in that nostalgic garden of ruins that the Forum has become.

THE BATHS OF CARACALLA

Caracalla, the fratricide, succeeded his father in 211 and, happily, reigned only six years. A bloodthirsty madman and a ranting demagogue, he sought to flatter his soldiers, it was said, by eating with them out of a wooden bowl. He granted the status of Roman citizenship to every man in the Empire who was not a slave—an act that did not serve to add luster to a rank of which the old Rome had been so jealous. In the effort to increase his popularity, Caracalla built the baths whose gigantic ruins "made us think of the remains of a Cyclopean city blasted by the lightning of the Titans." Not only was it an establishment for baths; it was augmented with promenades, gardens, peristyles, gymnasia and stadia, theaters and libraries, shops, restaurants. A sophisticated and idle society made these baths its major preoccupation: every pleasure could be found there, every luxury was to be had there. The most valuable marbles and the finest mosaics adorned the walls and the swimming pools; the greatest masterpieces of sculpture embellished its porticoes. What remains of the marvels of every kind that Caracalla gathered together to eclipse his predecessors? Naked walls, broken archways, shattered columns, enormous pillars supporting nothing. But artistic relics of these baths are to be found in every museum in the world. Rome has kept its share of them: the precious statues that adorn the Museum of the Baths and the Vatican Museum, the two huge granite basins made into fountains in front of the Palazzo Farnese, the great mosaic panels reconstructed in the Lateran Museum, which represent forty well-drawn and modeled gladiators with brutish faces. Then, too, the tremendous walls have survived, though they seem to have been hurled there by some cataclysm; their reddish ruins testify to the superhuman grandeur of the Roman Empire's official architecture. The arch dominates everything, the arch whose secret had to be sought in the mud of the Etruscan sewers. It is employed here with complete honesty, without any of the artifices that enabled Filippo Brunelleschi and Michelangelo to erect their domes. The use of the vault lent itself to the enlargement of surfaces. So Caracalla's halls were enormous: they had sixteen hundred marble seats, and two thousand bathers could use them at the same time. The four façades of the baths covered more than four thousand feet. They were not alone. A whole series of buildings, of which only fragments lie now among the greenery, ran as far as Porta Capena, along a broad artery, one hundred feet wide, that Caracalla laid out, the Via Nuova. This vanished quarter was endowed with an "archeological promenade," a kind of park strewn with relics of an earlier antiquity.

SANTA MARIA TRASTEVERINA / THE TROPHIES OF MARIUS / THE ARCH OF GALLIENUS

Roman decadence gathered speed with Caracalla's successors. "Heliogabalus gave Roman vices the proportions and the distortions of the Orient": his reign marked the nadir in the debasement of morals. It seemed that the last days of the Empire were at hand. The descent was halted for a moment by the rectitude of Alexander Severus. He was the first emperor to show any respect for Christianity, and his tolerance was the origin of one of the first Christian buildings—certainly the first Roman church to be dedicated to the Virgin. A Christian community had established a place of worship in a few shops in Trastevere, from which its eviction was sought in order to change the premises into a tavern. Having been informed of the dispute, the emperor resolved it in favor of the Christians, saying: "It is better that these premises be used for the worship of God, no matter in what manner."

Like all the old churches in Rome, Santa Maria Trasteverina has known sufferings. Nevertheless, in spite of fires and successive rebuildings, it has retained its deep mystic atmosphere: in no other sanctuary is Christmas Mass so intimate and so moving. This impression is due quite as much to the very special physiognomy of the residents of this quarter as to the appearance of the place itself. They claim to be the sole descendants of the ancient *quirites,* a claim that could be supported by their character and their customs. The men have very strong features and energetic ways; the women have brilliant eyes and a proud bearing: it is they who have always been sought out as models for painters.

In connection with Santa Maria Trasteverina, we should point out that the earliest churches in Rome were established on the sites of the original sanctuaries, fitted out by whatever means was possible in artisans' premises or in ordinary houses of which they occupied only part; and this was not always the ground floor. There were already some twenty of them in the time of Severus, usually known by the names of the individuals who had made over part of their houses for liturgical purposes. These places of meeting and prayer, which were identified by their locales, constituted centers of regular parishes that had their own clergy and that were consolidated under the authority of a bishop. This meant that the Christian community had made considerable progress: rich and poor were commingled in it. The senatorial class had opened its doors to the new religion, and even the imperial palace had done so, for already, under the Flavian dynasty, a cousin of Domitian, followed by his two sons, heirs presumptive to the Empire, had been converted.

There is no monument in Rome that can be directly linked to the creative thinking of Alexander Severus except perhaps those trophies inaccurately ascribed to Marius, of which some decorate the balustrade of the Capitoline Square while others were used to adorn a fountain whose ruins can be seen in Piazza Vittorio Emanuele. This formless mass of material is all that has remained to us of the one thousand three hundred and fifty-two public fountains that existed in Rome at the end of the third century, a fact that tells us a great deal as to the extent of the depredations carried out through the ages. The case of the trophies of Marius also enables us to understand the mechanics of the depredations. The fountain still existed in the time of Sixtus V, who removed its decorations for the benefit of the Capitoline in 1590; two years later, Marchese Orazio Savelli persuaded the Municipal Council to allow him to use what remained; he left only what we see today—in other words, virtually nothing.

Alexander Severus was not a destroyer. This enlightened despot devoted special attention to the maintenance of public buildings, especially the theater of Marcellus. It was he, too, who brought together in the Forums of Nerva and Trajan the statues of the most famous men that adorned streets and squares. He had an abundance of choice: three thousand seven hundred and eighty-five statues of men with claims to honor encumbered the city at that time, and special officials were charged with caring for this population in bronze and marble.

Alexander Severus drew plans for a large basilica that would have been more than one thousand feet long; obviously he was not immune to the lure of the colossal, which gained in architecture in proportion as the solidity of the Empire declined. In fact, a state of military anarchy prevailed. The emperor was its first victim, assassinated by his troops in 235. This was followed by battles among the armies, each striving to make its commander the emperor. It was then that foreign tribes began to cross the borders, which were no longer guarded by the legions; the Persians penetrated into Syria and the Alemanni got as far as Milan.

The emperors who followed one another during this period enjoyed only brief reigns and had no time to beautify the capital. Nonetheless the memory of the greatest zero of all of them, the emperor whose reign was the most deadly and who opened the gates of Italy to the Barbarians, Gallienus, was perpetuated by a triumphal arch. It still stands at Porta

Esquilina, while those of Marcus Aurelius and Trajan, who sallied out to defeat the enemy on his own ground, have disappeared. This is one of the jokes of the history written in Rome's monuments.

There was almost another in the theory that Gallienus undertook to honor the gods at a time when the most noble of Roman institutions were being shamefully profaned (in the triumph that he awarded himself, there were chariots filled with third-rate actors and twelve hundred gladiators dressed as women). It was a really curious idea in modern times to describe as a temple erected by Gallienus the ruins in Via Giolitti that are still inaccurately given the name of the temple of Minerva Medica. We know today that this was only a large nymph grotto in the gardens of Lucullus. Its dome was the model for the cupolas of the Renaissance. In 1826 it threatened to collapse; a guidebook published in Rome at the time mentioned the fact and added that the incumbent Pope "has issued orders for its restoration." One must conclude that little effort was made to follow these orders: the dome fell two years later.

THE ILLYRIAN EMPERORS / AURELIAN'S WALL

Once again the Empire was snatched from ruin, this time by the harsh fist of Aurelian, who was born in Illyria and who restored internal order and repelled the invasions. After his victory over Zenobia, queen of Palmyra (who spent the rest of her life, it will be recalled, in Villa Adriana, in whose vicinity her memory is kept alive by the names of several villages), Aurelian erected a temple to the sun whose enormous remains are scattered through the gardens of Palazzo Colonna on the Quirinal. This temple was surrounded by porticoes that were storage places for the wine kept for public distribution.

Aurelian has given his name to a fortified enclosure, rebuilt by Honorius and many times repaired by the popes down the centuries, that often checked the invader. In Aurelian's time the old wall of the republican period had disappeared and the Romans had not replaced it, relying, the ancient authors say, on their own valor for the defense of the city. Indeed there was a time when Rome, having become the master of the world, had no need for ramparts. By the third century that time was over, and the incursions of the Barbarians made it necessary to establish defenses. That was the purpose of the wall that Aurelian built in 271. Although it extended a dozen miles, it did not enclose the whole of the perimeter of the fourteen zones set up by Augustus; it followed no administrative boundary line and was limited to the protection of the city's vital areas, incorporating whatever structures stood in its path. The pretorian camp, the pyramid of Cestius, certain parts of aqueducts and many other buildings were thus made integral parts of it. In many areas of Rome one still sees the wall's curtains (between bastions), the asymmetrical succession of its turrets and its great sections of brick masonry. Jérôme Carcopino said of these remains that, "catching glorious fire in the flames of the sunset, they imbue the most insensitive tourist with the immediate sense of the majesty that still made Rome glorious in its decline." The wall was pierced by nineteen gates set at irregular intervals. Most of them still exist, though some have been extensively refashioned and many have new names. Thus Porta Flaminia became Porta del Popolo; Porta Tiburtina, on the road to Tivoli, was renamed Porta San Lorenzo; Porta Ostiensis, near the pyramid of Cestius, is now Porta San Paolo. As for Porta Proenestina, it became that Porta Maggiore that Michelangelo so admired and of which Giambattista Piranesi left splendid drawings.

It was customary in antiquity to give aqueducts a special magnificence wherever they intersected public thoroughfares. Aurelian and Honorius appropriated these decorative constructions as the gates of their wall. Porta Tiburtina supported the first-century aqueduct that Titus and Caracalla had restored; Porta Maggiore was formed from two arches of the Aqua Claudia aqueduct that bestrode Via Proenestina in a magnificent arch of triumph that is still in an excellent state of preservation.

From Aurelian to Diocletian the emperors were men of the Danube, almost all of them removed from the world stage by military risings. They kept the Empire alive in the midst of growing difficulties. The pomp of Oriental despotisms spread through Rome in direct porportion to the disappearance of the virtues that had assured its real greatness. The festivals in the Colosseum and the Circus Maximus grew to inordinate proportions. At the celebration of the thousandth year of Rome's existence, two thousand pairs of gladiators battled. To celebrate the victories of Probus the Circus was filled with an incredible horde of ostriches, wild boars, and gazelles for the people to hunt. At the same time, two hundred leopards, two hundred lions and three hundred bears were slaughtered in a single day. There had never been such a consumption of gladiators. Now Christians began to be handed over to the animals; this was the time of the most violent persecutions. Then came Diocletian, who, as we know, carried them to the ultimate heights of savagery.

THE CATACOMBS

Imperial paganism could not remain unaffected by the growth of the Christian religion, which it saw as a menace both to the Roman state and to ancient civilization. This was the root of the persecutions that were unleashed against Christianity throughout the whole third century, at shorter and shorter intervals, until those of Diocletian, which were the last but also the most cruel: Christians who refused to sacrifice to false gods were martyred and their places of worship were destroyed. This was when some of them took refuge in the catacombs to find sanctuary with their dead and to carry on their worship. These practices, which were born wholly of necessity, have given rise to some misconceptions as to the function of the catacombs, and it may not be unhelpful here to clarify their nature and their true purposes. "Archives of the Faith and trophies of the Church, the catacombs are the great emotion of Rome. But it must be experienced with full knowledge" (*Itinéraires romains—Roman Guidebooks,* by Jean Maury and René Percheron).

We know that the civil law prohibited burial within the city limits of Rome itself; therefore the cemeteries were laid out beyond the green belt, along the twelve Roman roads, so that they would be easily accessible. In the beginning, pagans and Christians alike were buried in them without distinction. St. Paul had been buried in the cemetery of Lucina, on Via Ostiense, and St. Peter had been entombed in the Vatican cemetery. This state of affairs was not to endure beyond the first century A.D. At that time the catacombs were established as purely Christian burial places; they were to grow to such a degree that there would be more than five million burial vaults distributed along almost three hundred and fifty miles of galleries.

Undoubtedly the first Christians rebelled at the thought of being mingled with the heathen in death; but the catacombs were born out of a different concern, which had nothing to do with clandestinity, contrary to an extremely widespread belief that has been reinforced by fine apocryphal documents. The visible facts give the lie to the legends; there are catacombs whose entrances are hard to find, but most of them open freely on large public roads: they date from a time when the Christians relied on the tolerance of the authorities. These corridors, so narrow that one bruises one's elbows on the walls, these winding galleries in which one can never see a dozen feet ahead could never have furnished asylum to the throng of the believers. No more than they served to "hide the church during the persecutions" did the catacombs function as the headquarters of the Christian community; they offered only a minimum of open spaces, in the least confining of which not even twenty persons could have found room. The catacombs were simply cemeteries.

The heathen practiced cremation, and their ashes required very little storage space. The Christians, on the other hand, were faithful to the rite of burial by virtue of their faith in resurrection. Hence their cemeteries required large areas that the Roman countryside could not conveniently provide. It was this factor that gave birth to the underground necropolis that made it possible to superimpose one grave on another in galleries that were themselves superimposed one on another. These labyrinths were hollowed into the layers of granular tufa.

There are almost sixty catacombs around Rome: the largest are those of St. Calixtus, on Via Appia, which contain the tombs of the first popes; the catacombs of St. Sebastian, on the same road; on Via Tiburtina, the catacombs of San Lorenzo or Cyriachus, which can be reached through the basilica of San Lorenzo; those of St. Pancras on Via Aurelia; Priscilla's catacombs on Via Salaria, where, it is said, Santa Pudenziana and St. Prassede were buried; those of St. Agnes, on Via Nomentana, are the best-preserved catacombs in Rome. The very curious church of St. Agnes Beyond the Walls was built above them.

All contain the same kinds of galleries and crypts. They are the first manifestation of Christian art, in the form of extended frescoes on vaults and walls, mosaics, carved stone, sarcophagi decorated with sculpture. These ornaments are done with an ingenuous, primitive art; proportions are not observed, and movement is lacking. Yet they date from a period when the city teemed with excellent frescoes. Must we suppose that the Christians were interested only in symbols and rejected any esthetic sentiment? Were these things, rather, the humble work of *fossores,* carried out in haste by relatively unskilled men in dark and inconvenient places? Whatever the reason, it is surprising that Christian art was so slow in breaking the yoke of ornamental conventions in the Greek-Latin style. There are indeed innumerable pagan subjects in the catacombs: the sun, the seasons, Cupids. Gospel scenes and symbols were handled in a manner that makes one wonder whether these are Christians' graves. "A eucharistic *agapé* looks like a profane banquet; a decorative arabesque might have come from the Palatine; young women crossing a room with vases of flowers belong in a Pompeian villa" (Maurice Paléologue).

Another occasion for astonishment in the catacombs is the total absence of crosses and crucifixes. We know that the ancients invested crucifixion with a certain ignominy; to the heathen the cross on Golgotha was an object of mockery. Therefore the early Christians depicted not the agony of Christ but his apotheosis. It was only in the twelfth century that they began to portray "the image of the bleeding, emaciated Christ nailed to his cross." The most ancient depiction of the crucified Saviour was not done by a Christian hand. It was found in a cartoon scrawled on a wall of the Paedagogium on the Palatine. The *graffito* shows a young man kneeling in adoration before a donkey-headed man on a cross. Beneath, the artist wrote: "Alexamenus prays to his god."

THE BATHS OF DIOCLETIAN

To return to Diocletian, who in other respects owes his fame to tragic causes, let us point out that it was this emperor who was responsible for the tremendous baths whose ruins are the first signs of Rome's antiquity that the traveler sees when he leaves the central railway station. They covered half of a section of the city and themselves resembled a city: their site is occupied today by the Roman National Museum, a large square, a monastery, barracks, and the biggest cloister in Rome; not to mention two churches, St. Bernard and St. Mary of the Angels, established in the upper rooms, where very little alteration had to be made for the new function.

Challenging his predecessors in the domain of the colossal, Diocletian wanted to outdo the Baths of Caracalla. Indeed, Diocletian's could accommodate more bathers at a given time, and the sections intended for cognate diversions were also greater. The theater was huge, and the library was so vast that it could swallow the big Ulpia library that had been moved into it from Trajan's Forum. Technique had reached its highest peak of perfection: the water ran hot from two thousand tanks at the same time; athletes had luxurious halls for their sports; the cultivated could spend whole days listening to philosophers or attending literary and artistic discussions. A thousand entertainments of every kind were available for the merely curious: loungers told stories, lawyers retried their cases, and scandal and gossip ran through the throng. Competitors of amphitheater and circus, the baths were meeting places in the unlimited chaos of Rome. They were much more than a café, a stock exchange, a school, or a theater is for us. They were all these, and they served as hospitals and houses of prostitution to boot. The life of a Roman citizen in the late Empire was voluptuous and free: fed on the grain of Africa, he was amused, from the circus to the baths, at the expense of the public treasury. The emperor saw to everything through his levies on the provinces, his exactions from the rich, and his inheritances from those who committed suicide at his command. It is extremely understandable that, thus relieved of every care, the Romans should have filled the air of the baths with their joyful songs and laughter and loud discussions.

The clamor of those days has given way to the hush that greets the visitor to the Roman National Museum. Sometimes it is a bore to visit museums. Most of them are like prisons for masterpieces. Too many beautiful things, often disparate, compete at once for our attention; and, besides, the fact that they were made elsewhere is a barrier that sensibly diminishes their power of suggestion. That is why we have not lingered over descriptions of the Roman museums. But that of the baths is exempt from all these strictures because of the frame in which it is set. It radiates the intellect of antiquity in the long sequence of its arcades, the long luminous cloister of Michelangelo, the garden with its centuries-old cypresses, where the incomparable masterpieces of Greek-Latin sculpture are displayed. Everything unites to show them to advantage, from the enormous, mutilated, pillaged structure that houses them to the flowers that spring from the capitals, the wisteria and the creepers that embrace the truncated columns. Everything must be seen, stone by stone, in this museum, one of the most beautiful in the world, where every inch arouses an artistic emotion. A long slow stroll through its halls, courts, and gardens is one of the most delightful experiences that can befall anyone in Rome who has any curiosity for the relics of his past. It is here that one can best grasp the nobility of marble and its ability "to confer eternity on perishable forms."

CHAPTER 9

THE AGONY OF THE EMPIRE

THE ARCH OF CONSTANTINE

After Diocletian's abdication, the tetrarchy that he had established ceased to function, and the generals began again to battle for the throne. After complicated struggles, only two rivals remained in the field: Maxentius, who was backed by the pretorians, and Constantine, endorsed by the army of the Gauls, who finally restored the unity of the Empire to his own profit in 324. Constantine was the son of a Christian mother, St. Helena, whose body was taken from Palestine to Rome in the magnificent porphyry sarcophagus that has been preserved in the Vatican opposite the tomb of St. Constance.

In spite—and perhaps because—of the persecutions, the Christian community had increased so much that it embraced a very considerable part of the Roman population. The Christians had pursued a very skillful policy of infiltration into the machinery of the state. (Tertullian wrote: "We are filling the municipal offices, the tribunes, the palace, and the Senate.") Thus they had created a *de facto* situation that sooner or later would have to lead to recognition of their rights. This was all the more the case because the organization of the Christian church, patiently evolved over three centuries, had transformed that community into a solid and cohesive society. A clergy of one hundred and fifty priests, deacons, acolytes, and exorcists served more than forty parishes. Thirty-one bishops had been their successive leaders since the death of the Apostle Peter. The bishop of Rome enjoyed special prerogatives.

Constantine felt a sympathy for the Christians that went so far that ultimately he embraced their faith. Eusebius, who enjoyed his confidence, reported that he had appealed for their help against Maxentius as the result of a miracle: in the sky above Rome a glowing cross had appeared, bearing the inscription: *"In hoc signo vinces* (In this sign shalt thou conquer)." The Christians responded in a body to his appeal, for in their eyes Maxentius was the enemy. One account, which may be partly legend, gives some idea of the hatred that he felt toward them; he said that he had locked up Pope Marcellus in the Vivarium, where the pontiff was to be the keeper of the savage beasts. A Roman matron, Lucina, was supposed to have rescued him and harbored him in her home, which she had converted into a Christian chapel that became the church of San Marcello del Corso. In a word, Constantine's cause was also that of the Christians, and they shared the victory.

The decisive battle was fought on the banks of the Tiber at some distance from Rome, near the bridge of Mulvius (Ponte Molle). The combat was furious, and a large number of the vanquished were hurled into the river. Such was the death of Maxentius. He is depicted at the mercy of the current in the great fresco by Giulio Romano in the Vatican's Hall of Constantine, which also shows the appalling battle of Ponte Molle adapted from a drawing by Raphael.

The emperor proved his gratitude to the Christians by issuing his famous Edict of Milan, which granted them freedom of worship. He did still more for the new religion by protecting it against the heresies that threatened it, notably that of Arianism. It was thanks to him that it was possible in 325 to convene that assembly of bishops that is known as the Council of Nicaea, which proclaimed the basic dogmas of the Christian religion in the Nicaean Creed, or Symbol. The preparatory meetings for this council were held in the chapel that Pope St. Sylvester had built on the ruins of Trajan's baths and that became the church of St. Martin of the Hills. A Christian edifice commemorates the victory of the bridge of Mulvius near the place where it was won: this is the church of the Holy Cross, built in 1913 by Pope Pius X to mark the sixteen hundredth anniversary of the event that changed the world. In certain respects it might be argued that Constantine's great arch of triumph, erected near the Colosseum, marked the victory both of the emperor and of the church. The ambiguity of the dedication, which declares that victory was gained "by the inspiration of the divinity," offers only shaky support for the theory. In addition, the structure bears no other trace of Christian inspiration; the bas-reliefs are devoted to heathen deities. This is not surprising when one reflects that Constantine had simply arranged that an arch erected to Trajan be altered to honor himself. But the bas-reliefs that Constantine added are equally profane in spirit. Let us add that they derive from a completely bastardized art; the poverty of their execution is in painful contrast to the borrowed fragments, which are excellent examples of Roman historical sculpture. In spite of its uneven decoration, the arch of Constantine is impressive in its noble proportions. Even in this twilight of Empire, Roman architecture preserved its harmony and its grandeur.

In front of the arch there was a fountain erected by Titus, the Meta Sudans, whose traces still show in the pavement. It was a marble cone topped by a bronze sphere pierced with tiny holes through which the water dripped like sweat.

CONSTANTINE'S BASILICAS

Constantine's Christian tendencies were inscribed elsewhere in Rome's monuments, above all in the venerable shrine that is the basilica of St. John Lateran. First among all the churches of Rome and the universe, the episcopal domain of the Supreme Pontiff, the seat of innumerable councils, St. John Lateran was the center of the Christian world until the end of the Middle Ages. The primacy of this church, *caput et mater* of all the Catholic churches in the world, is declared in the inscription on its façade.

Constantine decided to build it in part of the imperial park, the great estate of the Laterani, formerly owned by one of Messalina's lovers, Plautius Lateranus. It bore the name of Basilica Constantiniana until the twelfth century, when Pope Lucius II dedicated it to St. John the Baptist and St. John the Evangelist. It was to survive in its original form for almost a thousand years, until it was destroyed in the great fire of 1308 that led Clement V to rebuild it as it is today. In order to make room for the basilica, the emperor had closed the *equites'* garrison that had provided the officers for the army of Maxentius. This garrison had itself been built by Septimius Severus on top of a country house belonging to the Laterani. Excavations in 1936 beneath the present basilica brought to light the decorative frescoes of the Laterani apartments, the walls of the garrison and the foundations of the original basilica—another and most curious instance of that archeological stratification that makes the soil of Rome an inexhaustible treasure of discoveries.

All the organs of a great religious institute were grouped round St. John Lateran: the palace of the popes, a cloister, and the baptistry in which, according to legend, Constantine received his baptism in 326 at the hands of Pope St. Sylvester. Actually it was not until ten years afterward that Constantine was baptized, just before his death; and the baptistry was not completed until a much later period. It is the only surviving testimony in the Lateran to the times before the popes' flight to Avignon. Its octagonal wall was the model for the baptistries of Florence, Parma, and Pisa.

Through strange and devious ways the great red granite obelisk that stands in front of Piazza Laterano, the largest in Rome and no doubt in the entire world, is also directly associated with Constantine's memory. It was not erected on this site, however, until 1588, under the rule of Sixtus V, having been discovered in three sections in the Murcia Valley, where it had lain for eleven centuries after having stood on the crest of the Circus Maximus. But it was Constantine who had it shipped down the Nile from Thebes to Alexandria and then to Rome aboard a ship built especially for the purpose.

Another shrine whose foundation dates back to Constantine is Holy Cross of Jerusalem, one of the seven basilicas that are included in what is called the pilgrimage "of the seven churches," which is rewarded with special indulgences. St. Helena, the emperor's mother, had built it in the center of a large complex, the Sessorian Palace, which was her residence. Undoubtedly it is a grotto of this palace from which come the ruins that can be seen in the enclosure of the nearby garrison known as that of "the grenadiers." The Castrense amphitheater, whose columns and capitals survive to the right of the church, was a small arena intended for spectacles of the imperial court and as a drill ground for the imperial guard. The basilica of Holy Cross of Jerusalem was built to house the relics of the Passion which St. Helena had brought back from the holy places. Soil from Jerusalem was laid beneath the stone floor of the sanctuary.

Later it was to be the site where, on the fourth Sunday of Lent, the popes blessed the golden roses with which they rewarded illustrious foreigners outstanding for their devotion to the Holy See. Holy Cross of Jerusalem has been restored so often that it has completely lost the mark of its venerable origin.

St. Helena had also brought back from Jerusalem the stairway of Pilate's house, which Jesus had climbed on the day of the Passion. This is the *scala santa* that the faithful climb on their knees, opposite the Lateran Palace at Piazza di Porta San Giovanni.

The church of St. Agnes Beyond the Walls, on Via Nomentana, was also built by Constantine, in response to the prayers of one of his daughters and in memory of a little twelve-year-old patrician girl, who, hearing the trumpet that announced the opening of the trial of some Christians, had thrown herself into the Forum to affirm her faith. The church was built on the former ground level, and today it must be reached by descending a broad staircase of forty-three steps, built in the sixteenth century. The walls are covered with inscriptions gathered in the neighboring catacombs (those of St. Agnes). The interior of the church, rich in its very great antiquity, affords the closest model of the basilicas in the Roman Forum that were used as markets or courts. Situated below ground level, as we have said—as if it had been interred—St. Agnes seems almost a sepulcher welcoming the living: the sun never shines on its mosaics, which go back to the seventh century and are one of our rare illuminations of the very obscure early Middle Ages. A hundred paces from St. Agnes is the monumental tomb in the form of a rotunda that Constantine erected for his family and from which the sarcophagus of his daughter, Constantina, was taken for its present display in the Vatican. It is the best preserved of all Christian monuments of the earliest times. The circular shape of this little temple, converted in the thirteenth century into a church dedicated to St. Constance, shows the first Byzantine influence in Italy. The vault of its nave is decorated with the oldest Christian mosaics—partly redone—that are known in Rome; we are amazed at their mixture of Christian, profane, and pagan decorative elements.

As for the basilica of San Lorenzo fuori le Mura, also built by Constantine, in 330, on the martyr's tomb, it has best preserved the precious tradition of the rituals of the early centuries. At the end of the Middle Ages it was to be joined to the next-door church of the Virgin. The original change made in it at that time transformed it into a church of two stories, not one above the other but side by side, "the one merely crossing the other without covering it." Ionic capitals from the original basilica bear in their ornamentation two unexpected little figures, a frog and a lizard, an eloquent hieroglyphic translation of the names of the two Corinthian artists whose status as slaves forbade their signing their work. If the exterior of San Lorenzo looks like a hay loft, the interior is the finest example of the classic basilica. Its serene simplicity is anything but appropriate to the dazzling tomb of Pius IX that it houses.

The huge basilica of St. Paul Beyond the Walls, whose successive reconstructions have made it the largest church in Rome after St. Peter's, was originally a little shrine that Constantine built on the spot where St. Paul's disciple, Timothy, had laid the body of his martyred master.

As we see, it was outside the walls of Rome that the first sanctuaries were built in which the religion could be openly practiced. This exodus echoed the Christians' desire to rejoin their dead along the great Roman roads where they were buried.

The last shrine that Constantine built—and it is not the least important in the history of Christendom—was the Vatican basilica on whose site today St. Peter's of Rome stands. A very ancient tradition has it that the first Christian emperor built his basilica on the very spot where the apostle had undergone his martyrdom and been buried. Vast excavations carried out on the instigation of Pius XII transformed that tradition into a fact of history. In fact, they revealed, beneath the basilica, the existence of a cemetery dating from the first and second centuries in which both Christians and pagans were buried. It is known with what revulsion the Christians contemplated the mingling of their dead with those of the pagans, a revulsion that in part explains the catacombs. If many Christian families overcame this scruple to bury their members at the Vatican, it could have been only because they wanted them to lie near the sacred place that held the first head of the church.

The same desire to add both eminence and tribute to the Apostle Peter dictated Constantine's choice. He could have had no other reason for situating his basilica in a place that was the least adapted of all to the construction of a sanctuary. Situated, in fact, outside the walls of Rome, so that it must have been more difficult to maintain and protect, it stood also on sloping land containing much clay—that is, as unfavorable to building as it could be. And in addition, in order to lay its foundations, a cemetery had to be destroyed—a sacrilege in Roman eyes. The emperor could persist in such a determination only because he, like all Christians of his time, believed in the existence of St. Peter's tomb at the Vatican, at the exact point where the "Apostle's Confession" stands today. What was only a belief then has been made a certainty by the recent excavations. Indeed, it was at the very spot cited in tradition that they uncovered human bones in a recess carefully faced with slabs of marble. According to Jérôme Carcopino, "the precautions with which they were surrounded would be incomprehensible if these had not been relics, and if these relics in the basilica of St. Peter's had not been his." The presence of a red protective wall round the "trophy" attests to the concern of its builders for the preservation and isolation of a holy area. The old basilica of Constantine, whose only physical survival is in the substructures of the present church, derives an incomparable historical and emotional importance from these discoveries.

THE BASILICA OF MAXENTIUS AND THE TEMPLE OF THE DIVINE ROMULUS

Other traces of Constantine's architectural contribution survive on the ridge of the Quirinal, in the form of a few fragments of a frieze from the baths that the emperor erected there. The whole was still in existence in the sixteenth century, and disappeared in the foundations of the palace that Scipione Cardinal Borghese built in 1603 and that later became the property of Cardinal Mazarin; it is known today as Palazzo Pallavicini-Rospigliosi. It was from these baths that the statue of Constantine was taken that is now in the vestibule of the basilica of St. John Lateran, as well as the two colossal heroes, holding their rearing horses by the bridle, who are part of the group gathered in the center of Piazza Quirinale by Popes Sixtus V, Pius VI, and Pius VII.

As for the basilica called Constantine's, whose imposing ruins dominate the Forum at its northeastern end, it was erected by Maxentius before his defeat, and it was simply dedicated by the people to the victor, Constantine. It is the last great creation of imperial art. What remains of it (the vast platform, the three gigantic bays with their haughty vaults, the red porphyry shafts of the shattered porticoes) gives some idea of the magnitude of the building, which engenders a host of reflections on the Romans' tendency to construct larger and larger monuments as their capacity for great deeds became less and less. Its general construction, completely different from that of the older basilicas, was modeled on the great halls of the imperial baths: four enormous pillars separated the building, which was some four hundred feet long, into three naves. Its huge vaults tower above not only the buildings in the Forum but also the plateau of the

Palatine. At one time they were surmounted by a story of which some vestiges still exist. Of the eight columns that divided the interior, only one survives: it stands now in front of Santa Maria Maggiore. These columns were so broad that in one of them Simone Marchisio could carve the large sculptural group that shows Alessandro Farnese wearing a victor's crown, the River Scheldt in chains and Flanders at his feet. It was in the apse of the central nave that Constantine had a statue of justice, wearing a diadem and seated on a golden throne, separated from the public by a marble railing of which a few pieces have been found.

While he converted to his own glory the basilica that Maxentius had intended to exalt himself, he demonstrated more taste with regard to the temple that his unfortunate rival had begun to build in memory of his son, Romulus, who died in childhood in 307. Not only did Constantine complete the temple; he respected its debatable name, for young Romulus had only the scantiest claim to deification. This led to a curious confusion, as a result of which the founder of Rome, Romulus, and his brother, Remus, were long honored in a sanctuary intended for his namesake. It was after this false attribution that the temple was chosen in 527 by Pope Felix IV as the site of a church dedicated to two martyrs who were also twin brothers. The temple's *cella* is still the vestibule of the church of Saints Cosmas and Damian, which holds the tomb of the last French pope, who brought the Holy See back to Rome from Avignon.

THE FOUNDATION OF CONSTANTINOPLE AND THE PEACE OF THE CHURCH

Constantine had carried Oriental absolutism to its highest point and he had surrounded it with a wholly Oriental luxury. His way of living was much more like that of the ancient kings of Babylon than the styles of Augustus and the Antonines. This taste for Asian despotism led him to move the capital of the Empire and its political center to Byzantium on the Bosphorus, which he renamed Constantinople in honor of himself.

On the day when Constantine made this great decision he delivered Rome to the Barbarians, and the inscription on his triumphal arch that proclaimed him the liberator of the city became a mockery. For, in a system in which political centralization was carried to the absurd, the departure of an emperor laid a capital open to cupidities that had already become perilously manifest. In fact, it would not be very long before

Rome would be invaded and trampled, while Constantinople would hold out for eight centuries against invasion.

In every way, once abandoned by its emperors, Rome ceased to be the center of the world. It became, as some have said, a capital of the past, and all the more as the new capital aspired to supplant it in all things and even to take its name. Constantinople wanted to have its own seven hills and called itself the new Rome. It had its Capitol, its baths, its basilicas, and its fourteen municipal districts. It decked itself with an enormous number of Greek masterpieces removed from the banks of the Tiber.

The deaths of Constantine in 337 and two of his three sons over the next eighteen years were followed by an attempted restoration of dying paganism, whose zealous champion was Julian the Apostate. He applied himself to ridding the old religion of its most vulgar superstitions and to endowing it with a learned and virtuous clergy. It was in pursuance of this policy that a Roman prefect, Pretextatus, built the portico of the Dii Consentes on the edge of the Clivus Capitolinus: its nine white columns can still be seen from Via del Foro Romano, forming an angle crowned by Corinthian capitals adorned with trophies. Beneath the arches of the portico there were golden statues of the twelve gods, two by two (Jupiter and Juno, Neptune and Minerva, Mars and Venus, Apollo and Diana, Vulcan and Vesta, Mercury and Ceres). It is paganism's final monument.

After the defeat of this last reaction, there was no further halt in the growth of Christianity. In 370, on the advice of St. Ambrose, Gratian renounced the title of Pontifex Maximus and ordered the statue of freedom removed from the Senate. Twenty-two years later (392), Theodosius ordered the pagan temples closed and made Christianity the official state religion. The old beliefs persisted—for a time—only in the countryside, and it was for that reason that thereafter the word *paganism** would be used to designate the ancient faith.

The triumph of Christianity was consecrated with a monument erected in the Forum near the temple of Castor, behind the fountain of Juturna. It was the chapel known as the Forty Martyrs, an apsidal structure whose floor is paved with fragments of marble taken from neighboring buildings; the walls are decorated with paintings, some of which—these are of later date than the first construction—show the martyrs of Sebaste, in Armenia, being plunged into the frozen pond in which they were condemned to die.

---

*From the Latin *paganus,* a villager or rustic.—Translator.

It was also in the time of Theodosius that St. Paul Beyond the Walls was rebuilt on considerably enlarged foundations, which are reproduced in the present building, erected after the great fire of 1823. It has been said of it that it is not a church for a crowd: it is a shelter for an army. The eighty columns that carry the enormous nave prolong it out of all proportion; its interior is glacial and the decoration accentuates this frigidity. True, this St. Paul's is new; but it is equally true that it merely repeats its predecessor.

THE CHRISTIAN BASILICAS

Henceforth the only public buildings would be the shrines that the triumphant church would erect to its God and its martyrs. The burgeoning of religious structures had begun with the peace of Constantine. St. Mark had been founded in 336 (near the Palazzo Venezia), Santa Maria Trasteverina in 354. Santa Pudenziana dates from 384, St. Prassede, St. Eusebius, and St. Caesarius from virtually the same period, as well as San Lorenzo in Damaso, whose forty-four antique columns were to be given to the Chancellery Palace.

One feature common to the majority of these early churches was the fact that, established originally in private dwellings, they retained that character even into their most remote renovations. In many of them this character remains quite visible even today. That is why, for example, Santa Pudenziana and St. Prassede, dedicated to the two daughters of the senator, Pudens, who, according to tradition, offered his hospitality to St. Peter, have retained elements of the house in which was set up the chapel on which they were superimposed.

The most curious temple that has been handed down to us among these houses thus converted is the church of Saints John and Paul on the Caelius. The street that it overlooks is that ancient Clivius Scauri, so well preserved that one could "feel oneself a contemporary of Cicero walking under the arches that support the ancient walls that border it." These walls are the façade of an old *insula* (apartment house) whose stories of windows are still recognizable, and that was the home of two palace officers whom Julian the Apostate ordered beheaded. The ground floor contains a series of small rooms decorated with pagan frescoes; a stairway leads to a wine cellar and a bathroom, both well preserved. Above the original "house of the church" was built the chapel dedicated to the two martyrs, followed by a basilica that Adrian IV, the only English pope in history, altered in the Middle Ages and beside which he erected a little monastery. Cardinal Spellman, the titular of this church, endowed it with new improvements. But its real interest lies in its capacity to help us to grasp, "in a rare continuity, the whole sequence of cultural adaptations" (*Itinéraires romains*).

The basilica of Liberus, which was to be rebuilt and moved in the next century to become Santa Maria Maggiore, the fourth of the patriarchal basilicas, owed its foundation in 352 to a miracle. The Virgin appeared to Pope Liberus and a patrician, Giovanni, to bid them erect a church on a spot that would be found covered with snow on the following day. Although it was August, the miracle occurred on the summit of the Esquiline, and work began at once at the appointed site. The church was first called Santa Maria della Neve (St. Mary of the Snow). Its reconstruction in 342 was Christendom's cry of joy in response to the dogmas of the Council of Ephesus, which had proclaimed Mary the Mother of God. It was renamed Santa Maria Maggiore (Greater) because it was the most important of the Roman churches dedicated to the Virgin. The memory of its miraculous foundation is celebrated on August 5 with a Pontifical Mass during which petals of white flowers are dropped from the gilded piers of its ceiling to float like snowflakes through air full of incense.

St. Clement was a contemporary of the basilica in its first reconstruction above a chapel that dated from this third successor to St. Peter. It remained buried until 1857 under the church that had been superimposed on it in the twelfth century. It was undoubtedly this circumstance that kept it unmarred and that affords us a faithful image of the early basilicas. Sinners who considered themselves unworthy to mingle with the other worshipers remained in its little porch; the portico adorned with a fountain received those whose moral state was less dubious. The elevated chancel was separated from the rest of the church. Behind the balustrade that railed it off, the faithful clustered round the officiant and the episcopal chair. The Holy Scriptures were read aloud from the ambos, pulpits placed in the chancel.

One of the first Christian churches had been built about one and a quarter miles outside Rome on the Via Appia, at the place where, during Valerian's persecutions, the remains of St. Peter and St. Paul had been hidden in a quarry called Cata-Tumbas, which was to become the catacomb of St. Sebastian and to give its name to all the other places of the same kind. When freedom of Christian worship was proclaimed by

Constantine, the two apostles' bodies were taken back to their tombs, on which the emperor built the two basilicas of St. Peter and of St. Paul Beyond the Walls. But the site of their temporary refuge was still venerated, and a basilica was erected there in the first half of the fourth century. Dedicated at first to Peter and Paul, in the ninth century it was placed under the patronage of St. Sebastian, a Gallic centurion from Narboniensis who was martyred under Diocletian and buried in a nearby cemetery.

When Theodosius made Christianity the religion of the Empire, the churches multiplied. Among the notable churches dating from this time are St. Bibiana on the Esquiline, and St. Sabina, built in 432, and not on the temple of Juno on the Aventine, as was long believed, but on an ancient chapel in the house of a matron named Sabina. The twenty-four fluted columns that carry its three naves were borrowed from another temple on the Aventine. Originally the church was decorated entirely in mosaics, of which only one remains, above the entrance door. St. Anastasia was built at the same period on the old Vicus Tuscus, whose course is more or less followed today by Via di San Teodoro. One can still see the substructure of the old house on which the church was built. It was a Frenchman, Cardinal de Vitry, who rebuilt it in 1510. We should once more mention St. Pancras on the Janiculum, near the catacombs of the same name, which was twice to suffer from the presence of the French; ravaged in 1798 by revolutionary troops, it was sacked again in 1849 by the French army that had rushed to defend the pope against the new Roman republic. Let us be careful not to overlook San Pietro in Vincoli, one of the most visited churches in Rome because it contains Michelangelo's *Moses*. It was built in 455 on a pre-existing church by Empress Eudoxia to house the chains of St. Peter, and they are still displayed for the veneration of the faithful. San Pietro in Vincoli was to become the church of the cardinals of the della Rovere family, who were to enrich it with major works of the Renaissance.

Let us also mention St. Cecilia in Trastevere, built on the house of the saint, martyred under Marcus Aurelius, whose life was spent *"in hymnis et canticis."* Rebuilt in the eighteenth century, it is now nothing but a cream and gold drawing room. On November 22 young girls veiled like the Christian virgin perform a sacred concert there in honor of the musical saint.

Let us append to this very incomplete catalogue Santa Lucia in Selci, at the foot of the Quirinal, and St. Crisogono in Trastevere, to which the Cosmati added the bell tower and the beautiful pavement in the thirteenth century. This church prides itself on its possession, as supporters of its triumphal arch, of the two tallest porphyry columns in Rome.

We shall have many occasions to mention all these sanctuaries again, often in detail, in connection with the events of Rome's history with which they are associated. Therefore at the moment we shall mention only the characteristic that is common to all of them. With the single exception of the round church of St. Stephen, which is a reproduction of the church of the Holy Sepulcher in Jerusalem, all belong to the basilica type that would remain classic in medieval Rome. That is, they are rectangular in shape, the side opposite the entrance ending in a semicircle. There has been much debate as to the origin of these Christian basilicas. Their plan includes parallel naves bounded by rows of columns that support a flat roof. At the end of the central nave a high arch, which was later to be called the triumphal arch, opens, either directly or separated from the nave by a transept, on the large vaulted *cul-de-four* niche of the apse. A portico surrounds an uncovered court, in the center of which is the fountain for ablutions. This is a departure from the plan of the secular basilicas, which were surrounded by porticoes on all sides and which had a rectangular great hall in which the apse was lacking and the transept was unknown. Are the origins of these first churches to be sought rather in an imitation of Roman houses? Their resemblances are many: the *tablinium,* often vaulted, was a true apse; the plan of the *atrium,* with its lateral porticoes and its "wings," is the plan of the nave of the church, with the colonnades and the transept. Furthermore, the large court surrounded by porticoes that stretched before the entrance to the basilica played exactly the same part as the peristyle that preceded the *atrium* in large Roman houses. The first meeting places for the faithful, as we have pointed out, were private houses; it was normal that the churches that replaced them should have retained their major arrangements. It is not that they owe nothing to the secular basilicas, for it was in imitation of these that the Christian architects built their naves, and it may be assumed with certainty that the Basilica Julia and the Ulpia gave them the idea of dividing a large nave into several smaller ones with columns. In short, we must believe that the Christians borrowed the design of their churches from various sources to meet new needs: the Christian basilicas respect the old forms while adapting them to the new rituals. The population that had just undergone a change of soul was still attached to its most remote past. But, contrary to a rather widely held notion, the Christians did not take over secular basilicas as places of worship; they left them available to the public for the uses for which they had been traditionally intended. The bishops of Rome who built sanctuaries after the Peace of the Church showed themselves possessed of extreme caution in the utilization of ancient structures. The first churches in the Forum—St. Mary the Old and Saints Cosmas and Damian—took over only abandoned buildings. As for the temples consecrated to pagan gods, even though they had been closed by order of Theodosius, they were never put to Christian use at that period. It would not be until the sixth century that Rome could provide an instance of a temple transformed into a church: this was the Pantheon. The scruples of the popes, however, might occasion some regret when one reflects that, if the new religion had taken over all the heathen temples, ancient Rome would still be standing almost in its entirety. It must also be noted that their architects remained faithful to the most ancient Roman tradition in neglecting the vault, although there was an abundance of examples of it before them, including the very recent one of the basilica of Maxentius. The vault was to reappear in the Middle Ages, when it was relearned from the Barbarians as if it were a novelty.

A last trait in common in all the basilicas of the end of the Empire was the extreme richness of their interior decoration. Simplicity was confined to the architectural lines, but the great bare walls of the nave were covered with mosaics or with Oriental hangings of embroidered silk enriched with gold thread and stones; the altars gleamed with precious marbles and gilded bronze; the tabernacles were monuments to the goldsmith's craft. "The interior of a great Roman basilica of the fourth or fifth century was a kaleidoscope of colors and riches" (Emile Bertaux). Many of these radiant decorations are known to us only through the descriptions of contemporaries. The hangings have vanished, like the greater part of the goldsmiths' work and the statues in precious metals. The inventory of what remains of these marvels is soon made. The major item is the famous black bronze statue of St. Peter in the Vatican basilica, whose foot has been worn down by the kisses of pilgrims and worshipers. The gates of St. Sabina are the masterpiece of early Christian sculpture. Eleven of the wreathed columns that Constantine sent from Byzantium for the adornment of his basilica have found asylum in the new St. Peter's. One of them is venerated (in the chapel that contains Michelangelo's *Pietà*), under the name of Colonna Santa, as that to which Christ was tied to be whipped. A later relic hidden in the basilica's treasury is the votive cross donated by Emperor Justin II to be hung before the *Confession of St. Peter*. It alone, among all the gold objects that were accumulated in the churches of those days, has escaped the melting pot.

THE MOSAICS

Of all the arts that contributed to the ornamentation of the basilicas, mosaic is the only one that is still represented by large creations that are almost intact. Mosaic was the traditional decoration of rich residences under the Empire; just as they had adapted its plan, the Christian artists transposed into their churches the customary adornment of the Roman house. The walls of the nave and the conch of the apse were decorated with series of multicolored images, at first in imitation of Greek and Roman forms until a purely Christian art was born. Exactly like the frescoes of the catacombs, the mosaics of St. Constance, the most ancient Christian mosaics in Rome, are in every respect faithful to the ancient mode and offer only profane portrayals: scenes of grape harvests and dancing Cupids. This reached such a point that sixteenth-century archeologists took the mausoleum of Constantine's daughter for a temple of Bacchus. In order to remove these profane scenes from the sight of the faithful, a pope ordered them concealed beneath a thick layer of stucco. Such errors are no longer possible, now that the sarcophagi of the early Christian periods have revealed to us the mystic meaning of the grape harvest.

There are still a number of profane allusions in the mosaics of the chapels built during the fourth century round the Lateran baptistry. The apse of the chapel of Santa Rufina spreads a whole green foliage over a conch topped by symbolic animals; the vault of the neighboring chapel, consecrated by Pope Hilarus, is decorated with mild allegories, in which the souls of the faithful are represented by doves, while birds surround the lamb of God.

Santa Pudenziana contains a major work in the history of Christian art: the mosaic in its apse. It is a fascinating example of the new ideal: for the first time the artist achieves Christian types. True, the apostles, "broad of shoulder and of forehead," still have the gravity of pagan Senators, and Poussin had to admire "the Roman grandeur" in their powerful faces. Nevertheless the Syrian veil that the painters were later to give the Virgin already covers the heads of the women ranked beside the throne. Christ is not the handsome figure like a young Greek god "borrowed from the accessories of ancient art" that we see in the frescoes of the catacombs. Black of hair and beard, like a Syrian, he looks as the first Christians might have seen him. Even the background has changed: it is no longer a quarter of Rome or some imagined city, it is Jerusalem or Golgotha.

From the masterpiece of this Christian art to the first signs of its decadence is no great distance either in time or in space. The mosaic in the apse of Saints Cosmas and Damian is only fifty years later than that of Santa Pudenziana, and it is already a technically marred work. But the coloring retains a magnificent intensity. The appearance of Christ with a golden nimbus against a blue sky streaked with the purple clouds of the sunset is one of the most moving scenes that Christian art has ever given us.

The mosaics of the triumphal arch and the nave of Santa Maria Maggiore, contemporary with that of Saints Cosmas and Damian, though their design is no stronger, are no less admirable on more than one ground. Those of the nave tell the story of Genesis in a great number of episodes. "It seems," Emile Bertaux wrote, "as if the mosaic artist had merely enlarged, in order to unroll it above the coping, one of those scrolls covered with miniatures of which the Vatican Library has a precious example that tells the story of Joshua." As for the mosaics of the triumphal arch, spread over three panels, they recall the early episodes of the Gospel story. The Virgin is given the attitudes and the dress of a Byzantine queen. The infant God is seated not on his mother's knees but on a throne. Christian art had by now repudiated not only Greek-Roman traditions but also the ingenuous popular inspiration of its first stages; it was entirely penetrated by Oriental influence. The hieratic art of the mosaics was to interpret sacred history with limitless resources and to create a rigid world of amazing majesty. If one enters certain Roman churches just when they are filling with darkness, the figures in the mosaics, stereotyped in their golden atmosphere, enchant the eye and the mind.

THE HIERARCHY OF BASILICAS AND CHURCHES

If virtually all the sanctuaries that were built after the peace of Constantine assumed the form of the basilica—which many other churches were to adopt later—they are not all called basilicas. The religious authorities have kept that title for certain among them in order to make them the dignitaries of that nation of temples that is made up by the Roman churches. The basilicas are divided into major and minor. The major basilicas are nine in number. Five of them hold a higher rank; these are the so-called patriarchal basilicas, in which the pope officiates as if he were the cardinal-archbishop of each of them (San Lorenzo fuori le Mura, Santa Maria Maggiore, St. Paul Beyond the Walls, St. John Lateran, and St. Peter's). The four others have only the privilege of the *"porta santa,"* the walled entrance that is opened only in a time of jubilee by the Holy Father himself, who strikes it with a golden hammer. As for the minor basilicas (Santa Maria Trasteverina, San Lorenzo in Damaso, the Holy Apostles, San Pietro in Vincoli, and a few others), they became basilicas only by assimilation: they were "ennobled." The patriarchal basilicas have the monopoly of a privilege inaugurated by Pope Simplicius in the fifth century: in the confessionals there are penitentiary priests who strike with a long rod the faithful who come to kneel before them. An indulgence is attached to this act of humility. Visits to certain churches at periods of jubilee are a condition prescribed for the acquisition of a plenary indulgence. Seven churches are included in this pilgrimage, in memory of the seven times when Christ bled during the Passion.

Rome's ordinary churches are themselves ranged in a hierarchy that begins with the private chapels, going on to the churches confided to religious orders and then to the parish churches. The *Stationales* form a higher category: these are the churches built on the site of a saint's burial place or martyrdom. Above them are the churches known as *cardinalices.* Each cardinal has his own and is supposed to see to its spiritual and material needs. In each of them the arms of the titular cardinal are displayed beside those of the reigning pope.

THE LAST DAYS OF THE ROMAN EMPIRE

By making Christianity the official religion of the Empire, Theodosius made it possible for the church to erect its temples and establish its own organization on solid foundations, the same bases that in the centuries to come would give it authority and power and make it the rampart of civilization. But at the same time this same emperor precipitated the destruction of the old order by making the division of the Empire a reality. Become the capital of the Occidental Empire, Rome was to sink into decadence. The new emperors did not even establish residence within its walls: they were to live in Ravenna, in Milan, in Trèves. While these new centers were made richer by a few monuments, no more were constructed in Rome. At the very most, its emperors, who had become virtual foreigners to the capital, would occupy themselves with the maintenance of the monuments of the past. Honorius repaired Aurelian's Wall, Gratian rebuilt the Cestius Bridge and gave it his name. These were shoddy repairs, testifying to the decadence of the arts; the columns of the temple of Saturn, re-erected in this period and rebuilt with unmatched sections, are the most visible index of the mediocrity of a sterile age. The Eastern emperors lured the artists, the talented architects, and the skilled workers. The monumental history of ancient Rome had ended.

Nevertheless, if no new edifices were erected, no old ones were demolished. At the dawn of that fifth century that would see the arrival of the Barbarians, the city's monumental appearance was still magnificent. It was the time when a foreign visitor adjudged it "something immense that speech could never equal." A poet said in 420: "Thanks to the gold that covers the temples, the sky of Rome surpasses every other sky in brilliance." And Themistius* spoke of an "ocean of beauty."

But all that Rome had preserved of itself was its monumental exterior; its inhabitants were lost now in the vast spaces of its baths and its porticoes. The libraries were deserted, the basilicas had become useless. Wealth had emigrated to Constantinople; the great families had fallen. The decline in trade had ruined the economy, and taxes had become too heavy for an impoverished population. The number of functionaries had grown, the armies were only mercenaries, and the security based on the *Pax romana* was a mere memory. The great proprietors had withdrawn to their estates, where they were beginning to fortify their villas, already foreshadowing the strong castles of the Middle Ages. Workers sought only to escape a situation that had become intolerable. All that remained, kept alive by the free distribution of food, was the lazy Roman *plebs,* more assiduous than ever in keeping up with the spectacles in the circuses. Stagnation reigned in a depopulated Rome. The city whose population had reached almost 2,000,000 had hardly more than 400,000 in the fourth century. Rome was nothing more than "a vast shame spread before the eyes of men." After having conquered the world, it was to be an easy prey for the Barbarians, who were already at hand.

* A fourth-century Greek philosopher.—Translator.

They had been there before. The Gauls had burned the city, Hannibal had appeared before its walls. Since then the old Roman virtues, and above all the warrior spirit, had vanished; the division of the Empire, the enfeeblement of power, financial ruin, economic disorder, the disintegration of the army made further resistance impossible. Already the Barbarians (the name was given to all the peoples that were not Roman) had overrun the provinces; Gaul and Spain were in the hands of the Vandals, the Burgundians, the Swabians. The Goths had thrust as far as Venetia; in 408, under Alaric's leadership, they marched on Rome without encountering any obstacles. They opened siege, and they would not leave until they had exacted payment of a heavy indemnity. In order to meet its burden, the bronze statues that adorned Hadrian's tomb had to be melted down. Two years later Alaric returned, and this time he entered Rome and sacked it. This disaster plunged the world into a stupor. "The light of the world is extinguished," St. Jerome wrote, "and the entire universe is about to perish in the midst of the ruins of a single city." Then came the Vandals, and Rome barely survived their visit in 442. Soon there was a fresh menace: the Huns! An embassy of senators headed by Pope Leo I managed to divert their chief, Attila, from Rome; he died in the same year and his empire crashed in a single day. But the Barbarians were pouring in from everywhere. In 454 Genseric's Vandals appeared once more at the mouth of the Tiber; they took Rome, they sacked it for two weeks, and they left under a burden of booty. During this time hordes from every part of Europe, thrusting farther in their invasions, became the masters of everything that had been the Occidental Empire. Its agony was paced by assassinations, pillages, fires, devastations of every kind. In 476 the last emperor, Romulus Augustulus, who through an irony of fate bore the names of the founder of Rome and the founder of the Empire, was deposed and interned in Campania. Thus ended the history of the Roman Empire and, in the general opinion, the history of the ancient world.

PART TWO

MEDIEVAL ROME

CHAPTER 10

GOTHIC ROME [476–553]

THE WARS OF THE BARBARIANS AND THE EMPERORS

When the long period of the Middle Ages began, the Goths were masters of Italy. Odoacer, chief of the Heruli, who had established the center of his rule at Ravenna, granted the city on the Tiber the status of a republic that was, if not independent, at least empowered to govern itself with officials chosen from among its own citizens: a prefect assisted by a Senate. The prefect and the senators were chosen by the Barbarian king, but they were Romans of the old great families, all Christians, who turned for guidance on policy to the head of the church. Thus, far from regarding themselves as the subjects of the sickly Roman government, the popes were to make it more and more the instrument by which they would dominate.

In the beginning the Christian church had been a spiritual republic, with neither a secular arm nor a temporal power. But the bishops' power had progressively broken free of the democratic forms of its inception. After having first profited by the protection of the Empire, it had striven to be free of that as well. Occasionally the church's desire for independence had impelled it to welcome the Barbarians as liberators. Nor had the Barbarians rejected its support: Alaric and Genseric had negotiated with the popes, and Odoacer had allowed a Roman republic to remain out of respect for the sacred city that was the seat of the chieftain of a moral power with which henceforth he would have to reckon.

The collapse of the Occidental Empire, in fact, left only the papacy as an active, organized force. Still unarmed, it had inherited the prestige of Rome, which was unimpaired in the eyes of peoples everywhere in spite of the city's decline. This situation had given rise to the popes' first notion of an independent temporal realm: their every act thereafter was to be aimed at the construction of its bases. For centuries this aim would dictate the policy of the Roman church, which would consistently strive to prevent the establishment of a powerful kingdom in Italy, for that would be a threat to its independence.

The popes were friendly with the Heruli only until they began to fear the invaders were growing too strong; then the church called on the Eastern emperors for help, on the theory that faraway and weak masters would let them continue in the autonomy that they were in danger of losing. But the sovereign in Byzantium was so weak at this time that he assigned the task of reconquering Italy to Theodoric, king of the Ostrogoths. Theodoric routed the Heruli in 493, restored the Roman traditions, renewed public celebrations, and resumed the public distribution of food. He even repaired the imperial palace, the Circus Maximus, and the Colosseum. But he very quickly forgot that he was the emperor's deputy, and he ruled Rome as its absolute master for his own account. In 526 he threw Pope John I into prison and assumed the right of selecting his successor.

This time Rome's appeal to Byzantium was not in vain. A forceful sovereign, Justinian, ruled in Byzantium, and he made the restoration of a united empire the great goal of his reign. His best general, Belisarius, arrived before Rome in 536 at the head of an excellent army, and with great pomp the pope surrendered the keys of the city to him after having solemnly pronounced the forfeiture of the Gothic kings because they had not deigned to defend it.

This was only a false victory. A year later the Goths returned in force under the leadership of a new king, Vitiges. A strict blockade was imposed on Rome. The Goths did not stop with closing all the roads that fed the city; they cut the aqueducts in the countryside, and the mills on the Janiculum were halted. Hunger took over Rome, beset with a defeatism that Belisarius harshly denounced. An inflexible leader, he had his troops well in hand. On March 21, 537, he hurled back a fierce assault by the Goths, on whom the garrison at Hadrian's tomb hurled the bronze statues that still decorated the top of the monument. The colossal heads of Hadrian (now in the Vatican) and Antoninus (preserved in the museum of Castel Sant'Angelo) served on that memorable day as projectiles.

The attack having failed, the blockade was resumed, and the Romans bore it so badly that, in order to prevent insurrection, Belisarius had to depose Pope Severus and exile several senators. But malaria decimated the Goths and they were compelled to raise the siege on March 12, 538.

For the first time real protection had been provided by Aurelian's Wall, whose line Emperor Honorius had somewhat adjusted when he strengthened its defenses. It must also be added that Belisarius had fortified it with a knowledgeable system of trenches and battlements. Out of respect for a popular belief, he had not fortified the *Muro Torto:* it was said that St. Peter would personally guarantee its defense because it had bent of itself while the apostle was being led to execution. This section of the wall of Honorius, which runs from Porta del Popolo to Porta Pinciana, has always looked as if it were on the point of falling, but it has survived for eighteen centuries as if miraculously upheld by invisible supports.

Eight years later a surprise attack overwhelmed Aurelian's powerful wall. The Goths had by then re-established their control of the peninsula; arriving at Rome, they penetrated its gates by a ruse on the night of December 17, 546. When daylight came, their king, Totila, commanded the population to abandon the city and disperse through the countryside. In moments Rome was transformed into a vast desert; a chronicler declares that not a single living creature remained, neither men nor beasts. The city called eternal almost never recovered from the blow. A kind of miracle prevented it from vanishing out of history after fifteen centuries of greatness; Belisarius saved it by reoccupying the city without striking a blow: Totila had not even posted a garrison in that deserted and dismantled city. At an appeal by Belisarius the fugitives returned, and feverishly they rebuilt the walls. A shaky revival! Once more Totila made himself master of Rome in 549: Belisarius was no longer there to defend it. The re-establishment of Gothic rule was celebrated with games in the amphitheater and the circus.

It was too soon to hail victory so enthusiastically, for Justinian had not abandoned the reconquest of Italy. In 550 he sent his best general, Narses, to the peninsula. Narses recaptured Rome and, four years later, he rescued it from the vast danger into which it was cast by the arrival of seventy thousand Alemanni, sent for by the Goths. Narses defeated them at

Vulturna and returned to Rome in triumph. The entire city joined in celebrating the restoration of the Empire and the victory of Catholic orthodoxy.

For two centuries Rome was to become Byzantine.

ROME UNDER THE BARBARIANS

The decadence of Rome was accelerated during the Gothic period. Such a tragic succession of sieges, famines, and invasions had inevitably been followed by a procession of devastation and ruin.

But it is rather difficult to assay the Barbarians' share in the "sack" of Rome. During the Renaissance it was the fashion to hold them exclusively responsible for all the depredations that the Middle Ages had perpetrated. There were the marks of their spears even on the walls of the Baths of Caracalla; it was said that their axes had a hammer head on one side and a sword blade on the other, a sufficient symbol of their love for destruction after they had killed. The word *Goth* was a synonym for *highwayman* and *looter*. When it was demonstrated in the nineteenth century that the Renaissance itself had taken a very large hand in the destruction of the ancient monuments, it became almost fashionable to rehabilitate the Barbarians and describe them as harmless.

In reality they deserved neither such severity nor such leniency. First of all, it would be most unjust to judge them as a mass: their attitudes varied with the circumstances and with the moods of their chiefs; if the passage of Vitiges and Totila was destructive, Theodoric protected Rome's riches. It must be observed in addition that in general the Barbarians restricted their deeds to the theft of objects of small size and light weight, easy to carry. Nor were they alone in stripping palaces and temples of their valuable vases and their statues: the Byzantine emperors organized large-scale transfers of Roman works of art to their own Oriental residences. As for the mutilation of statues, it seems that this cannot be imputed to the Barbarians. What is most often lacking to the statues is their noses, which the peasants broke as they dug them out of the ground, for fear of their "evil eye."

Nor did the Barbarians indulge themselves to any greater degree in the systematic destruction of buildings. If they cut the aqueducts and dismantled Aurelian's Wall, those were acts of military necessity. But they did not burn or demolish a single temple; since they were not builders, they had no need of materials. There is an inventory of Rome's monuments that dates from the seventh century—in other words, after the Barbarian invasions. It shows that no major monument had perished and that the Forum was still peopled with a large number of statues. It was to be only when a new Rome would be built that the ancient Rome would vanish under the attacks of enemies more civilized than the Goths.

Obviously the ancient monuments suffered from a total lack of maintenance during the Gothic period, and this was enough to bring a number of them to the point of ruin. No doubt the turmoils of the time sufficed in themselves to make maintenance difficult. A further factor was the Christians' aversion to the buildings of heathen Rome. To them the temples suggested a heathen worship, the amphitheaters and the circuses symbolized the blood of the martyrs. There was no organized destruction, however. The Christians contented themselves with closing the temples after having removed the statues of gods and heroes. But they showed no enthusiasm for the maintenance or restoration of these buildings.

They saved their meager resources for their own religious sanctuaries. With the exception of the hospitals annexed to the three basilicas of St. Peter's, St. Paul, and St. Lawrence, the only new monuments of the Gothic era were churches, and these were quite few. The only one that seems to have been a totally new structure is St. Agatha (on the Viminal), the national church of the Goths, which was served by Arian heretics. It was not consecrated to Catholic worship until 592, by St. Gregory the Great. The other churches of this period were renovations of Empire buildings no longer in use. Marking the new religion's conquest of the center of the city, the church of Santa Maria in Cosmedin took over the offices formerly occupied by the supervisors of the imperial markets. The old Forum Boarium was brought under the rule of "the gentleness of Christianity in its pure state." In the modesty of its appearance and the ingenuity of its design, this "treasure of poor aspect" recalls the Parisian church of St. Julian the Poor. It is regarded as the best example of the smooth transition from pagan art to Roman art. Saints Cosmas and Damian, whose mosaics we have mentioned, had occupied one of the rooms of the library in Vespasian's Forum since 530 and not, as is often said, the Templum Sacrae Urbis. No more was St. Theodore once a temple of Vesta, a notion born of its rotunda form; it stands on the site ascribed by legend to the sacred fig tree under which Romulus and Remus were found. In ancient times ailing children were taken there to be cured. Popular belief has preserved this heathen tradition while somewhat denaturing it, for it is now St. Theodore who is expected to perform the cures once sought from the Sacred Twins.

Santa Maria Antiqua, set back below the brow of the Palatine, represents a renovation of the former library of Augustus. With its awkward liturgical figures, its rudimentary altar, its grotto-like coolness, and even the skulls in rows behind the gratings, it is "the most touching first step of Christian art." It was entombed for seven centuries; we owe its resurrection to the bold action of archeologists who did not hesitate to sacrifice an entire building in order to bring to light works of superior artistic interest that were imprisoned by it. Damaged by an earthquake and laid waste by the Saracens, Santa Maria Antiqua was in such piteous state in the twelfth century that it was abandoned and a new church, Santa Maria Liberatrice, was built on its ruins; its walls required shoring up in 1901. At that time the remains of the original church were discovered, and Santa Maria Liberatrice in its turn was demolished. Then Santa Maria Antiqua reappeared in all its original freshness.

It was also during the Gothic rule that, on either side of the access stairs to St. Peter's, the first dwellings were built for the pope and his court— humble beginnings of a huge cluster of palaces.

CHAPTER 11

BYZANTINE ROME [553-751]

BYZANTINE GOVERNMENT AND THE GROWTH OF THE PAPACY

After its reconquest by Narses, Rome became the center of Byzantine Italy; it was a fleeting period of happiness for the city. But Narses occupied the imperial palace on the Palatine for only twelve years, and his successor established himself in Ravenna with the title of exarch. Then Rome lost its rank as a capital and became once more a provincial city, as in the Gothic days. It found this demotion all the less tolerable in that the emperors strove, through the intermediary of their exarchs, to impose on the church a jealous authority that was exercised in particular whenever the pontifical throne became vacant but that also intervened occasionally in matters of dogma. Thus Byzantium endeavored to enforce the Monophysite heresy on the papacy with brutal measures that went even as far as an attempt to assassinate the sovereign pontiff while he was celebrating mass in Santa Maria Maggiore. On another occasion the popes had to take up arms to defend their rich Lateran treasury. In 653 Constans II launched a special attack: suspected of insubordination, Pope Martin I was brutally deposed and exiled after savage indignities.

This having been accomplished, the emperor journeyed to Rome for the solemn proclamation of his omnipotence and of the wardship imposed on the papacy. He led a dazzling parade and graciously acknowledged, at St.

Peter's and Santa Maria Maggiore, honors that were not rightfully his. He did not go home without a rich harvest of the treasures that remained among the Roman monuments. In particular, he ordered the removal of the gilded bronze tiles that covered the roofs of the temples. Having generously donated the tiles from the temple of Venus and Rome for the decoration of the basilica of St. Peter's, he kept those from the Pantheon for his palace in Byzantium. The accuracy of the old proverb "ill-got gains are never profitable" was demonstrated again in this instance: the loot from Rome never reached Constantinople. Falling into the hands of Saracen pirates during the voyage, it was diverted to Alexandria.

Rome had felt mortally outraged by the emperor's violence. Too weak to fight back, the church had still to endure many humiliations. But, the more strained its relations with the emperors grew, the more the papacy enlarged its temporal power. The pontificate of Gregory the Great at the end of the sixth century was decisive in this respect. The Byzantine officials and even the exarch's representatives, paralyzed by their distance from the central authority, were progressively stripped of their prerogatives. It was at this period that the popes began to play the major part in the government of the city. They saw to the regularity of food shipments, they maintained the streets, they formed a militia, they organized defenses. Their power, which was never specifically stated, established itself side by side with that of the official authorities, but in fact the papal power was paramount. These popes could well be called "Consuls of God," as the inscription on the grave of one of them put it.

This temporal power, gaining strength with each new pontificate, was to manage gradually to contain the demands of Byzantium and finally to overthrow the imperial dominance. It was in the first half of the eighth century that a maneuver began that was to open a new era in Rome's history. Two circumstances aided it: the Eastern Empire's ordeals in its conflicts with the Arabs, and above all the Lombard menace.

Already masters of Venetia, Liguria, and southern Italy, the Lombards were resolved to destroy Byzantine power in the peninsula in order to make it a great kingdom under their own domination. Rome had come to hold Byzantium in horror, but respect for its tradition imbued it with a determined aversion to the Lombards.

Impotent to resolve the situation with his own resources, Pope Stephen II called to the defense of Roman independence that Pepin the Short, the son of Charles Martel, whom he had consecrated as king two years earlier. The alliance was effected virtually instantaneously. Pepin the Short had not forgot the papacy's eagerness to armor the advent of the Carolingian dynasty in its authority. The Frankish army appeared in Italy in 751 and turned back the Lombard threat. The Frankish king restored to the pope the lands that he had just seized from his enemies, particularly the exarchate of Ravenna. This was the origin of the Papal States and of the temporal sovereignty of the popes, which was to persist until 1870.

In gratitude for these good offices, the Holy See gave Pepin the symbolic gift of the relics of St. Petronilla, that Roman martyr who was supposed to have been the spiritual daughter of the Apostle Peter. Established as the saint's spiritual sister, France was able, through this mystic union, to proclaim herself the eldest daughter of the church, a title that a dozen centuries of history have not cast into disuse.

The chapel of the basilica of St. Peter's, in which St. Petronilla's sarcophagus is kept, became French soil. A solemn mass is celebrated there every year on May 31, in a tradition that was interrupted by the Revolution and revived by Chateaubriand in 1829, then "restored in all its magnificence" in 1949 through the highly praiseworthy efforts of the then ambassador, Wladimir d'Ormesson. The mass revived by Chateaubriand was only a low mass; now a solemn mass is celebrated, during which liturgical honors are rendered to the French ambassador to the Holy See. This is one of the most moving of all the French traditions of Rome.

ROME IN THE BYZANTINE ERA

After the influx of the Barbarians, sieges and famines had made the Romans' existence very precarious; after their mass eviction by Totila in 546, many city people had definitively established themselves in the country areas. Rome's population density had then lessened to such a point that it was possible to develop large open spaces in the city.

On the other hand, the destruction of the aqueducts had made the heights uninhabitable by depriving them of water. In order to replace the wheat mills on the Janiculum, floating mills had been set up in the narrowest parts of the Tiber, and these had caused floods. The consequent bursting of the drainage pipes had led to the formation of marshes that rapidly became breeders of disease and were to give Rome a reputation of unhealthiness that was to be deserved for centuries. As a result of these upheavals, whole zones were depopulated, and their residents crowded into the lower parts of the city. Having taken over the facilities of assistance, food supply, and security, the church deemed it advisable to revise the internal administrative division of the city on the model of its own organization. The city was divided into seven ecclesiastical regions, each under the authority of a deacon; these became quarters, the distribution of which was more suited than the old fourteen regions to the existing situation.

The highway-maintenance system was in no better state, given the lack of facilities. The maintenance of official buildings also suffered from the lack of resources. Gradually the ancient temples disappeared. Those of Jupiter Capitolinus and Juno Moneta were already no more than ruins at the beginning of the eighth century. It was extremely difficult to find a proper residence for Pope John VII in the Forum when he decided that he was too isolated in his distant Lateran quarters. This momentary transfer of the papal residence briefly restored some animation to the old seat of Roman greatness. There were duels on Via Sacra in 713, and the ephemeral assembly of all classes of the population that Pope Stephen II convoked was held before the ancient Curia.

The only active quarter then was the Field of Mars, favored because of its proximity to the Vatican, whose importance was rising as the influence of the church mounted. In addition the nearness of the Tiber was a great advantage, since the river was still the sole source of water supplies. The increasing population of the Field of Mars led to the construction of new churches there. One house, in which Pope Paul I was born, was not far from Via Lata, the quarter's great artery (now the Corso). He converted it into the church of San Silvestro in Capite, which, rebuilt in the seventeenth century, is assigned to the English Catholics. Its *atrium* protects it from the noise of the neighborhood. The adjoining convent has since become the Post and Telegraph Building. Not far away, near the present Palazzo Colonna, the church of the Holy Apostles was built to commemorate the victory of Narses; destroyed by an earthquake in the fourteenth century, it was rebuilt by Julius II, who added its arcaded portico, and it was so completely remodeled in 1702 that nothing but six of its original columns remains.

In 608 the Pantheon was consecrated for Christian worship and dedicated to St. Mary of the Martyrs by Pope Boniface IV, who took the occasion to entomb there twenty-eight wagonloads of martyrs' bones collected in the various catacombs. This was the first instance of the church's appropriation of a temple of paganism for the practice of its own rites. To this symbol of the definitive victory of the true faith Gregory IV was to add another and prouder token on November 1, 830. The Pantheon had been dedicated to "all the gods"; Gregory IV made it the church of all the saints, and he decreed that on this date of every year the entire Catholic world would celebrate a holy day that would be called All Saints'.

The Field of Mars was not the only quarter of Rome to be enriched with churches during the Byzantine period. St. Saba was built on the Aventine, on the site of the house of St. Sylvia, the mother of Gregory the Great; near Porta Latina, which Belisarius had rebuilt and flanked with towers, St. John at the Latin Gate was erected; after various debatable renovations, it remains a delightful church. The little square, shaded by an old cedar, on which it opens is one of the most picturesque in Rome. It is probable that St. George in the Velabrum also dates from this period: this is the church coupled with the Arch of the Silversmiths dedicated to Septimius Severus. It has a disconcerting feature: its rows of columns tend to converge toward the apse, in defiance of parallelism.

The Forum quarter also had its churches, above all that of St. Adrian, in the Curia. It was to be demolished in 1931 in order to permit the restoration of the imperial Senate's meeting place to its original state. St. Adrian's ancient doors, which had been the Curia's, were removed in the eighteenth century in order to be used, with modifications, for the great gate of the basilica of St. John Lateran. The Secretarium Senatus, which dominated the Forum, became the site of two superimposed churches, one dedicated to St. Luke, the other to St. Martina, who was thus honored only a few steps from the triumphal arch of that Septimius Severus who had ordered her beheaded.

The Capitoline was also opened to Christian worship with a chapel that was called Santa Maria in Capitolio before it became Santa Maria in Ara Coeli at the end of the Middle Ages. The church stands on the site of the ancient citadel of Rome; a legend has it that the Virgin appeared there to Augustus to announce the birth of the divine Savior. Awed by this vision and the words that accompanied it—"*Ecce ara primogeniti Dei* (Behold the altar of God's first-born)"—the emperor is supposed to have raised an altar (*ara filii Dei*—the altar of God's son) on the exact spot where today, in the new church, in the left branch of the transept, the eight antique marble columns of the Holy Chapel, St. Helena's chapel, stand.

It cannot be said that secular architecture was entirely neglected by Byzantine Rome, since Narses was responsible for the reconstruction of two bridges over the Anio, Ponte Salario and Ponte Nomentano, both of which had been destroyed by Totila. Ponte Salario, a relic of the republican era, has since been often rebuilt and enlarged, but Ponte Nomentano (one and a quarter miles from the gate of the same name) has retained its original appearance. When Charlemagne entered Rome on April 2, 774, he was to cross this bridge, which is near Monte Sacro and those meadows where Nero committed suicide.

In this troubled period, ignorance prevailed even among the clergy. Only a few monks went on copying the ancient manuscripts, the language of which they alone understood. The arts were dead, except for music, which was still taught in the Lateran school.

THE ANGEL OF HADRIAN'S TOMB / THE PILLAR OF PHOCAS

It was during the Byzantine epoch that the miraculous event is supposed to have occurred that gave Hadrian's tomb its new name of Castello Sant'Angelo. Rome being under the scourge of the plague at the end of the sixth century, Pope Gregory the Great had ordered a huge procession to appeal for heaven's intercession. When the procession was passing the mausoleum, an angel alighted on its summit and sheathed his sword to show that the Eternal had agreed to put an end to the scourge. The plague ceased, it was said, at that precise moment, and even those already infected by it were miraculously cured. In honor of this prodigy, the statue of the archangel St. Michael was erected on the mausoleum; it was to be replaced several times in the ensuing centuries.

We shall not leave Byzantine Rome without recalling that in 608 the last monument in the Forum was erected: the pillar of Phocas, which commemorates the transfer of the Pantheon to the pope for conversion into a church. This Phocas, to whom an untruthful inscription attributes "numerous good works," was in reality by far the worst of the Byzantine emperors, a bloodthirsty usurper and a revolting drunkard. Nonetheless his statue (which has since disappeared) was placed in the Forum on a fluted marble column that is still there. No one took the trouble of cutting it (who could have done so in the eighth century?), and it was merely taken from some ancient monument, no doubt the round temple ascribed to Vesta, near the Tiber.

This monument of falsehood has been the subject of passionate debate among archeologists. Theories on its origin long clashed amid a storm of invective before anyone thought of questioning the stones themselves. Unearthing the pedestal would have been enough to provide the key to the mystery. This basic investigation was not undertaken until 1813, during the systematic excavations ordered by Napoleon I. Then a barely buried inscription was found, which very explicitly and clearly identified the monument. A satirical sonnet pointed the moral of this ridiculous episode. In it Phocas was made to cry: "Learned idiots, the volumes that you have written on the name to be given to my pillar, set one atop another, would equal its height; how much more clever and less boring you would have been if you had laid aside the pens and reached for spades."

The pillar of Phocas concludes the monumental history of the Roman Forum. Now brambles would invade what had been the center of the greatest empire in history and, century by century, turn it into that dizzy pile of stones and marble in which nothing would remain whole. Men would be stirred only by the shadows evoked by the ruins.

CHAPTER 12

CAROLINGIAN ROME [751–911]

THE MOSAIC OF THE TRICLINIUM OF LEO III

By establishing the temporal power of the popes and making them "the present and efficacious servitors of the public necessities," Pepin the Short did not sweep their road clear of rivalries and plots. To gain control of the papacy and use it for gain was to become the ambition of families as of nations. The history of the Roman Middle Ages is synthesized in an uninterrupted series of cabals and armed assaults that kept all Europe in turmoil. Since it is our intention to limit this study to the boundaries of the city, we shall recall here, among so many events of every nature, only those that, taking place in Rome itself, had a direct effect on the lives of Romans. They will be many, for the enemies of the pontiffs continually maintained confederates and informers among the population. The ground was always favorable to such intrigue, and many of the plots against the papacy were to be born of purely local circumstances. The Roman nobility, which until then had dominated the army, adjusted poorly to the new situation that had placed the public services and the militia under the direction of the ecclesiastical power. On the death of Paul III in 767, plotters forced their way into the Lateran Palace and installed one of their number, Constantine, who was not a member of the clergy, on St. Peter's throne. Violent opposition to this improvised pope broke out at once. Called upon to remedy the iniquity, the Lombards appeared at the Janiculum and, under their protection, a new pope was chosen; his first act was to order the usurper and his confederates blinded. Then a synod decided that henceforth the people would have no voice in the election of the popes, who would be chosen by an electoral college composed exclusively of the upper clergy.

This, it was thought, would prevent incidents injurious to the institution's good name. But as history went on there were to be periodic recurrences of such challenges, as the result of which there were to be some thirty anti-popes—that is, priests contesting for the Holy See, often sword in hand, against its canonically elected incumbents. This in turn has occasioned some confusion in the nomenclature of the popes, for historians have not always agreed on the list. The disturbances ended only when the Frankish king, Charlemagne, intervened and constituted himself the official protector of the papacy, confirming, with notice of the fact to all the powers, the full temporal sovereignty with which his father had invested him. It was this important event that was commemorated in the famous mosaic of Leo III, which Pope Clement XII in 1730 ordered put back into the great pediment-crowned niche that opens on the Lateran promenade beside the Scala Santa. It shows St. Peter handing the pontifical stole to Leo III and the standard to Charlemagne, the political chief of Christendom. This equitable division of the symbols of spiritual and civil authority was a great victory for the church. Through arduous and secret labors the popes had created a Catholic state by dint of little touches that had seemed insignificant; these fragmentary efforts had finally been concerted in the brilliant explosion that opened the great road of its future to the Holy See.

CHARLEMAGNE'S VISITS TO ROME

Relations between the two powers were not to change in the lifetime of Charlemagne, who made five journeys to Rome without having to intervene in the city's affairs.

One of these visits, that of 800, was to mark an important date in the history of the world. Its sole purpose was to purge Leo III of certain accusations that were being made against him at that time. The pope took the occasion to crown "the magnanimous king of France" as emperor. He had kept his plan a secret in order to spare his guest "any suspicion of having solicited this honor." On Christmas Day, Charlemagne, who was supposed to hear mass in the Vatican basilica, was requested to have the goodness to dress himself in the old patrician style "in order to please the Romans' pride." When he entered the church, he found it filled with the most brilliant gathering of princes and barons. Without further prelude the pope placed on his head a crown sparkling with precious stones and administered the sacrament of holy oil. Charlemagne walked out of that Christmas mass a Roman emperor. He was "extremely displeased," a well-informed witness reported. Not so much perhaps by his elevation as by the fact that it had been received as the gift of a pontiff. In effect, the pope's action acquired a tremendous historical importance: for centuries the church was to consider it dogma that "imperial power could neither be consecrated elsewhere than in Rome nor be separated from Rome, and that the order and the progress of the world depended on the union of pope and emperor." For medieval Rome, Léon Homo wrote, "the scene that took place in 800 was pregnant with six centuries of history."

Become once more the center of the world, Rome derived great profit from that "charter of protectorate" as long as Charlemagne could enforce respect for it. The difficulties were renewed when the Carolingian empire was parceled out by the treaty of Verdun (843). The Roman factions, whose appetites were no longer held in check by a higher authority, returned to their intrigues. When Pope Gregory IV died, two popes were elected to succeed him. The Lateran Palace became a battlefield, and Rome experienced a period of inordinate agitation.

It was at this moment—and there was no hesitation in descrying the hand of God in the matter—that Rome was put to the appalling test of the Saracen invasion.

DAYS OF STORM / THE CITADEL OF LEO

Starting from Africa, the Saracens had gained a foothold in southern Italy. It was to be expected that the lure of its riches would impel them to attack the Eternal City as soon as they regarded it as being in no position to resist. Preoccupied exclusively with the plots centered on the papal tiara, and a prey to almost anarchic disorder, Rome offered an easy target in the summer of 846. It was then that the Saracen fleet of seventy-six vessels landed a veritable army of eleven thousand men at the mouth of the Tiber. The city's strong wall inspired considerable respect in the invaders, but all the surrounding countryside was subjected to the most savage devastation. The two large basilicas of St. Peter's and St. Paul, which were outside the walls and undefended, were the great victims of this plundering. Not one object of value escaped the methodical pillage of the Saracens—not the gold and silver offerings, not the precious facing on the walls, not the great golden altar of St. Peter's. Their job done, the Saracens withdrew with their rich booty (three tons of gold and thirty tons of silver), but it never reached its destination, for a frightful storm destroyed the fleet.

The immensity of the catastrophe was the more cruelly felt by all Christendom because the Saracens had not only pillaged but profaned, as no other race of Barbarians had yet dared to do. The Saracens were fanatical Mussulmans; they had danced before the altars, mutilated the holy images, thrust their lances into the mosaic head of Christ that decorated the apse of St. Peter's; and then, it was said, the blood had spurted from the Savior's wounds.

The capital of Christianity had very nearly become a Mahometan village. It owed its salvation more to the sturdiness of its walls than to the courage of its defenders. The firm stand of Pope Leo IV when the danger was at its height earned him the designation of Rome's savior. The storm having passed, he dedicated the treasures of the church and his own fortune to the construction of strong walls round the Borgo, the Vatican quarter; some vestiges of them remain near St. Peter's. This quarter was then called the Citadel of Leo and, with Castello Sant'Angelo, it became the citadel of the papacy, within and round which raged the battles that the sovereign pontiffs had to endure for centuries.

The second half of the ninth century was not to give Rome much respite; the city was constantly pulled in varying directions and occasionally cruelly persecuted by the emperors, who remained nevertheless its official protectors. The decline of the Carolingian family had given rise to long struggles for the imperial succession. The popes were involved in them, not without sometimes compromising their authority and their prestige, the more so because the Roman nobility incessantly played the blundering part imposed on it by its own turbulence. As if to symbolize this disastrous epoch, the basilica of the Lateran collapsed in 897; all that remained of the venerable structure was a heap of ruins. In 911, when the last representative of the Carolingian dynasty died, a new period of history began: that of the Holy Empire, which, for Rome, was not to be a happy one.

THE ACHIEVEMENTS OF THE CAROLINGIAN PERIOD

In spite of the turmoil of its closing years, the Carolingian period had been essentially fruitful from the architectural point of view—the most fruitful period, perhaps, that Christian Rome had known since Constantine.

The two papal residences of St. Peter's and the Lateran were enlarged, and the Lateran was endowed with the vast dining hall that was to house, until its transfer to the neighboring promenade, the great mosaic celebrating the union of the Empire and the Holy See. In addition, the aqueducts that Vitiges had cut were partly repaired, thus restoring to Rome the Trajana, Claudia, Junia, and Virgo waters and making a most welcome improvement in Roman living conditions.

The quality of the military architecture was demonstrated by the fact that the walls of Rome had discouraged attack by the Saracens in 846. Aurelian's old fortifications had been so well reinforced that they formed an impregnable defense. The fortifications of the Citadel of Leo and of the basilicas of St. Paul and San Lorenzo fuori le Mura, erected with amazing speed, were a new proof of the competence of the papal architects of that time.

It was in religious architecture above all that they showed their industry, if not their talent. They did not build a single church *ex novo*, however, but a great number of those already in existence were so extensively improved that often the work amounted to complete rebuilding. Such was notably the case of San Pietro in Vincoli, formerly known as the basilica of the empress, which Adrian I ordered rebuilt on its present plan in the eighth century. Pope Paschal I, similarly, had St. Cecilia in Trastevere completely rebuilt, and its apse was covered with mosaics recounting the saint's glories.

About 830 Gregory IV undertook a complete renovation of St. Mark. He was responsible for the beautiful mosaic in the apse that shows him in the flattering situation of being introduced to Christ by the Evangelist Mark.

Leo III had ordered the reconstruction and splendid decoration of the church of Saints Nereus and Achilleus, first built in the fourth century on the Via Appia at the place where St. Peter, fleeing Rome, supposedly lost the bandage that bound the sores made by his prison chains. Santa Maria in Cosmedin (in the Forum Boarium) was substantially altered by Adrian I and enlarged with two lateral naves equipped with apses.

It was also in the Carolingian period that Santa Maria in Domenica was rebuilt from bottom to top by Paschal I and adorned with the apsidal mosaic that is still there. Leo X was to add a portico designed by Raphael, as well as the graceful *Navicella* that has given its name to the square and occasionally, in popular usage, to the church itself. It reproduces an ancient work found in the vicinity, which, depicting a boat, seems to have been an *ex voto* to Isis, the patroness of navigators. It is believed to have been presented by sailors brought to Rome to work the rope mechanisms of the awnings that protected spectators in the Colosseum.

Another complete reconstruction was that of St. Prassede, carried out by Paschal I in 817. It is possible, too, that the rebuilt church was not placed precisely on the site of the old one. St. Prassede contains a number of works of art and precious relics: Giulio Romano's *Flagellation,* three thorns from Jesus' crown, the porphyry disk that covered the pit in which St. Prassede collected the martyrs' blood, the whipping post brought back from Jerusalem after the Sixth Crusade. The high altar is approached by old red marble steps, the most beautiful in Rome. Napoleon, it is reported, wanted them for his throne and they only narrowly escaped being shipped to Paris for his coronation. The chief ornament of the sanctuary is still its mosaics, which are highly representative of Carolingian art. Those of the triumphal arch and the apse reproduce the great composition in Saints Cosmas and Damian, done four centuries earlier. It is a literal transposition except that the two Arab saints' faces are replaced by those of the daughters of the Senator, Pudens. But the faces are expressionless, the bodies lack form, and the colors are mediocre. In contrast, the mosaics (the sole example in Rome) that completely cover the chapel of St. Zeno are rich in inspiration and evidence a much bolder art. The saints and the flowers that alternate on the walls give a serene charm to this solitary, silent chapel, to which a popular tradition has given the wholly appropriate name of Garden of Paradise.

None of the reconstructions that we have mentioned, any more than the renovations that were carried out in a number of other Roman churches in the same period, offers any originality: the basilical type continued to prevail. At the very most there was some replacement of antique columns, which were beginning to become rare, with masonry pillars. These are numerous in the lateral naves of Santa Maria in Cosmedin built by Adrian I.

No one in those days gave a thought to the restoration or the maintenance of the monuments of antiquity. Demolition of them had not yet begun, but time had accepted the task of destroying them slowly. While Via Sacra was still the great route for pontifical processions, it was flanked by nothing now except dismantled buildings. Little by little the Forum was being entombed beneath a bed of rubble whose level was to be raised by six feet when a dignitary of the papal court ordered his house built on the Vestals' *atrium* in the beginning of the tenth century. As for the imperial palaces on the Palatine, they were now the property of the brambles; not a single room there was adequate to receive Charlemagne when he was in Rome.

Its monuments in ruins, its schools closed, its literary language dead, its libraries destroyed, Rome sank in this time to the lowest level of its intellectual and artistic decadence. Only religious solemnities gave it life and animation. We shall describe their splendor presently.

The pope's presence attracted a considerable number of pilgrims and travelers. They would have been lost in the labyrinth of ruins and Christian shrines if in those distant days "guides"—the remote ancestors of those that we see in tourists' hands today—had not been compiled. The oldest that is known to us, Einsiedeln's eighth-century itinerary, offers a series of routes (exactly eleven) to the traveler. The ancient ruins are cited in almost meticulous fashion, a detail that deserves mention, for the time would soon come when the monuments of the past would be so completely unrecognized that they would be given arbitrary identifications.

In order to reach that point we must plunge deeper into what is very unjustly called the "night" of the Middle Ages.

CHAPTER 13

ROME AND THE HOLY EMPIRE [911–1273]

THE DISORDERS OF THE MIDDLE AGES AND THE SACK OF ROME BY ROBERT GUISCARD

The tenth century was a period of crisis for Rome. Events followed one on another in a chaotic pell-mell; never thinking in terms other than their own immediate interests, men changed cloaks and characters constantly. A dual ecclesiastical and secular feudalism had been born, whose components battled fiercely in the service of confused and fluid interests. Since the Empire had become the prey of obscure adventurers, the papacy, which could neither do without it nor live in peace with it, allowed itself to be absorbed in the minor intrigues that rose and fell round it. Papal vacancies—extremely numerous, since there were twenty-eight popes in less than a hundred years—were created and filled by violence. Many pontiffs were poisoned, strangled, suffocated under pillows, stabbed, or starved to death in cells; one was killed with a hammer in the hands of a jealous husband. Women ruled the Roman court; for sixty years the papal tiara was bestowed according to the preferences of three courtesans of high degree, the two Theodoras and Marozia, who, it was said, "promoted their lovers from their beds to the pontifical throne."

Rome, which Charlemagne had made the center of the church and the empire, no longer obeyed either the emperors or the popes. Violence was everywhere, and the approach of the year 1000 brought only a passing respite. It was believed that the world would end in that year, and there was considerable haste to build expiatory chapels, none of which has been preserved. Superstitions did not spare the person of the sovereign pontiff. The pope in 1000 was Sylvester II, an Auvergnat from Aurillac, the first Frenchman to sit on St. Peter's throne, and the first pope to conceive the idea of a crusade for the liberation of the holy places. He was an extremely learned man and, for that reason, suspect in the eyes of his contemporaries. The astronomical observatory that he set up in his Lateran Palace, even though it was quite modest and primitive, gave rise to accusations of sorcery. He was charged with having sold his soul to the devil in return for his election: one of the clauses in the contract of purchase and sale, it was said, forbade him, on pain of instant death, to make the journey to Palestine. Now it happened that, having gone to celebrate mass at Holy Cross of Jerusalem, he fell dead as soon as his foot touched the floor of the church in which St. Helena had buried holy earth brought from Golgotha. Before he breathed his last, the legend says, Sylvester recognized the trap that the Prince of Darkness had set for him, and he confessed his crime. It was only after ten years that his body was admitted to St. John Lateran. One cannot say that it reposes there, for popular belief has it that the accursed pope's bones clatter noisily whenever the reigning pontiff is in danger of death. For centuries this was the criterion by which the seriousness of popes' illnesses was gauged.

Once the fateful year of 1000 had passed, all the old quarrels were renewed in all the old complications; there was fighting in the streets for trivial and often ridiculous reasons. Rome was again an easy prey. In 1082 it was captured by Emperor Henry V after a relentless street battle during which the Septizonium was in large part destroyed. Pope Gregory VII appealed for help to Robert Guiscard's Norman bands, whose triumphant intervention unleashed a vast catastrophe. Certain quarters having risen in revolt, they were subjected to a methodical repression that the Norman troops in their zeal extended to the entire city, which was so thoroughly sacked that centuries were needed to efface the marks of a single day of pillage. Men were massacred in huge numbers, women and even nuns were violated, houses were burned. The churches were spared neither profanation nor pillage: those of St. Clement and the Four Crowns were destroyed, as was Porta Asinaria, which was renamed Porta Perasta (Burned Gate).

The victory of Henry V claimed fewer victims, but it hurt Roman pride more cruelly: the German king's knights led a procession in which, roped to one another at the neck, there marched one pope, sixteen cardinals, the chiefs of the Roman nobility, and a host of priests. These tumults were part of the famous war of investitures that set all Europe aflame and in which the rival parties of Guelphs and Ghibellines had so many bloody clashes.

For two centuries Rome again endured the ordeals of the dethronements and imprisonments and assassinations of popes, of the excommunications of emperors, of riot-torn coronations: the basilica of St. Peter's was taken by storm by Frederick Barbarossa's troops in 1167. In those dramatic days there were many battles in Rome, and often between Romans. For the Roman population, far from offering a united front against the assaults on the papacy, divided its loyalties between the rival parties. Bristling with their bastions and towers, the city bore the mark of their warlike antagonisms. Not only did the enemies of the church find welcome and support in its capital; in those times when it was temporarily free of foreign mastery, the papacy was still exposed to the invariably conflicting demands of Roman factions. When the great German interregnum freed the Holy See of imperial interference at the end of the thirteenth century, new problems arose before the popes. For all that they were virtually always purely local in character, they were no less onerous.

THE ROMAN *COMUNE*

In the middle of the twelfth century there was a development that considerably aggravated internal dissension: the formation of the *Comune* of Rome. Ever since the establishment of the temporal power, the government of Rome had been in the hands of the popes and under the protection of the emperors. The sovereign's physical remoteness and the progressive decline in the imperial power had consolidated the pontifical power. The Senate had disappeared, though the title of Senator had persisted as a purely honorary attribute. Unquestionably the Roman aristocracy had often managed to hold the papacy in check, but it had governed the city only in the name of the papacy. Consuls and dukes were still under the authority of the Holy See and subject to its dominance. This essentially aristocratic government allowed no voice to the middle class or the mass.

The oppressed elements of the population rebelled in 1143 against the nobility's monopoly of government. As the result of a popular rising that seized the Capitoline by force, the *Comune* was created. It restored the Senate, minted coins with the old legend, *SPQR,* and stripped the Holy See of temporal authority over the city. The popes and the nobility rose in their turn against this totally new situation. The Capitoline was besieged once more; there was fresh fighting. The strife was resolved in a compromise arrived at in 1188. The *Comune* recognized the sovereignty of the pope, who administered the oath of office to the Senate and took its pledge of loyalty. Conversely, the pope recognized the *Comune* and municipal autonomy.

This rather loose arrangement left an open field for intrigue: the nobility, abandoning all hope of overthrowing the *Comune,* set itself to taking it over. A whole succession of popular reactions followed: there was an attempt at legal dictatorship under Brancaleone degli Andalo, Count of Casalecchio, a Ghibelline from Bologna, but this was shattered by the aristocracy in 1255. Five years later, Charles d'Anjou, king of the Two Sicilies, became senator for life, but, exercising his power only through deputies, he was unable to restore order. In spite of repeated constitutional changes, Rome was to remain until the end of the fourteenth century an autonomous republic under the supreme sovereignty of the pope, who appointed the prefect of the city, while the *Comune* elected the Senate, whose principal concern was the gradual extension of its powers in derogation of the papal authority. As was to be expected, this rivalry of influences was never without friction and conflict.

OMENS OF THE RENAISSANCE

In the tenth and eleventh centuries the arts allied with architecture were lost. Builders did not know how to use anything but the ancient ruins. The manufacture of tiles, so widespread during the classic period, had disappeared, and houses were roofed with those wooden planks with which Rome had been satisfied in the early centuries of its existence. Waste areas spread like leprosy. At the very most there was a highly rudimentary construction of the first feudal fortresses. As for churches, in two centuries only four were built—badly. The oldest of these is St. Mary of the Priory of Malta on the Aventine, which Piranesi was to alter in the eighteenth century, adding the elegant façade with four piers supporting a triangular spandrel adorned with the symbols of the order. Then came

San Cosimato and Santa Maria in Cappella, in Trastevere. The last was St. Bartholomew, on the Tiber island, which recalls the memory of the first French pope, Sylvester II, who built it on the site of the old temple of Aesculapius. This church introduced another architectural novelty, the fashion for which was to be even greater than that of the campanile, or bell tower: the porch, where the poor could be sheltered from the weather while they waited to receive the alms of the faithful.

The beginning of the twelfth century marked a revival of the arts in which the signs of the Renaissance could already be perceived. The erection of buildings of all kinds was to take on decided momentum, which would not be lost until the departure of the popes to Avignon. This was the period of the reconstruction of the bridges of Cestius, now destroyed, and Mulvius, the symbol of Constantine's victory over Maxentius and now known as the Ponte Molle. The new *Comune* was also responsible for the building of hospitals: those of the Holy Spirit at the Vatican, St. Anthony the Abbot on the Esquiline, and St. Thomas on the Caelius. Five popes in succession made extensive additions to their Lateran residence.

Feudal towers and fortresses multiplied, to the great detriment of the ancient monuments, which they directly utilized or from which they borrowed their rich materials. We shall list elsewhere these works so characteristic of their time, the depredations to which they gave rise, and the remains of them that survive. It was principally in the religious sphere that the architectural renewal distinguished itself. All the churches destroyed or damaged during the sack of Rome by the Norman bands were rebuilt or restored, as well as many others whose names alone would fill many pages.

A huge church was built on the site of the large temple to the Egyptian goddess Isis, assimilated to Minerva. This was Santa Maria sopra Minerva, "the Minerva," whose convent was long to be the Dominicans' general headquarters. Two monks of the order, Brother Sisto and Brother Ristoro, were its architects; at the same time, in Florence, they built the church of Santa Maria Novella, with which the Minerva has many similarities. Their Roman work had the peculiarity—alone in the city—of Gothic design. But this amounted really to no more than an adaptation of Italian taste to the Gothic. This attempt was to have no imitators: born under dark skies where light is elusive, Gothic art loses its sense in Italy. With very rare exceptions, the Roman churches, in Camille Mauclair's words, are "horizontal symphonies." They know nothing of the ogive that makes the vault something more than a mere roof for the structure—"a thrust, an aspiration toward heaven."

It must also be pointed out that the Gothic tendencies of Santa Maria sopra Minerva were accentuated by its complete restoration in 1847, which was intended to return it to its original appearance and which in fact resulted in making it only a kind of mixture. Between its creation in the thirteenth century and its restoration in the nineteenth, the Minerva had been given its façade and its lateral chapels in the fifteenth century. Carlo Maderno, a Swiss, had rebuilt its chancel in the taste of the seventeenth century. In sum, it is less interesting for its architecture than for its ornamentation, which makes it one of the richest museum churches in Rome. The authors of the *Itinéraires romains* point out that, "if one does not mind running back and forth, one can devote oneself here to a complete study of the evolution of funeral art from the Middle Ages to the eighteenth century."

The restorations that date from the period that we have now reached, it should be clearly noted, were not mere repairs; the sanctuaries received new decorations. The art of mosaic, lost for centuries, was revived, as was that of bronze, which had emigrated to Constantinople. It was the celebrated Cosmati, or Cosmas, family that was responsible for this revival. These men had invented a method that was to give birth to a decorative art that, while perhaps minor, was delicate and charming, using marble fragments in all colors and blending their harmonies in order to create antique or primitive designs for pulpits, tabernacles, and chancel railings. The works handed down to us by the Cosmati are innumerable. Among the best known are the elegant ciborium of Santa Maria in Cosmedin and the two ambos of the Ara Coeli. Their art was often applied to entire pavements, tracing rare arabesques, as in San Lorenzo fuori le Mura and San Benedetto in Piscipula, the smallest of the Roman basilicas. They were builders as well; in testimony to that we have the cloisters of St. Cecilia and St. Lawrence and the graceful chapel of Sancta Sanctorum, all that is left of the former Lateran Palace. For successive generations this family enlarged the original conception. This dynasty had pupils, imitators, and rivals: this was the foundation of the great school of the Roman marble makers. Their guild had its own church, that of the Four Crowned Saints. In the adjoining cloister they achieved one of their most suggestive creations.

Ornamental and even great sculpture, the secrets of which had been forgot for ten centuries, were to people churches and cloisters with altars, tabernacles, thrones, tombs, and statues of great richness in material and execution. Let us particularly note, in all this great flowering, the tabernacles of San Lorenzo fuori le Mura and Santa Maria in Cosmedin, the stone lion in the portico of the Holy Apostles, the candelabrum of St. Paul's, the episcopal throne in Holy Cross of Jerusalem, the altar and the pulpit in St. Cesarius.

The architecture of the basilicas called on the arts of painting and mosaic for the decoration of interior walls. Byzantinism had reigned over these two arts from the sixth to the eleventh centuries, but it had not everywhere stifled in its hieratic forms and its rigid conventions that old pictorial tradition that came from the catacombs and that had been expressed in the earliest Christian shrines. The old humanism had reappeared in the twelfth century and progressively freed itself from outside influences. The communal revolution of 1143, which had been an act of political emancipation, was also the source of the complete liberation of pictorial art. Specifically Roman painters emerged. In the following century the ascendancy of the people brought a triumph of individualism in painting as in social life. It was then that the great Pietro Cavallini appeared, in whom the genius of Roman art of the Middle Ages was epitomized. His master work, the frescoes in St. Paul Beyond the Walls, of which only the sketches have survived to us, disappeared in the great fire of the nineteenth century; but the scene of the *Last Judgment* can still be seen in St. Cecilia; the decoration of the apse in St. George of the Velabrum survives, as well as a number of Virgins scattered among the churches of Rome (*della Strada* in the *Gesù, della Nave* in Santa Maria Maggiore, *of Mercy* in Santa Maria Trasteverina). Then came the Tuscans—Cimabue, who left nothing in Rome but the precepts of his art, and above all Giotto, whose Roman work, though it was considerable, is represented now only by the reredos of the old altar of St. Peter's (now in the hall of the Capitulary) and by the portrait of Boniface VIII proclaiming the jubilee of 1300 in St. John Lateran.

To return to religious architecture, let us point out that the fashion of porches and bell towers, introduced in Rome as early as the eleventh century, became widespread in the next two centuries. It was then that St. Clement, St. Prassede, and St. Saba in particular were given their porches and that Pope Calixtus II gave Santa Maria in Cosmedin the graceful *propylaeum* that leads to a porch that was the site of the *Bocca della Verità* that enjoyed a very special celebrity in Rome. It is a round slab representing a Triton's mask, whose mouth, it was said, would close to bite the hand of the liar or the perjurer. The legend is very old; perhaps its origin should be linked to a fountain of Mercury that was near and at which the cattle merchants purged themselves of their false oaths. Was the *Bocca della Verità* one of the mouths of that fountain? Some archeologists have been inclined to regard it as a mere sewer cover. It was the fashion to decorate the enclosed places in front of churches with these "miraculous things" (*mirabilia*) that had absolutely no connection with religious conceptions. This was certainly the case of the *Bocca della Verità,* and even more of the two whale jawbones that are its neighbors and the imperial eagle that adorns the portico of the Holy Apostles. The porch of San Lorenzo fuori le Mura was garnished with sarcophagi and religious paintings. In the vestibule of St. Sabina, access is given to the aisles by the famous door of eighteen panels in sculptured cedar that are considered the oldest portrayal of scenes from both Testaments.

As for the brick bell towers that are the enchantment of medieval Rome, at least seventeen of them were built in a single century—all graceful, illuminated by windows, overlaid with faïence, mosaics, and porphyry. They drew their inspiration from the Roman shapes in northern Italy, but they took their specifically Roman character from the splendor of their polychrome decoration. Santa Maria in Cosmedin, Santa Francesca Romana (then called Santa Maria Nuova), Santa Maria Maggiore, Santa Pudenziana, Holy Cross of Jerusalem, St. George in the Velabrum, and St. Alexis all possessed such bell towers, to name only the most beautiful or the most famous. Let us add also that of San Lorenzo fuori le Mura, which rises above the cypresses of the cemetery as if to create a Florentine landscape. With that of Santa Maria in Cappella in Trastevere it is the oldest in Rome. The smallest is that of San Benedetto in Piscipula, already mentioned, but it has the honor of possessing the oldest bells in the Eternal City. As for that of St. Cecilia, it leans like Pisa's tower.

In spite of the political upheavals, the twelfth and thirteenth centuries were a time of illumination in Christian thought. Prayer became more ardent. It was the time of the Crusades; it was also the time of St. Dominick, of St. Francis of Assisi, of St. Claire. It was the golden age of the Roman cloisters. The best known are those of St. Paul Beyond the Walls, with their sparkling twin columns; St. John Lateran, which mingles delightful fantasies with Benedictine simplicity; San Lorenzo fuori le Mura, decorated with bas-reliefs taken from the catacombs of Cyriachus.

But there are many others that in their own way sing of the glory of God—those of St. Saba, St. Sixtus, Saints Vincent and Anastasius of the Three Fountains, the Four Crowned Saints, as well as those of San Cosimato, where St. Francis lived, and of St. Sabina, which piously preserves St. Dominick's cell and the orange tree that he planted with his own hands. Precincts of reverie and silence whose arched passages open on gardens where water murmurs among the flowers, all breathe the same pervading Roman serenity.

The Renaissance gave no such perceptible foreshadowings in the realm of literature. The literary awakening that was general throughout Italy manifested itself in Rome only in production that was very limited in quantity and very meager in quality. Culture penetrated only the circles of the ecclesiastics and the noble families. It was still in Paris and Florence and Bologna that it must be sought. But there was one evidence that the city had broken out of its torpor: it sent its sons abroad to be educated, while the popes were beginning to fill their courts with scholars and men of letters who had gained renown elsewhere. Little by little, intellectual groups were formed in Rome. Abélard was to go there; St. Bernard was to establish a cloister Ad Aquas Salvias in Via Ostiensis; the University of Rome was to be founded; and St. Thomas Aquinas was to teach for a time in the convent of St. Sabina on the Aventine.

CHAPTER 14

HOW ROME LOOKED AND LIVED IN THE MIDDLE AGES

THE DESTRUCTION OF THE ANCIENT CITY

Before we enter on the dramatic period of the popes' sojourn in Avignon, the disintegration of the medieval world, and the physical ruin of Rome, it would seem not unhelpful to linger a moment in contemplation of what the city had become eight centuries after the collapse of the Roman Empire. First of all, what was left of that fabulous city that had been the marvel of the universe? In truth, it had undergone progressive degradation under the influence of many factors. Natural forces had played a large part, but men had contributed remarkably to the destruction of monuments by systematically using them as quarries.

The medieval sculptors found it at once convenient and anything but difficult to levy on the ancient ruins for whatever materials they needed. Indeed there were enterprises that specialized in this form of vandalism, which was the more productive because it had built up markets in the whole of Europe. The cathedrals of Pisa, Lucca, and many other Italian cities had been adorned or built with Roman marbles, on which the baptistry of Florence had made very large inroads. Even the cathedral of Aachen and Westminster Abbey had had a hand in this. As early as 1140, the famous Abbé Suger, when he was rebuilding the basilica of St.-Denis, had contemplated having the granite columns of Diocletian's temple transported to Paris.

Yet, in spite of its wickedness, this exploitation retained a somehow rational character. But there was a far less defensible kind of depredation that consisted in reducing the ancient marbles to lime. Furnaces were set up near the large ruins; they operated in the imperial palaces on the Palatine, in Diocletian's baths, in the Basilica Julia. There were so many of them that their traces remain in many Roman street names. Such words as *carcarario, alle carcare,* and their derivatives evoke the memory of such furnaces in the neighborhood. And this destruction was practiced not only on slabs of facing or building materials but also on statues, as is shown by the discoveries, in a number of places, of statues all ready for processing and, in some cases, carefully broken into small pieces in order to facilitate it. Such was the fate of the Vestals' statues, which were discovered in a furnace set up in their *atrium.*

These ravages had made profound changes in the city's appearance. Temples, baths, and lordly mansions, stripped of their rare marbles, stood naked in their common stone or brick. Even the color of Rome was changed; it was "tinged with old age." This was all the more the case because the new houses, built with materials taken from their predecessors, already bore the darkening tones of old stone.

At the end of the Middle Ages, the Forum, the seat of ancient Roman grandeur, was buried beneath those enormous masses of earth that caused Stendhal to wonder again, eight centuries later, where they could have come from. They covered the greater number of the monuments, at least in part, even those that had been built on higher sites. It was the work of time and the neglect of man. When Rome's population shrank in the Middle Ages, the Forum quarter had been the first to be abandoned, and street maintenance there had been dropped. The dust piled up; mud blocked the sewers, which were no longer kept functioning: the lowest-lying areas became swamps again as they had been in the time of Romulus. Weeds and brambles made a firm bed for the soil that increased from year to year. The neighboring quarters that were still inhabited used the area as a garbage dump. "The broken sewers erupted with mud." This mudhole, which changed its appearance with the seasons, grew so thick that it almost effaced the former topography. Cattle were led to pasture thirty feet above the glorious streets. For in the end the mud had become fertile humus. A new kind of city planning emerged from this change:

vegetable gardens were planted above the Forum, and the people went there to take their walks. From the arch of Septimius Severus to the arch of Titus, both half entombed, there was a tree-flanked avenue that became the route of processions. The ruins that still thrust above the ground harmonized with the appearance of the area, which breathed that melancholy poetry that led to cries of "sacrilege" when the first excavations threatened the romantic beauty of the Campo Vaccino (Cow Pasture).

ROME OF THE TOWERS

The damage was aggravated by the transformation of ancient monuments into fortified places. Every noble family wanted to have its fortress, from which it could keep a jealous eye on its rivals. The most powerful sought to be the best fortified: the tomb of Augustus passed first into the hands of the Colonnas, Domitian's stadium to the Sanguignis, Pompey's theater to the Orsinis, Marcellus' to the Pierleonis, the Circus Maximus to the Frangipanis, like the arches of Titus and Constantine and the whole of the Palatine, which represented a powerful citadel. On the Quirinal the Colonnas had the baths of Constantine, while the Capoccis took over Trajan's on the Oppius. Families of lesser merit contested for the other edifices, and the rivalries among them were so acute that nothing escaped the feudal grip except what was indisputably too far away. The greediness of the "barons" did not spare even those structures that had been converted to pious purposes. A number of religious buildings were equipped with defensive additions, such as the churches of the Four Crowned Saints on the Caelius, Santa Balbina on the Aventine, and San Nicola in Carcere in the Forum Olitorium, whose massive bell tower is nothing but a military construction.

At the same time, for their own safety, the nobles built strong houses topped with battlements, some remarkable specimens of which still exist: Cola di Rienzo's house in the Forum Boarium, the Savellis' palace (almost in ruins) on the Aventine, the Anguillaras' palace in Trastevere, the Caetanis' near the tomb of Cecilia Metella, itself converted into a turret. The house of the Knights of Rhodes, which overlooks the forum of Augustus, was the best example of these fortified dwellings, with its barbican windows and its crenelated walls (before the addition of its loggia).

Considered an indispensable adjunct of the fortifications, at once in order to reinforce their defense and as a boastful mark of power, towers rose by the hundreds in medieval Rome. A pilgrim of the Middle Ages professed to have counted ten thousand of them. He was surely wrong: Poggio* mentions only seventy-nine in the walls and eight hundred within the city. Occasionally they were close together, so that Nerva's forum was nicknamed Campo Torreggiano (Tower Field).

Many have survived, distributed throughout the city and often integrated into later constructions. We shall not attempt to list them, limiting ourselves to mentioning those that deserve attention by reason of their size or some peculiarity of their history. The highest and best preserved is the tower de' Conti, at the beginning of Via Cavour; it made a deep impression on Petrarch, who said that it had no equal on earth. He saw it as it appears to us in a fresco in the old San Spirito hospital, much different from what it has become. For the earthquake of 1348 destroyed its upper stories, and it should be noted, in a curious coincidence, that another earthquake is supposed to have caused the erection of the very ancient Roman temple on whose ruins it stands: it was to appease the goddess of earth, Tellus, that this large temple was built. It had had its time of glory: the Senate met there occasionally in the last centuries of the Republic, and Cicero had often orated there.

Not far from this tower is the Militia Tower, inaccurately called Nero's, which leans slightly, a little behind Trajan's markets. Although its summit was destroyed by lightning, it still rises as high as the bronze *quadrigae* of the Vittoriano. It is the best elevation from which to look out over the whole of Rome and its environs.

The Torre della Scimmia (Monkey Tower), near the church of St. Anthony of the Portuguese, recalls a miraculous occurrence in the seventeenth century: a little girl was carried to the top of it by a monkey that swung her dangerously out over the void; the madonna rescued the child from this dangerous situation. She was thanked with a statue at the foot of which a lamp has burned night and day for more than two hundred years. The Anguillaras' tower in Trastevere competes in height with its neighbor, the brick bell tower of St. Crisogono. The Sanguignis' tower, converted into a residence, was the home of St. Ignatius Loyola.

Dominating more or less extended areas, and occasionally an entire

* Poggio Bracciolini, a Renaissance Florentine writer and scholar.—Translator.

quarter, these feudal fortresses divided Rome into a mosaic of sectors: within each lived a lordly baron surrounded by his servitors and his men at arms. Rivalries were continual in "that unquiet, seditious, intractable race," as St. Bernard called it. Skirmishes and limited sieges were the currency of the day: the defeated saw their towers razed and took the first political opportunity to rebuild them. When the disorders grew too great, the reigning power—the pope, the *Comune,* or the occupying foreign power—took it upon itself to dismantle the fortresses. In 1257 Brancaleone had 140 towers demolished at the same time; in a few months, with a change in government they had all reappeared.

Within the shadow of these feudal families, most often involved in their quarrels but tending more and more to busy itself with its own concerns, there was a middle class that filled the city with new houses, often built on Roman foundations and always borrowing the greater part of their materials from the ancient buildings. Rome has a tremendous number of these apartment houses that abound with antique fragments: colonnades, marble frameworks of balconies or windows, stair railings. There is an admirable group of them at the corner of the two streets of the theater of Marcellus, as well as another near Trajan's market, and a third in Trastevere, in the narrow alley of the Atleta that opens out into a real popular atmosphere: "Beautiful black eyes, little hawkers on the sidewalk, orange peel, dark doorways under the stone arch, huge fishing nets hung out to dry" (Y. and E. R. Labande).

As for the mass of the people, always on guard, sometimes joining in the quarrels of the nobles and sometimes rising against them under leaders from its own ranks, it was compressed into those dark narrow streets of Suburra, the Trastevere, or the Field of Mars, the course of which has hardly changed over the centuries. Some are perfectly preserved evidences of the time in which they were built, such as that Via Biberatica that emerged intact when Trajan's Forum was cleared. The building numbered 15 in Via della Portica di Ottavia can be regarded as the type of popular housing in the Middle Ages. The twisting streets of the old quarters still offer those vaulted passages known today as *archi,* which were characteristic of the medieval periods: Arco de' Cenci, Arco de' Ginnasi, Arco de' Sinibaldi in the Field of Mars, Arco di Tolomeo in Trastevere. Every one has its picturesque history, and their legends are often strange.

CELEBRATIONS AND SOLEMNITIES

In spite of the political turmoils, the Middle Ages was a period of religious and popular celebrations in Rome. There were so many of them and they were endowed with such splendor that they make it impossible to qualify the city of the popes with the epithets ordinarily employed for the life of a period that is reputed to have been difficult and dark.

The most brilliant of these celebrations were certainly those of the emperors' coronations. Unparalleled luxury reigned in the ceremonials and processions, when they were not marred by serious troubles; incidents arising out of the political situation of the moment were not unusual.

There was more occasion to crown popes than emperors, but the rapid succession of sovereign pontiffs did not weary the Roman people's enjoyment of the ceremonial of their coronations. This included, after the ritual consecration in St. Peter's, a splendid procession that was the most magnificent spectacle that could be offered to a people that has always been a lover of pomp.

What was remarkable in the procession was the fact that virtually all its participants were on horseback, even ecclesiastics of the highest rank in their sumptuous sacerdotal habits. The order of the procession was established in an unalterable rite. It was led by a richly caparisoned horse without a rider. This was the horse of the pope, who for the moment was relegated to another part of the parade. Behind this horse came the cross bearers, the standard bearers, the judges and lawyers in their long black robes. They were followed by the pupils of the Lateran singing school, then a host of deacons and subdeacons, and the abbots of Rome's twenty abbeys, preceding the bishops and archbishops. At last the pope appeared, riding a white horse led at the bridle by the most influential notables of the moment; if the emperor or a few kings were in Rome, this honor fell to them by clear right. More deacons escorted the pope, as well as the prefect of the city at the head of an impressive delegation of judges. The guilds came next, followed by the militia. The line of march was closed by the Roman nobility in all its splendor, coats of arms on display. Every participant did his best to make the procession still more splendid by the richness of his dress and the beauty of his horse. The city was decked in keeping; arches of triumph were erected at brief intervals. The good people packed the route, especially at its prescribed stopping places, so that the chamberlains could carry out their ritual largesses of money. One of these stops was at the foot of the arch of Septimius Severus, where the Jews, headed by their rabbis, stood on a luxuriously beflagged platform. When the pope arrived before them, they greeted him and offered him the Pentateuch, which the sovereign pontiff pretended to bless, at the same time being careful to indicate a gesture of protest, a double symbolic manifestation that demanded a real theatrical talent in its executant.

The final rites of the coronation were performed in the Lateran. Under the portico, the pontiff cast three handfuls of gold, silver, and bronze coins to the people, saying: "Gold and silver are naught to me; what I have, I give to ye." After having received the homage of the chapter, he went to take solemn possession of his palace, seating himself turn by turn on a first chair of porphyry, where he accepted the scepter and the keys of the church, and then on a second, where he turned over his symbols to the prior. After having received the great sash of red silk with the homage of the dignitaries of the palace, once again he tossed three handfuls of coins to the people. Each prelate who now came to kiss his foot received a present in money, the *presbiterium*. The celebration ended with a banquet served at small tables. The pope sat alone at his own, served by the highest notables of the city or by such kings as might be in attendance.

After 1227 the splendor of the pontifical procession was enhanced by the new red color of the cardinals' vestments. Red was Italians' favorite color, a token of power. Dante usually wore red, Michelangelo wore red stockings, and Cosmo de' Medici was accustomed to say that one could get a great deal out of a man "by giving him a little red."

RELIGIOUS CELEBRATIONS

In medieval Rome there were still many celebrations, both secular and religious, on the occasion of which there were brilliant processions through the city, to the delight of great crowds. The most frequent were the great parades, some of which were followed by the entire population. Some were improvised at the occurrence of some unforeseen event—a visit by a notable foreigner, a public calamity, a supposedly miraculous apparition. Others, periodic in character, followed rigid rules and unchangeable routes. These were led by the pope, a crown on his head, escorted by his cardinals; but disputes over precedence in the ranks occasionally ended in bloody brawls. Carved in the marble of the Conservators' Palace is one of the many rules made by the communal legislature for the procession of the Assumption; one cannot be sure that it was any more observed than the others. Besides, it is extremely obscure.

On the first day of Lent the pope walked barefoot from St. Anastasia to St. Peter's, but this custom was rather soon abandoned. St. Sabina was the point of convergence for seven processions, each having started at a different church, in which the faithful were divided into seven groups: the clergy, the men, the nuns, the married women, the widows, the poor, and the children. On April 23, at St. George in Velabrum, the blessing of the city's flag was the occasion for a deafening uproar of trumpets and drums. On the night of St. John's Day all the streets near the Lateran were the scene of huge bonfires that occasionally burned down the surrounding houses. Although it was presided over by the pope, the Coromania that was also celebrated at the Lateran was more than half a heathen festival: there was dancing in the square, and clergy and people mingled indistinguishably in the diversions. This mixture of the sacred and the profane recurred in the popular celebrations of which the Testaccio was the scene. Sacred performances, such as re-enactments of the crucifixion of St. Peter or the beheading of St. Paul, alternated there with races of pigs harnessed to light carriages. In the Colosseum there were mystery spectacles, but also tournaments in which the noblemen dedicated their feats of arms to the lovely ladies in the audience. On September 3, 1332, it was the scene of a Spanish-style bullfight that has remained famous: eleven bulls were killed, but eighteen men of gentle birth, matadors for a day, were also killed, while nine others were seriously injured.

PILGRIMAGES AND THE JUBILEE

Bathed in the aura of its rich Christian past, Rome had become in the Middle Ages a place of pilgrimage that drew the faithful from all Italy and the whole of Europe for devout visits to churches and catacombs and the hope of seeing the pope in the full splendor of his pomp. Their offerings were favorably received by the treasurers of the Holy See, and the entire city profited by their influx.

It was in order to encourage such things, as well as to accomplish a kind of apotheosis of the papacy, that Boniface VIII decided to open the fourteenth century with "a solemn demonstration of faith." For the whole year of 1300 he proclaimed a plenary indulgence for visits to the basilicas of St. Peter and of St. Paul. This was the inauguration of the "jubilee," which was crowned with enormous success. Two million pilgrims went to Rome in that year, and it has been estimated that at any given time there were always 200,000 in the city at once. This meant that the faithful did not restrict themselves to quick visits: travel was so arduous and so protracted in those days that one did not undertake it for a short stay. Besides, the pope had been careful to establish a fifteen-day minimum for a pilgrimage.

This unaccustomed volume of visitors included a number of old persons, invalids, and cripples on litters. How did they all live in a city ill equipped to receive them? Quite badly, without doubt, but that meant nothing, since Christians of the Middle Ages undertook their pilgrimages principally out of penitence and made their sufferings a tribute to God. And indeed none of them died of hunger, food supplies having been seen to through emergency measures. But housing left much to be desired, and whoever managed to find a corner in a bad tavern paid through the nose for it. The influx was so great that pedestrian traffic had to be regulated and one-way rules had to be enforced on the Aelian bridge, which led to the Vatican. In the basilicas of St. Peter's and St. Paul the offerings were so many that two clerics, rake in hand, could not gather them all in. The pontifical treasury was incalculably enriched, and, according to Villani,* all the Romans made fortunes. The visitors of note included Giotto and Dante, neither of whom created as much stir as a hundred-year-old Savoyard whose fine patriarchal appearance was much admired. Having acquired a taste for this sort of thing from its excellent financial results, the Romans demanded a repetition of the jubilee fifty years later. It was equally rewarding. When Petrarch arrived in Rome at the end of the summer, he saw such an invasion of pilgrims that he wrote to Boccaccio that "it was a wonder that the earth, which was supposed to be depopulated, could still supply so many"; twelve persons died of suffocation during a display of Christ's shroud. These first jubilees left so splendid a memory that subsequently the interval between jubilees was to be reduced to twenty-five years.

The pilgrims of 1300 had the opportunity to admire the new basilica of St. John Lateran, whose main altar had been paid for by King Charles V the Wise of France. Since it was intended that the pilgrims should regard the basilica as the marvel of the Christian world and the symbol of the

---

* Giovanni Villani, born 1267, was a traveler and chronicler of events of the first half of the fourteenth century.—Translator.

papal power, it had been so thoroughly restored that it seemed completely new. Awed by its splendor, Dante preserved an overwhelming memory of it. "There is no work of man," he wrote, "that is not surpassed by the Lateran." We must take his word for it, since the building was wrecked by fire in 1308, a catastrophe that was to be repeated fifty-four years later, destroying the greater part of Giotto's frescoes. No other church in Rome has known so much glory and at the same time so many woes.

The tide of pilgrims who, having accomplished their devotions, became sightseers led to the publication of "guides" intended to introduce the tourists to the marvels of Rome. The interest of these books today lies in their errors, which are occasionally droll; they are innumerable and they show an unbelievable degree of ignorance of their city's monumental history in the Romans of the time. Baths and basilicas are called palaces; theaters and arches of triumph are listed as temples; names are distorted or travestied; monuments are invented that had never existed. In their ingenuous desire to explain everything, the editors of these "guides" resorted to the legends that the popular imagination of the Middle Ages had elaborated in so great a quantity. The Colosseum became a temple of the sun, which was supposed originally to have been covered by a golden dome. The pyramid of Cestius, identified as the tomb of Romulus, owed its shape to its builders' concern with "keeping dogs away." The temple of Romulus on Via Sacra was identified with the Asylum of the city's earliest period, as the result of a confusion between the son of Maxentius and the founder of Rome.

It is hardly surprising that the past was embroidered with legends when the present was woven of them. The appearance of the archangel St. Michael was so firmly accepted as historical fact that it was commemorated by the erection of the statue that gives its name to Castello Sant'Angelo. The legend of Pope Joan still has its echo in the papal coronation ceremony, in which there is meticulous verification of the candidate's sex. The Middle Ages never doubted that the ghost of Messalina continued to lead her dissolute life in Suburra. As for Nero, he was so persevering in venting his ill humors at Porta Flaminia that Pope Paschal II erected an altar to the Virgin there in order to rid the quarter of this unwanted presence; the altar was subsequently to be replaced by the church of Santa Maria del Popolo.

CHAPTER 15

ROME DURING THE "AVIGNON CAPTIVITY" AND THE GREAT SCHISM [1309-1420]

THE RIENZO EPISODE

For Boniface VIII the jubilee of 1300 was only a success without a tomorrow; the papacy was already at grips with King Philip the Fair. Now that the emperors, absorbed by their German concerns, no longer had the time to go to Rome and claim their historic rights, internal dissensions had grown much greater and made the pontifical throne the prize of the great families' rivalries. For thirty years the Colonnas and the Orsinis, backed by their traditional allies, went through the alternations of defeat and success. The election of Boniface VIII had been a triumph for the Orsinis, who had had their rivals excommunicated and exiled; the Colonnas had then sought the intervention of the king of France. Philip the Fair laid hands on the person of the pope in his temporary residence of Anagni; a popular uprising rescued the pontiff, but, shaken by the brutality of the abduction, he returned to Rome only to die there in 1303. His successor, Benedict XI, won over to the French cause, moved the seat of pontifical power to Avignon, while the Colonnas regained wealth and influence.

Rome was to remain without a pope from 1309 to 1377 and to suffer cruelly from the absence of its protectors. The nobility and the people battled fiercely for power, and the Capitoline was taken and retaken. Aristocratic and popular governments, unstable and ephemeral, succeeded one another in a climate of constant violence until, in the person of Cola di Rienzo, the people found a leader who could assure his supremacy for a longer time.

The saga of this washwoman's son is miraculous. He was nothing more nor less than a poet, and the only explanation of his success lies in the lyric movement on which he was borne. In thrall to the antique glory of Rome, he cherished the fixed idea of restoring its ancient splendor to the city. This sentiment, as they say, was "in the air" then. Dante had died in 1321 and his poem had become the object of all but religious adoration throughout Italy. Petrarch played on the chord of memory when he sang of "the splendid queen of the world." On Easter morning of 1341 the people of Rome invested him with the honors that it had often "sold to the Caesars": clad in a purple mantle, the poet was carried to the Capitoline to receive a victor's laurel wreath.

This latent nostalgia for a dead past was to become a doctrine to Cola di Rienzo. A genuine scholar, a real lover of the ancient splendors of Rome, a magnificent speaker, he was to preach his crusade on a somewhat simplistic sentimental theme that contrasted the shame of the present with the glory of the past. In his view, re-establishing in Rome the old forms of government described by Livy (what he called "the good ways of the old days") would be sufficient to bring back fortune and greatness.

Eloquent and vehement, Rienzo's propaganda aroused the enthusiasm of an easily stirred people that still saw round it the traces of Roman greatness. It was the more enthusiastic because its hero made no secret of his determination to destroy the system of nobility that continued to predominate in the *Comune* in spite of the periodic popular insurrections. It was for the people's benefit that he wanted to alter Roman institutions. The people was to follow him blindly. The nobles, who had nothing but mockery for his person and contempt for his mission, left him in peace to prepare his revolution; one day he posted the plans and the date on the portal of St. George in Velabrum. A Colonna headed the communal government at the time; it never occurred to him to take this bluster seriously.

Nevertheless, on the day stipulated—Pentecost, May 30, 1347—the people attacked the Capitoline at the signal of church bells. Cola had spent the night in prayer in his parish church, Sant'Angelo in Peschiera. He arrived at the Capitoline and addressed the crowd, which acclaimed him dictator, charged him with reforming the state, and invested him with all powers for its conduct. The revolution had succeeded without the shedding of a drop of blood, without even the slightest gesture by the government, taken entirely by surprise at the suddenness of the insurrection. Confronted with the accomplished fact, the great noble families could find no other course than to adhere to the new government, the Orsinis and the Colonnas at their head.

"The good ways" were inaugurated at once: finances, militia, courts, police—everything was reorganized. Public granaries were established in order to maintain supplies, and a generous welfare system was improvised. Petrarch, the glory of his time, congratulated the "tribune of the people" and gave him his poetic blessing. His every move aroused a remarkable enthusiasm; the people, Léon Homo wrote, "seemed to have arisen from the grave." And not only the Roman people, but the people of all Italy, in whom Cola di Rienzo's enterprise had wakened an exalted fervor. All the cities of the peninsula paid tribute to the illustrious liberator "of the Holy Roman Republic": Florence, Siena, Perugia sent him soldiers, Viterbo and Orvieto dispatched deputies, and Gaeta contributed six thousand gold florins.

Intoxicated by so fervent a reception, Rienzo then committed the error of raising his ambitions to the level of his sudden renown. He proclaimed the independence of all the Italian cities; he summoned to appear before him Louis of Hungary and Joanna of Naples, who were rival claimants for the Empire; and he called on the pope to return to Rome. He was seized with a kind of delirium, "in which Christian mysticism was strangely mingled with the evocation of pagan antiquity." He conceived of himself as the representative at once of the old and the new Rome. He assumed the dalmatic of the emperors and issued an edict proclaiming Rome the capital of the world. He appeared at a ceremony in the Lateran wearing white silk embroidered in gold and carrying a naked sword, with which he designated the four points of the compass, crying: "This is mine." He then took a solemn oath "to judge the world according to justice and the people according to equity." The emperors had had only one crown: he desired seven, to symbolize the seven virtues, decked with the wild plants that were growing under the arch of Constantine. All this was accompanied by lavish celebrations that ignited the popular ardor afresh; during one of these, wine flowed from the nostrils of the bronze horse of Marcus Aurelius.

The most concrete effect of the tribune's theatrical posturings was to incite a violent opposition. The nobles consolidated their forces with a view to the common defense of their ancient privileges; they won the Avignon pope to their cause, and he issued a thunderous bull against the usurper. A conspiracy for his overthrow was formed in Rome. Nothing lasting, of course, could have emerged from a movement based on nothing more than an exaltation of spirit. When the situation turned critical, Cola di Rienzo found no real support in the mass of the people, disappointed at the fact that there had been no return of the golden age. Having plumbed the depths of his illusions, he resigned his powers on December 15, 1347, and fled to Naples, where he became a monk.

The house in which he is supposed to have lived (*la casa di Rienzo*) stands near the temple of Fortuna Virile. It is a square tower adorned with outside galleries supported by piers. Its entablature is composed of a salad of ancient fragments and remnants of all the Roman styles. This hodge-podge was in complete accord with the tastes of the orator who was forever invoking inscriptions and ruins in the name of "liberty." The name of *casa di Pilato* (Pilate's house), which is also given to Rienzo's house, is one of those insults that followed the tribune after his fall.

This intermission of popular democracy having been concluded, the earlier system was restored. But the nobility did not regain its traditional prerogatives: the middle class was now challenging its political supremacy. The city government was laboriously resumed amid a disorder of institutions and minds. After seven years of exile, Cola di Rienzo reappeared in Rome in 1354 as a senator, but very soon he was killed in a riot and his body was hanged by the feet from a balcony of the Colonna palace.

One symbol of this sterile epoch survives, intact and magnificent: the great marble stairway of the Ara Coeli, built in 1347 by Cola di Rienzo in thanks to heaven for having preserved Rome from the terrible plague called the Black Death that was then laying Italy waste. The church had been rebuilt in 1250, in the style that it has retained to the present. Its austere façade is still waiting for the mosaics that were supposed to cover it. For centuries, with its adjoining monastery, it was to be the chief establishment of the Franciscans. It is still deeply moving to see the house of a God of peace erected on the very spot that symbolized the warlike power of Rome. A whole literature has been born of that contrast. It was the direct inspiration of Gibbon's *Decline and Fall of the Roman Empire.*

THE STRANGE CONCLAVE AND THE GREAT SCHISM

Disillusioned with the dream of a universal republic with which for a moment Cola di Rienzo had deluded it, Rome now looked only to its popes for its salvation. Powerless to give itself a stable government, fallen from its rank as a capital, a prey to economic and financial stagnation, the city had seen its population drop to the lowest figure it had ever known (seventeen thousand in 1375). All the arts whose revival had been so strong in the previous century had fallen back into decay. The aversion to them in all classes of society was complete, and the *Comune* had many other concerns than vigilance for the preservation of the city's artistic treasures. The earthquake of 1359 had knocked down a whole section of the Colosseum: a number of other monuments had been damaged by the cataclysm. "The statues are in pieces," a Greek wrote; "sometimes some of them are used as steps for mounting a horse, or as thresholds or troughs in stables." Petrarch said of the ancient monuments: "Aside from Agrippa's Pantheon, all that holds them to the ground is their own weight." Abandoned by its masters, the Citadel of Leo was empty; its wall was crumbling; rubble blocked access to St. Peter's. At night wolves roamed through the Vatican gardens.

In all this misery the nostalgic memory of the popes and their good works was cherished. As long as they had remained in Rome they had striven to restore order and peace: their court and the flow of foreigners that it attracted were a double source of wealth: the Romans had found ecclesiastical employment the doorway to respect and wealth. No misfortune struck the city without the Holy Father's endeavors to help the afflicted. Rome offered everything, and "on its knees," for the return of its protectors: the keys to its fortresses, the principate of the Republic, the right of feudal sovereignty over Trastevere and the Citadel of Leo, over the city's bridges and gates and even over its wealth. The pope was still hesitant to plunge himself into the Roman furnace. It was a woman's will that determined his decision. A young religious, Catherine of Siena, ardent and zealous, assumed the mission of bringing back the papacy to the seat of the first apostle. She made many appeals and wrote many letters; in 1376 she undertook the journey to Avignon and, in their mystic talks, she prevailed on Pope Gregory XI to return to Christendom's traditional center.

After a troubled voyage, the papal galley anchored in the middle of the

Tiber, and the next day, at sunrise, the pope disembarked, the cross in his hand. A huge crowd was waiting for him—nobles and burghers, soldiers of the militia, monks, and men of the people. From St. Paul to the Vatican the procession traversed "the solemn desert of Rome." Romans had posted themselves on the roofs of the houses; the women wept with joy; a rain of flowers fell round the Holy Father. It was dusk when they reached St. Peter's: eighteen thousand lamps were shining in the basilica. Catherine of Siena was not present at this triumph, and she could take part only in thought and in her prayers in this universal rejoicing; she was to die in Rome in 1380, in the little room that the visitor can enter behind the sacristy of the Minerva. Her body lies beneath the main altar of the church.

The high relief that adorns the tomb of Gregory XI in Santa Francesca Romana, at the upper end of the Forum, depicts the pope's return to Rome and shows the procession that accompanied him. Gregory XI was to be the last French pope; Santa Francesca Romana, of which he had been cardinal-deacon, was long thereafter regarded as the attribute of the French cardinals.

When the eighteen thousand lamps that illuminated St. Peter's had been extinguished and the sound of the acclamations had died away, the papacy was once more at grips with the problems that had brought on and prolonged its exile in Avignon. They were so grave in character and they raised so many insoluble problems that momentarily Gregory XI thought of going back to Provence, for which he was homesick. He foresaw the schism, and, when he was very near death, he established rules for conclaves in order to prevent his death from becoming the occasion for a spectacular rupture between the opposing tendencies. In vain; the catastrophe befell in spite of these cautious maneuvers.

Rome had suffered too much by the absence of its popes, it had had too much difficulty in getting them back, to accept a new exodus. The surest guaranty against the recurrence of the incidents that had led to ruin was to give the throne of St. Peter's to an Italian pope, and, better still, a Roman pope. At the beginning of the conclave that followed the funeral of Gregory XI, in 1378, the Sacred College, meeting in the Vatican, heard the roar of an ultimatum from the crowd outside: *"Romano o italiano lo vogliamo* (We want a Roman or an Italian)," which was soon put into stronger terms by the captains of the militia who forced their way into the conclave's chapel: "Give us a Roman pope who will stay with us, or else we will give you heads redder than your hats." Impervious to the threats, the majority of the Sacred College, which was French, elected the man whom it preferred, Archbishop Prignano of Bari, who, though he was an Italian, paraded Francophile sentiments that testified to his position as a client of the house of Anjou.

Nevertheless, whether in a spirit of bravado or in some tortuous effort to roil matters, Cardinal Orsini announced the elevation of a Roman pope, Tibaldeschi. At this news, the crowd pushed through the barriers, tore down the doors of the palace and charged into the conclave to adore "its pope." The frightened cardinals, seeing no other way of averting popular vengeance, resorted to the stratagem of pretending to enthrone Tibaldeschi. The poor man was virtually hurled on to St. Peter's throne, hastily capped with the pontifical miter, while, amid the rolling notes of a hasty *Te Deum,* the trembling cardinals sneaked away *"sine capis et capellis."* So now there were two popes, one genuine, who, swooning with fear, was hidden no one knew where, and one false, who protested, threw his miter on the ground, and answered the Romans' tributes with solemn curses. He revealed the deception and identified the real pope. Enraged at so base a fraud, the people set out after the wicked cardinals, but it could not find them; some had taken refuge in Castello Sant'Angelo and others were fleeing through the countryside, still bareheaded and without their cloaks.

The tumult was at its peak. The cool heads of the *Comune's* leaders reined the population's excesses. The cardinal of Florence called for resignation: was not the new pope an Italian, after all? The excitement dissipated and gave way to meek submission. On Easter Day, Urban VI could be crowned without incident. The conclave that had elected him was nonetheless to remain the strangest in history.

Urban was not an altogether restful pope; although Catherine of Siena called him "her most gentle father," he was endowed with a pride and a violence that were not long in provoking the gathering storm. Tired of his sharp ways, the French cardinals declared his election void and chose in his stead Robert of Geneva, under the name of Clement VII. This was the beginning of the great schism that was to rend Christendom for fifty years.

Urban VI's successors were determined to become the absolute masters of Rome, and they succeeded by destroying the city's freedoms one by one. This process did not go forward without interruptions and rebellions. An abortive plot by the Colonnas led to the confiscation of the family's possessions. There was fighting during the conclave of 1404, and there was a popular rising the next year during which the basilica of St. Peter's was besieged and the cardinals' palaces were burned. The pope having fled to Viterbo, the rebels were split by dissensions: there were barricades everywhere in the city and anarchy prevailed. All this turmoil was concluded by the return of Innocent VII, who abolished Roman autonomy. Papal absolutism was then threatened by the nobility. In 1407 the Colonnas attacked Castello Sant'Angelo, which was defended by the Orsinis. King Ladislas of Naples took a hand in the matter: he arrived before Rome with a strong army that was not called on to prove its valor, for the Orsinis came to financial terms with it, in accord with the deplorable custom of the time.

A sterner ordeal befell Rome five years later. The schism that divided the church was at its climax; there were now three popes: the Council of Pisa, which had undertaken to restore unity, had chosen a new one, Alexander V, who was supposed to replace the two others. He attempted to do so without success, but his successor, John XXIII, who in his youth had been a brilliant practitioner of the profession of piracy, managed to establish himself in Rome in 1411. Thereupon Ladislas hastened up with a powerful army to indulge himself in a sack of Rome that was quite as harsh as that of Robert Guiscard and that exceeded even the great pillages of the Gothic times.

The sequel was no less painful; three parties were battling one another in Rome: that of the pope, that of the king of Naples, and that of the defenders of freedom. There was a succession of conspiracies and of executions. One group's leader, Braccio di Montone, profited by the anarchic condition of the city to proclaim himself its protector, a pleasant euphemism for an omnipotence of which he was preparing to take full advantage when a Neapolitan army under the high constable, Sforza, threw him out of Rome.

The Council of Constance ended the great schism in 1418. The new pope, Martin V, who had been recognized by the whole of Christendom and who had at first established himself in Florence, made his solemn entrance into Rome on September 29, 1420, through Porta del Popolo. After so many complots, so many rebellions, so many tempests, Rome had at last regained its popes. It was never again to lose them.

With the definitive return of the papacy Rome's Middle Ages ended. We have seen how intensely the city suffered under its ordeals. Feudal struggles, communal movements, savage customs, there as elsewhere, had followed the passionate, dramatic course that was characteristic of the age. Nevertheless, in many respects the history of medieval Rome remained dominated by the obsession with the great past. Still present in its memories, its legends, and its monuments, ancient Rome had retained its prestige; it had been the inspiration of the founders of the *Comune,* of Cola di Rienzo, and of all who had sought to regenerate the Roman people. In spite of its decline, Rome had retained in the world's eyes the universality and the primacy that were the heritage of twelve centuries of greatness. Throughout its ordeals the medieval city had preserved the traditions of the ancient city, adapting them to the new era. This, Léon Homo wrote, was what made "its historic interest and its imperishable greatness."

PART THREE

THE RENAIS-SANCE

CHAPTER 16

THE BEGINNINGS OF THE ROMAN RENAISSANCE

THE FIRST ARTISANS OF RENEWAL

The beginning of the Renaissance in Rome can be dated from the arrival of Pope Martin V. But he found his city in the tragic condition that we have described. Fewer than twenty thousand persons were living wretchedly within the walls with which Emperor Aurelian had sought to protect a population of two million. Many quarters were totally deserted; the scenes that had been the seat of Roman greatness were now no more than a spectacle of desolation and ruin. Flocks were pastured among the wreckage. The Forum was a meadow for cattle, *campo vaccino;* the Capitoline had become that hill for goats that is still remembered in the name of a street near the Tarpeian Rock, Monte Caprino. "The country had invaded the city." But already there were strange visitors wandering among these fields of ruins, making sketches of the scattered blocks and the prostrate statues. These were Florentine artists (Filippo Brunelleschi and Donato di Betto Bardi, known as Donatello, among others), who, without servile imitation of the ancient art, were to make the study of it the source of the elements of a new art that would be the art of the Renaissance. If Florence had been the first home of that art, Rome was to be its first school. It has been very aptly said that it was not antiquity alone but its alliance with the Italian and especially the Roman spirit that regenerated the West.

Rome was awaiting only the return of its popes to come back to life: the tithes and the offerings whose sources had been stopped by the great schism began to flow again and brought back prosperity. Occupying a throne that had been consolidated and reinforced, Martin V could assist this renewal with his wise measures. Having seen in Florence the joyous intellectual and artistic flight that illuminated the city of the Red Lily, he intended to join Rome to that movement, to lead the city back to a respect for antiquity that would inspire a new flowering of art. He undertook to restore the artistic riches that centuries of neglect had gravely sapped. On an old medieval structure in the square of the Holy Apostles he erected the great palace of his family (the Colonnas), which was to be entirely rebuilt in the eighteenth century. He repaired the worst-damaged churches, and he spent huge sums on the construction of the Conservators' Palace on the Capitoline and the reconstruction of the basilica of St. John Lateran, whose nave had twice been burned in the preceding century. For its decoration he called on artists from Verona, Umbria, and Tuscany. With them the spirit of the Renaissance entered Rome with its living art, rich and gay, in which nature and life had their places, and the histories of the saints were unfolded in "brilliant landscapes peopled with animals and birds." Clouded but fascinating, the first example of this Roman art has come down to us in that *Crucifixion* that is fading on the walls of a chapel of St. Clement.

Let us point out, as a turning point in the history of Rome, that Martin V did not install his residence in the Lateran, which had been the first home of the papacy. Fleeing its distasteful memories, undoubtedly desirous of renewing the institution, of purifying it, and of bringing it closer to St. Peter's, he established himself in the Vatican, thus preparing the way for the vast enlargements of the palace that would be carried out by his successors.

To the first of these, Eugene IV, we owe the bronze gate that still closes the main entrance of the basilica after some additions that harmonized it with the modern church in 1619. Eugene IV commissioned a Florentine artist, Antonio Filarete, to execute this work, which was set in place on June 26, 1445. It is also to this pope that we owe an intelligent restoration of the Pantheon: the dome, loosened by an earthquake, was reinforced; the columns of the façade were cleared of the hovels built against them. The approaches to the temple were cleared, and it was during this work that the soil beneath the square yielded the great porphyry urn that became the tomb of Clement XII in St. John Lateran and one of the two lions that Sixtus V later ordered installed at his fountain of Acqua Felice.

Eugene IV did not have the leisure to devote himself at length to the work of restoring the churches that were dear to him; nevertheless he commissioned the construction of the church of Sant'Onofrio (on the crest of the Janiculum) that still preserves "the charm of a hermitage that was in the spirit of its foundation." This pontificate was marred by conspiracies, revolts, and even a schism. The Colonnas were active once more, but without success; their palaces were sacked and their accomplices were drawn and quartered in St. Peter's Square. These violent actions led to a popular revolt to which the pope replied with a major excommunication and the closing of the churches. The Vatican thereupon was taken by storm in a riot and the pope was obliged to flee to Florence, where he died after having been replaced by the anti-pope, Felix V, on whom he incessantly called down maledictions.

In 1447 Nicholas V succeeded both the pope and the anti-pope: the latter was quite willing to resign for a high price. The conclave that elected Nicholas V had a comic aspect that is unique in the annals of the papacy. During his ceremonial investiture, the pope was supposed to take three coins from a purse and toss them to the crowd, saying: "Money is naught to me; what I have I give to the faithful." Taking the statement at face value, the crowd would then storm the residence of the prelate invested with the supreme honor and ransack it of everything: furniture, dishes, pictures; there would be nothing left but the walls. It goes without saying that, in anticipation of this foray, every cardinal who thought that he had any chance of elevation to the papacy would always take the precaution of removing everything of value from his house before the conclave began. Now it happened that the election of Nicholas V was announced by Prospero Colonna from the very window of the conclave hall. Since this window was quite high, the crowd did not hear the new pope's name clearly and assumed that it was Colonna himself, and his sumptuous palace was at once put to the sack. This, however, was no protection to that of Nicholas V, which was also thoroughly pillaged as soon as the truth became known. For the new pope's election was so great a surprise not only to the people but to himself that he had neglected the traditional precautions. Thus the misunderstanding gave the Roman throng a double chance at very rich prizes.

THE FIRST PLANS FOR ST. PETER'S

Nicholas V was the forerunner of that celebrated phalanx of popes who were to become "the Maecenases and the fathers of modern civilization in the west." It was the beginning of a time when the human spirit was filled with a passion for reconstruction out of its own ruins. In this vast desire for rebirth, a Greek scholar redeemed from oblivion, a forgotten manuscript rediscovered, an ancient marble brought to light were to be celebrated as so many victories. Perhaps this was illusion, but occasionally mankind is carried up by such illusions, which become the passion of an era. Cosmo de' Medici had dedicated himself to fostering this passion in Florence, whence it had spread over the western world. Nicholas V was the most complete personification of the Renaissance on the papal throne. He launched a genuine crusade against ignorance. Thanks to him, three thousand manuscripts were rescued from destruction; he paid five thousand ducats for the Hebrew manuscript of the Gospel According to St. Matthew. He was responsible for the foundation of the Vatican Library.

His enlightened love for the arts led him to conceive a project for the beautification of Rome that surpassed the ambitions of his greatest predecessors: a new city was to rise in the Citadel of Leo, "all in palaces, straight avenues, and porticoes." All of Rome was to be rejuvenated in huge construction undertakings. The basilica of St. Peter's was to be rebuilt on a new design and to be given a dome rivaling that of the cathedral of Florence. In order to carry out this magnificent program, the pope summoned a galaxy of Florentine artists to Rome under the direction of Leon Battista Alberti, one of the most talented artists of the Renaissance.

There was not enough money. But it poured in on the occasion of the jubilee of 1450. It has been remarked that these jubilees are the finest financial enterprises that the popes ever conceived. Nicholas V neglected nothing for the success of this one: circulars were distributed in every Christian kingdom. The ceremonials were to be of a splendor never before known: indulgences were assured to everyone who went to present gifts to St. Peter's and to pray in the three main churches of the apostle's city. The pilgrims responded to this appeal; a prodigious number of them poured into Rome; the success of the jubilee of 1300 was at least equaled. But the celebrations were darkened by a dramatic episode: several arches of Ponte Sant'Angelo collapsed one evening under the weight of the crowd, and many perished. But the jubilee had brought prosperity back to

Rome. A host of artists and merchants had flocked to the city and grown rich there. The population figures were rising from one day to the next: a thriving middle class and a competent artisan class were soon to reanimate a city that was once more alive and happy.

The pontifical treasuries were filled beyond all expectation, and the pope soon had his works in progress. Ground was broken in the apse of the basilica of St. Peter's; work began on the preparation of the great square that was to open in front of the *atrium* and in the center of which it was planned to erect the obelisk from Nero's circus. The death of Nicholas V in 1455 interrupted this laudable endeavor, and all that was left was magnificent plans and a chaotic unfinished project.

The only structure that had been completed in the Vatican was the austere brick building that looks out on the court of the Belvedere and that contains Raphael's "rooms." The escutcheon with the two crossed keys still adorns the pediment of the simple, severe structure, which was to be the popes' residence during the most brilliant period of the Renaissance. Nicholas V had had its walls decorated by the greatest painters of his time. Only one has preserved its original decoration: it is in the chapel in which Fra Angelico portrayed the lives of St. Clement and St. Lawrence in beautiful high colors. Everything here is calm and serene, "even," as some have put it, "the torturers." The Florentine monk's eyes were receptive to the new art, but perhaps he lost some of his freshness of soul in contact with it. He was to die in Rome in 1455; his modest gravestone is in the Minerva among so many more grandiose monuments. Perhaps it would be more at home in Florence, in that cloister of the monastery of St. Mark where he decorated each cell with a scene from the Gospels, reserving for his own the depiction of the kiss of Judas.

Nicholas V was to die only a little time after the painter of madonnas and angels who was his friend and whose epitaph he composed. Though time was lacking to him for the completion of his great designs, it was at the same time he who was responsible for the shaping of certain quarters, notably the Campo dei Fiori. He had this area, abandoned to cattle, cleaned and paved; new houses rose there at once, particularly the Albergo del Sole, one of the oldest hotels in Rome. It was during his pontificate that work was begun on the charming Palazzo Capranica, near the Pantheon, whose remains, with the Palazzo Venezia, constitute the sole Roman evidences of the transition from medieval to Renaissance architecture.

The fall of Constantinople on May 29, 1453, undoubtedly hastened the pope's death. The Turks' appearance in force on the European stage was a major event, and it manifested a danger whose extent was understood by the popes alone. Henceforth their great concern was to be the task of forcing the princes of Europe to abandon their petty ambitions and uniting them against the new enemy who was threatening all of them. Nicholas V was not the least dedicated in the call for union of all Christian souls against the infidel.

THE PALAZZO VENEZIA AND THE CARNIVAL

While the popes who succeeded him in the fifteenth century were as steeped as he in the spirit of crusade, none of them before Sixtus IV thought of resuming the work of beautification that had been left barely begun at the death of Nicholas V. The only one of them who had a liking for large construction, Paul II, a Venetian, neglected the Vatican in order to concentrate his effort near the Capitoline, where he erected the gigantic palace which was known as Palazzo Venezia after Pius IV granted it to the Most Serene Republic to be used as the latter's embassy. It is the great architectural achievement of the fifteenth century; it still makes a noble appearance in Rome. Its severe façade is topped with battlements, like a fortress; the dawning art of the Renaissance displays its refinements in the great courtyard, where stories of triumphal arches recall the relief and the power of the Empire's monuments. The palace included an annex, the little palace of St. Mark (or Venice), which was demolished in 1911 because it was hiding Victor Emmanuel's monument. Rebuilt at the end of the *piazzetta,* it is now the headquarters of the National Institute of Archeology. In a corner of this *palazzetto* there is an antique bust that may be part of a huge statue of Iris but that Romans have familiarly christened Signora Lucrezia. In the seventeenth and eighteenth centuries it was used as a place on which to post satirical pamphlets, like other so-called speaking statues (Pasquino, Marforio, and Abbot Luigi) whose remarks we shall have ample occasion to recall.

At the same time that he was building the Palazzo Venezia, Paul II ordered the restoration of the church of St. Mark that adjoins it. This was an ancient shrine founded in the fourth century, and repaired once in the Middle Ages, when it acquired its Roman bell tower. Paul II endowed it with its very noble façade of a double row of archwork, probably the creation of Alberti. When the Palazzo Venezia was completed, Cardinal

Barbo hired the artists who had worked on it to decorate the house of the Knights of Rhodes with the elegant loggia whose archways dominate the whole landscape of the imperial forums.

In order to build the Palazzo Venezia, stones had been torn out of the Colosseum; for its decoration the ancient buildings had been stripped of all the objects of art that they still held. Paul II added many others taken from his private collections, which were extremely rich. His emissaries scoured the world in pursuit of antique sculptures, Byzantine paintings, precious manuscripts, and miniatures. The time was favorable to such searches; the Ottoman invasions were inundating the West with artistic works rescued from monasteries.

Paul II has been called at once the Narcissus and the Lucullus of the popes. Indeed he loved all forms of luxury: his table was opulent, his dress was elegant, he had ordered his tiara from Ghiberti* and had it adorned with precious stones valued at one hundred and twenty thousand gold ducats. It was he who granted the cardinals the privilege of having red silk miters, purple *birette,* and golden stirrups. In love with splendor and highly skilled at using it for the enhancement of his reputation, he introduced the celebrations of the carnival in Rome; he wished these to be gay but in good taste, in the style for which his compatriots, the Venetians, had set the model. Having enlarged and straightened the Corso that is named for him, he inaugurated the cavalcade of the *barberi* (Berbers) there in 1468. The Romans, unfortunately, possessed none of that Venetian secret of buffoonery that retains a certain wit. They had a predilection for vulgar spectacles and this was to be reflected in their carnival. It was only a few years before it was augmented with horse, buffalo, and donkey races, then with children's and old men's races in competition for the *pallio,* a piece of fabric presented by a senator to the most agile. Later the carnival was enlivened with Jews' races. As time went on, the pleasures of the carnival were to become more and more frenetic, finally deserving the harsh judgment of Goethe, who wrote at the end of one day of it: "I have spent the day with madmen." Paul II died of apoplexy in 1471, when he was only fifty-five years old. Let us remember that he confirmed Louis XI of France and his successors in the title of "eldest son of the church."

* Lorenzo Ghiberti was a Florentine architect, sculptor, and painter.—Translator.

CHAPTER 17

THE GREAT REIGN OF SIXTUS IV

THE INCEPTION OF THE PAPAL COURT

The three popes who reigned during the thirty final years of the fifteenth century had to concern themselves extensively with temporal matters. We need not go into the details of their politics. Their domestic work is enough to occupy our attention: a vast body of work that was to bring about a complete transformation of Rome. In three decades the city was to lose its characteristics of a medieval citadel and to become a modern capital. This evolution was to affect external appearances quite as much as the manners and morals of its inhabitants. A whole luxurious papal court was to be created and all classes were to cluster round it in order to serve it and to profit by its expenditures. Gradually the noblemen would abandon their plotting in order to become the gentlemen of this court; the mass, busy with lucrative employments and plentifully amused, would show only the rarest tokens of independence. Men of letters and arts were to become courtiers. Rome was to be covered with palaces; literary salons and studios would become as numerous as public holidays. Life was to become easy and gay in spite of some dramatic resurgences of disorder.

But the first successor to Paul II, Francesco della Rovere, who became pope in 1471 under the name of Sixtus IV, did not seem destined to put much life into his capital. His religious career had shown proof of a high degree of piety, and he had made himself famous for the zeal with which he had defended what was later to become the dogma of the Immaculate Conception. He was considered highly competent to maintain the spiritual interests of the church, and there was no reason to expect that his pontificate would be directed toward any other ends. Contrary to all anticipations, from the moment of his elevation he revealed an aggressive character that he dedicated to high political aims. His wars have been ascribed to his deep desire to provide a large fortune for each of his nephews. But such an attribution confuses the means employed with the ends in view.

The exile of the popes had not benefited their temporal affairs. When they returned to Rome they found a nobility in turmoil, constantly determined to work only for its own ends. Having become inordinately rich, the Colonnas and the Orsinis were maintaining veritable armies; they had even entered into alliances with neighboring princes, just as if they were themselves sovereign states. What was even more alarming was the fact that they were no longer such bitter rivals that the popes could rely on the one in order to subdue the other. Outside Rome the situation was no more favorable. A number of papal cities had profited by the popes' absence, and then by their problems, to become independent. Some had become feudal domains or independent principalities; others had stopped paying the Holy See the taxes stipulated by their vassaldom. Thus far no pope had attempted to rectify this deplorable situation; the majority of them had come to St. Peter's throne in their declining years and had reigned only briefly. Sixtus IV was only fifty-seven years old when he was elevated, and he was in exceptional health; he set himself the mission of regaining mastery over his states and even of enlarging them. It was his dream to expand the pontifical realm into new territories that would be bound to it by ties of obedience and that would in a way serve as its satellites.

To this end he required reliable men, and he believed that his nephews (of whom he had many; some were supposed to be his sons) would be more devoted than others to his purposes. That was why he took great pains to give them the highest ecclesiastical offices and the richest benefices, until such time as he could name them princes or kings. Such generosity was by no means unusual, but thus far the popes had confined themselves to relieving their relatives of want when they were poor or of assuring respect for them when they were rich. In defiance of these traditions, Sixtus distributed offices to them so lavishly and so shamelessly that it is legitimate to say that Roman nepotism in its most cynical form goes back to him.

Thus established, the popes' nephews lost no time in setting up luxurious modes of living. It was not that their new wealth went to their heads; their prodigalities were calculated, designed to overawe Italy and enhance the renown of the Holy See and its magnificence. It was in pursuance of this promotional plan that Sixtus IV himself had installed a luxurious court. Although he did not share his predecessor's taste for precious stones and jewels, his tiara was as sumptuous as that of Paul II. For his private apartments he had splendid tapestries sent from Bruges, and he commissioned rare marbles and precious silverware in Italy. This sumptuous environment was to determine what would be the morals of the Roman court for centuries: the conspiracies veiled in the splendor of the ceremonials, the stratagems cloaked in mildness, the wary maneuvers, the perfidy masked in politeness.

In the pursuit of his chimerical political ends, Sixtus IV was to commit himself to an unending series of military operations that were seldom successful. The recruiting of armies and the price of his exigent *condottieri* soon bled the papal treasury dry. He had to increase existing taxes and then to levy new ones. When these revenues were no longer adequate, he did not hesitate to open bidding for posts in the chancery and the papal court that had hitherto been awarded for merit alone. But his needs continued to rise, and so he created new offices in the apostolic chamber and sold them at high prices. When he died, though he had been unable to accomplish his arrogant plans, his debts amounted to more than 150,000 ducats.

In spite of these serious financial problems, he was never frugal with the church's money or his own. His liberality, which was often rash, earned him among the Romans a popularity that was not impaired by certain inconsistencies: he issued sumptuary decrees to restrict the luxuries of women and celebrations even when his own court was offering the spectacle of the most extravagant prodigality.

The dignitaries of this court—the pope's nephews, incredibly rich cardinals, ostentatious Roman princes—extended the pontifical splendor to their own huge and luxurious palaces, and often their pleasures overflowed into the streets, to the great joy of the population. There were exotic dances at street intersections, tournaments in the square of the Holy

Apostles. Sorrowing minds deplored a reversion to paganism, but their criticisms were blown away in the great wind of the Renaissance.

THE JUBILEE OF 1475 / THE PONTE SISTO / THE SISTINE CHAPEL

Sixtus relied heavily on the jubilee of 1475 to refill the papal treasury. In order to strengthen the prospects for its success, he launched vast enterprises for the beautification of the city as soon as he had been crowned. Paraphrasing the famous remark of Augustus, a flatterer observed that, having received a capital of mud, Sixtus intended to leave a capital of brick. There is no question that the pope allocated vast sums to great city-planning projects and that he contributed his own effort, his vigilance, his tenacity, and his laudable desire to involve the most eminent artists of the time in his work.

One of his first acts was to give the city of Rome some ancient statues of great value, or, rather, to return them to the municipal authorities, since it was generally held that all the relics of its past greatness were the city's property. Restitution or gift, these statues were to represent the beginnings of the Capitoline museums. The Capitoline already had the lion devouring a horse, and two urns that came from the tomb of Augustus; one of the urns had held the ashes of the first Agrippina, the wife of Germanicus. This embryo of a museum was enriched by Sixtus IV with a number of pieces that are still its jewels, such as the statue of the thorn remover, the colossal head of Nero, and above all the famous Roman wolf that, after having adorned the temple of Jupiter, had endured numerous wanderings. The inscription that records the generosity of Sixtus IV does not exaggerate his merits. He was indeed the creator of that Capitoline Museum in which Greece and Rome are as splendid as in the Vatican or in the Museum of the Baths.

As in the previous period, Rome's streets were still narrow, twisting, unhealthy; the squares were too often used as dumping grounds; the churches, which were far too many, were crumbling everywhere. In the brief time remaining before the jubilee, Sixtus IV could not hope to make any perceptible change in the appearance of his capital. He had to confine himself to what was essential. The most urgent need was the improvement of communications between the two banks of the Tiber, which was crossed by only three bridges. In order to prevent the repetition of a disaster like the one that had cast a pall over the jubilee of 1450, it was decided to match Ponte Sant'Angelo, which was most used by pilgrims, by rebuilding the ancient bridge of Aurelius, first built by Caracalla, from which it had been the custom to hurl Christians into the river during the times of the persecutions. The rebuilt structure was named by the pope for himself: Ponte Sisto. Inaugurated with much pomp, the span had been built quickly—no doubt somewhat too quickly, for it had to be extensively repaired in 1477 because of serious flaws.

To give air to the old city, Sixtus IV cut through the Field of Mars with the long, straight road that has become Via dei Coronari, one of the most picturesque streets of Rome. It still has houses contemporary with its construction: freed of the defensive works that burdened the houses of the previous period, they open freely on the street, and they were already decorated with the *grisaille* paintings* that were to become the fashion of the next century. Such were the dwellings of the humanists of the Renaissance, the most finished model of which is the pleasant house of Cardinal Bessarion with its large Guelph-cross windows looking out over Porta San Sebastiano; its large loggia of four arches supported by antique columns; its garden blooming with roses—the delightful setting where learned friends met to discuss Plato in comfort.

The great concept of Sixtus IV was the transformation of the Vatican. Throughout his reign he was unceasingly to make it the object of substantial expenditures, which were to increase every year until they reached two thousand gold florins. The greatest task was executed before the jubilee in the legitimate endeavor to let the faithful see their pope in a residence that was worthy of him. The work of Sixtus IV continued that of Nicholas V; it retained the warlike aspect of a brick bastion pierced with rare windows and topped by battlements. But the interior arrangements contradicted the severity of the outside with the richness of the woodwork and stained glass, the sumptuousness of the pictorial decoration. The jewel is the great chapel, which has become the Sistine Chapel and which was the pope's favorite among all his endeavors. On the day of its inauguration in 1473 so huge a crowd pressed into it that for a moment it was feared that none would get out alive. It was only at the end of the pope's reign that it was to acquire the admirable frescoes that made it the marvel that we know. Similarly, the library was to be completed only later; nevertheless, it was

---

* A technique intended to create bas-relief and sculptural effects.—Translator.

already equipped at the time of the jubilee with twenty-five hundred volumes that had to be protected by a papal bull against the casual ways of bishops and humanists, too often inclined to keep the books that they had borrowed from it.

In anticipation of the pilgrims' arrival, the most dilapidated churches had been hastily repaired, the filthiest quarters had been cleaned, the squares had been cleared of their garbage, and a number of feudal towers had been torn down. And the pope had been scrupulous in affixing his signature to each of these admirable improvements, strewing the arms of his family everywhere; many of these shields are still set into modern walls. Thus, by giving it an unprecedented diffusion, he established the fashion that has endowed the pediment of every Roman building with the arms of the pope or the cardinal who erected it, beautified it, or simply repaired it. The visitor to Rome quickly learns to recognize the five balls of the Medicis, the oak of the Roveres, the eagle and the dragon of the Borgheses, the bees of the Barberinis, the *fleurs-de-lys* of the Farneses. All these benefactors of the arts have made certain that posterity should not be ignorant of their good works. It was a mania that sometimes led to rather ridiculous excesses: Stendhal professed to have seen on the Quirinal "some bad benches in painted wood, worth perhaps twelve francs," that bore the name of the pope who had had them put there.

Sixtus IV seemed all the more the "founder of a new Rome" because he never missed an occasion to reiterate his resolve to spare no expense in order to make the city worthy of its rank as the capital of the world. In the jubilee year, eminent visitors thronged to Rome one after another throughout the summer. They included Eleanor of Aragon, King Christian I of Dacia, the king of Naples, the duke of Urbino, the marquis of Mantua, and all the important princes and potentates of the peninsula. The cardinals insisted on offering them the hospitality of their palaces. The pope's nephews made a special effort in magnificence: one of them, Pietro Cardinal Riario, had hung all the rooms of his palace with damask and tapestry; the square in front had been entirely roofed and boarded over for the service of exquisite banquets followed by spectacles.

Each arrival of a visiting prince or sovereign was celebrated with processions and illuminations. There was a revival of the mule trains that in antiquity carried the tributes of conquered countries to Rome. Loaded with imitation treasures, the animals wore the papal arms. There were performances of Christ's birth and of His resurrection. Secular pleasures, especially horse racing, were not overlooked.

These brilliant feasts with all their color brought out the pope, the cardinals, and the upper clergy in all possible pomp. Nothing was left undone to celebrate the glory of the papacy and of Rome. Nevertheless, in spite of great tides of pilgrims at certain times, the total of visitors remained consistently well below expectations. In those troubled times the roads were anything but safe, for war was always going on somewhere in Europe. The offerings collected were not enough to fill the pontifical vaults, the huge food supplies that had been collected lay untouched, prices tumbled so hard that, instead of making fortunes, the merchants found themselves ruined. To climax all the ill fortune, a dramatic flood of the Tiber cut short the jubilee and sent the pilgrims into disorderly rout.

The flood destroyed the crops; hunger followed, leading to a disastrous epidemic. In order to escape infection the pope had to leave Rome on June 10, 1476, and wander from city to city throughout the summer. In his absence misery increased, the epidemic redoubled its force, deaths became so many that there were no longer men to carry away the corpses. Soon came the disorders that are the mandatory corollary of great crises: violence in the streets, pillage in the houses.

The pope's return in October, the timely measures that he took to assure the city of food, the end of the hot weather, which terminated the epidemic—all these factors helped Rome to regain its balance and its calm. Once again the streets gleamed with the gold of princes' and cardinals' processions through the city. Burghers, shopkeepers, and workers left their tasks whenever there was an opportunity to take part in a celebration, and for this an occasion always offered. In 1477 there was a particularly splendid one to inaugurate the market in Piazza Navone. The recently created Communal Council took part in its full strength; it was subsequently to play an important part, but at this time its 155 members had neither a place in which to meet nor a function to perform, except one that they had devised for themselves: to confer the title of "Roman citizen." Gerolamo Riario, the pope's nephew and the chief instrument of his military policy, was the first foreigner to be invested with this honor.

THE GREAT WORKS OF SIXTUS IV / SANTA MARIA DEL POPOLO / SANTA MARIA DELLA PACE

At one and the same time the pope was busy with his diplomatic intrigues, his military expeditions, and his transformation of the capital, in which he expended an indefatigable zeal. Under his guidance, the narrow little alleys gave way to new arteries built at great expense. The sewers were restored to operation, the breaches in the city walls were repaired, the aqueducts were made to function again. The San Spirito hospital had been rebuilt and had become the leading such institution in Europe. The Tabularium had been completely renovated for its new function as a salt storehouse. The Lateran Palace had been restored; the side aisles of the basilica had acquired stone pavements. Not even Marcus Aurelius' horse was overlooked in the solicitude of Sixtus IV. It had been lying in the dirt in the Lateran Square, in piteous state; it was erected at the site now occupied by the Lateran obelisk: it is shown there in Filippino Lippi's fresco in the church of the Minerva.

Sixtus IV had sworn a great adoration to the Virgin. It is not surprising that he showed special interest in the churches dedicated to her. On the sanctuary that Paschal II had built in the eleventh century in order to exorcise Nero's soul, which, according to popular belief, was unpleasantly haunting the area, Sixtus built the church of Santa Maria del Popolo, which is very representative of various aspects of Renaissance art; its chapels are a veritable museum of it. Since this is the first manifestation of the custom, let us mention here the habit that was to lead every great family of Rome to reserve as its own a chapel bearing its name in the church that it most preferred and to assume the cost of its decoration. The chapels of Santa Maria del Popolo are filled with masterpieces; they contain works by Caravaggio and by that Pinturicchio whose art appears again in the Sistine Chapel. Raphael's work dominates in all its three aspects (sculpture, painting, architecture) and makes the Chigi chapel one of the most interesting in Rome.

In the period of the most virulent quarrels among the Christian princes, Sixtus IV had taken a vow to build a church to Mary if peace could be established among them. It is to the execution of this vow we owe the precious church of Santa Maria della Pace, near Piazza Navone, where Raphael's Sibyls are. The pope had the miraculous image of the madonna of peace placed above the main altar, where young bridal couples often go to hear their first mass in order to assure the harmony of their marriages.

Sixtus IV also built (in Via Carlo Alberto) the church of San Vito. Set into its wall and worn by the hands of the faithful is the *Pietra scellerata*, which was supposedly employed for the agony of so many Christians. It is interesting to trace the origin of this legend in a simple modification of language. San Vito is built on the site of the ancient market of Livia (Macellum Liviae). Now in the Middle Ages the word *macellum* changed its meaning from *market* to *slaughterhouse* (Italian *macello*). Hence the name of San Vito in Macello stimulated the popular imagination to scenes of carnage, and it was this confusion that gave the *pietra scellerata* its undeserved reputation. We might add that it is reputed to cure the bites of mad dogs.

Sixtus IV rebuilt a great number of churches: St. Susanna, San Vitale, St. Balbinus, and many others. These restorations bore the stamp of the new architecture: the transposition of the medieval silhouette into Renaissance forms is clearly visible in it. The graceful bell tower that Sixtus IV added to the San Spirito hospital when he rebuilt it is very characteristic of this evolution. The pope was actively seconded in his work by the very wealthy cardinals of his court. To one of them, a Frenchman named d'Estouteville, he had entrusted the supervision of all the great projects in Rome. Since this Frenchman was the richest among all the princes of the church, he naturally added his own contribution to the funds that had been allotted to him. He even, at his own expense, built the church of St. Augustine, whose very dignified and beautiful façade, in travertine taken from the Colosseum, is one of the outstanding ones of the Renaissance. It was inspired, like that of Santa Maria del Popolo (both are by the same architect, Pietrasanta), by those Florentine façades whose model had been provided by Alberti in Santa Maria Novella. Its pride is the richest madonna in Rome, the Madonna del Parto, which sparkles with diamonds, rubies, and topazes, and which heals children and makes women fertile. Behind it the wall disappears in an armor of *ex-voto* offerings in the form of hearts. These treasures eclipse Bernini's main altar and even more the tomb of Santa Monica, which attracts hardly any attention from the faithful.

However generous Cardinal d'Estouteville was, he was unable to keep all the promises that had been got out of him. When it was felt necessary to establish a market in Piazza Navone, he declared himself willing to finance its construction, but no one ever saw his money. Sixtus IV himself was inclined to dodges of this nature. When he was reproached for the nonpayment of a pension that he had awarded, he replied: "I did indeed promise it to you, but I never committed myself to see that it was paid to you." It was a time when the pledged word did not count for much.

The pope often tried to disencumber the papal treasury of enterprises that he urged others to finance instead. Thus he was at the origin of the church of St. Louis of the French in that he donated the site on which it was to be built; but no one was in a hurry, and the first stone of the French national church in Rome was not put in place for forty years. Sixtus IV was luckier with the devout sovereigns of Spain, who built the church of San Pietro in Montorio about 1475 on ground that he had given them on the Janiculum; more than a century later the remains of Beatrice Cenci were to be buried there. Until the end of the eighteenth century the main altar was adorned with Raphael's *Transfiguration* (now in the Vatican). Next to this church stands Bramante's little round temple, through which a Franciscan monk now guides visitors as he bewails the fact that it is no longer regarded as the site of St. Peter's crucifixion.

SIXTUS IV AND FOREIGN ARTISTS

The work of Sixtus IV was not restricted to the building and restoring of churches; it was above all their interior decoration that was to enrich Rome's artistic heritage during his reign. All the arts were to collaborate in adorning sanctuaries and palaces with masterpieces. But the least part of this artistic flowering was that of artists native to the city. The popes' exile in Avignon and the troubled periods that had followed had interrupted the Roman artistic tradition. At a time when the smallest cities in Italy were enjoying flourishing schools, Rome was sterile. It was in order to remedy this deficiency that Sixtus IV invited to Rome the artists of all the Italian cities. In point of fact, the Florentine sculptors and painters had begun flocking there during the pontificate of Nicholas V. It was this trend, much augmented by Sixtus IV and continuing after his death, that was to place the city of the popes, especially in terms of sculpture, at the head of the Renaissance.

Even a huge volume could not list all the riches of this Roman sculpture of the fifteenth century. It included not only the vast gallery of the tombs of great men; tabernacles, statues of saints, mural friezes that are real pictures in marble survive in very great number, adorning churches or prisoned in the Vatican grottoes beneath the pavement of the basilica. Restricting ourselves only to the time of Sixtus IV, let us mention the railings of his Vatican chapel, the tomb of Cristoforo della Rovere in Santa Maria del Popolo, and that of Cardinal Forteguerri in St. Cecilia in Trastevere, all the work of Mino da Fiesole, as are also, probably, the bas-reliefs in the chancel of Santa Maria Maggiore, of which it has been said that they join the richness of a Renaissance procession to the artlessness of a children's story. Andrea Bregno of Lombardy, who lies in the church of the Minerva not far from Fra Angelico, has left us Pietro Riario's tomb in the church of the Holy Apostles, Giovanni Battista Cardinal Savelli's in the Ara Coeli, and many others.

The foreign contribution was even more important in painting. The pope had established the San Luca academy of painting in Rome, but it was not to the members of that brotherhood that he entrusted the task of decorating the Vatican palace. He summoned Melozzo da Forlì from Umbria to paint his library: only one part of the frescoes that clothed its halls has come down to us; it is now in the Vatican's picture gallery and it shows the pope investing Platina with the function of papal librarian.

The success of these frescoes was so tremendous that it is impossible to understand why Sixtus IV barred their inspired creator from the gigantic work that he was about to undertake: the decoration of the great Sistine Chapel, which had finally been completed after twelve years of toil. But politics has its own exigencies, which, in this instance, did not coincide with artistic taste. The great conflict between the Holy See and Lorenzo il Magnifico had ended in a spectacular reconciliation. Sixtus IV deemed it expedient to organize artistic exchanges between Rome and Florence as an overture to more intimate collaborations. For the decoration of his chapel he called on three Florentine painters—Cosimo Rosselli, Sandro Botticelli, and Domenico Ghirlandaio—and an Umbrian, Pietro Vannucci, known as Perugino. They arrived accompanied by their assistants, who were by no means mediocre artists—their number included Piero di Cosimo and Pinturicchio. They completed their work in 1483; it was of such quality that it can still be seen in the chapel, with the exception of the frescoes in the chevet, which have been covered by Michelangelo's *Last Judgment,* and those of the far wall, which vanished when the wall collapsed in 1522. Sixtus IV had stipulated the theme to be illustrated, while at the same time allowing complete freedom of execution to the artists whom he had chosen. The Sistine frescoes would be enough to assure their glory, even if the churches and museums of Florence, Perugia, and other cities were not filled with their works. It seems, however, that the painters of the Sistine lost something of their ease in Rome, just as Fra Angelico had lost something of his animation there. They had exchanged the Medici court, which was then at the peak of its brilliance, and their joyful, enthusiastic towns for an austere palace, bartering a free life for a rather confined existence. The pope was offering them only money, whereas the princes whom they had left had paid them as well with friendship. It is not surprising that Botticelli's frescoes did not have the charm of his *Primavera* and that Ghirlandaio's *Vocation of the Apostles* does not overshadow Oggioni's *Supper.* Nonetheless the Sistine frescoes are magnificent in their sumptuousness; the art of the Renaissance bursts out of them in the fullness of its "insolent and profane" vitality. Never, it has been said, have walls been hung so splendidly.

From now on the Italian painters would flock to Rome and make it the great studio of the Renaissance. Overwhelmed with commissions, they could not execute them entirely themselves; so they looked for collaborators in the city. It was their studios that would be the training grounds for a galaxy of Roman artists who would bring back to life the tradition of their ancestors of the previous century. At the same time, under the patronage of St. Luke the Evangelist, an association of painters and miniaturists with a dozen patrons was being formed. But it seems likely that very few of the members of this corporation were real artists. They painted pictures, perhaps, but they were chiefly concerned with selling them and with destroying the competition of the second-hand dealers and the color sellers. Whence one must conclude that the sale of objects of art was a profitable business in Rome under Sixtus IV.

There were others: the substantial rise in the population had brought prosperity to the artisan trades and to commerce; workshops had been opened almost everywhere by wool merchants, dressers of skins, potters, iron workers, saddlers, and candle makers. The cardinals and their retinues and the officials of the papal court were the best customers of the luxury trades. The middle classes saw to the rebuilding of their houses and spent large sums on decorating them; their women took a lively interest in jewelry. As prosperity went on and on and Rome grew rich again, it paid little attention to the political and military movements with which its pope was always busy in his unremitting pursuit of his dream of hegemony.

THE UNEASY END OF THE PAPACY OF SIXTUS IV

Unfortunately, the king of Naples led his armies to the walls of Rome in the spring of 1482; access to the neighboring countryside was barred to the Romans, who, from the tops of their towers, could watch the enemy harvesting for himself the wheat that they had sown. The papal forces had been consolidated inside the wall. For a while burghers and artisans were pleased by the presence of the men at arms: it was entertaining to visit their camp, to be invited to dinner in their tents, to marvel at their cannon as at curiosities of some sort. Idlers treated themselves to the pleasure of watching from the ramparts the spectacle of skirmishes in the neighborhood of the aqueduct of Claudius. But these pleasures soon palled when their inescapable price had to be paid in the form of the soldiery's debauches, the higher cost of food, and then its strict rationing. Then came what was regarded as the heroic sacrifice of suspending horse racing, and recrimination set in; eating black bread, which everyone said was bad for the health, people began to accuse the pope of speculation in wheat. Soon there was an epidemic, which was ornamented, according to the custom, with the name of *plague,* and which damaged the morale of the besieged quite as badly as the terrible storm of August 16, 1482, which incited a panic: men went mad, and others were sure they were dead.

Five days later the pope's *condottiere,* the invincible and magnificent Malatesta, defeated the Neapolitans in the brilliant but not very bloody battle of Campo Marte. The Romans forgot their sufferings in the intoxication of victory. The pope ordered them to rejoice in celebration of the triumph: he was obeyed with zeal. The explosion of joy was premature; the war was resumed and Rome was invested again at the beginning of the winter. Once more the Romans were short of food; in addition, there was no more wood for heating. To crown the catastrophe, the taverns had to close because they could get no wine. All these things so irritated the people that the sovereign pontiff no longer felt safe in his own capital. But the so-called perpetual peace was proclaimed unexpectedly on November 28 and the popular irritation was transformed into enthusiasm. In all these excitements the Romans had regained their traditional talent for quarrels. In the time of Cola di Rienzo they had been known to kill one another in competition for a look at a dromedary. During the carnival of 1483 the residents of the Monti quarter and those of Trastevere fought a pitched battle that was motivated (if one dare use the word) by some trivial discussion about the bulls that were supposed to run in the next day's races. The funeral of the old Cardinal d'Estouteville on January 22, 1483, was the occasion of fierce fighting when the Dominicans of Santa Maria Maggiore battled the Augustinian brothers for possession of the gold brocade cloak in which the corpse was wrapped. The crowd having joined in, there was general fist fighting, spiced with sword play. When the corpse finally arrived at the church it was naked of all the ornaments with which it had started out. Not only the brocade cloak, the original *casus belli,* but also the miter and even the rings had vanished.

Disorders acquired a graver course in the following year, when the Colonnas and the Orsinis took it upon themselves to settle in Rome that controversy over the city of Alba that divided them. Sixtus IV, aligning himself with the Orsinis, ordered the sack of all quarters loyal to the Colonnas; every Roman who had a taste for looting stormed their palace and overwhelmed it after having killed forty of its defenders. Before they set it on fire—it was to burn for five days—they stripped it of everything that was in it: silver, furniture, carpets, jewels. The Colonnas' other houses in Rome were subjected to the same fate. The churches of which they were the patrons were also sacked, and sacred objects and relics were destroyed or stolen. Their friends' houses were also devastated. The violence continued for months and claimed victims all over the city, Paolo Orsini having hired foreign thugs who impartially attacked friend and enemy. Soon there was not a cow or a donkey or a sheep left in Rome. This would have been only a minor misfortune if the looting had not been accompanied by murders.

In the midst of all these things Sixtus IV died an edifying death on August 12, 1484; his palace had been so thoroughly looted during his brief illness that neither his vestments nor his pastoral cross could be found. He was dressed in borrowed vestments and a guard had to be posted over the corpse to prevent the theft of the papal ring.

Antonio Pollaiuolo was to devote ten years to the creation of his tomb, which has been relegated to the Vatican grottoes since 1924. It is a work of audacious originality. For the first time, the deceased was portrayed stretched out on a large state bed of black bronze with a unique patina, surrounded by the theological and cardinal virtues. The pedestal of the monument was adorned with figures symbolizing the sciences whose study the pontiff had encouraged: theology, philosophy, arithmetic, dialectic, astronomy. In an allegory that is far from transparent, they carried quivers full of arrows.

CHAPTER 18

PRELUDE TO THE BORGIAS

MANNERS AND MORALS UNDER INNOCENT VIII

As successor to Sixtus IV the conclave selected Giovanni Battista Cibo (Innocent VIII), whose courtesy and gentleness were in happy contrast to the imperious nature of the defunct. These qualities of spirit had none of the happy results that were expected of them. The internal disorders that the rude ways of Sixtus IV had been unable to settle were aggravated by the lack of authority that the new pope evidenced beneath the disguise of his horror of conflict and his desire to displease no one. Even during the ceremony of his coronation the popular excitability burst out in significant demonstrations; the pope had barely dismounted when his horse and his scarlet portfolios were stolen; the traditional banquet was held amid extreme confusion. And yet Innocent VIII had thrown so much money to the people that he did not have even a florin for the traditional offering on the Lateran altar.

The lack of a supreme authority spurred the Colonnas and the Orsinis to renew their battles: again there were political murders and pitched battles in the streets of Rome. The war that the pope, in spite of his love of peace, intemperately launched against the king of Naples heightened the internal strife, which was made worse by the hunger that set in and by the plague that was its natural consequence. This time the Colonnas were on the side of the Holy See, while the Orsinis were now its enemies. Their troops were masters of the countryside, cutting off food supplies, threatening the city gates every day, occasionally infiltrating into the city. Cardinals escorted by men at arms could be seen going through the streets to maintain their safety. Their laudable efforts were no deterrent either of theft or of murder, or even of sacrilege. For it had now become a custom to force church doors at night and steal their valuable objects and even the sacred relics, as happened in Santa Maria in Traspontina. The Lateran treasury itself was not immune to search by freebooters. There was no great risk in this sort of thing: the pope issued bulls against the evildoers, of course, but justice was impotent to chastise them. The Capitoline magistrates and the ecclesiastical judges, who were divided by deep jurisdictional disputes, were concerned only with reducing each other to impotence. Furthermore they were equally venal: a death sentence could be bought off easily with the payment of two hundred ducats. "The sovereign," the governor of Rome declared, "desires not that the criminal die but that he pay." From time to time, it was true, there were bodies hanging from the windows of the Capitol or the gibbet on Monte Caprino, but there was never any way of knowing whether these were real criminals who had been unable to buy their way out or poor devils sacrificed to make an example. The archives of St. John the Beheaded throw no light on this question. A brotherhood attached to this church had assumed the mission of assisting criminals and keeping a register of executions. In compensation therefor it received title to the ropes used in the hangings.

Criminals of some importance found refuge in certain cardinals' palaces, and then they easily acquired papal bulls of absolution. In short, violence was tolerated and protected. Brutality was the rule of this strange society of the end of the fifteenth century. It dominated the highest ecclesiastical circles; the canons of St. John Lateran publicly battled the Conservators of the Capitoline and, in 1486, Rodrigo Cardinal Borgia and Cardinal de la Balue pummeled each other in the Sacred College itself.

Amid all this turmoil, Roman life was paradoxically organized according to a merry rhythm of entertainments and celebrations. The frenzies of rejoicings were so great that every year the period of carnival was lengthened. In 1487, although Easter fell on April 15, there were masquerades as early as Christmas. Overflowing the Corso, games were organized in every quarter. Those of the Testaccio were the most popular. From the top of the hill wagons were sent hurtling down, with pigs attached; the competitors' task was to try to detach the pigs as they passed and make off with them. It is easy to imagine the noise and the chaos of this sporting event.

Even while showing no aversion whatever to these coarse diversions, the people had a passion for spectacles of solemn pomp. This was a taste that the popes cultivated: each arrival of an ambassador, each princely visit, each investiture of cardinals produced a greater ostentation of bunting and triumphal arches along the route of the processions. And they were innumerable in those declining years of the century: the sojourn of Ercole d'Este; the wedding of Franceschetto, the pope's son, to the daughter of Lorenzo il Magnifico; the visit of Lorenzo's son, Pietro; the solemn entrance of the young Cardinal dei Medici. None of these events aroused more delight than the Turkish delegations. The first, Mustapha Bey's, had been accompanied, however, by certain fearful omens (stars had been seen in broad daylight) that had caused some to think that God might be vexed by the presence of Mussulmans in the capital of Christendom. For all that, the Romans had enthusiastically adopted the Turks and Turkishness. At carnival time there was nothing but Oriental costumes; the chronicles of the period talk only of the Turks, of their pleasant appearance and their sympathetic manners. Their popularity rose exceptionally in 1492, when a new deputation arrived to give the pope a piece of the spearhead that had pierced the side of Jesus. The precious relic was paraded through all the great arteries of Rome to the frenetic acclamation of a huge crowd, somewhat stimulated from having drunk the wine that was coming out of all the fountains that day instead of water. What it was most difficult to make the Romans accept was the absence of the Turks from the pope's procession: they were quite ready to accept the juxtaposition of infidels' turbans and bishops' miters. But the Turks were lustily cheered all the same.

While secular and religious celebrations kept the streets lively with popular rejoicing, Romans of all classes pursued less innocent pleasures in private. The city boasted more than six thousand courtesans of all categories, over whom absolutely no control was exercised. They were known as *donne di buon tempo* (good-time women), and the most sophisticated of them had made their way into good society. The clerics themselves did not find it unworthy of their sacred calling to have part- or full-time mistresses.

A certain corruption, in fact, had penetrated the papal court. Certainly it had not become that "sink of all the vices" that was denounced throughout Europe by propaganda with an ulterior motivation. But its morals were not restrictive. It was said that swindling was practiced even in the apostolic chamber, where there was supposed to be an organization of forgers complete with its own decoys and confidence men. No doubt there was a good deal of exaggeration in such stories; similarly, it was inaccurate to accuse all the members of the Curia of leading unfit lives. Truth compels the admission, however, that some cardinals were rather ostentatious in their luxury. That they were now clad "not in wool but in silk and brocade" would not have been a major matter, though a somewhat ingenuous chronicler of the time reproached them for it. But the very free tone of their way of living was certainly not overly edifying. Some were preceded by musicians and followed by a troop of gentlemen and jesters whenever they walked abroad in the streets. Ladies of convenient virtue and questionable young men were not always forbidden their company. They had in addition a true passion for gambling: Cardinal de la Balue lost eight thousand ducats in one night and Cardinal Riario won fourteen thousand in the same time. In short, the high clergy was beginning to earn by its conduct the reproaches of those who were already saying that "the church needed to be reformed."

THE PALACE OF THE CHANCELLERY

Just as "the elegant vice of the courtesans" stimulated the progress of the arts in the Renaissance, so the prodigality of the princes of the church encouraged the artists. In the eyes of an indulgent pope there could be no better pretext for exactions than the dedication of their proceeds to the enrichment of Rome with a palace, a church, a fresco, or a statue. When Rafaele Cardinal Riario won a fortune by gambling, the pope called on him to relinquish so ill-got a gain; the papal thunderbolts were silenced as soon as the nephew of Sixtus IV promised to invest his immoral winnings in the stones of a palace.

This palace, bigger even than Palazzo Venezia, was to remain the major work of secular architecture in the Renaissance: it is the Chancellery that stretches the calm and pure lines of its long façade along Corso Vittorio Emanuele. For the first time there is a sort of rhythm in the succession of bays: another innovation is that of the two foreparts "that enliven the wall with the play of light that they produce." The interior court is the most harmonious in Rome; "on the two stories of light archways, the wall garnished with pilasters inevitably recalls the upper part of the Colosseum" (*Itinéraires romains*). The nobility and the simplicity of the architecture are thrilling, like the majesty of the whole. It is the perfection of order and design. It has been said that architectonic forms "have never spoken a clearer language." The marble for its construction came from the recently unearthed arch of Gordianus, and forty-four columns of granite were taken from Pompey's portico. In spite of the objections based on the artist's biography, there can be no question that for the greater part the Chancellery was the work of the great Bramante, then just making his start in Rome, who was to leave so many marks of his genius in the Eternal City. Since the sixteenth century this palace has been the seat of the papal Chancellery. This occupancy was interrupted only during the time when Rome was the capital of a department of France: the inscription above the door, in which the words *Cour impériale* (imperial court) can be barely discerned, is a trace of the Napoleonic occupation.

At the same time that he was building this palace, Cardinal Riario commissioned the construction, on an ancient shrine of the fourth century, of the church of San Lorenzo in Damaso, which adjoins the church and communicates with it through the celebrated door of Giaconio da Vignola. This church was to be modernized by Valadier, then to be seriously damaged by fire in 1944; but its interior retains Bramante's curious design, a quadrilateral surrounded by a double portico.

Few members of the papal court could display splendor comparable to that of the Riarios and the della Roveres, whom their uncle, Sixtus IV, had loaded with wealth before he died poor. Many cardinals were to restrain their desire to leave some mark of magnificence for posterity to more modest evidences. Painters, sculptors, and marble makers served them well in these intentions. Rome's churches abound in altars, reredoses, and funeral monuments of the period. They came from the chisels of Antonio and Piero Pollaiuolo, Luigi Capponi, Andrea Bregno, and other talented artists. Altars and tabernacles in Santa Maria del Popolo, St. Agnes Outside the Walls, the Minerva, and the tombs of Cardinal de Coca and the Rusticis in the same Minerva are among the most striking works. For its paintings Rome had to summon back some of the artists who had worked for Sixtus IV and who had gone to various other cities after the dedication of the Sistine Chapel. In 1491 Perugino painted the charming triptych that is now in the collections of Villa Albani; Pinturicchio decorated the Bufalini chapel, in the church of Ara Coeli, with frescoes retracing the life of San Bernardino of Siena. Cardinal Caraffa had sent to Florence for Filippino Lippi, who gave the Minerva its frescoes consecrated to St. Thomas Aquinas, which are the finest jewels of his art. Since it was a custom of the time for the artist always to show in his works the generous donors who were paying for them, St. Thomas Aquinas has Cardinal Caraffa's face.

As for Innocent VIII, the chronic malnutrition of the pontifical finances hardly enabled him to embellish his capital. He managed nevertheless to complete the work that his predecessor had left unfinished in the Vatican; he even added a new wing whose four stories gave the palace the imposing aspect that until then had been wanting. This wing ran as far as the place where today the "bronze" gate is. At the summit of the Vatican hill, the pope had an old oil-storage place torn down and replaced by a small fortified villa from which the view was so extended and so beautiful that it was named Belvedere. A few years later Bramante was to join it to the Vatican through a magnificent complex of buildings.

On the Capitoline the pope ordered the restoration of the Tabularium and the tower ascribed to Nicholas V, which has since borne his arms. He enriched the museum with some antique ruins, notably a huge marble foot that had just been discovered and that was believed to have belonged to a statue of Apollo.

Throughout Rome substantial maintenance tasks were undertaken; streets and squares were paved, notably the Campo dei Fiori, which was the most popular open area in the city. During the repairs on the arch of the tribune of Santa Croce in Gerusalemme, workmen found the scroll of the cross that St. Helena, Emperor Constantine's mother, had brought back from the holy places.

In order to finance these undertakings, the pope created and sold new offices. Since these did not fulfill any need, he justified their creation by increasing the number of situations in which it was necessary to obtain a papal brief. Thus there grew up a papal bureaucracy whose exigencies were not to the taste of the Roman population. Always short of money, Innocent VIII was irregular in the settlement of his debts. Vasari* reports that one day the pope asked Andrea Mantegna what he intended to represent in a face that he had put into one of his pictures. His salary being long overdue, the artist replied that it symbolized parsimony.

---

* Giorgio Vasari was a contemporary painter, architect, and biographer and critic.—Translator.

"Well," the pope said, "give it patience for a neighbor; it will be in good company."

Innocent VIII had attracted scholars to Rome, such as Angelo Poliziano, a poet and humanist, and the Venetian Daniello Barbaro, whose scientific knowledge was the admiration of all Italy. He did not pay them, but he found work for them so that they could live. The Vatican librarians were Hellenists; reporters were added to the corps of apostolic secretaries. With a strange inconsistency, this pope, who loved literature, allowed the printing industry that Germans had established in Rome to decline, after a brief prosperity, and it emigrated to other Italian cities, such as Florence, where it received greater encouragement. On the other hand, the Holy Father fostered the theatrical art. The Gonfalon company was authorized to stage performances in honor of God and the saints. Other theatrical companies were established, but they did not restrict themselves to sacred dramas. Plautus and Seneca were performed on the stage to the great delight of the public. This led to the staging of topical and occasional plays, showing the capture of Granada and the attempt to assassinate Ferdinand the Catholic. The plays were performed in the Forum or Piazza Navone. The pope did not disdain to attend the spectacles that were given at Castello Sant'Angelo in the courtyard that is still called the Theater Court.

He was an avowed enemy of superstition. In the Via Vestra, which ran from the Lateran to the Colosseum (now Via San Giovanni), there was an ancient statue (now in the Vatican) that portrayed a woman suckling a child. A legend of the Middle Ages declared that it marked the site where the woman who had become pope under the name of John VII by concealing her sex had stopped to give birth during a procession. The content of this tale had been assumed as rigorous truth for five centuries: therefore the popes were forbidden to use Via Vestra. Innocent VIII scorned this prohibition, thus incurring the reproof of the people and the clergy. But nothing untoward resulted, the prejudice was undermined, and after that the popes were allowed to use Via Vestra, which was a logical route for them. The strange story of Pope Joan was to find a belated defender in the person of Stendhal. In the imperial armies he had seen women disguised as soldiers win the Legion of Honor, and he said that there were not so many differences between the face of a young man and that of a certain kind of woman of firm and daring character, "such as would be required," he added, "to aspire to the papacy."

Innocent VIII died on July 25, 1492. His tomb, the work of the Pollaiuolo brothers, is in the basilica of St. Peter's. In 1621 an inscription was added to it, stating that America was discovered during his pontificate. An amazing error: Christopher Columbus' little fleet did not in fact set sail until August 3, 1492, and it was not until sixty-five days later that he reached the New World.

CHAPTER 19

ROME UNDER THE BORGIAS

ALEXANDER VI

"It is easier not to mention Alexander VI at all," Nardi wrote, "than to speak of him with moderation. With the greatest of vices he combined scant virtue, or, rather, absolutely none." On the basis of this opinion, Alexander VI would have to be regarded as the worst pope in history. But recent studies have made it possible considerably to lighten the blackness of his character without at the same time basically improving the bad reputation of his family. Unquestionably Alexander VI laid himself open to criticism, but a whole army of authors, closer to legend than to history, have devoted their efforts to disgracing him in order to attack the papacy through him.

Although Cardinal Borgia's misconduct was notorious and he fathered four bastards destined to regrettable infamy, his election had aroused enthusiasm. He was a pleasant man who spoke with distinction. In his long conduct of the high office of vice chancellor of the church he had demonstrated ability and character: it was on his instigation that his uncle, Calixtus III, had rehabilitated Joan of Arc. Above all, he was the richest of the cardinals, a fact to which the members of a conclave were not indifferent; for it was a tradition that the new pope should divest himself of all his dignities and all his prerogatives in order to bestow them on those who had elected him. Overwhelmed with the benevolences of four popes, Alessandro Borgia had enough to gratify everyone's appetite. His elevation was the most profitable in history, the more so in that he had endowed his abbeys with a great deal of money; the patriarch of Venice alone received five thousand ducats. This simony laid the foundations for many cardinals' fortunes. An edifying version of it was offered: the new pope, it was said, "divided and gave his goods to the poor."

Alexander's great design was to overthrow Roman feudalism in order to assure the Holy See's independence. After having filled the Sacred College with Spanish cardinals, he set the Colonnas and the Orsinis against each other so masterfully that they launched a series of small wars that finished by discrediting both sides. The long continuation of inconclusive battles and more or less successful sieges of various places was brought to an end in a compromise that left both families equally weakened. Free of their unwelcome agitation and assured by their age-old hatred that they would never combine against him, the pope employed the same divisive tactic against the petty Italian tyrants. In turn the ally and the enemy of Milan, of Naples, and of Venice, he made and unmade compacts with and against them. He enlisted, helped, and battled at various times the French kings engaged in Italian adventures, Charles VIII and Louis XII. In this tortuous strategy Alexander was striving at once for the best interests of his family and the preservation of the papacy's independence. If he was not always successful, at least he earned the reputation for duplicity that has always been associated with his name.

Anticipating trouble, Alexander VI concerned himself from the start of his pontificate with the reinforcement of the defenses of Castello Sant'Angelo. He constructed a battlemented wall on top of the circular mass of the imperial structure. He sought even to divert the course of the Tiber so that it might surround the castle, but he had to abandon so costly a scheme and limited himself to strengthening the fortifications of the quadrangular surrounding wall, which was to survive until the Tiber quays were drastically remodeled in the nineteenth century. A supposedly secret passage already connected Castello Sant'Angelo with the Vatican. Alexander VI had it replaced by a long enclosed corridor, built on arches, in the form of an aqueduct. From this vantage point the panoramic view of the city was marvelous: each quarter in turn could be seen from the successive bays of the watchtower.

THE BORGIAS' GREAT FESTIVALS AND THE OTHER SIDE OF THE COIN

As for the dissolute life that Alexander VI is supposed to have led without interruption within his entirely secular court, one must be careful not to assess it on the basis of the fables to which it has given rise. Nor should one ever lose sight of the fact that the papal court was also a princely court and that it was frequented by men and women whose condition did not obligate them to modesty and meditation.

At the same time it is indisputable that at times Alexander VI gave that court a rather free aspect, to say the least. It was in such manner that he held a party in the Vatican to celebrate the betrothal of his daughter, Lucrezia, to Giovanni Sforza. The guest list included 150 Roman ladies. It was the first time that the papal palace had been opened to women in so official and so broad a manner. The party was a splendid one: there were flattering comments from a stage on the most important of the guests, followed by the performance of light comedies interspersed with songs and dances. The evening was climaxed with rather vulgar diversions; it appears that one amusement was to pour the contents of all the silver cups inside the fronts of the ladies' extremely low-cut gowns. On many other occasions the Vatican glittered with celebrations that did not always observe the restraint that was the due of their setting. On the day when "the illustrious lady Lucrezia," widowed a second time as a result of undisclosed circumstances, took as her third husband the heir of Ferrara, a ball was given in the courtyard of the palace and was followed by so enthusiastic a tournament that five gentle participants were wounded. The chronicles have given much attention to the fifty courtesans who were supposed to have danced for the papal court on that day on ground strewn with chestnuts, undressing progressively as they moved. Without attaching any credence to such gossip, one must concede that Alexander VI was a very worldly pope, that he always made an extravagant public appearance, and that Roman life under his reign was a whirlwind of pleasures. The first carnival of his pontificate was the gayest that had ever been seen until then, with military displays and races whose brilliance was not to be surpassed.

The Romans had acquired a new taste—that of the military parade. Foreign perils having mounted round the Holy See, the pope had consolidated his army within Rome. Since he had augmented it with a corps of cannoneers and garbed them in gleaming red uniforms, their parades were the delight of the crowd.

Their splendor was to be eclipsed by the entry of the French army on December 31, 1494. Embarked on the conquest of Naples, Charles VIII, who had already crossed church soil, was requesting free passage through Rome. Alexander VI was apprehensive about having the king of France as his neighbor in Naples, but he was equally hesitant to resist a monarch quite capable of having him deposed by some council in which he would find few defenders. Racked by these mortal anxieties, he looked to his fortifications, called for help on the Neapolitans and even on the Great Turk,* pleaded with Charles VIII not to come, and threatened him with the bludgeon of major excommunication. At this moment a section of the city wall collapsed, and the pope saw in this accident a token from Providence that bade him yield. This he did at once, protecting his safety and his pride as well as possible. The Romans could then admire at their leisure the fine discipline of Charles VIII's troops, their huge drums and little fifes, their splendid golden halberds, their plumed helmets, and above all their great bronze cannon that made those of the pope seem like a child's toys. Rome's welcome was warm: the streets were so well lighted with torches and lanterns, a chronicler declared, that it was as if "the city were on fire." Every house was decked with the arms of the king of France. Cheers rose wherever his soldiers went.

This enthusiasm was quickly succeeded by great vexation. The French were completely lacking in respect for the traditions and the protocol that played so large a part in Roman life. "They could be seen storming the altars, taking over the places set aside for the clergy," and interrupting the decorum of the liturgy. Above all they looted the houses in which they were billeted, smashing the furniture and especially the new globes of the earth that had been made fashionable by the discovery of America. What was more, they manifested an excessive interest in women, and this was the major cause of the brawls that soon broke out almost everywhere. The solemn reconciliation between the pope and the king of France wiped out the resentments and restored the relations between the people and the army to their earlier cordiality. Charles VIII was acclaimed when he visited the Capitoline, Trajan's Column, the Ara Coeli, and the Minerva, where he heard mass in the company of his bodyguards and his nobles. "There was great marveling to see him employ his miraculous power to

---

* The contemporary Christian designation for the Ottoman emperors.—Translator.

cure the king's evil [scrofula] for the sake of 500 assembled sick." He was forgiven for the lack of formality with which he had treated the sovereign pontiff, sometimes resorting to all kinds of pretexts to avoid kissing his foot, sometimes keeping him waiting for some important ceremony "until the king had finished dining." When he left Rome on January 28, 1495, blessed by the pope, clothed in gold brocade, and covered by a white hat, he took with him the genuine good will of the population.

The Romans loved visits and adored parades. They felt rather lonely after the departure of the French, who for a whole month had made their city so lively. The licentious habits brought by the French persisted so vigorously that it was readily conceded that the terrible Tiber flood of December 4, 1495, had been wrought by Providence in punishment of the Romans for their evil ways. It must be admitted that the suddenness of this cataclysm deprived it of all semblance of a natural phenomenon. The sun was shining when the river sent its torrent into the streets. Cardinals who were just leaving a consistory could not make their way to their homes. The tremendous crest reached by the inundation is still marked on the Venetian ambassador's house in Via del Paradiso, near the Campo dei Fiori. The lower stories of buildings were ruined, as were the cellars especially, and a sardonic chronicler observed that "the overabundance of water created a shortage of wine."

This warning from heaven, however, made no change in the immorality, which in fact became both worse and more widespread. The papal court offered virtually no resistance to the tide of corruption. Eager for wealth, even at the cost of dishonorable means, prelates engaged almost openly in trafficking in holy things. One forged papal bulls, another sold ecclesiastics the advancements that they were seeking without being entitled to them, a third released them from their vows for a price. Crimes were committed in the pope's retinue, occasionally before his eyes, such as the assassination of Pedro Calderón, whose blood spattered the Holy Father's mantle. Very strange explanations were offered for the crimes. When the son of Sultan Mahomet II was poisoned, it was said that he had been given "a drink that was not adapted to his constitution." According to Jean Burchard, who was the historiographer of the pontifical ceremonials, a man who had been flung into the Tiber "fell into the river against his will." Similar euphemisms were employed to excuse the perilously rising number of assassinations. The pope himself forbade investigation of the most suspicious instances. When Cardinal della Rovere's majordomo came to complain that his daughter had been raped by a man whose name he gave the pope, the pontiff replied with a smile and no more. After the mysterious murder of the pope's own son, Giovanni, duke of Gandia, in 1497, he limited himself to notifying the bereavement to the various sovereigns of Christendom without further inquiry into the matter. (Perhaps, it has been suggested, he was only too well informed about it.) Let us remark in passing that this unpunished crime was to be popularly linked with the thunderbolt of October 27, 1497, that shattered the statue of the archangel St. Michael that dominated Castello Sant'Angelo; it was alleged that the saint had flown away in order to escape the scene of so many heinous crimes.

The crimes of the court were far exceeded by those of the city. Nocturnal skirmishes, private vengeances, duels and riots, banditry and ambushes claimed new victims every day. Popular imagination, furthermore, supplemented facts: if one had not seen an acquaintance for a day or two, that was enough to give birth to the rumor that he had been murdered. Rodocanachi reports that this happened to Burchard himself, who had to show "considerable activity" in order to convince his friends that he was still alive.

This state of insecurity did not impair the success of the jubilee of 1500, for which the pope had a special brilliance in mind. He had created a new means of access to St. Peter's, Via Alessandrina, which is called Via Borgo Nuovo today, and he had encouraged the erection of houses that would be "ornaments" to the city. The jubilee attracted a great number of pilgrims, not all of whom had reason to congratulate themselves on their zeal. The innkeepers robbed their customers; a physician in the Lateran hospital killed his patients in order to acquire their possessions: "the hospital's confessor pointed out the richest for him." Highwaymen of every variety practiced their trade at will; every day pilgrims disappeared. A few malefactors were arrested and punished; eighteen thieves were hanged twice on Ponte Sant'Angelo: the gibbets collapsed the first time, so that the operation had to be repeated.

On Easter Day 200,000 persons crowded round St. Peter's to receive the papal blessing. There were such crushes at the doors of the basilicas that the pope decreed that praying on the steps or even in the vicinity of the churches would be enough to gain indulgences. The jubilee had to be extended for twelve days after the end of the holy year. The offerings filled the treasury, but the proceeds had to be turned over to Cesare Borgia, whose exigencies had no limitations. Only an infinitesimal fraction was reserved for the construction of the ceiling of golden panels that covers the central nave of Santa Maria Maggiore. This is one of the most beautiful decorative achievements of the Renaissance, in which the first gold to be received from America was used in abundance. Nothing could be more splendid and more in harmony with the religious pomps that that epoch adored. This magnificent work was the extent of Alexander VI's contribution to the beautification of Rome's churches.

THE BORGIA APARTMENT

Alexander VI was not an Italian; that was no doubt the reason why he was not greatly interested in the embellishment of Rome. The opening of a new street, the fortification of certain gates, some improvements in Castello Sant'Angelo—these were utilitarian projects, conceived and executed without regard to any esthetic concern. Quite the contrary was the case with the famous apartment that Alexander VI established in the Vatican and that still attracts as many visitors as the Sistine Chapel and Raphael's rooms. Bounded by the courtyards of the Sentinella, the Belvedere, and the Parrot, it occupies the second story of the austere palace of Nicholas V for the whole length of the wing to which the pope had just added the square battlemented tower that still bears his name (Torre Borgia). It was Pinturicchio, who had just completed the paintings in the chapel of Ara Coeli dedicated to San Bernardino, to whom Alexander VI entrusted the decoration of the five rooms that make up the apartment. The program laid out for the artist was the same as the one that Raphael was to carry out twenty-five years later on the third floor of the same building. Aided by his numerous pupils, Pinturicchio completed the task in less than three years. The Umbrian master's frescoes are a treasure of precious colors. The Sistine painters may have looked on life more seriously, but here the brilliance of the costumes and the marvelous natural settings give the lives of the saints the poetry and the richness of fairy tales. Lucrezia Borgia appears here as St. Catherine in a setting of an earthly paradise, and Pope Alexander (in the fresco of the Resurrection) is portrayed "in prayer in the midst of a landscape dotted with buttercups."

The decoration of the Borgia apartment marks the first appearance of grotteschi—"grotesque"—those grotto paintings whose models the Renaissance artists had just discovered in their feverish explorations of the ancient ruins. The craze for these underground investigations had been born with the dramatic discovery made in 1485 near Via Appia: the body of a young girl that retained every semblance of life after fifteen centuries of repose in a sarcophagus; the body was still supple, the hair was shining, the lips were pink, the features were intact. The discovery made a great stir, it was immediately acclaimed as a miracle, and the body of the unknown pagan, displayed in the Conservators' Museum, attracted a remarkable number of viewers. But the girl's body became completely black within a few days of its exposure to the air, and the pope ordered it speedily reburied in order to cut short the excitement. All that remained of this occurrence was the taste for exploring the underground rooms of the ancient palaces and baths in search of unsuspected curiosities. This led to the discovery of a lost system of decoration in the paintings that here and there still adorned the walls: arabesques mingled with figurines, which were given the name of *grotteschi*. The walls of the crypto-portico of Nero's House of Gold, hidden under the ruins of Trajan's baths, still bear the signatures of the Renaissance artists who went there to copy the antique designs.

The spirit of these designs is repeated in the Borgia apartment as it is in Raphael's *stanze*. On the massive vaults of the palace of Nicholas V these animated arabesques celebrate a new victory of the Renaissance. It is true that there is no other place in Rome that better evokes the spirit of that age as well as the private life of the papal court: it was there that the light played in Lucrezia's blond hair and that the "invincible" Cesare Borgia strutted in his gilded armor. It was there that Alexander VI in his brocade cloak elaborated his political schemes. The apartment was so thoroughly steeped in his presence that, when he died, it was closed as a sign of the aversion attached to his memory. Its rooms were in the most desolate abandon when Pope Leo XIII decided to restore them and to reopen them to visitors.

THE BORGIAS' PALACES AND THE FOREIGN CHURCHES (TRINITÀ DEI MONTI, SAN CARLO, SANTA MARIA DI MONSERRATO) / MICHELANGELO'S *PIETÀ*

It would seem that the pope did not take great care of the palaces in which he had lived in Rome before his election. Palazzo Cesarini (in Piazza Sforza Cesarini), which he ordered built when he was vice chancellor of the church and which for a time was called the Chancellery

Palace, was in very bad condition when it was restored by one of the della Roveres in 1508. As for Palazzo Borgia, its medieval tower has become the belfry of San Francesco di Paolo, on the stairway that leads from Via Cavour to San Pietro in Vincoli. What is left of the palace would be of no particular interest if Alexander VI's former mistress, that Vannozza who bore him five children, had not embellished it with a balcony in the Renaissance style whose poetry and grace have been celebrated by many poets.

Aside from the apartment in the Vatican, Alexander VI's artistic contribution is meager. It is fortunate that his contemporaries were less indifferent than he to the beautification of the capital of Christendom. At this point notice must be taken of the contributions made by foreign nations, which were beginning to pride themselves on the construction of churches worthy of them in Rome. During his visit, Charles VIII had used the money that he had received from the pope for the purchase of a vineyard that was to be the site of the Minims' monastery (it was transferred later to the Sisters of the Sacred Heart) and of the French church of Trinità dei Monti. The first stone was laid in 1496; but the kings of France were to be very slow in completing the church, and it was not consecrated until ninety years later.

Santa Maria dell'Anima, similarly, became the church of the Germans and Dutch, who built it near Piazza Navone. Its ample Renaissance façade is attributed (erroneously, some say) to Giuliano Giamberti da Sangallo. Although all the interior decoration is the work of Italian artists, it is irresistibly reminiscent of Germany: one feels that one is in a church beside the Main or the Danube. The Milanese built San Carlo, the great church on the Corso, of which Stendhal said that it was very much visited in his time because, seen from the Pincio, its dome showed to advantage and seemed almost as high as that of St. Peter's. The Spaniards built their national church of Santa Maria di Monserrato (in Via Monserrato), whose name recalls Catalonia. St. Ignatius Loyola was to preach there. It contains the tombs of Alexander VI and the last of the Spanish kings, Alfonso XIII.

Contemporaneously with Bramante a young Florentine artist had appeared in Rome who was to leave immortal masterpieces in the city: Michelangelo. Lorenzo il Magnifico had been the first to descry the promise of his genius; but it was as the result of a French undertaking that Rome was to possess the first of his great works. A worthy successor to the benefactions of Cardinal d'Estouteville, Cardinal Villiers de la

Groslaie commissioned Michelangelo to carve the famous *Pietà* that visitors crowd to see in the first chapel on the right in the basilica of St. Peter's. This work rich in human tenderness is the vanguard of two centuries of art. It has been said that it was conceived and carved by a believer the force of whose feeling makes one forget the perfection of his technique. He made a daring innovation: the Virgin, who has retained the young face of the Florentine madonnas, is the same age as the child lying on her knees. The courtyard of Palazzo Capranica yielded, among its ancient busts and bas-reliefs, a badly hewn block of marble that is the first sketch of the *Pietà*. Displeased with the quality of the marble, Michelangelo had abandoned it in this condition.

Casa del Burcardo, which the erudite prelate, Jean Burchard, built on Via del Sudario in imitation of contemporary German houses, dates from the same period, and is altogether on the fringe of Roman architectural tendencies. Today it houses the museum and library of the Teatro Argentina. Burchard was a native of Strasbourg, the ancient Argentoratum, and he bequeathed the name of his city to the square near which he lived; thus it has become Largo Argentina through a curious phonetic distortion quite similar to that by which Burchard himself became *il Burcardo*. Roman pronunciation lent itself awkwardly to the Germanic endings and accommodated them to its own convenience.

The reign of Alexander VI was only the beginning of the vast movement that was to make Rome the city of palaces. A host of foreign artists and a whole army of skilled artisans had flocked in, not only from Florence, which the fall of the Medicis had plunged into stagnation, and from Milan, now stripped of its ducal court, but also from Switzerland, Germany, and France, in spite of the insecurity and the exorbitant cost of living. This was because economic progress was becoming solidified in spite of unfavorable political conditions. Commercial activity was intense; guilds were growing and new ones were being organized. This renewal was preparing the brilliant period that was to be the golden age of the Italian Renaissance.

CHAPTER 20

THE "HELMETED" RENAISSANCE [JULIUS II]

CITY PLANNING UNDER JULIUS II

Alexander VI Borgia had done much to strengthen the papal state: Giuliano della Rovere, a nephew of Sixtus IV, who was to occupy the throne of St. Peter for nine years, beginning in 1503, under the name of Julius II, was to establish the authority of the Holy See on broader foundations and to impose it on the states of Europe. Machiavelli summed up the results of this pope's policy, as they appeared in 1512, with a short sentence: "There was a time when the least of the barons believed it his right to hold the pope's power in contempt; today it commands respect from a king of France." The world knows well enough how Julius II subdued Cesare Borgia, how he manipulated Emperor Maximilian and Louis XII of France, whom he finally drove out of Italy. Deposing rebellious cardinals, excommunicating kings, unceasingly hurling all the violence of his character into the service of limitless conceptions, this warrior pope, "in whom all that was priestly was the robe and the name," was to build the modern church and to make the Eternal City the center of the political universe.

He was also to make it "the citadel of the arts, the metropolis of the mind, and the center of pleasures," and it is this part of his work that we should like to examine. Let us note at the start that he introduced it by remedying the evils that constituted his inheritance from his predecessor. The misery of the lowest classes was appalling; he relieved it through energetic measures quite in keeping with his bold nature. At the same time that he was sending a requisitioned fleet to distant countries in quest of grain, he was imposing rigorous rationing. Entrance to his domain was forbidden to foreign workers. In a more draconian move, he threw the useless mouths out of Rome. These exiles of an unprecedented category filed through the gates in long, heart-breaking lines, bound like convicts and escorted by prison warders. To put an end to the dangers of the streets, the pope instituted a harsh police force that harassed robbers and those who protected them. Any kind of misconduct was punished without mercy, and it was possible again to walk through Rome without being robbed and beaten. This was a great novelty. In order to assure his own safety, Julius II provided the papal palace with that corps of Swiss mercenaries that still guarantees its security. Their weaponry has changed little since the time of the Renaissance, no more than their uniforms, which make them look like the jacks in a deck of cards. There has been much mockery of this well-dressed and overly healthy-looking garrison: it has been said that it must never have faced any fire but blanks. "Sun and moon," de Brosses wrote, "are the usual enemies that put them to flight." This was a cheap witticism: the Swiss Guard has not often had to offer proof of its military valor for the very simple reason that the palace to whose defense it is assigned has been only rarely attacked. But, when attack has come, the Swiss have done their duty: in particular it was thanks to their courage that Pope Clement VII was saved in 1527 from the German infantry of the Bourbon Constable.

In spite of the efforts of Nicholas V and Sixtus IV, Rome was still quite wretched when Julius II became pope. Except for the Capitoline, the hills were covered with ill-defined properties strewn with ruins; only a few low houses round churches maintained the semblance of a cheerless life. The heights of the Quirinal were planted with olive trees. On the Pincio the scaffolding of the church of Trinità dei Monti stood alone, surrounded by woods. The traveler who entered Rome through Porta del Popolo, then a shabby sight, gained a sorry view of the capital of the Christian world. It was only after he had passed through vast almost deserted areas that he reached the inhabited part of the city, which began in the vicinity of the Pantheon and included, besides the Field of Mars, the Capitoline and the lower slopes of the Aventine and the Quirinal. Between Piazza Navone and the Tiber there were lordly residences, most of which still preserved their medieval appearance and their ancient defenses. The rest of the city was still that network of sordid, narrow, tortuous streets and irregular squares filled with garbage that we have already described. Looking down on this tangle from their bell towers, the overnumerous churches were falling to pieces. The city's filth was caused both by the paucity of water available to its residents and by their lack of interest in cleaning the streets. This service was left to the municipal government, whose activity was never noticeable except on great occasions. It required a visit by the pope to get a quarter cleaned. Only then were things done properly: the chief official of the Sant'Angelo quarter was given twenty-five gold ducats for this purpose when the pope was to be crowned in March, 1504.

In less than ten years the secular activities of Julius II were to make Rome a well-regulated, beautified city, in every way worthy of its mission. At the end of his life the pope was to take justifiable pride in his accomplishments, to which he himself paid tribute when he affixed to a house in Via San Spirito, where it can still be seen, an inscription that describes the scope of his work.

One of the first measures that he took was to open new streets, following the example of Sixtus IV; the most famous, which still bears his name (Via Giulia), runs from Ponte Sisto to San Giovanni dei Fiorentini. The pope intended to make it the center of Roman life, and he had plans drawn for a huge palace that would house both the municipal services and the offices of the Holy See. These plans have been preserved in the Uffizi in Florence. Medals, struck for propaganda purposes, show the façade of the palace. The hope was false: the walls had barely begun to rise above the ground when Julius II died, and his successors gave up this great project. In this connection we should observe that it has been rare for any pope to carry on his predecessor's work, "either because his character and his aspirations were different or because some question of rivalry or jealousy arose." Nonetheless many buildings, including the Palazzi Sacchetti and Raphael's house, were to be erected along Via Giulia, as well as several churches: San Biagio della Pagnotta, in particular, and San Giovanni dei Fiorentini, which was to be erected by Leo X. Many other streets were laid down or widened by Julius II, such as Via della Botteghe Oscure and Via Rua, where an inscription of 1508 listed the buildings that had had to be demolished to make way for it.

Via della Lungara was opened in Trastevere; it ran from Porta Settimiano to Porta San Spirito. It was on this street that the banker Agostino Chigi, known as Il Magnifico, began in 1509 to construct that graceful residence "worthy of paradise" that became the Farnesina when acquired in 1580 by Alessandro Cardinal Farnese. It stood opposit palace on which Domenico Cardinal Riario had been working for ye and in which Christina of Sweden was to die. Today this is Palazz Corsini, rebuilt in 1730 by the cardinal of that name. Somewhat later, other buildings were to be erected on Via della Lungara, some of which were quite important, such as Palazzo Salviati, various churches, and convents. The area was very desirable because of its unusual charm: from the bank of the Tiber to the top of the Janiculum it was terraced with the gardens and woods where Septimius Severus had had a villa built for his son, Geta.

Julius II also gave his attention to a vast number of minor traffic problems. When a house projected so far into the line of a street that it created an obstacle, the pope ordered it demolished; when the overhang of a balcony prevented light from reaching an alley, he had it altered. And he did not intend his orders to remain dead letters. Cardinal von Auch learned that by experience: his house was blocking the street; in spite of his protests, it was torn down so quickly that the unfortunate prelate had to rush for shelter to friends. On the other hand, the pope encouraged new building that was designed to lessen the congestion in the old quarters: he exempted the owners from taxation and often he gave them the sites. This was how a large number of comfortable and pleasant-looking apartment houses came to be built in quarters that until then had been sparsely populated.

Not only was the city improved and given access to light and air; it was also cleaned. Repairs to the aqueducts made the water flow again from the fountains, a great many of which were restored, notably the Fontana di Trevi, which was still all simplicity and rusticity. Among Julius II's urban improvements we must also include the dredging that made the Tiber accessible to ocean-going vessels.

CHURCHES AND PALACES

As a result of lack of maintenance, many churches were facing total ruin. Julius II restored them, occasionally at the cost of very extensive undertakings. San Pietro in Vincoli, whose titular he had been, was the object of special solicitude; after radical alterations, he entrusted its maintenance to the regular canons of the Lateran. He restored Constantine's baptistry, and he had Giuliano Giamberti da Sangallo, a pupil of Bramante, start work on the church of Santa Maria di Loreto, one of two churches in Trajan's square, whose appearance was to be changed in 1580 by a remarkable lantern above its dome. Like its neighbor, the church of the Holy Name of Mary, which dates from the eighteenth century, it is one of the churches of the Bakers' Brotherhood.

In 1509, a few steps from Porta Latina, an unknown architect built the delightful little octagonal church of San Giovanni in Olio in the spirit of Bramante, on the site where, according to tradition, St. John the Evangelist miraculously emerged unharmed from boiling oil. St. John of Porta Latina is the official church of the Paris printers. The little chapel was erected at the expense of a French auditor of the Rota, Benoît Adam, whose motto, "For the pleasure of God," is carved above one of the doors.

For the cardinals it was a point of honor to follow the examples set by the Holy Father. The most opulent among them, Giovanni dei Medici, rebuilt Santa Maria in Domenica (la Navicella) from the foundations up and presented it with a new door executed from plans by Raphael. Cardinal Caraffa entrusted Bramante with the execution of the beautiful cloister of Santa Maria della Pace with its double cloister. These princes of the church had so many rivals that almost all Rome's churches were in good condition by the end of Julius II's pontificate. This was not a minor achievement, in view of the fact that their great number was out of all proportion to the requirements of the faithful.

While they spent a great deal of money in the restoration of churches, many cardinals were to devote even more to the construction of their own palaces. The annual income of the Sacred College at that time was in the neighborhood of 490,000 ducats, so that each member had approximately 12,000. This was augmented by the pope, who was generous, with private gifts, often quite large. In addition, many high prelates had extensive properties of their own, especially the della Roveres, the Medicis, the Farneses, to name only the best known.

Julius II believed that the public display of the cardinals' wealth contributed to inspiring in the people a high idea of the power of the church. They never went to the Vatican without brilliant processions, preceded by drums and bagpipes; their servitors bore with great pomp the red case that was the symbol of their dignity (and that is perhaps the origin of the ministerial portfolio); behind their richly equipped horses marched their escort of familiars and gentlemen, who were beginning to be called their "creatures." The people crowded the route to admire them and pay honor to them. In private they gave costly entertainments and lavish banquets that lasted so long that the guests had to stand up at table "in order not to fall asleep."

Nor were they alone in leading such luxurious lives. With the exception of the very greatest (the Colonnas, the Orsinis, the Savellis), the old families, impoverished by their rivalries, had withdrawn into obscurity. But a new elite was coming into being, composed of municipal officials, great merchants, bankers, and moneychangers, usually of foreign origin; they threw themselves into ostentatious prodigalities in order to dazzle the Romans and divert attention from their own foreign origins. All that concerned cardinals and financiers was the adornment of their houses; the richest built palaces. A great number were constructed under Julius II, more or less lavish but always beautiful, because there were so many artists of great talent and good taste in Rome. Aside from the Farnesina and Palazzo Corsini, which were to be completed only later, let us mention, among many others, Palazzo del Governo Vecchio, Palazzo Torlonia (formerly Giraud, a reproduction of the Chancellery on a smaller scale), Palazzo Sacchetti, which was Sangallo's residence. They were indicative of the change in customs. The day of fortified houses flanked by towers was over. Always firm and sober, architecture was becoming more delicate. Henceforth the Renaissance was to express itself fully in its best medium.

The holy father heartily encouraged the rich Romans in their prodigalities, took an interest in the furtherance of their projects, and stimulated them to competition. Visiting Agostino Chigi one day at the site where the banker's summer residence was being built—it was to become the Farnesina—the pope asked whether this house would be as luxurious as that of the Riarios, which was just being completed not far away. The powerful banker, whose income was greater than that of a state, replied that "his stables would be more beautiful than the Riarios' dining room." This jest was to give rise to the picturesque stables, now vanished, whose luxury is hinted at in another anecdote: Chigi gave so sumptuous a feast there for Leo X that the guests were mute in admiration, and the pope reproached his host for this excessive display, saying: "I had thought that you were on a more intimate footing with me." The banker replied: "Your opinion was quite correct: look at the humble surroundings to which I invited you."

All these splendors were paid for with much destruction. The ancient monuments provided not only the materials for the new buildings but also the lime required for their assembly. Until this time it had been almost always only the stone and the marble that had fallen away from the ruined monuments that were used. Julius II authorized the demolition of ancient monuments that were still standing. It was with his consent that the Colosseum was assigned to the function of an inexhaustible quarry. The most venerable relics no longer inspired any respect because they were considered useless. "The right to remain standing was no longer recognized for baths that had no custom, for temples that had no worshipers, for altars that had been attacked by weeds" (*Vita Romana*).

Raphael drew up an inventory of the demolitions that he actually observed. This long list includes the temple of Ceres, large parts of Nerva's Forum, and Diocletian's baths. Seven thousand ancient columns, intact or fragmented, were incorporated into new structures at this time, and no one knows how many others were swallowed up in the lime kilns with priceless statues and mountains of marble tablets bearing inscriptions whose texts would be a treasure to us.

THE TOMB OF JULIUS II AND THE NEW ST. PETER'S

The first thought of a Pharaoh when he ascended the throne was to build the pyramid that would house his remains. The Roman emperors, such as Augustus and Hadrian, had revived this tradition. Following their example, Julius II decided, as soon as he had assumed St. Peter's throne, to build his own mausoleum, which he wished to be grandiose, like everything else that he conceived. This was neither presumptuousness nor arrogance on his part. This bellicose pontiff, who was to make the papacy the leading power in the whole of Italy, never intruded the thought of his own renown on his great purposes. He carved out no kingdom for his kin; he did not make his family wealthy. But he did expect his works to redound to the glory of the Holy See, and, as a man of the Renaissance, he assumed that a grandiose monument ought to be erected in his memory. In the impatience of his ardor it did not displease him to contemplate in his lifetime the magnificent symbol of his achievements that he intended to hand down to future generations. That explains his desire to invest his tomb with an epic character even though he had not yet embarked on any epic enterprise and was celebrating the success of undertakings that he envisaged on a gigantic scale but had not yet begun.

His mausoleum was to be a veritable palace, adorned with forty triumphal statues representing the provinces to be conquered. Images of Victory and Renown would symbolize the pontiff's military successes even before the start of the first campaign. This poem in marble, celebrating the history of his reign in anticipation, would in short be something of a prophecy. Only the porphyry sarcophagus that was to receive the pope's remains represented a reality that, it was true, was still to come but that was certain. This project was the result of the collaboration of Julius II and Michelangelo, the one contributing his immoderate love for the colossal and his feverish transports, the other the flame of his dominating genius. These were two men of the same race, two "terrible" men, as each said of the other. It is seldom that harmony endures long between such imperious personages.

Michelangelo himself went to Carrara to select the marble blocks and to supervise their preparation. It was there that he was seized with the idea of carving into one of the mountains a colossus that would dominate the sea. On his return to Rome he soon recognized that the pope had been diverted from his project and had lost interest in his tomb. His frenzy had found another object and his favor had found another artist. Bramante had profited by Michelangelo's absence to convince Julius II that the great accomplishment of his pontificate should be the reconstruction of St. Peter's so that Catholicism would have a shrine worthy of it. Opposition among the clergy and the faithful had been sharp: so many venerable memories were associated with the old basilica that there was a reluctance to see it disappear. Bramante was able to counter the objections and allay the anxieties. He was a gentle, accommodating, helpful man, and also extremely clever and ingratiating. His professional name and nick-name—his real name was Donato d'Agnolo—was the present participle of the verb *bramare,* which means *to court, to plead, to entreat,* and also *to covet.* Michelangelo anticipated nothing good from this intrusion by a competitor whose character was diametrically opposite to his own. He abruptly gave up the studio that had been arranged for him on St. Peter's square, and he left in the middle of the night for Florence. In addition to resenting his rejection, he wanted to escape from imagined perils. "If I had stayed in Rome," he wrote, "my grave would have been needed before the pope's." He was to return and to be reconciled with Julius II, though he never stopped holding Bramante responsible for all the unpleasant-nesses with which his career was filled.

Bramante's plan for the reconstruction of St. Peter's was unbelievably daring. It called for a total rebuilding on an entirely new design. The old basilica built by Constantine and enriched over twelve centuries of piety with an unequaled series of mosaics and sculptures was condemned to disappear. Its place would be taken by an enormous square church that would embody the synthesis of all the architectural styles of the known world. From a central dome, itself flanked by four Byzantine cupolas, four equal arms were to radiate, forming a Greek cross. At the four corners of the square, four towers would recall the style of the old Germanic cathedrals. The naves would have the gigantic proportions of the basilica of Maxentius that dominated the Forum. Above these immense vaults Bramante proposed "to suspend in the air a dome comparable to that of the Pantheon." The Orient, Byzantium, the North, Roman antiquity, and the Renaissance would be combined in this Babel "fantastic in its silhouette and classic in its detail." For artists as for believers, as Emile Bertaux has observed, Bramante's St. Peter's would indeed have been "the universal church."

Julius II was excited by a project as grandiose as his own ambitions, and he ordered its immediate execution. The foundation of the new sanctuary was announced by special emissaries to all the sovereigns of Europe. The Holy Father expected a great deal from their generosity, and he felt a certain disappointment at the modesty of their contributions. The king of England contented himself with sending tin; as for Ferdinand the Catholic, he sharply refused to sacrifice for the construction of the basilica one-quarter of the tithe collected from his states, for that was the lofty figure on which Julius II had fixed for Spain's contribution. All the clergy of Christendom busied themselves in furthering the Holy Father's intentions. His zeal led him, indeed, to the use of questionable means: indulgences were promised to whoever would offer money for the construction of the new basilica. In plain language, they were sold. Under the pressure of his enormous needs, Julius II approved and perhaps encouraged this traffic, which was to revolt Luther and engender the Reformation. It was not without reason that it was remarked that the religious wars of the sixteenth century, St. Bartholomew's Night, and the English revolution "were born of the fantasy of a pope maddened with magnificence."

On April 18, 1506, the first stone was put in place for the first of the four pillars intended to support the great dome; the stone was aspersed with holy water in a splendid ceremony during which the Holy Father ventured alone into the deep excavation whose "unstable and crumbling supports" foreshadowed the tremendous difficulties that would be encountered as construction proceeded. The work went forward throughout the reign of

Julius II, in alternate feverish spurts and inexplicable delays. The technical problems that would have to be faced were aggravated by the requirement that the existing structure could be demolished only section by section. For the pope did not wish to incur the reproach of having interrupted worship. Mass continued to be celebrated in clouds of dust and frightful drafts, to the bitter complaints of the higher prelates. The major obstacle to the progress of the work lay in the marshy character of the soil. The excavations had to be taken to an extreme depth in order to assure a solid base for the foundations, but they were periodically flooded by seepage. Most of the twenty-five hundred workmen who were busy at any given time on the job (there were enough of them, the pope said, to stage a parade) were assigned to draining the water from the foundations. This explained the inordinate delays in progress. When Julius II and Bramante died, a year apart (in 1513 and 1514), the four enormous pillars for the dome were still all that had been built, and they dominated the half-destroyed roof of Constantine's basilica. Now the work was to be interrupted for fifteen years; it would be resumed on new designs. So all that remains of the marvelous edifice conceived by Bramante, aside from the pillars, is the plans and a medallion that reproduced them.

THE BELVEDERE AND THE ANTIQUITY CRAZE

Under the plan of Julius II a new Vatican was to rise beside the new St. Peter's, so that the papal city might equal in solemnity and size the imperial city whose ruins covered the Palatine. Only a part of these ambitious plans was to be realized; even that part was subjected to alterations that changed its character. Before it occurred to him to demolish the palace of Nicholas V (he did not have time to carry this out), Bramante had used the large area that lay free between the medieval castle and the Belvedere of Innocent VIII. There was a hollow in its center; he had it filled, and thus he had available a large site about one thousand feet long. He bordered it with two tremendous three-story galleries forming the open colonnades whose walls were to be decorated with frescoes. He did not have time to finish this part of his work, which Pius IV was to complete fifty years afterward.

Bramante's buildings served as an enclosure for a kind of stadium where the pope could stage splendid celebrations, tournaments, and even bullfights in the Spanish style imported by the Borgias. Behind the stadium there was a flowered terrace that was reached by broad flights of stairs whose angle of climb was so slight that they could be taken, up or down, on horseback (Bramante was asked whether he would not design a similar staircase to heaven). The background decoration was the huge niche, similar to the apse of a temple, that hid the villa of Innocent VIII. The vista from the hemicycle that spread at the foot of the palace extended as far as the terrace of the Belvedere. This grandiose view no longer exists: Sixtus V, with his library, and Pius VII, with the Braccio Nuovo, cut the tremendous courtyard of Julius II in two, separating the court of the Belvedere from the melancholy garden of the Pigna, ornamented with the venerable pine cone taken from the summit of Hadrian's tomb and flanked by the two large bronze peacocks that decorated its gate.

Cardinals, bankers, and all Romans who prided themselves on their modernism had adopted the fashion for gardens, as they were then admired: intermingled with groves of orange and pomegranate, enlivened with aviaries of rare birds, populated with exotic animals, adorned with antique statues and columns. The most famous were the gardens of the Coluccis, the Chigis, the Colonnas, and the Bembos. Those that Julius II created in Bramante's great courtyard were the most sumptuous by virtue of the remarkable works of art that he assembled there.

The craze for antiques was carried so far at that time that no one recoiled at the most shocking procedures in their acquisition. "Robbery was praiseworthy, theft was honorable," Baldassare Castiglione wrote in 1507. As for forgers, their trade was booming. It was even better for the diggers who combed the soil of Rome and even the bed of the Tiber. Not to mention the merchants who scoured Greece or spent huge sums to bring back from the Orient by the shipload the treasures with which Byzantium had enriched itself under the Empire at Rome's expense. The fever of the treasure hunt was universal; as soon as a statuette came on the market the bids for it rose incredibly. It was then that every palace in Rome began to become a museum.

Julius II, as might well be expected, did not hold aloof from all this; in fact, with regard to the finest pieces, he asserted a pre-emptive right in the Holy See, which he himself had given it. Thus he managed to snatch the famous *Laocoön* group away from the greedy hands of his cardinals after its discovery in a vineyard near the baths of Titus in 1506—a discovery that filled Rome with an indescribable rapture of patriotism. Before it was placed in the Belvedere, the *Laocoön* had to be exhibited in the Capitoline, where it was made the object of an amazing veneration. Its transfer to the Vatican was a triumphal procession: a huge crowd hailed it as the symbol of the classic past, to the accompaniment of church bells and the thunder of the artillery of Castello Sant'Angelo. The chance discoverer of this treasure, Felice de Fredis, was rewarded by the pope with the inestimable privilege of being buried in the church of Ara Coeli, where a bombastic inscription assures him of immortality. In the court of the Belvedere the *Laocoön* was to join two other windfalls of Julius II, the *Apollo* and the *Venus,* in a kind of sacred triad. The torso of Hercules found in the Campo dei Fiori was also placed with them in 1507, as was the sleeping *Ariadne* in 1512, as well as the thirteen masks taken from the Pantheon, and the *Tiber* that, as a result of political events, is now in the Louvre. Most of these works, undoubtedly, are not the apogee of antique beauty that they were long considered to be: one has only to compare them with other beautiful Greek fragments that later enriched the Vatican Museum and the Belvedere courtyard itself. Nonetheless Michelangelo and Bernini were their devoted students: they were to "stimulate all the baroque attractions" of sculpture.

THE VAULT OF THE SISTINE CHAPEL

Two years after his flight into Tuscany, Michelangelo made his peace with Julius II—an armed peace, one might say, that was still to be marred by violent storms. The Signoria of Florence had decided that this reconciliation would be helpful to its own policies. In Bologna, which he entered as a master "with his cardinals, his court, and his army," the warrior pope greeted the rebellious artist, whom at bottom he deeply respected, with a rude welcome: "It was you who should have come to meet Us, but it was We who had to go to meet you." The pope thereupon imposed the yoke on him again with the assignment of a crushing commission: to decorate the vault of the Sistine Chapel. Michelangelo, who had been dreaming of resuming the execution of the great mausoleum of Julius II with its forty marble statues (the dream and the preoccupation of his whole life), boggled, seeing in this unexpected commission a treacherous maneuver by his enemy, Bramante, and adding the objection that he knew nothing of painting (*essendo io non pittore*), as he would never stop reiterating in defiance of the fullest evidence to the contrary. But in the end he yielded, and, when he returned to Rome in March, 1508, he found the scaffolding in place for the beginning of his work. It was suspended from the ceiling on ropes that went through the roof.

Another trick of Bramante! It was not difficult for Michelangelo to demonstrate its illogic: once the work was finished, he said, how would the gashes in the roof be repaired? He won permission to set up his own arrangements; but his "system," however ingenious it might have been, required him to lie on his back as he painted, while the colors that he placed on the dome dripped into his face "in a rich mosaic." He allowed himself only brief intervals for rest, during which, still lying down, he read Dante's *Inferno* and Savonarola's sermons. He himself has described the discomfort of this position and the ill effects that he suffered: "I gave myself a goiter through this assignment, so that my belly touched my chin; my chest was caught between them and my kidneys moved up into my ribs, while I acquired an enormous hump on my backside." Whenever he came down from his scaffold, he was tormented by agonizing cramps: he walked without seeing where he was going and he felt that his skin had been stretched.

This physical suffering, which he had to endure for years, was aggravated by anguish of another kind. The pope, who was no longer concerned with his tomb, was impatient to see the decoration of the Sistine Chapel completed—he was to be portrayed in it several times; he made frequent visits to the artist, who found the Holy Father's encouragement as difficult to suffer as his criticisms. He was to write later that "he would have done better to become a match seller: painting was done not with the hands but with the brain, and his was being racked." Between these two "terrible" men, in spite of the discrepancy in their positions, it was inevitable that conflicts should erupt and grow bitter. One day a prelate who tried to mediate was beaten with a stick by Julius II himself. Once he cried to the painter: "Do you want me to have you knocked off your scaffolding?" It was not much after this that Michelangelo, at the end of his rope, dropped a few planks as the pope was entering the chapel; he was credited with the diabolical wish to make His Holiness believe "that the whole scaffolding was about to fall on him." Certain cardinals whose visits the artist found unwelcome were similarly greeted with cascades of plaster, which were very seldom accidental. Michelangelo's tremendous work was introduced to the public on the eve of All Saints' Day in 1512. The crush of the crowd was such that it was extremely difficult to enter the chapel and even more difficult to get out.

The frescoes with which Michelangelo covered the great ceiling of the Sistine Chapel represent the first occasion on which sacred history was no longer depicted in anecdotes but "rendered in comminatory judgments." Each confronted man's mind with the problem of his destiny. "It came down finally to the soul," René Benjamin wrote, "finally to life, finally to death." The great drama of the human adventure was indeed the vast subject that Michelangelo took. The complete exploitation of the idea, the total disdain for landscape, the stubborn renunciation of pictorial graces combine to give the work a greatness that has few equals in the history of art. And yet there is nothing severe or rigid in it. The sublime is attained without effort, the greatness is wholly spontaneous; it is as if the artist had fulfilled himself "by playing." It is one of the great mysteries of artistic creation that Michelangelo should have given this character to a work executed under the deplorable conditions that we have mentioned, whereas twenty-two years later, exempted by his glory from all restrictions and working in a climate of tranquility, he was to paint that agonizing and terrible *Last Judgment* on the high wall of the chapel that makes such a dramatic contrast with the frescoes on the ceiling.

RAPHAEL'S ROOMS

At the same time when Michelangelo was decorating the Sistine Chapel, another Titan of painting, Raphael, was covering the walls of the apartment of Julius II with frescoes. After his elevation the pope had taken over the apartment that Alexander VI had had decorated by Pinturicchio. A few months later he said publicly that "he could no longer endure the sight of that Borgia hypocritically kneeling before Christ." The rooms above the Borgia apartment were at once cleared so that they might be remodeled for his use and turned over to a team of painters that included, in particular, Luca Signorelli of Cortone, Perugino and Sodoma (Giovanni Bazzi). Impetuously volatile as he was, Julius II soon sent away all these artists and replaced them with a twenty-five-year-old painter who had recently arrived from Urbino and whose genius he had discovered. This new arrival was Raphael, who was to reign over Rome for twelve years. Assisted by a swarm of young collaborators, among whom was Giulio Romano, the young master of Urbino embarked in 1508 on a task as tremendous as that imposed on Michelangelo. He was to continue at it until his death (in 1520) and to multiply its "effects of grace and tender femininity." In complete contrast to Michelangelo, the spokesman of masculine strength, the tormented Christian, and, as he has been called, "out of tune with his time," Raphael was content with his lot, fascinated by the spectacle of the world, full of trust in human nature, dedicated to the portrayal of its harmonious development. All this led him later to take advantage of his facility. But it did not prevent the Vatican frescoes from being regarded as Raphael's masterpiece of painting and representing in some opinions "the absolute of beauty."

Julius II was not to see the conclusion of the undertaking, but before his death he was able to use several of the rooms, notably the one called the Signature Room, in which, beginning in 1511, he affixed the innumerable signatures "that necessity and routine demand of every chief of state." During his lifetime the sovereign pontiff had ample opportunity to see himself portrayed in many of Raphael's figures, sometimes as an old man representing Gregory IX, sometimes full of youthfulness and strength of success as in the scene of Heliodorus being driven from the temple. Raphael took more pleasure than any other painter in reproducing the faces of the notables of his time. That is why his frescoes have given rise to so many hypotheses and speculations, justifying the Goncourts' observation that "nothing in the world can produce so much stupidity and empty chatter as a painting."

PASQUINO AND THE SPEAKING STATUES

Authoritarian in his dealings with princes and kings, Julius II was liberal in his government of Rome. He accorded new freedoms to the city and broader powers to the conservators. He put an end to the jurisdictional tangles that were hamstringing justice, and he made plaintiffs themselves defend their claims and their property. The source of much murder and "grave injury" having been uprooted, Rome became an orderly and calm city. Jews enjoyed a tolerance there that was refused to them elsewhere. Anyone who did not challenge dogma could express his views on everything. A humorous stone cutter near Piazza Navone was able to shower the city government, the cardinals, and even the pope with satire without being molested. His style made him well known, first in his own neighborhood and then throughout the city. After his death he was credited with more wit than he had possessed. Near his shop a very mutilated ancient statue was found, and the scholars debated whether it represented the torso of Menelaus or that of Patroclus; the people resolved the question by baptizing it Pasquino. This illegally awarded identity was ratified by the municipal government; the so-called Pasquino was erected at the corner of Palazzo Braschi in a square that also bore its name. Protected by darkness, furtive hands were to take over its pedestal at night as a bulletin board to which they attached satires and pamphlets that were the joy of the city next morning and that often shaped its views. Pasquino became the voice of public wit. Roman malice was to give him an interlocutor as amusing as himself in the person of a colossal antique statue from Caesar's Forum that represented a river deity and that was christened Marforio. Today Marforio cools his heels, as if "to expiate his long spurts of speech," in the courtyard of the Capitoline Museum, of which he seems to be the doorkeeper. Pasquino and Marforio were to be joined by other speaking statues—Faquino, Abate Luigi, and Signora Lucrezia—to form that *Congresso degli arguti* (Congress of Wits) that in papal Rome was to represent the freedom of the press and, as some have said, "the press itself."

In the days of Julius II, grounds for accusation and subjects of criticism were not too numerous. It was a delightful period in Rome's life, and unfortunately quite short. Pleasures of every nature were abundantly available to all, and everyone was free to enjoy them fully in accordance with his condition and his rank. At this banquet of life the dignitaries of the papal court and the great burghers of Rome certainly had the choicest places. Sumptuous dinners and magnificent spectacles were constantly being given in the great halls of the palaces or under the cypresses in their gardens. Poets, men of letters, and artists, then very numerous in Rome, were welcomed with open arms by the new aristocracy and contributed to these occasions "the light and witty tone that had hitherto been lacking." No one imagined, Castiglione wrote, "that the pleasure and the delight that come from congenial and sympathetic company were ever so highly prized anywhere else."

Some idea of the freedom of manners may be gained from the fact that courtesans were extremely numerous. The Romans of the Renaissance enjoyed their company as the Athenians had done. They were to be seen everywhere: in splendid carriages in the streets, magnificently jeweled in the drawing rooms, at the spectacles, and even in the churches; their homes were filled with works of art. The drawing rooms of one of them, the beautiful Imperia, "the pride and the marvel of Rome," were frequented by the most eminent citizens (she is buried in St. Susanna). She was reputed to be modest, and her colleagues were respected and highly regarded. We know very well how much the Renaissance owed to these *donne di buon tempo:* the painters took them as their models, the poets took them as their inspirations, the great lords took them as their advisers; and yet one may wonder whether the Italians of the sixteenth century gave certain words the same meanings that we attach to them.

THE DEATH OF JULIUS II

Julius II took the occasion of the carnival of 1513 to arrange his own apotheosis, even before his death, in a triumphal procession that hailed the glories of his papacy. These allegories were marvelously suited to a character that had been, as Vettori* said, that of an emperor rather than a pontiff and that had done more to exalt the church in the temporal realm than in the spiritual.

While the celebrations of his triumph were taking place, Julius II was busy in one of Raphael's rooms with the plans for his funeral. He knew that he was close to death, and his stormy life ended, in fact, three weeks later, on February 21, 1513. His tomb, the first of his great designs, still consisted only of a few statues by Michelangelo, barely roughed out. His coffin had to be placed in the tomb of his uncle, Sixtus IV. It was to remain there for more than thirty years, almost anonymous, under the black bronze bed worked for another by Pollaiuolo. On reflection, such a conclusion to a tempestuous life is quite in accord with the man and rather aptly represents the defects of his achievements. This man who had a passion for building left only unfinished works. His tomb was to be completed only thirty-two years after his death, and in a place that had not been intended for it; it was not to have the majesty of which the pope had dreamed, and, in the end, it was never to contain his body. His apartment was to be completed by his successor, as was the Belvedere courtyard. The fantastic palace, huger than the Venezia, that he had wanted to build on Via Giulia was never to rise out of its foundations, and they were never to be used for the purposes that had brought about their excavation. The dome of St. Peter's was not to be raised for fifty years on Bramante's pillars; and it too was to be very different from the original conception. Even the great municipal improvements of Julius II were far less than

---

* Francesco Vettori, a highly gifted political adviser to the Medicis.—Translator.

various forceful inscriptions would lead their readers to believe. In politics there were the same imperfect conclusions to great projects. The most concrete result of the late pope's bellicose tendencies was the fact that all the great powers turned to Italy as their private tilting ground and no one could imagine how to rid the peninsula of their armies.

CHAPTER 21

THE AGE OF LEO X

A HUMANIST POPE: LEO X

Giovanni Cardinal de' Medici gave the lie to the old adage according to which "he who enters the conclave as pope comes out a cardinal." Even though everything pointed to him in advance to succeed Julius II, an irresistible tide swept up rebellious spirits and his election was triumphal.

The son of Lorenzo il Magnifico, he seemed to have inherited that prodigious man's talents. It was in his childhood that that education had begun that already determined his special character as a pontiff who would be the patron of letters and arts. He was in addition tremendously rich, and this detail counted for much, beyond any challenge of doubt, in the enthusiasm that was aroused on his behalf. Rome was illuminated for a week; the many Florentine merchants in the city kept popular spirits high with frequent distributions of wine and money. It was understandable that throughout that triumphal week all that they heard round their houses was "serenades, songs, and the sound of rejoicing."

Crowned on March 19, 1513, at the temporary main altar of St. Peter's under the name of Leo X, the new pope took possession of the basilica and the Lateran Palace on April 11. This was the occasion for one of the most magnificent parades that had ever been seen in Rome. The splendors of the procession indicated the luxurious tastes of the new pope: his court was to be the most brilliant in the world and to be, as Stendhal said, "the ornament of the world."

Leo X was not handsome; he was painted many times by the artists of his day, and especially by Raphael, but, even though these state portraits owe more to flattery than to truth, he appears in them as a man grown thick and old before his time, with a heavy body on legs that were too frail, almost deformed. His physical misfortune was aggravated by a perpetually open fistula, which made it unpleasant to go too near him. But in the splendor of his ceremonials greater attention was paid to his rich attire and his miter glittering with precious stones. Even more attention was paid to the clerics of the apostolic chamber, who threw handfuls of money to the crowd. The Romans were extremely susceptible to this munificence.

In any event Leo X would have benefited by a predisposition in his favor. The replacement of a tumultuous pope by a humanist was highly welcome. In this respect Leo X was to disappoint none of the hopes invested in him. His name has been given to an age in which, however, he reigned for only a few years, and hence this is no doubt an exaggeration. It must be conceded, nevertheless, that the magnificence of his court and his lavish encouragement of arts and letters made Rome the center of the artistic universe. At his death the decline of the Renaissance began.

In contrast to so many popes who pretended to deprecate the work of their predecessors, Leo X, who was responsible for few new creations, was unfailingly dedicated to the realization of the projects that Julius II had conceived, or at the very least to the prosecution of those that he had launched. For a time he took some interest even in his predecessor's tomb, and Michelangelo moved back into the studio on St. Peter's square that he had given up under duress so many years before. But there was an incompatibility of temperament between the sybaritic pope and the rough, gloomy artist, always locked in his austere thoughts. The time of their collaboration was short, and after a few months Leo X sent Michelangelo back to Florence, this time to work there as an architect. He was to remain there eighteen years, employed against his will in undertakings that for him were the source of new disappointments. His departure from Rome left unfinished the statue of Christ that was to be placed in the church of the Minerva in 1519 after having been clumsily completed by a mediocre sculptor. This was the sole work by Michelangelo that was incorporated into Rome's artistic patrimony under the reign of Leo X.

Another artist won the pope's favor: Raphael. Young, of a mild nature, he was able to accept a master's wishes with charming grace. Completing the decoration of Julius II's rooms, his obliging brush "gloriously illustrated" the acts of Leo X in his last frescoes. This was indeed the man whom this pope needed, and he was made a kind of superintendent of fine arts.

First of all he was assigned to the work on St. Peter's when Bramante died. This choice created much surprise, for Raphael had made his early name as a painter. But he had already given some evidence of his architectural talents in 1509 by building in Via dell'Armata, the church of St. Eligius of the Goldsmiths, a delicate masterpiece and a charming example of the intellectual studies of the Renaissance. Did Raphael feel that the immensity of the task that was assigned to him exceeded his capabilities? In any case, he was hardly enthusiastic about St. Peter's. It was his idea to alter the original design and give the basilica the shape of a Latin cross. He decided to reinforce the pillars of the dome, and he turned over to his assistants the planning and execution of the work, which was not very actively forwarded.

In reality he had many other projects in mind; he was receiving a tremendous number of commissions from all quarters. The courtiers of Leo X besieged him for their portraits; he painted a great number of them, which are now scattered and of which none is still in Rome (the one that is exhibited in the Doria gallery is only a bad copy). No palace was decorated without an appeal for his collaboration. "He could direct such varied undertakings," Bertaux wrote, "only on condition of executing nothing more himself." In painting, as in architecture and sculpture, he no longer produced anything but designs. Besides, this was what the pope wanted of him. Leo X was concerned less with surrounding himself with the works of masters than with a setting that would gratify his curiosity and his vanity.

It was in fact this tendency that led him to have Raphael execute the sketches for a series of tapestries intended to complete the decoration of the Sistine Chapel. Executed in Brussels, the tapestries vanished in the sack of Rome in 1527 and were scattered throughout the world. Some have been reassembled in the Vatican Museum in a side room near the Antiquities Museum. They gained nothing by their travels; the fabric is threadbare and faded, the designs are often deformed. As for the original sketches, they are not in Rome but in London, having been purchased by Rubens on behalf of King Charles I.

RAPHAEL'S LOGGIE / THE SIBYLS / THE CHIGI CHAPEL

Julius II, as we know, had hoped to extend to the Vatican the program that he had made it his duty to accomplish with the basilica: to make a clean slate of the past in order to erect new buildings. Having been unable to tear down the buildings of Nicholas V, he had remodeled their interiors while at the same time hiding their uneven masses devoid of beauty. It was in order to mask them to viewers from the city that Bramante had constructed those stories of open galleries (loggie) that, continued during the sixteenth century, were to achieve the fine harmony of the present court of San Damaso. The second story of the original wing communicated with the pontifical apartment, which it extended into a sumptuous gallery with sixteen bays, from which one could easily look out over the river and the countryside as far as the Alban Hills. The buildings that now face the gallery did not then exist, any more than the conservatory windows that the Murat king was to install in order to close the arches, in a belated concern for the protection of the mural paintings. It was an aerial *belvedere* where Leo X enjoyed relaxing in the company of his cardinals and his favorite poets. He charged Raphael with decorating it in a style in harmony with the softness of the surroundings. This was the origin of the celebrated loggie, which, even though they have been the victims of weather, still provide a good glimpse "of the luxury and the refinements of a princely residence in the best years of the Renaissance." The pleasant age of Leo X is there in its entirety with the image of a world "that had not yet been spoiled by puritanism."

The elegant ornamental paintings, composed of arabesques peopled with nymphs, dancing girls, and satyrs, were directly inspired by the "grotesques" whose ancient models had just been discovered. Undoubtedly they did not come from the hand of Raphael, who had to confine himself to providing designs and supervising their execution by his pupils. As for the series of panels portraying scenes from the Holy Scriptures that decorate the vaults and are inaccurately termed "Raphael's Bible," it is now believed that only the first episodes, those of Genesis, benefited from the master's personal attention, although the others reveal the inexhaustible fertility and the inspired invention of pose that are admired in his greatest works.

The famous banker Agostino Chigi, the creditor of princes and popes, was the equal of the Medicis at that time, as much in his wealth as in his interest in the arts. Though he had become an intimate of Leo X, he retained an almost filial devotion to the memory of Julius II, who had largely assisted him in his early days. It was as a mark of gratitude to that pope's family that he commissioned from Raphael the sumptuous decorations of the della Rovere family's two churches, Santa Maria della Pace and Santa Maria del Popolo. One chapel in Santa Maria della Pace was adorned with the famous fresco of the Sibyls, which is regarded as the artist's masterpiece and a peak of poetry and art. The movement of the supple, harmonious bodies ripples through the austere style of their draperies; it has been said that in their spiritual expression the Sibyls transcend human reality. One of them, the Phrygian, however, is the faithful portrait of a person who was in no way dissociated from mundane considerations: the beautiful Imperia, who had just died at the age of twenty-six. This tribute in a church rendered to a notorious sinner shocked no one. There was another example of these intrusions of the profane on the sacred in Santa Maria del Popolo, which Raphael enriched with the magnificent Chigi chapel, whose dome, in miniature, reproduces that conceived by Bramante for St. Peter's. The mosaics of this cupola are also adorned with heathen images whose presence in a sanctuary was considered no more out of place. Still, they show the gods of Olympus being blessed by the God of the Christians.

This was not the only digression of the kind that Raphael allowed himself. Aside from the profane subjects that he included in his great works for the Vatican, in the popes' palace itself he decorated Cardinal Bibbiena's bathroom with pictures of the amatory life of Venus. It is well known that the Renaissance was steeped in paganism. Nevertheless, every pope since Leo X has regarded that bathroom as a scandal and has carefully kept it invisible to visitors. It still exists, but it is a secret place inaccessible to the public.

THE VILLA FARNESINA

Chigi, who had been nicknamed *Il Magnifico,* wanted to have his villa just like the greatest princes. Begun under Julius II and completed under Leo X, it stood between the Tiber and Via della Lungara. Baldassare Peruzzi, regarded at the time as the Raphael of architecture, made it the most graceful and the freshest work of the Roman Renaissance. Vasari said of this building that it was born as if by enchantment and that it was a creation rather than a construction. Villa Farnesina (it acquired this name when it became the property of Alessandro Farnese in 1580) no longer enjoys its former amplitude, for the construction of the Tiber quays mutilated its gardens; today it is lacking in perspective. But its casino has not been touched; the purity of Greek art is brought back to life in it, with what the Renaissance added in its originality of interpretation of the antique. It is a unique place for relaxation and celebration, a true temple of pleasure.

In this "golden house" of the prince of Roman banking, magnificent parties were given; splendid banquets there brought together the pope, the prelates of his court, the ambassadors, the cream of the poets and artists, and all the noblemen and beautiful ladies of the aristocracy. A detail will indicate the prodigality of the house: the silver dishes were thrown into the Tiber after every course. It remains a superb gesture even if, as is also reported, there were nets in the river that made it possible to get the silver back.

All the great artists of the time took a hand in the interior decoration of the Farnesina: Giulio Romano, Sodoma (Giovanni Bazzi), Sebastiano del Piombo, who had been summoned from Venice, to say nothing of the master of the project, Peruzzi, who was also an excellent painter. This group of artists was to be joined belatedly by Raphael, who in ten pictures portrayed the fable of Psyche and the triumph of Galatea. Once again he demonstrated the fecundity of his genius. He triumphed by playing, by completely abandoning himself to his pagan inspiration. Psyche and Galatea recount their adventures, Tritons embrace nymphs at whom flying Cupids loose their arrows. And yet "the spectacle of love remains chaste in its Virgilian grace." The nude, it has been said, "is purified by its plastic perfection." A beautiful Trasteverine woman, *la fornarina* (the baker), was Raphael's model and inspiration. His love for her assures her of a share in his immortality. He has left many portraits of her, the finest of which is in Palazzo Barberini.

In the hall of Galatea's triumph, a charcoal face of a faun has been added to the fresco and is obviously alien to it. It has been said that Raphael sketched it there in order to leave some sign of his visit for Sebastiano del Piombo, whom he had not found there. It has also been called the work of Michelangelo, who supposedly wanted to give his competitor a lesson in style. Whatever its origin, this fortuitous addition contributes in its own fashion to the evocation of that happy time of the Renaissance of which the delightful Farnesina affords us the most attractive and the most accurate conception.

SAN GIOVANNI DEI FIORENTINI / ST. LOUIS OF THE FRENCH / THE PALAZZO VIDONI

Now that one of their own was pope, Florentines were coming to Rome in great numbers, and many of them were establishing themselves there. A great celebration, which Leo X never failed to attend, brought them all together every year on the anniversary of their city's patron, St. John the Baptist; riderless horses competed for a golden *pallium* and in the evening there was a fireworks display in Piazza San Celso. It was near this area, along Via Giulia, that a papal bull of January 29, 1519, authorized the Florentine colony to build its church. This was San Giovanni dei Fiorentini. In reality, the Florentines were merely permitted to assume the cost of it, the pope himself taking charge of everything else. He had set a competition for several architects, and he chose the design of Jacopo Sansovino. Though he had not been admitted to the competition, Raphael participated in the final arrangements for the building, though it is impossible to identify exactly what his contribution was. Antonio da Sangallo and Giacomo della Porta were to carry on and complete the construction. Hence it is hardly surprising that San Giovanni dei Fiorentini is a remarkably finished work; the lateral chapels in particular are most remarkable. As for the façade, it was to be erected in the eighteenth century by another Florentine pope, Clement XII.

While a few churches were given notable embellishments by Leo X (in particular, he gave the chapel of Castello Sant'Angelo its lovely lateral façade at the end of the angel courtyard), no other church aside from San Giovanni was erected during his pontificate. The first stone for St. Louis of the French was indeed set in 1518, but the start of work had to await the arrival of funds from Catherine dei Medici, so that the church was not completed until 1589. The construction of Santa Maria di Loreto, begun in 1507, was similarly left in abeyance, and it was seventy-five years before the church was to be completed. On the other hand, a sanctuary especially favored by devout Romans, San Marcello in Corso, was lost. It was destroyed by a fire that miraculously spared the wooden crucifix, which was reinstalled on the main altar of the new church (rebuilt in 1550), where it is the object of special veneration. San Marcello, which owed its façade to Carlo Fontana, houses the curious tomb of Cardinal Orso, who had donated his library to the adjoining convent: it portrays the prelate lying on a bed of books.

Raphael's artistic majesty was exercised in so sovereign a manner, even in the field of architecture, that most of the palaces that were to rise in Rome in his time were to profit by his collaboration, which was sought after by everyone. For the closest intimates of the Vatican he prepared designs of a great many houses, but, since his many concerns prevented him from personally seeing to the execution of works that he had conceived, they bear only the names of their builders. It is because of these very special conditions that Raphael enjoys universal admiration as a painter while at the same time he is one of the least known of Renaissance architects. Aside from the fact that his great talent is displayed in many parts of Rome, his superiority can be verified by comparing his work with that of his successors in the same structure. Palazzo Vidoni (Via del Sudario, 10–16) makes such a comparison possible. Raphael had designed it for the Caffarellis; his plans were followed as far as the top story; then, after a long interruption, work was resumed with a new design and a disastrous result: "the ridiculous superimposed on the sublime."

PALAZZO FARNESE

The finest creation of this period, Palazzo Farnese, escaped Raphael's influence. It was the work of Antonio da Sangallo the Younger, who received from Alessandro Cardinal Farnese, later Pope Paul III, the chance to show his full talent when he was commissioned to build this palace in the Campo dei Fiori; it is now the French embassy. Riddled with doubts of the cardinal's financial solidity, the neighborhood proletariat hung a box on Pasquino's pedestal with this inscription: "Alms for the construction of the palace." Georges Gromart wrote: "What Peruzzi did with the *Farnesina* on the inspiration of the villas of Florence was accomplished here by Sangallo for a great city residence; adopting the general basis of Florentine architecture, he created the finished model of a great Roman palace." There are no more piers, as in the Chancellery, but austere walls reinforced at the corners by powerful bossages. There would have been more sturdiness and grandeur than grace in this building if Michelangelo had not later been enlisted to crown it with his broad cornice. The square courtyard is embellished with several stories of pilastered porticoes; it imitates the arrangement of the theater of Marcellus and it is not unworthy of its model. Some of the material used in its construction came from the Colosseum and the theater of Marcellus, a fact that prevented de Brosses from recognizing the beauties of Palazzo Farnese: "Must a man not be possessed of a devil to perpetrate such a deed? Would it not have been a hundred times better to invest all that thought and labor in repairing the Colosseum . . . and to have no Palazzo Farnese?" One might as well argue that it would have been better to leave in the ruins of the Baths of Caracalla the two monolithic Egyptian granite basins that became the fountains of the square in front of the palace. The insensate Cardinal Farnese, as de Brosses called him, was after all not alone in looking for cheap material; at least the use to which he put it was highly honorable, for his palace, a classic example of Renaissance architecture, is the best illustration of that rule that another cardinal set for his architect: "*Semplice, ma pomposo* (simple, but stately)." The interior decoration of the palace is also very beautiful; the reception halls have magnificently paneled ceilings and the ballroom is decorated with the celebrated frescoes of Annibale Carracci, in which once again the Renaissance yields to the temptation of pagan subjects. As for the two basins in the square, over which the cardinal erected heraldic lilies to make it clear that they belonged to his palace, no water was to flow from them until 1613, when Pope Paul V extended the Acqua Paola to the Regola quarter.

ROMAN LIFE IN THE SIXTEENTH CENTURY

During this brilliant epoch, delicacy and elegance had reached farther and farther into the different classes of society. It was a long time since the Florentines had been able to dismiss the vulgar burghers of Rome as herdsmen. The Romans had so thoroughly lost their old rusticity that they were now being reproached for their effete manners and their esthetic preoccupations. Furthermore, in spite of the censors, Rome was enjoying itself, and its pleasures had become gentler and often intellectual. The air was almost impregnated with a sensuality that seemed to have become an essential element of life.

Unquestionably the sophistication of the arts did not suppress the ardor of the passions. The memoirs of the period are full of tales of violence in which artists were often involved. It was the time when Benvenuto Cellini calmly killed colleagues for senseless reasons. And the popes absolved these crimes too easily: "You must learn," Leo X said, "that men like Benvenuto who are unique in their arts should not be subjected to the usual laws." The era was the crossroads of two ages, and the most amazing contrasts erupted in the blend of savagery and culture that was the Renaissance—except that, beginning in the sixteenth century, the lover of antiquities had precedence in Rome over the man of the sword. More advanced than the other cities of Europe in the quest of the beautiful, Rome was more and more to renounce private violence and to take pleasure in masquerades, processions, and festivals.

The time of the Renaissance was the golden age of popular celebrations in Rome; they had never been more frequent or more brilliant. They were enhanced with theatrical performances, re-enactments of the ancient games, historical processions, tournaments, and sporting contests. The balloon game, a distant ancestor of football, which had arrived with the Florentines, had a large public: it was played by two teams of thirty-five men each on the site where Julius II had intended to build his great government palace. The game was occasionally played even in the Belvedere courtyard, in the presence of the pope and his court.

Every day there was some procession. It might be the arrival of an ambassador, a cardinal's first visit to the Consistory, the inauguration of a municipal magistrate, the canonization of a saint. All the guilds, which were more numerous now that commercial activity had increased, organized ceremonials, processions in which the publicity given to their work was mingled with religious pomps. As for the return of a pope to Rome from a campaign (it was always called victorious), it was celebrated with indescribable splendor, and the crowd pressed in on the pontiff's passage so closely that it took him three hours to go from Piazza del Popolo to the Vatican. A contemporary, generally thought to have been Erasmus, has left us a description:

Never had anyone seen so many cardinals in their purple followed by so many servitors, so many horses caparisoned better than the horses of kings, so many mules covered with linen, with gold, and with precious stones; some were even shod with silver and gold. The pope sat on a golden chair carried by soldiers, the crowd prostrated itself when he lifted his hand. One had to hear the thunder of the salutes, the ringing of the bugles and the trumpets, the crashing roar of the cannon, the acclamations, the cheers of the crowd, one had to see on all sides the gleam of the torches, the flames of the bonfires.

In these celebrations, in which good taste and magnificence met, all classes joined their talents in common. The smallest artisan shared in the euphoria. "There was a popular feeling," Taine wrote, "for beautiful forms, for great harmony, for picturesque ornament; a carpenter would talk about them to his wife in the evening, they were the subject of discussion in the tavern, at the work bench." Religious and profane pomps were commingled in allegorical presentations in which drama and pantomime were joined; choirs of angels sang for the entrance of an ambassador, and strong men performed their feats in the wake of the processions. Sometimes it happened that all these additions were not enough to enhance the processions, and they were replaced by parades of maskers.

Luxury was everywhere, in the celebrations as in the arrangements of the palaces. And also in the sumptuous dress of the great ladies, who had to have servants to carry their long trains. The dressmakers of that time were honored as artists, and the hairdressers already enjoyed a virtual dictatorship over elegant women. The fashion for blond hair, which had come from Venice, predominated, but mastery of *l'arte biondeggiante* (the art of bleaching) was limited to a very small number of specialists. There was rivalry for the services of cooks and bakers. Goldsmiths, silversmiths, perfume dealers made fortunes. The consumption of candles was so high that the candlemakers' guild became one of the richest in Rome. From the luxury industries prosperity seeped down little by little into all fields of activity.

Life became a continuous feast of body and mind. In this feast pure intellectuality had its place. Audiences flocked to the debates of the humanists and the verse readings of the poets. When word went round that Bernardo Accolti was preparing to recite a poem, the shops closed.

Delightful customs gave Roman life that quality of graciousness that has always made it so attractive. Let us limit ourselves to mentioning only a few of them. Certain weddings were held in groups—those of the girls educated by the nuns' orders. The richest of these staged thirty weddings every year, dressing the girls in borrowed gowns and transporting them on horses borrowed from the papal stables; preceded by a troop of little boys dressed as Cupids, they went through the city in a procession, to the sound of trumpets, and escorted by the clergy of St. Peter's.

On May Day lovers decorated their girls' houses; "they gilded the doors, they decked them with flowers, leaves, and wreaths, they nailed up sonnets, and they planted a laurel with a gilded trunk, filling it with pieces of fabric, mottoes, little presents, and birds. People went from house to house to admire and compare the tributes" (Rodocanachi). On Epiphany the cardinals loosed live birds over the heads of the crowd to symbolize the descent of the Holy Spirit, in imitation of the canons of St. Peter's, who released a dove in the basilica on Pentecost.

Thus Rome had become an idyllic resort; foreigners flooded the city, and left only with regrets that have come down to us in their letters. Erasmus wrote to the French ambassador: "If I had not simply torn myself away from Rome, I could never have made up my mind to leave." Isabella d'Este, on her return to her own domain, summed up the whole magic of the Eternal City in one sentence written to Cardinal Bibbiena: "My body is here but my spirit remains in Rome."

CITY PLANNING UNDER LEO X

Leo X was the first pope who relied on the Communal Council for the administration and development of the city. This body, which had existed since the end of the previous century, consisted only of the conservators and the *caporioni* (heads of quarters). Leo X added a corps of useful advisers. He consolidated the council's powers and even broadened them. Above all, in a remarkable innovation, he relieved it of interference by the religious authority. Thus the council became in fact the center of urban government, and Rome ruled itself. Processions and festivals were no longer occasions of scandal or disorder: women of bad reputation were kept away from them, crowd movement was regulated. A city police force, the *maestri di strada* (street masters), saw to it that the streets were kept clean. Great improvements were initiated, at the head of which must be listed the enlargement of Piazza del Popolo and the opening of a new street that was first called Via Leonina and then Via Ripetta; it has retained the later name. At the same time the modern Via del Babbuino was laid out in such manner that Via Flaminia was divided at Piazza del Popolo into three major arteries leading to the center of the city; each kept its own character, which was to be accentuated in their subsequent evolution. It was to be said later that travelers entering Rome at Porta del Popolo could choose for their journey into the city the route that corresponded to the reasons for their journeys; for the poets there was Via del Babbuino, for the merchants the Corso, for the priests Via Ripetta. Via del Babbuino is in fact the artists' quarter; the Corso is flanked by shops; Via Ripetta leads to the Vatican through a double hedge of churches and palaces. This sort of specialization was already indicated in the days of Leo X.

Many other streets were laid out or widened at this time; rules were formulated for the destruction of buildings that impeded traffic or impaired the good appearance of the city. All this was the fruit of the complete collaboration between the pope and the Communal Council, which decided to show its gratitude to the sovereign pontiff by erecting a statue to him. After numerous tribulations, it now stands in the left-hand transept of Santa Maria in Ara Coeli. To tell the truth, it has none of the qualities of a masterpiece, and the least that can be said of it is that it does not give a very attractive portrait of its subject.

On Good Friday in 1520 Raphael died of exhaustion in his graceful palace in the Borgo, amid the court of artists that had taken shape round him. He was only thirty-seven years old and had just finished that *Transfiguration* that is considered his masterpiece. Placed first on the main altar of San Pietro in Montorio, this famous painting, which was taken to France in 1797 and briefly exhibited in the Louvre, is now in the Vatican picture gallery. It still stood on its easel when Raphael died and it presided over his wake.

The great artist departed from life early enough to remain "always young in men's memories." The friend of all, he had never hated anyone, being too busy with his love affairs and his work. His death was a public sorrow, and his funeral was worthy of a pope. A huge, deeply moved crowd accompanied his body to the vault of the old Pantheon, where it rests beside that of his betrothed, Cardinal Bibbiena's niece, who had died three months earlier. Later he was joined in the Pantheon by a number of other artists: Annibale Carracci, Baldassare Peruzzi, Giovanni d'Udine, and others.

His death was to mark the end of "the free and joyous life that the court of Rome and the elegant among its citizens had led under the eyes of the happy gods." Leo X died a year later, stricken with a mysterious disease that gave rise to fantastic diagnoses. Brantôme* contends that the pope died because he choked with laughter when he learned of the defeat of a French army.

Dazzled by the splendor of his life, history has endowed the memory of Leo X with an excess of honor. In reality he was a vacillating politician,

---

* Pierre de Bourdeille, *seigneur* de Brantôme, was a French historian and biographer of the sixteenth century.—Translator.

concerned above all with the interests of his family; the scant zeal that he invested in combatting Luther's heresy makes him seem a feeble champion of Christian doctrine.* But he established academies and libraries, encouraged the arts, and gave a new aspect to Roman life.

He lies in the chancel of the Minerva, beneath a monument designed by Antonio da Sangallo and adorned by a rather mediocre statue by Montelupo.

* The adjective is used here in the restrictive sense of "Catholic" by a Catholic author.—Translator.

CHAPTER 22

THE DECLINE OF THE RENAISSANCE

THE INTERVAL OF AUSTERITY

If the conclave convoked at the death of Leo X had sought to give him a successor who would be his opposite in every respect, it could not have made a more significant choice than that of Adrian VI. But the cardinals were in no way motivated by a spirit of reaction; they confined themselves to elevating to St. Peter's throne the man who had been forced on them by Charles V. He was the son of a brewer in Utrecht, a former tutor to the emperor, who had twice made him regent of Spain—an honest German of the kind that the sixteenth century bred, "steel-clad from head to toe in theology and scholasticism." In Roman eyes there could be no calamity to match the election of a "savage" Pope. The Romans made this very clear to the cardinals, whom they assailed with insults when the conclave adjourned. The sight of their new pope did nothing to mitigate their anger: he looked like a begging monk, with bowed shoulders and a harsh face. His actions were not to belie his appearance. The people, dazzled by the splendors of the two preceding reigns, was quite as appalled by his attitudes and his deeds as the enlightened, elegant, frivolous class that set the tone. He was especially disliked for his rigid aversion to the fine arts. The sight of the frescoes in the Sistine Chapel revolted him. He recoiled in horror at the ancient statues "as if he had walked on serpents." He gave away a great number of these remains of heathenism to anyone who wanted to make lime of them. While he did not order the destruction of the *Laocoön,* he had its gallery locked. In order to have no further traffic with the Venuses and Jupiters that encumbered his palace, he went to live under its eaves with his old serving woman and his seedy clerk. As for celebrations, spectacles, banquets, and amusements of all categories, they were naturally out of the question. All forms of luxury were mercilessly hunted down and a monastic simplicity spread over Rome.

It pleased no one's taste, and, when the collapse of a vault in St. Peter's almost killed "the barbarian," there was public cursing of Providence for having saved his life. This "savage" pope, who was to be the last of this hated kind, fortunately vindicated after a decent interval the then widespread belief that a foreign pope could not long endure Rome's climate. His decease was viewed as an incalculable blessing. His physician's door was hung with garlands of flowers bearing an inscription ascribed to Pasquino: "From the Senate and the Roman people to the liberator of the fatherland."

Adrian VI was buried in Santa Maria dell'Anima, in the midst of other notables of Germanic origin. The two years of his reign had been enough to change Roman life completely. The swarm of poets that had surrounded Leo X had scattered; the artists and their assistants had gone to find employment elsewhere for their talents; a number of wealthy men had abandoned living in Rome as too unhealthy. The inns were going bankrupt. Desolation was everywhere. Once again vindication was claimed for the proverb that declared that "Rome always suffers when its pope is numbered VI."

The city thought that it was saved when, after fifty days of bitter deliberations, the conclave elected Giulio de' Medici, the cousin of Leo X and the bastard son of Giuliano, the victim of the Pazzis' plot.* Everything was expected of this new pope: the restoration of the Holy See's power, the end of the cruel wars that were bathing Italy in blood, even the return of the golden age. Perhaps never, Pastor said, "were higher hopes more completely dashed." The pontificate of Clement VII, in fact, was to be one of the most unfortunate in history. The reason was the pope's involvement in political machinations with the same passion and the same

---

* The Pazzis were a Florentine family of Ghibellines who arranged the murder of Giuliano de' Medici in 1478 because of the feud between the two clans.—Translator.

duplicity as Leo X but with an even more indecisive character. But this time the reverses that he suffered were terrifying, and Rome was to live through the most painful page of its long history.

The reign began well, however. Romans at once plunged back into that life of pleasure that they loved so much. The carnival of 1524 was splendid and gay. Unfortunately it had a sorrowful sequel: a plague broke out and raged throughout the summer with the utmost intensity; four cardinals died, the courts and even the Consistory had to suspend their sittings. Of the nine thousand houses in Rome, seventeen hundred were contaminated. It was then that the little church of Santa Maria in Augusta had a particular influx of the faithful. Antonio da Sangallo the Younger had just completed it, in the Horseshoe Square, near Via Ripetta, and popular belief assured entry into heaven to anyone who died at worship there. Since then it has been called St. Mary Gate of Heaven.

Once the plague had passed, Rome remained supine and as if paralyzed in expectation of a new catastrophe. The construction of St. Peter's, resumed *pro forma,* was only desultorily pursued for lack of money. The only signs of activity were at Castello Sant'Angelo, where Montelupo was working on the reconstruction of the statue of the archangel St. Michael. The emptiness of the pontifical treasury and the apprehensive inertia of the city were no inducements to the artists whom Adrian VI had driven out to go back to Rome. The Trattoria della Fontanella—the restaurant still exists, at Via del Banco San Spirito, 19—where they were accustomed to gather in the time of Leo X, waited in vain for their return. Those who somehow had not left Rome were chiefly engaged either in attacking or in defending Raphael's work in innumerable arguments that often ended in fights. The rest of their time was spent in studio fakery and good eating. Associations were formed (Benvenuto Cellini was the president of one of them) with no other purpose than to organize these diversions. There were also a few literary groups in which minor poets met to shower praises on one another. All these brotherhoods were to be routed by the sack of the city in 1527.

THE SACK OF ROME AND ITS SEQUELS

The defeat of Francis I at Pavia (February 25, 1525) had delivered Italy to the imperial forces. In this situation Clement VII had been unable to do more than cling to an incoherent policy that in the end left Rome isolated before the terrible menace of the imperial troops. These were mercenary forces whom the adventurers who were supposedly their leaders could control only by furthering their basest instincts. The Bourbon Constable, a traitor to his country, was the leader of one of these brigand bands. The Prince of Orange commanded another, composed of Spaniards and Belgians. Frondsberg, a German who wore round his neck a golden chain with which, he boasted, he would strangle the pope, led the Lutheran mercenaries. The one thought that occupied all of them was to sack the city of the popes; they called it "the glorious sack" in order to cloak their lust for rapine in the highly fallacious pretext of a crusade "against impiety." In the spring of 1527 these hordes poured down from Lombardy, where there was nothing left for them to eat; in the afternoon of May 5 it was possible, from the top of Rome's walls, to see them in Nero's meadow and on the slopes of Monte Mario.

To counter them the pope had been able to muster only a laughable force commanded briefly by a strange general, Francesco Maria, who knew only one tactic, that of refusing to fight. "It is more prudent," he said, "to conquer with the sheathed sword." For Rome's defense within the walls the pope had only troops who knew little of war and who were frightened, to boot, by the grim omens that foretold the chastisement of the Eternal City: lightning had shattered an infant Jesus in the arms of a marble madonna in Santa Maria Traspontina, an invisible hand had stolen the Host from a tabernacle, a city wall had collapsed from no apparent cause. The papal troops' resistance was virtually useless, although it cost the lives of four thousand Romans, whose corpses reddened the water of the Tiber. On the evening of May 6, 1527, from the terrace of his refuge in Castello Sant'Angelo, the pope could see the enemy army making camp in the Campo dei Fiori, and the fires of its bivouacs brightened the Roman night.

The sack of Rome began on the following day. It exceeded all the previous tragedies of history in its atrocity, even the destruction of Jerusalem and the capture of Constantinople. Houses were ransacked one by one; their inhabitants were put to the sword, women in the sight of their children and nuns on the steps of the altars. Churches were pillaged and crucifixes were hurled down with halberds. Wine-inflamed brutes reeled out of looted monasteries with miters on their heads and chasubles over their armor. Cardinals were dragged through the streets until they could borrow enough money for their ransom. At Ara Coeli one of them was placed alive in a coffin, which the soldiers paraded through the city as they sang the office for the dead. The halls of the Vatican were turned into kitchens, and the soldiers' fires stained Raphael's frescoes. The basilicas of St. Peter's and St. Paul became stables: the altar ornaments were dragged through the horses' litter, pell-mell with the relics of the saints. No one has ever succeeded in listing the works of art and the precious manuscripts that were destroyed during those insane weeks. For the hideous saturnalia lasted an entire month, and the only change made by the armistice of June 6 was to transform the disordered, violent rapines of the beginning into more formal requisitions. Above all it put no end to scenes of impiety; foot soldiers in cardinals' hats were still riding through the city on donkeys, or strutting in brocade garments beside trollops decked with jewels stolen from a monstrance. The mercenaries' insolence knew no limit; their lack of discipline brought on the worst disorders, and soon a violent epidemic was raging in the city. The conquerors viewed it as revenge by the Romans, who in turn regarded it as the vengeance of heaven; consequently everyone did everything in his power to further the plague instead of uniting against it. Bodies were thrown into sewers or left in the streets, thus spreading the infection. The peasants ceased to bring in food; famine set in and intensified the virulence of the epidemic; "at times it carried off in a single night all the soldiers who had chosen the same palace or monastery as their barracks." The death rate rose so sharply that the imperial troops finally felt compelled to release their prey "lest they be entombed in their triumph." When they abandoned Rome they took with them twenty million gold pieces.

It was sheer luck that the emperor's ruffians had not cut the throats of the pope and his cardinals. In disguise, Clement VII had managed to flee to Orvieto, where he was held prisoner until the full payment of the enormous ransom that had been set for him. His absence lasted ten months, during which the Romans longed constantly for his return. It took place on October 5, 1528, a foggy day, and the spectacle of his capital "crucified his heart." The population had been reduced by half. The sack and the woes that had followed it had claimed thirty thousand victims; many of the survivors had fled; four-fifths of the houses, pillaged or burned, were uninhabitable. Food was in short supply and wine could not be found; the Germans, it was said, had drunk it all.

The pope's return initiated the revival of the city; the fugitives came back, the city officials resumed their duties; taxes were levied and work was begun to restore traffic in the ruined streets, to rebuild the houses, to reopen the churches. The German invasion had spread the Reformation among certain lay circles in Rome: "the pestilential heresy" was hunted down and all the faithful were called on to take part in the defense of the faith. It was this new impulse that set off the Counter-Reformation.

Roman life had barely begun to return to normal when the city was suddenly flooded by the Tiber in the middle of the night. More than three thousand Romans were drowned, and four hundred houses were destroyed. Ponte Sisto was carried away; the water rose halfway up the doors of Santa Maria sopra Minerva. All Rome, a chronicler said, was navigable.

Reduced to total dependence on Charles V, Clement VII embarked on the task of winning his favor and assuaging his rancors. It took him less than two years to forget the humiliation of the Holy See and the sufferings of Rome. In 1529 he placed the two crowns of Italy and the Holy Empire on the head of Charles V with his own hands. It was through his desire to advance himself in the emperor's favor that he cast England, after Henry VIII, into the camp of Luther. His last political act was to marry his niece, Catherine dei Medici, to the dauphin of France in 1534.

THE ARTS UNDER CLEMENT VII

In Rome, as in all Europe, he was the object of increasing hostility. Demands came from all sides for a complete reform of the church, and they made it sharply plain that its head was not to be exempted from this. The dialogue between Pasquino and Marforio became more and more biting.

An occurrence in the spring of 1534 excited the whole of Rome. The pope's nephew, Lorenzino dei Medici, perpetrated an act of vandalism that already pointed to the disorder of his mind: he thought to gain fame by beheading the eight statues of barbarian kings that decorated the arch of Constantine. He may also have had something to do with the head injuries of the muses that adorned a sarcophagus in the church of St. Paul. There was great resentment in Rome, where respect for antiquity was almost superstitious; the angriest Roman of all was the pope himself, who ordered that the perpetrator of these profanations (whose identity he had not yet learned) was to be "immediately, without further trial, hanged by the neck." When he learned that the criminal was his nephew, he reduced the penalty to expulsion from the city, though not without rebuking his infamy: "See," he cried, "his way of following the other Lorenzo, *il Magnifico!*"

Clement VII was genuinely sorry that a man of his family should have dared to damage Rome's artistic patrimony. He himself would have devoted his efforts to enriching it if his reign had not been rent by the horrors of war. When he was still only a cardinal, he had demonstrated the attachment to the arts that was traditional in his family. He had always given a warm welcome to all the Florentine artists who fled from the conflicts to which their city was then a prey and who sought refuge in Rome; he had protected even the most disorderly among them, Benvenuto Cellini, who regarded himself as the most important man in Italy after he had killed with his own hand—or so he claimed—the Bourbon Constable on the eve of the sack of Rome.

It was Clement VII who had commissioned Raphael's *Transfiguration* and his design for the villa, worthy of a Roman emperor, that Clement had built on the slopes of Monte Mario. It is called Villa Madama in memory of Marguerite of Austria, the sister of Charles V, who lived in it. Long abandoned, often mutilated, Villa Madama has been restored by the Italian government for the accommodation of important state visitors. Its portico is one of the most exquisite works of the Renaissance; from its balcony there is a very beautiful view of the city and the winding course of the Tiber. Its garden, long the finest in Rome, served as the model for the majority of the gardens of that epoch. It still contains the fountain by Giovanni d'Udine, in the form of the head of an elephant that was very popular then. The ambassador of Portugal had presented the animal to Leo X; because of its good nature and its almost human intelligence, the placid pachyderm was the darling of the populace. Raphael included its head in a fresco in one of his *stanze*.

In Rome the Medici family also owned the vast Palazzo Madama, which in 1870 became the seat of the Italian Senate (in Corso del Rinascimento). Leo X and Clement VII lived in it when they were cardinals. Catherine de' Medici spent her youth there. Its tenancy by Marguerite of Austria gave it its name. When they became popes the Medicis virtually lost interest in their old Roman residence. It was to be Grand Duke Ferdinand of Tuscany who would restore it in 1642.

Clement VII had established his court on a footing of luxury; it seemed as if the days of Leo X were returning when the catastrophe of 1527 put a brutal stop to everything. With the return of peace the pope spent the last years of his reign in repairing the disasters of the siege. In a short time the ruins were rebuilt and the wounds were bandaged. The pope had found a temporary refuge in Castello Sant'Angelo; the danger having passed, he improved the castle in order to make his stay in it more comfortable. These improvements included the two halls ascribed to him, the hall of Apollo decorated with grotesques and the charming setting of paintings and stucco in the bathing hall.

In 1533 Clement VII summoned Michelangelo back from Florence, where he had just finished the Medicis' tombs. After his absence of twenty-five years the old master found the Vatican wrecked by the pillagers and stripped of the works of art that the popes had accumulated there since Nicholas V. The frescoes of the Sistine Chapel were intact, except for those on the entrance wall, accidentally damaged during the reign of Leo X. Clement VII asked Michelangelo to repair the damage and to create a complementary decoration that would compensate for the loss of Raphael's tapestries, stolen during the sack. Surpassing the pope's intentions, the artist thereupon set out to cover with tremendous frescoes not only the damaged wall but also the one behind the altar that faced it. He did not hesitate to erase either his predecessors' or his own works in order to give his genius a broader field of expression. It was this audaciousness that was to bring forth *The Last Judgment* "for the amazement of Rome and the world."

Following the pope's example, the great lords busied themselves with repairing other losses. Palazzo Ossoli, on which work had been started shortly before the cataclysm, was to display its beautiful rhythmic façade near Palazzo Farnese, in Via dei Balestrari, and Peruzzi created a work quite as famous as the Farnesina in his Palazzo Massimo (on the new Corso del Rinascimento).

Like many others, the Massimo family's palace had been sacked; when the question of rebuilding it arose, each of the two brothers, Pietro and Angelo, insisted on a separate dwelling. The narrow site was irregular in shape, and the street on which it faced had an inconvenient curve; in addition, the architect had been instructed to retain the foundations of the old palace. With stunning adroitness Peruzzi resolved this discouraging problem and made each house of Palazzo Massimo the purest type of the Renaissance town house. Nothing appeared irregular: the convex façades have a noble simplicity and the court is charmingly arranged. The perfection of detail is such that not even the slightest sign of aging after four centuries can be descried. "Here," G. Gramort wrote in a remarkable book on Renaissance architecture in Italy, "the elements have found their definitive expression; if one wished to do better, one would have to try to do something else."

On an artificial height named Monte Giordano, after Giordano Orsini, who had built a feudal fortress there in the twelfth century, Peruzzi erected Palazzo Orsini, somewhat lean in design but characteristic of the era. Its court is adorned with a very beautiful fountain. Unmatched buildings have been added to it, without depriving the whole of its charm and its picturesqueness. There is no great certainty as to the identity of the ancient monuments whose accumulated rubble formed the height called Monte Giordano.

In spite of his efforts to restore the Eternal City's prestige and to perpetuate its artistic tradition, Clement VII was not popular. Too many disasters had marked his reign. He died on September 25, 1534, and the beautiful funeral oration preached by the bishop of Segni, full of exaggerated praises, was coolly received. If the Medici family, which had regained its omnipotence in Florence, had not itself commissioned the monument that decorates his tomb in the Minerva, no one else would have raised a finger to honor a pontiff to whom Rome owed its worst calamity.

THE LAST JUDGMENT AND THE DOME OF ST. PETER'S

A better memory was to be left behind by his successor, Paul III (Alessandro Farnese), who did not disappoint the hopes reposed in him. His wealth went back to the time of Alexander VI Borgia, who had appointed him to the Sacred College at the age of twenty-six on the orders of the beautiful Giulia, Borgia's mistress: this had earned the young prelate the title of "Cardinal Skirt." An ostentatious patron of the arts and an elegant humanist educated at the court of Lorenzo de' Medici, he had given evidence of his taste for grandeur in the construction of Palazzo Farnese. When he became pope it was to the architect of that palace, Sangallo the Younger, that he entrusted the control of artistic investigation and endeavor; when Sangallo died, Paul III appointed Michelangelo to succeed him. These two appointments would be enough to prove the high quality of his judgment.

His achievements in politics were equally laudable. Determined to restore peace, which was still in danger, he spared neither zeal nor patience in his efforts to end the enmity between Francis I and Charles V. He went to great pains to fill the Sacred College with outstanding men, he stamped out abuses, he approved the formation of the Jesuits, he reorganized the Inquisition's tribunal. Above all he demonstrated his determination to effect a reform in Catholicism, of which everyone was talking without making a move, by convoking the Council of Trent. In internal affairs, his government so effectively re-established good order and abundance that no one thought of criticizing the shameless privileges that he lavished on his family. It was in fact his pontificate that was to give nepotism the pervasive character that was to transform Roman society by creating a new privileged class within it. There will be occasion to observe that these customs, however reprehensible from a moral point of view, were to have consequences for the artistic development of Rome that were not always deplorable.

Few popes incurred fewer reproaches than Paul III. He was forgiven even for receiving Charles V with great pomp when the emperor was returning from his expedition to Tunis. Yet this visit did great violence to popular sentiment. In 1536, the year in which it occurred, Rome's wounds were still far from having healed, and the people, unmoved by the devious course of pontifical policy, still regarded Charles V as the author of all its woes.

Everything had been prepared for a magnificent welcome. There had been no hesitation in demolishing two hundred houses in order to build the triumphal avenue that was to take the emperor to St. Peter's. But only the clergy and the nobility followed the gaudy procession; the people of Rome, usually so enthusiastic in such matters, stayed away. When the Holy Father blessed the emperor on the steps of the Vatican basilica "that his cavalry had stained with blood," a glacial silence filled the square like a rebuke. Charles V grasped the lesson; he stayed only two days in this city that was cursing him. During his visit to the Pantheon, he had bent over the great opening in the dome and a young papal officer had been violently tempted to hurl him through it. "I do not know how I resisted," he told his father, who replied: "My son, those are things that are done and not talked about."

It was Paul III who founded the hospital of St. Mary of Mercy for mental patients, the first institution of its kind in Europe. Until that time the insane had been abandoned to their unhappy fate on the pretext of a singular notion: "Our Lord certainly healed the sick," it was argued, "but he did not bring the mad to their senses, and therefore men must not meddle with them." Paul III wanted to give the hospital of San Spirito a church befitting it: Sangallo the Younger built it, preserving the beautiful campanile of the early Renaissance.

The memory of Paul III gains glory from his furtherance of Michelangelo's last works. In fact the Farnese pope assisted him mightily in the execution of *The Last Judgment* by assuring him of the means of devoting himself to it and above all by lavishing care and attention on him. So there is nothing shocking in the fact that the Roman people's enthusiasm extended to the enlightened Maecenas the recognition that he showed to the inspired artist.

When the wall of the Sistine Chapel was unveiled on Christmas Day, 1541, everyone in attendance knew that he was in the presence of a remarkable work that was to remain unique. It certainly provoked astonishment. Its tragic atmosphere, the beardless Christ with the body of an athlete and the face of a judge, the scramble of naked bodies, that human avalanche hurled from the dome, that show of physical force—it was indeed the celebration of the flesh that Delacroix was to call it. Michelangelo put behind him the sacred tradition in which the nude was the symbol of suffering and infamy and in which the heavenly hosts were represented in serene symmetrical arrays, rich in allegory and all haloed in mystic beatitude. But the Dantean and almost infernal power of the work swept away hesitations and resistances. Michelangelo's tormented genius imperiously overwhelmed them, leaving no room for argument or scruple. Only Cardinal Bragio insisted on making an outcry: that was because Michelangelo had included his face among the damned. He complained of this to the pope, who replied: "If he had put you into purgatory, I should have tried to do something to save you. But he has put you into hell, and nothing can be done about that." It was only later that the Inquisition was to lodge the ridiculous charge of Lutheranism against Michelangelo, that popes were to have shrouds of draperies painted over the herculean bodies of *The Last Judgment,* and that one pope was even to entertain the idea of destroying Michelangelo's colossal work and his final profession of faith.

Michelangelo, then in his seventies, had barely completed the great Sistine fresco when the pope appointed him to direct the work on the basilica of St. Peter's, which had been almost completely suspended for fifteen years. The Florentine master was to give the basilica its final form and to endow it with the famous dome that soars into the air and, in

Stendhal's words, "stuns us with admiration." He had gone back to Bramante's original design—that is, the Greek cross, which Raphael had sought to replace with a Latin cross. In spite of his oaths of loyalty, Michelangelo revised his predecessor's plans and made them more grandiose. In particular, the huge dome that he raised to a height of more than four hundred feet differed considerably from Bramante's conception; it was inspired by Brunelleschi and the dome in Florence, while at the same time it brought new and daring solutions to the problem created by such an undertaking.

Although Michelangelo devoted the last eighteen years of his life to the basilica, he was not to see its final completion. At his death in 1564 work had proceeded far enough so that his successors could no longer modify his designs; the two arms of the transept and the apse had been built, the dome had risen as far as the top of its tambour; the plans laid down for its completion had to be faithfully respected. The dome of St. Peter's, which tells the traveler from afar that he is approaching the Eternal City, is inseparably linked to the names of Rome and Michelangelo.

THE CAPITOLINE PALACES AND SQUARE

The great Florentine's thoughts hovered over another summit of Rome: the Capitoline. In Paul III's time, it was difficult to imagine that this could have been the inaccessible citadel of the masters of the world. Five centuries of changes had succeeded only in creating a border of confused and discordant buildings round an unshapely area that was difficult to reach. The honor of the city required that its municipal offices be lodged in an environment worthy of them and, even more, that the center of Rome's most glorious memories be given an appearance in harmony with the brilliant past of the Eternal City. Paul III entrusted Michelangelo with the task of preparing the plans for this new Capitol, and the master's designs were to give birth to the admirable collection of palaces, stairs, and terraces virtually as they appear today.

Michelangelo's project preserved the ancient structures, but it veiled them in a regular façade and banished their tangle of unmatched towers and roofs. Added to the Senator's Palace and that of the conservators, a third palace became, on the Ara Coeli side, a boundary of the narrow square whose small size was to be forgotten in its majestic setting. The square was to be reached by a great flight of stairs starting at the foot of the hill. Carved balustrades, antique statues, and allegorical figures were to decorate the square itself, the stairs, and the flat roofs of the buildings; a bell tower would overlook the Senator's Palace. The execution of this plan was not the work of a day. Michelangelo and Paul III could see only its beginnings, but over the next fifty years their successors were to carry it on, making only minor, though not always beneficial, revisions in the original conception. Thus, in particular, the campanile became much higher than Michelangelo had planned it, the windows of the second floor of the Conservators' Palace are uneven in height, and the Dioscuri that adorn the entrance to the square are not those of the Quirinal, which were much more beautiful and which Michelangelo wanted to move to the Capitoline. In all other respects his wishes were respected. The additions that have been made to the decoration do not diminish the magnificent sensation of triumph imparted by the great access stairway. The added pieces, for that matter, are very precious in themselves: the two Egyptian lions spurting water (replaced by copies in 1886) are said to antedate the conquest of Egypt by Cambyses; the trophies of Marius come from a fountain of Septimius Severus whose vicissitudes we have reported; one of the two milestone columns of the balustrade (the one on the right) marked the first mile of Via Appia; the two gigantic statues of Constantine's sons were discovered in the ruins of the theater of Balbus.

The only part of his immense project that Michelangelo saw executed in his lifetime was the erection of the equestrian statue of Marcus Aurelius, which is the central motif of the decoration, in the Capitoline Square. We have followed the tribulations of this statue up to its installation in front of the Lateran church. The Lateran canons had become so accustomed to its presence that for the second time they exerted all their influence to prevent its transfer to the Capitoline in 1548. They failed. Their resistance was overcome by the determination of Michelangelo and the pope. Michelangelo carved the pedestal for the statue from a huge block of marble taken from the ruins of Trajan's baths. As it was conceived by Michelangelo's imperious genius, the Capitoline Square is at once glorious and intimate, one of the most beautiful in Rome and all the world. It is so remarkably asymmetrical that academic critics have made it the subject of reproaches to which Stendhal gave their deserts when he said: "It is extremely irregular, and that is the criticism made of it by idiots with schoolbook tastes." Michelangelo succeeded in "embracing history in a village square," and this result was obtained without artifices of substructures and terraces, without *trompe-l'oeil* or falsification.

THE CORNICE OF THE PALAZZO FARNESE / THE PAULINE CHAPEL / *MOSES*

Thus, after Sangallo's death, Michelangelo officially governed Roman architecture. It was then that he added to the Palazzo Farnese its fourth story and the powerful cornice that crowns the building. He intended to add a loggia as well, similar to the one in the court, so that it would have overlooked the garden, which ran as far as the Tiber. The pope's death prevented the execution of this plan; all that remains of it is the three magnificent arcades of the loggia that Giacomo della Porta was to complete after Michelangelo's death and according to his designs.

Paul III enhanced his family's luxurious home with a collection of ancient marbles that is today the pride of Naples. Its jewel was the celebrated *Hercules* (the Farnese *Hercules*) that is one of the miracles of Greek sculpture. It had just been discovered in the ruins of the Baths of Caracalla. It had neither head nor legs; it was given an ancient head found in Trastevere and Guglielmo della Porta made legs for it. Now it happened that subsequently the authentic head and legs were discovered. The real head was put where it belonged, but not the legs, because it was considered that the legs carved by della Porta were more appropriate. It was only when the statue was moved to Naples in 1787 that its ancient legs were substituted for its newer ones, which remained in Rome, where they can be seen at the bottom of the plaster reproduction of the *Hercules* in Palazzo Farnese.

On Paul III's request, Michelangelo had taken up his palette for the last time to decorate the Pauline Chapel, which the pope had built to balance the Sistine, from which it is separated by the Royal Hall. Michelangelo adorned it with the conversion of St. Paul and the crucifixion of St. Peter, works that in their dramatic intensity are the equal of *The Last Judgment.*

In 1545 the mausoleum of Julius II, which had been the torment of Michelangelo and even, as he himself said, the tragedy of his life, was built against one of the side walls of the church of San Pietro in Vincoli. Originally intended for the basilica of St. Peter's, the reduced and impoverished monument thus ended in a sanctuary that, while it was indeed venerable in its antiquity, had no other claim to this honor than the fact that Julius II had been its titular when he was a cardinal. It bore no resemblance to the magnificent project conceived by Michelangelo in his youth. Mediocre in its architecture, it contained an effigy of the pope and allegorical statues that were the clumsy work of untalented students. At the very most, the master's weary hand sketched the outlines of Rachel and Leah. But between these two lifeless creatures "a giant appeared, like a ghost from another age." This was the *Moses,* one of the forty gigantic statues that were supposed to adorn the triumphal monument of the "terrible" pontiff. Michelangelo had to leave his scaffold in the Sistine Chapel to carve it; it has the stature of the prophets ranged round the *Genesis,* the power of the titanic figures in *The Last Judgment.* The Hebrew lawgiver is portrayed seated, turning his head and ready to rise. His whole person expresses the majestic pride of the man who has just withstood the sight of God, shattered the tables of the law, and reduced the golden calf to dust. Anger and scorn speak in the curve of his lips. Many interpretations have been sought for this Moses, "fierce and horned, running his menacing fingers through his disheveled beard." Was Michelangelo seeking to portray in this imperious leader of Israel the despotic master toward whom he nursed a bitter enmity? Was this his revenge for the insolences of Julius II? Why is it not possible to see in this statue the ideal representation of the genius that was incarnate in Michelangelo? In any event it seems impossible to detach this creation from its creator's personality. That is in fact, it has been said, what gives the statue "so clear and lofty a language."

The amazing grandeur of the style is coupled with the delicacy with which the marble is worked, chiseled like a cameo, causing one critic to declare: "The *Moses* is a miniature that is twelve feet tall." This remarkable mastery in execution, in combination with Michelangelo's sovereign qualities—universality, daring, and energy—makes the statue in San Pietro in Vincoli his masterpiece in the field of sculpture, on a par with *The Thinker* of Florence, and perhaps above it. A legend has it that, when he had completed *Moses,* Michelangelo struck the statue's knee with a hammer and said: "Now speak!" Tourists like to try to find the mark of this imaginary hammer.

RENAISSANCE GARDENS AND PLEASURES

Let us not leave the Renaissance without describing the beauty of Rome's gardens in that period. They had been laid out everywhere, within the city and round the villas in the nearby countryside. Not all were fairy-tale gardens like those that surrounded the Farneses' villa on the Palatine; not all had the splendor of the Farnesina's gardens or the sophistication of Villa Madama's. But all were derived from the esthetic ideas peculiar to the period.

It is not surprising that, in their zeal to revive the ways of living of antiquity, the humanists should have sought to reproduce the flowerbeds and lawns of the imperial gardens. Thus they came to achieve what Stendhal called "the finest fusion of the beauties of architecture with those of trees." The variety and the originality of these gardens, designed in harmony with their sites and their settings, were what most impressed Montaigne during his visit to Rome. The great ruins barely touched him, but the gardens entranced him: "One of the great beauties of Rome," he noted in his travel diary, "is the vineyards and the gardens." And he marveled that art "could make such excellent and appropriate use of lumpy, hilly, and uneven ground."

Many of these gardens survive after five centuries, no doubt altered by the growth of the great pines and the giant cypresses that have somewhat choked the dwarf trees and the trimmed yews that, long before Le Nôtre,* the Renaissance gardeners had made the basic element of their decoration. But the plans of the groups of shrubs have not been erased. The straight paths, leading to some point of interest (a fountain, a bowl, a grotto, an ancient sculpture), still accentuate the knowledgeable composition of these wholes, "their symmetrical distribution among spaces each of which has its own character." The close alliance between the upper and lower levels, the stylized treatment of the slopes preserved a classic simplicity from which the next two centuries were to depart in order, under the influence of the baroque, to achieve more rhythmic and brilliant compositions.

These masterly creations have often been harshly judged. The chief accusation against them is that they are not English gardens. Certainly we have given the word *garden* a new meaning, and the Roman gardens of the Renaissance express "a state of mind of which a modern man, and especially a northern man, has no conception." In the humanists of the sixteenth century the senses were "turned toward the outside." Taine has clearly explained to us that they had no feeling for the spirit of external things and that they enjoyed only their forms. Skillfully chosen and

---

* André Le Nôtre, a seventeenth-century Frenchman who designed the gardens of Versailles, Vaux, Chantilly, and Dijon.—Translator.

arranged landscapes gave them the same feeling as a tall, simple apartment, solidly built and well decorated. The Renaissance garden, exactly like that of the Empire, was an extension of the drawing room. It was the transition between architecture and nature. It was a part of each, and not the least of its attractions was its capacity to make one aware of the adaptation of nature at the same time to the amenities of social life and to reverie.

The wealth of ancient objects incorporated into these gardens attests to the esthetic pleasure that they afforded. "At intervals among the green, the whiteness of a marble gleamed. Sometimes it was a solitary Hermes or a broken column, sometimes a balustrade enlaced in vines or a sarcophagus in which a rose bush was growing." And what shall we say of the admirable fountains that add the song of their streams to these formal landscapes and occasionally, as in the Villa d'Este in Tivoli, take precedence over all the other decorations and become an animated spectacle rather than decoration? And Tivoli is not alone in the neighborhood of Rome in having been jeweled with gardens in those days. Albano, Castel Gandolfo, Frascati were other places where landscapes that seemed to have been made for Virgil's *Eclogues* grew up round princely villas. On a magnificent site in Caprarola, Sangallo the Younger built an amazing palace, surrounded by a garden with marvelous scenic effects, for the Farneses.

These gardens reflect the social conditions that had come into being in Rome in the second half of the sixteenth century. This was the time when Montaigne stayed in the Eternal City, comfortably installed in the inn at the sign of the Bear, beside the Tiber, where Dante and Rabelais had lodged and which is still the oldest inn in existence in the world.

The Périgord moralist's observations illuminate certain aspects of Roman life of those days. Prelates and financiers still set the style, but the influence of idle foreigners, who had come not only to visit the city but to live in it, was making itself felt in manners and morals. Rome had become a city "patched together with foreigners." There were so many of them that the beggars had learned to practice their profession multilingually. Everyone was completely at home there, and the populace paid no attention either to foreign dress or to unusual behavior.

This cosmopolitanism, like the progressive wealth of the men of the church, gave rise to those amenities that make life so pleasant. Montaigne was amazed that the city could be so well equipped and so rich without anyone's apparently doing any work. It was a city, he said, "that is all court and all nobility; every man has his part in the ecclesiastical leisure."

In this life of pleasure there was nothing trivial apart from the "follies" of the carnival. The high dignitaries and great lords who presided over it, while not always irreproachable in their morals, at least had good style. A much neglected writer, Bandello,* whom Henri II was to appoint bishop of Agen, has left us a very accurate picture of sixteenth-century Rome in tales that, though sometimes rather gay, are all based on real experiences. They show us that there were more wit and courtesy in the papal court than in that of any sovereign in Europe, even the kings of France, where there was considerably less refinement than is generally admitted.

But, in one of those contrasts of which the Renaissance offers so many instances, the celebrations of the carnival were then at the peak of their licentiousness. The crowd felt that it might do anything: beg for money, ridicule anyone, even commit profanations. Prohibitions had to be issued against pouring boiling oil on passers-by, throwing rotten eggs into their faces, making mock of magistrates and cardinals, and even wearing carnival costume to church. The popes themselves had to make deplorable concessions to popular caprices: it was Paul III who, "wishing to do things on a grand scale," added the Jews' races to the carnival festivities; under later popes, these runners would have to suffer the ridicule and shame of being stuffed with food before the race so that running would be more difficult for them; they were harassed with jeers, bad jokes, and occasionally clubs. In witness to the times and their contradictions, Montaigne was to attend this wretched spectacle in 1580 without being at all revolted by it: he found it only rather thin as an amusement.

To take leave of the Renaissance on a more pleasant note, let us accompany one of the last popes of this period, Julius III, on the boat trip that he so often took in order to reach his summer home, that charming Villa Giulia (on Viale delle Belle Arti) that Vignola had built for him. It is one of the marvels of sixteenth-century Rome. Everything in it preserves an unequaled rustic flavor in the midst of sophisticated art. The grace of the courtyard, the perfection of the gardens, the lightness of the decoration—everything concerts to enchant the eye, down to the nearby fountain that Vignola had designed, a little architectural gem beside the road, so

---

* Matteo Bandello was a writer of tales in the sixteenth century.—Translator.

that the *contadini* might water their horses before they entered the city. This pleasant establishment can be studied at leisure, for Villa Giulia has become a museum for antiquities older than the Roman epoch.

The last Roman work of the Renaissance meets the eye in the Vatican gardens, of which it is the finest ornament. This is the casino of Pius IV, a little pavilion of exquisite dimensions that preserves all the graces of the Renaissance. It is the seat of the Pontifical Academy: that means that it may not be entered by tourists. At least one can glimpse, through the windows of the map gallery, its delightful façade decorated with stucco and its always empty marble benches that "warm themselves in the sun" round the basin of a fountain in a rose garden that is always silent.

PART FOUR

THE COUNTER-REFORMATION

CHAPTER 23

THE AGE OF SEVERITY

ART UNDER THE COUNTER-REFORMATION

The lazy, carefree Rome that Montaigne had seen was living out its final days of joyousness. The final third of the sixteenth century was to bring it into an era of severity that would have no further room for the spirit of the Renaissance. For seventy-five years there were to be no more pleasure-loving popes who could not imagine that men lived, in the words of one of them, "without taking one another's teeth." The days of cardinals in ribbons and laces were over. The church was to become once more harsh and militant. This was the age of the Counter-Reformation.

In consequence of wars and of the rupture of Christendom by the Protestant heresy, the papacy no longer counted as a military and political power. On the other hand, the decisions of the Council of Trent (1563) had strengthened it in its apostolic prerogatives. Sternly resolved to make Rome once more the spiritual pole of the world, the popes were to bring to that reconquest a fervor and a force that would profoundly mark manners and institutions. The weapons of the church would be the Holy Office, the Inquisition, and the Index; its troops would be the Society of Jesus. A strict order was established, aimed at spiritual regeneration in the integrity of faith. There was no further question of populating pontifical palaces with mythological figures or churches with nudes. Prudery took over in religious art; Huguenot austerity was outdone. Fig leaves were put on the ancient statues. Michelangelo's audacities were harshly dealt with; since no one had the courage to efface them, the titanic bodies of *The Last Judgment* were draped in cloaks. Entrusted with this task, a pupil of the master, Daniele di Volterra, earned the nickname of *braghettone* (trousers maker). The popes crusaded against the relaxed morals of the time. Pius V forbade married men to eat in inns and nuns to keep male dogs in their convents; he segregated the courtesans in a special quarter and any who rebelled were whipped in public. His predecessor had already taken a similar step with respect to the Jews, whom he had restricted to the bank of the Tiber in the Sant'Angelo quarter, the principal entrance to which was in the square that the Romans named Piazza Giudea, in front of the church of Santa Maria del Pianto.

Whether this change in climate was to the Romans' liking is doubtful, if only on the basis of the enthusiasm with which one day they set to sacking the Inquisition's tribunal. It was not that this tribunal "tried the issue by torture and corrected the sinner with death." Its zeal was limited to a few arrests of suspects. But it was enough to make the pope's rod felt. In this new atmosphere the good population of Rome, which was so fond of festivities and songs, turned gloomy, became morose and fearful. The enterprises of the counter-reformers were to leave it quite lukewarm, and often it contributed no more than forced collaboration. Nonetheless the pioneers of re-Christianization were to pursue their work in a mystic efflux that would raise heroes and saints like Ignatius Loyola and Filippo Neri.

The prime movers of the Counter-Reformation intended art to serve in its ranks and to become a medium of apologetic. It was given the function of teaching the people and touching hearts. "The church," according to Jean Maury and René Percheron, the authors of *Itinéraires romains* (an extraordinary book from which we have borrowed a great deal), "was to offer as the structure for the pomps of its liturgy the edification and the appeal of its images, calling to mind heaven and the manner in which the saints had earned their places there." Everything that Protestantism had rejected—the papacy and the adoration of relics and saints—was to be exalted in the decoration of churches.

But what was lacking was creative geniuses. Scattered by the sack of Rome, Raphael's collaborators had trained hardly any pupils. As for Michelangelo, he had only scorn for anyone who claimed to derive from him: he had discouraged imitators in advance when he said: "My style is intended to create first-class fools." Furthermore, the atmosphere of the time encouraged coldness and dullness with the growing emphasis on formalities and the excess of conventional ornamentation. Techniques, it has been said, "lagged behind intentions." The painting and sculpture of this period were only a monotonous succession of official reports. The churches built then, like Santa Maria dell'Orto and Santa Maria in Trivio, however cleverly planned, consistently fall below those of the preceding period, and they became more interesting only when the next century had enriched them with exuberant decoration.

THE PALAZZO SPADA / SANTA MARIA IN TRASPONTINA

The structures that are regarded as the best expressions of the Counter-Reformation are the best evidence that it did not create a style.

Palazzo Spada, for example, where the Council of State sat, completely abandoned the vigorous sobriety of the Renaissance, in which ornamentation retained an architectonic character, in favor of an accumulation of superficial effects that were often gratuitous and occasionally pedantic. Statues, festoons, and insets were lavished on the façade to recall the war of the centaurs and the exploits of the Roman legionaries. It is all the less understandable that there should have been this total dedication to war when one reflects that the palace was built by Mazzoni to be the residence of a man of the church who had little of the warlike in his character, Cardinal Capo di Ferro.

It was the Spada that gave Francesco Borromini a chance, while he was still quite young, to display a curious and intelligent sample of his talent by creating the vista that is to be seen in the court behind the library; through a grill one perceives a gallery that is apparently very long and at the end of which stands a warrior's statue that seems gigantic. If one enters the gallery, one recognizes that it is less than thirty feet long and that the warrior is not even so tall as a child! A skillful use of arches and progressively smaller columns accomplishes this amazing optical illusion, which the "knightly" Bernini was to take as his inspiration for the Scala Regia in the Vatican.

The palace contains the statue of Pompey at the foot of which Caesar died under the wounds of the conspirators. Discovered in 1553 buried in the foundations of a party wall dividing two houses and claimed by both owners, it was the subject of litigation that the Capitoline judges resolved by decreeing that each owner should retain that part of the statue that had been found beneath his house. Having got wind of the judgment of Solomon, Pope Julius III satisfied both owners by buying the statue for five hundred crowns.

As for the church of Santa Maria in Traspontina, its façade and the decoration of many of its chapels are considered characteristic of the Counter-Reformation. It is more interesting for the memory that it recalls and for the curiosities that it houses. It was built on the site of the tomb of Scipio Africanus, who destroyed Carthage; the street that runs along it and that became Via della Conciliazione in 1936 is the one that in ancient Rome led to Nero's circus through a portico whose marble paving stones were used to floor the peristyle of the basilica of St. Peter's. Of very ancient origin and already rebuilt in the eleventh century, Santa Maria in Traspontina contains the two pillars to which, according to tradition, the Apostles Peter and Paul were bound. It also houses the tomb of Nicola Zabaglia, a strange person whose popularity has very justly persisted. A plain unschooled workingman, he had been endowed by nature with a mechanical genius. Employed in the construction of St. Peter's, he invented a tremendous number of machines all intended to simplify the masons' work and save their time. His successors constitute that very tightly closed group of elite workers called the *San Pietrini,* "the little men of St. Peter's," charged with maintenance work on the basilica: their highly skilled craft has been handed down from father to son since the sixteenth century. It is a guild apart, with its own laws, its own enforcement arm, and its seat on the platform below the dome.

MICHELANGELO'S LAST WORKS AND HIS DEATH

If the epoch of the Counter-Reformation was lacking in great creators, it continued to bear the unique stamp of Michelangelo. Remaining in the service of Paul III's successors as the artistic director of Rome, he directed Vignola's construction of Porta del Popolo in 1561 in the ancient rampart at the beginning of Via Flaminia; its inner face was later to be decorated by Bernini. In the same year Porta Pia was similarly built from a plan by Michelangelo. And he presented Rome with one of its most beautiful churches by creating St. Mary of the Angels in the library of Diocletian's baths. This hall, to which the Romans of the Empire repaired after their baths to read and discuss, was found virtually intact by Michelangelo, with its granite columns, its great semicircular arches, and its tremendously high walls supporting a great vault. Taking great care to move nothing, to destroy nothing, and above all to add nothing to so majestic a setting, he confined himself to a brilliant restoration of the ancient structure. Presently we shall describe how his work was deformed in the eighteenth century by a headstrong architect.

Next to the church Michelangelo built the famous cloister of the hundred columns, one of the largest in existence, for the Carthusians; it now houses the statues of the Roman National Museum. Taine said that there were few things in the world so grand and so beautiful. A solitary square courtyard is framed by white columns supporting small archways. Nothing more. In the center, the wall of a well is made to look like a tomb by the four cypresses, "battered by the centuries," that Michelangelo himself planted.

In his capacity as the Pope's artistic manager, he at least was familiar with the plans for the church (St. Bernard) built only after his death in one of the circular rooms that marked the corners of these same baths; with its paneled dome whose opening admits sunlight and rain, this church is like a Pantheon in miniature.

Michelangelo died in 1564 at the age of ninety, a half-century after Raphael. He had long outlived the movement of the Renaissance, but to the end he had emphasized its lessons to a generation of artists inclined to forget them. He had lived his whole life as a battle, against events and men and also against his own thinking. A cenotaph was erected in his memory in the corridor that leads to the sacristy of the church of the Holy Apostles. That was where his body was laid until it was stolen by Tuscan emissaries who secretly carried it to Florence in the form, it was said, of a bundle of merchandise.

THE GESÙ AND THE JESUIT STYLE

Released, if not from the influence, at least from the rule of the old master, an army of painters, sculptors, and architects with good intentions but without genius were to provide Rome with works that would express the zeal of the popes, the prelates, and the religious orders for the Counter-Reformation. There was no shortage of commissions, but there was strict supervision to make sure that the executions would inspire respect and serve the prestige of the church without the slightest concession to worldly ornament. The motivating thought was to incite to piety through the concrete portrayal of the pomps of religion, the display of a luxury that would be in itself a prayer, the appeal to the heart by way of the imagination. This complex of concerns was to give birth to the style that would be called the Jesuit. The society did not invent it and was to hold no monopoly of it; but its mother church, the Gesù, affords the most characteristic example of it. The conquering order was to adapt the improvements of religious structures to the exigencies of its rules. The Jesuits constituted a militia constantly prepared to go in search of opportunities to serve; relieved of the obligation of long prayers, they had no need of a large chancel. Their preoccupation with effectiveness impelled them to make the faithful understand the ceremonials; good light would enable the congregation to follow the celebrant's movements and to read in its missals the prayers that he was reciting. Proper acoustics were essential to the understanding of the sermons: the single nave would make preaching easier. Finally, a luxurious aspect for the edifice seemed an imperative necessary to the dignity of divine office. The style that could meet all these requirements was what the Jesuits would call *il modo nostro* (our style).

Built by Vignola (except for the façade, which is by Giacomo della Porta) under Pius V and Gregory XIII, the church of the Gesù contains a very broad nave, enhanced with high pilasters of colored marbles. The altar was placed at the end of the apse; little chapels opened off the nave, forming, it has been said, a succession of grooves. As a result of the rich embellishments of the seventeenth century, all these chapels, which were originally austere in the spirit of the Counter-Reformation, now vie with one another in splendor. The chapel consecrated to the founder of the order, St. Ignatius, is disturbing in its richness. The rarest marbles, agate, rock crystal, and precious stones are profusely distributed in it. The globe of the earth placed above the pediment was carved from the largest block of lapis lazuli ever known. Framed by four magnificent columns in the same stone, there is the monumental statue of the saint at prayer. It is a reproduction, in an alloy of less precious metals, of the work of the French sculptor Pierre Legros, which was in pure silver. The replacement was made under Pius VI, who melted the original statue in order to pay the war indemnity imposed by Bonaparte at Tolentino.

The Jesuit style has been often attacked, but every argument for its defense can be found in the Gesù. While the paintings of the altars and the vaults show signs of the taste of the period, the architectural whole is impressive. The sumptuousness of the materials and the extreme abundance of rare marbles are not alone in producing the impression of magnificence, which derives quite as much from the beautiful proportions of the structure and the perfect balance of its parts. The Gesù marked the origin of a new type of religious monument that was to impose itself on the entire Christian world. But it was inevitable that the merits of the original work should be lost in the very many imitations of it that were to be multiplied over two centuries.

The church of the Gesù adjoins the monastery that was long the society's professed house. St. Ignatius lived in the little apartment in it that can still be visited on his feast day, July 31. The arrangement of the streets leading into the little square before the church causes an air current that inspired the caustic spirit of the Romans to an irreverent fable: The devil and the wind were walking there together one day, and the devil went into the Jesuits' house. He never came out again, but the wind is still waiting for him in the square.

THE GREGORIAN CHAPEL / THE PONTE ROTTO / THE FOUNTAINS OF GREGORY XIII

In the spirit born of the Council of Trent, Rome was indeed the common fatherland of the whole Christian world. "The domicile of the Christian religion," as its popes proclaimed it, it was bound to attract and hold the faithful of the whole world. It was in order to assure it of the "material ornaments" of which Sixtus V would speak that churches were to be built in such great number. The population, moreover, had doubled in a half century. At the same time, splendid avenues would be opened, palaces and villas would be built. Aqueducts would be restored, and new fountains would sparkle where streets met.

In the succession of pontiffs who were to be the artisans of this development of the Eternal City, Gregory XIII (1572-85) was distinguished more for his praiseworthy industry than for the felicity of his creations. He marches in effigy in the nave of St. Peter's, surrounded by the mathematicians and astronomers whose erudite calculations gave us the calendar that he promulgated—a lasting reform, since time is still measured by the Gregorian calendar. This pope left us another monument that seems no less indestructible, the Roman College. Intended to house the Gregorian University, which was long directed by the Jesuits, it now contains a preparatory school, two museums, and the huge Victor Emmanuel library, with its wealth of almost two million books and manuscripts. Its architecture, wholly in the style of the Counter-Reformation, is particularly severe and cold. But we are indebted to Gregory XIII for less-forbidding creations, such as the splendid Gregorian chapel in St. Peter's, which still gleams with rare marbles, and the Vatican map gallery, still as picturesque and alluring. The majority of this well-intentioned pontiff's other achievements seem to have been haunted by the malice of fate.

The first blow was struck at the Palatine bridge, the oldest stone bridge in Rome. Gregory XIII had completely rebuilt it for the jubilee of 1575: the great flood of the Tiber in 1598 carried away two of its arches and even its name, for ever since then it has been known as Ponte Rotto (Broken Bridge).

Gregory XIII became the great dispenser of the Acqua Vergine: its fountains were to be the victims of the most unfortunate accidents. Only one remains intact, in Piazza Colonna, and it is not the most beautiful, even though it was carved by Giacomo della Porta. The Rotunda fountain in front of the Pantheon was to undergo substantial additions in the eighteenth century that made it unrecognizable. As for the two fountains with which Gregory XIII had adorned the opposing ends of Piazza Navone, they vanished completely in order to make room for Bernini's *Moro* and the modern fountain where Neptune battles an octopus before a large audience of Nereids and seahorses. The sufferings of the Terrina were more complicated. Gregory XIII had erected it in Campo dei Fiori, which was already the site of the crowded market that is still held there. From the start this fountain had been criticized by Romans for its graceless aspect. The lack of pressure had compelled the architects to sink a basin into the soil to receive the water, and it could be reached only by descending several steps. In order to improve its appearance, it had been topped with a travertine cover that earned it the nickname of Terrina. And in fact it looked quite like a soup bowl placed on a large table; the merchants of Campo dei Fiori treated it as such, decorating it with fruits and vegetables. They had quite forgot that in the Middle Ages the Campo dei Fiori had been the place of execution for heretics and sorcerers. Now the Terrina stood on the exact spot where Giordano Bruno had died at the stake. Then, when it was decided in 1889 to erect a monument to the relapsed monk, become "a hero of freedom," on the very site of his execution, the fountain was demolished without hesitation. It was only in 1925 that it was reconstructed under the trees before the Chiesa Nuova, without even thought of removing the inscription that some unknown stone mason had carved into it on his own authority: *"Ama Dio e non fallire, fa del bene e lascia dire* (Love your God and do not fail, do good works and let folk rail)."

Another fountain of the same period was to experience almost the same tribulations. It stood in Piazza Campitelli with its two superimposed basins. It had no history until Pope Alexander VII built the church of Santa Maria in Campitelli in the square as an *ex voto* after the terrible plague of 1656. There were already many churches in Rome, but some whim of fashion made this one the favorite of the Roman nobility. Beautiful ladies from all parts of the city went there to hear mass; afterward, they gathered round the fountain to gossip in pleasant company and show off their pretty dresses with their short sleeves and very deep necklines, the fashion that Maria Mancini had just introduced in Paris. But a harsh pope, Innocent XI, who had gone to Santa Maria in Campitelli in 1676 to say mass, took exception to these social gatherings; in order to put an end to them, he had the fountain moved to an obscure corner of the square. It remained there, alone and abandoned, until a modern city-planning project brought it back to the light of day in the admirable setting of Via del Mare.

The fountain of Gregory XIII that was best known in his day no longer exists. It provided water from the Acqua Vergine in the long street that connects Piazza del Popolo with Piazza di Spagna and that was then called Via degli Orti di Napoli. The main feature of the fountain was a fragment of an ancient statue, so battered that it was no longer possible to determine whether it portrayed a man or an animal. Some thought that it was a half-lying Silenus with his little goat legs; others considered it the portrait of a Roman god. Daria Borghese reports that Cardinal Dezza regarded this ruin as a statue of St. Jerome and made a devout reverence to it whenever he passed it. As for the good people of the neighborhood, they had made up their minds that the decoration of their fountain was simply a monkey, *"un babbuino."* They ascribed a mind to him, and credited him with all the satirical remarks that were current in the street. Thus the *babbuino* became the local Pasquino, and the French revolutionary troops who occupied Rome in 1798 so thoroughly endorsed this character that they smeared the statue with red paint, like all the other speaking statues. The name of the street was changed in honor of the monkey, and it is still called Via del Babbuino: it is now the antiquarians' district. But the fountain was demolished in 1870 after the entry of the Piedmontese troops, on the ground that it was blocking traffic. Its component parts were scattered; the great stone basin was used as a horse trough on Via Flaminia, but it lost all trace of the two dolphins with which it had been adorned. As for the Babbuino, he can be seen living in retirement in the courtyard of Palazzo Cesari at No. 51 of the street that bears his name.

To conclude the misfortunes suffered by the creations of Gregory XIII, let us add that he was (indirectly) responsible for an unprecedented work: the frescoes of San Stefano Rotondo that depict the torments of the martyrs with pitiless crudity: the entrails of St. Erasmus are strewn on the wheel, the head of a saint is crushed between two millstones, and there are many other atrocities of the same order. The pope had assigned the church to the German-Hungarian College, and this nightmarish spectacle was presented in order to arouse the zeal of the future missionaries. It is undoubtedly too frightful to be truly edifying, but it conveys one of the less attractive tendencies of the Counter-Reformation.

Let us mention, finally, that Gregory XIII authorized the erection of Palazzo Caffarelli by a page of Charles V whose family was the first to live on the Capitoline. The palace, which served as the German embassy until 1914, is believed to have been built on the site of Jupiter's temple. It was partly demolished in 1919 in an attempt to find beneath its foundations some traces of the sacred place that had dominated ancient life.

CHAPTER 24

SIXTUS V

A STRANGE "EXALTATION"

When Gregory XIII died in 1585, almost a hundred years old, the papacy was beset with grave problems. Orthodoxy was under attack by a number of enemies; the capital was full of bandits whose activity was beginning to be a dangerous menace to the tranquility that had prevailed there. To steer the papal ship the church needed a sturdy helmsman. Unfortunately, this need, which was obvious to everyone, made no impression on cardinals concerned above all with remaining the masters of the papal state. The conclave that began on Easter Day was divided into six rival factions, but all were ready to agree on that candidate who would be least competent to take a personal part in the management of affairs. There was indeed one who seemed to promise the best assurances in this respect because of his apparent debility. This was Cardinal Montalto, who was believed to be in his eighties and who himself always said that he was on the point of death. The son of a poor peasant, he had been a swineherd until the day when a Franciscan had made him put on the habit of that order under the name of Brother Felix. Becoming a rough fighter in philosophical disputes, the monk spent forty years in the ascent to the highest dignities. But in 1585 no one remembered his vigorous preaching or his harsh zeal as an inquisitor; ever since he had put on the cardinal's purple in 1570 with the title of Montalto, he had exerted every effort to make himself forgotten by effacing himself. Tending his vineyard of Santa Maria Maggiore, he had managed to acquire the nickname of the Donkey of the Roman Marches, wearing his purple like a pack saddle. "What brings that death's head here?" the cardinals said when he entered the conclave. What brought him there was simply the determination to be elected pope. All the factions in the conclave united all the more gladly behind this phantom candidate when he declared that he hoped to turn over to them the burdens of governing the church. His election was to be followed by a dramatic shock. The cardinals thought that it was a dream when they saw the sudden transformation of the gouty old man whom they had just made pope. Tossing away the stick on which he supported his bent body, the dying man instantaneously regained the agility of a youth as he dashed to the altar to intone the *Te Deum* "in so thunderous a voice that the whole chapel rang with it."

So at least the scene is reported for us by one who was there, Antonio Cicavella, a doctor in theology. It is likely that his picturesque account trespasses somewhat against truth, but the fact should not be too different from the fable. It is certain that Sixtus V owed his elevation to his obscurity and that, with the tiara, he recaptured the impetuousness, the violence, and the unshakable rigidity of his youth. Under his rod everything suddenly was reversed in the church's states. Unappealable sentences shut off brigandage in a few months; the perfidious maneuvers of the Protestant princes were undone by a firm policy. Security returned, industry gained a new impetus, agriculture prospered in amazing fashion. The finances of the Holy See having thus been rehabilitated, Rome enjoyed a brilliant period that brought its population close to 100,000. Once again the city became a gigantic building project. Although Sixtus V reigned only five years, he transformed Rome even more than Julius II had done. He took as his architect Domenico Fontana, who had made his professional start as a mason and who was devoid of genius. But the pope himself was more interested in immediate concrete accomplishments than in the great missions of the spirit; he found his attitude perfectly implemented by Fontana's industriousness and his methodical mind.

The affectation of modesty that Cardinal Montalto had practiced makes it quite improbable that at any stage in his shrewd upward progress he lived in the charming little palace in Via di Parione that is nevertheless known in Rome as *il palazzetto di Sisto V*. It is an elegant creation, with a picturesque *cortile* and a poetic hanging garden. Nor is it easier to imagine the future Sixtus V in that Casa dei Papassi (Popes' House—

Palazzo Crivelli, Via dei Banchi Vecchi, 22) that is also supposed nonetheless to have been his home.

THE GREAT PROJECTS OF SIXTUS V: THE VATICAN, THE LATERAN, AND THE QUIRINAL

By way of overture to his tremendous undertakings, Sixtus V announced that he intended to accomplish a task that would be comparable to that of the Caesars. He had the taste for grandeur and force. This meant that the architecture of his time would sacrifice the ingenuity of detail to the effects of mass. No project could have been closer to this pontiff's heart than the completion of St. Peter's, for his dominating thought was to celebrate the triumph of Catholicism in everything. He forwarded the work so vigorously that the dome was finished in May, 1590, under the direction of Giacomo della Porta. "An inscription in the name of Sixtus V, extending in a circle above the skylight, was the first decoration of its inner surface" (Bertaux).

Earlier the pope had carried out the old scheme of Nicholas V for setting up in front of the basilica the obelisk that Caligula had brought back from Egypt and that had occupied the mid-point of the axis of Nero's circus. The colossal monolith, one of the largest in Rome and the only one that was still intact, had lain for eleven centuries alongside the church. To move so huge a mass was so complex an undertaking that all the celebrated mathematicians of Christendom had been called on to submit proposals. Out of some fifty intricate suggestions, Fontana's was chosen, although for a long time its extreme simplicity gave rise to doubt of its chances of succeeding. Its success, however, was to enrich the architect (and the pope as well) with greater renown than all their other accomplishments. On April 30, 1586, all Rome had gathered to observe the first steps. The solemnity of the hour was enhanced by the profound silence in the square: the pope had commanded silence on pain of death to whoever opened his mouth. In this silence the sound of a trumpet rang out from the scaffolding where Fontana, who had thus given the signal, was directing the operations of his nine hundred workers, all of whom had gone to confession that morning. At this signal, thirty-five winches began to turn, and the obelisk rose from the ground to remain suspended in mid-air. Then the cannon of Castello Sant'Angelo thundered to announce the event, and all the Eternal City's church bells pealed at once.

At the most solemn point one man had dared, at the risk of his life, to violate the order for silence. *"Acqua alle funi!"* he had shouted. "Throw water on the ropes!" The friction had ignited one of them and it was threatening to break. Without this warning, Fontana's enterprise would have failed. The hero, a young mason named Bresca, from the Genoa area, was congratulated by the pope, who, in recognition of his action, granted him the exclusive right in perpetuity to provide the palms that are sold on Palm Sunday on the steps of all the churches in Rome.

Placed on rollers and hauled to the center of the square, the monolith was not set up there until September 14, to the cheers of a huge throng. For this solemn ceremony Sixtus V had chosen the day consecrated to the exaltation of the Holy Cross; it was his intention to dedicate the pagan obelisk to the symbol of redemption on the very site where the early Christians had been martyred. This conqueror—at least in spirit—gave all his actions the aspect of victories: in order better to attest to the triumph of Christendom, the obelisk of Caligula and Nero had been crowned with a brilliant cross.

In the same spirit, the pope had the statues of St. Peter and St. Paul placed on the pillars of Trajan and Marcus Aurelius, thus making the recital of the Roman conquerors' victories participate in the peaceful glory of the apostles. He imposed similar Christian baptism, by way of decoration with the cross, on three other obelisks that he re-erected, as much for the beautification of the city as for the perpetuation of his own glory. The obelisk that had adorned the entrance to the tomb of Augustus was moved to stand before the apse of Santa Maria Maggiore. Two others, buried under the ruins of the Circus Maximus and broken in three places, were skillfully repaired, and the taller was placed before St. John Lateran, while the one more richly decorated with hieroglyphics was erected in the center of Piazza del Popolo.

The Lateran Palace, which had been the popes' first residence until their departure for Avignon, had since stood abandoned. All that remained of it was a chaos of buildings that Sixtus V ordered torn down in order to replace them with the present palace, which forms an integral part of the Vatican State and contains three rich museums (the profane museum, the Christian museum, and the missions' ethnological museum), filled with ancient marbles, paintings taken from the catacombs, priceless epigraphical collections accumulated through the piety of the pontiffs and the faithful. In particular the visitor can examine a mosaic from the Baths of Caracalla and a tremendous series of Christian sarcophagi. The palace constitutes "a monumental landscape of melancholy solemnity, with an essentially Roman stamp" (*Itinéraires romains*). This enormous structure was never to be attractive to the popes, who always preferred the Vatican and the Quirinal.

The old medieval building that Fontana had demolished had contained a number of chapels and shrines in bad condition, but covered with paintings and mosaics that were mercilessly sacrificed. All that survived until the reign of Clement XII was the mosaics of the ancient *triclinium* of the old palace, recalling the long-ago alliance between the Holy See and Charlemagne. Redone in the eighteenth century to the point of unrecogniz-ability, they are in the apse that Benedict XV commissioned as their repository, near the Scala Santa.

The former Lateran was considerably larger than the present palace. When Sixtus V decided to demolish it, he preserved and moved the old palace's grand staircase from Pilate's house, which Jesus was supposed to have mounted on the day of the Passion. This the pope ordered trans-ferred to the monumental complex that he commissioned Fontana to build round the old private papal chapel, called the Sancta Sanctorum. This is the Scala Santa, whose twenty-eight steps, brought back to Rome, according to some, by St. Helena, and, according to others, not until the end of the Crusades, must be climbed only on the knees.

It leads to the chapel of San Lorenzo, built in the thirteenth century by one of the Cosmases. It is called Sancta Sanctorum because of the treasure in relics that it houses. The most precious is a Byzantine painting on cedar, dating from the sixth or seventh century, which is somewhat overshadowed by its elaborate gold frame. In the Middle Ages it was believed to have been painted by angels. It was the object of a special adoration: on Easter the popes went solemnly to kiss it, and a procession carried it to Santa Maria Maggiore on the night of August 15.

No additions had been made to the Vatican palace for a half-century, except a second branch of the loggie that Gregory XIII had begun at right angles to Bramante's. Sixtus V had them completed and at the end of them he erected the enormous characterless structure in which the popes have since lived. It is at one of its dreary windows that the sovereign pontiff appears at noon on Sundays to bless the public. Sixtus V es-tablished residence there, abandoning the "chambers" tapestried with masterpieces, which were now reserved for state receptions. Another infelicitous innovation by this pope was the construction of the library in the middle of the Belvedere courtyard, which, thus cut in two, lost some of its nobility and its charm, while the view of the flowerbeds was inaccessible to the apartments of Julius II. This new building included the ostentatious Sistine hall, decorated, with apologetical intentions, with frescoes and pictures narrating Sixtus V's accomplishments in the city. A notable feature is its depiction of the erection of Caligula's obelisk, with the picturesque deployment of girders and winches in front of the old façade of the basilica and its unfinished dome.

For such a pope, two palaces were not enough. Sixtus V carried on the Quirinal undertaking launched by his predecessor, in order to make it the papal court's summer residence. The palace served this purpose for two centuries before it became the home of the Italian kings and then of the presidents of the Republic. Sixtus V was to die in this unfinished palace, to which Bernini was to give the final touch by designing the great entrance gate and the apostles half-lying on the pediment. Many dignitaries were already living in the neighborhood; thus on Rome's highest hill a new quarter was created by a trend quite similar to that of the Middle Ages and the Renaissance that had led to the population of the Lateran and the Vatican.

In order to decorate the square in front of the Quirinal, Sixtus V ordered two statues of horse breakers erected there; these had been lying not far away in the ruins of Constantine's baths. They were not, as the inscriptions on their pedestals still claim, the work of Phidias and Praxiteles. They were Roman copies of transitional Greek works, quite remarkable nonetheless, and it is understandable that Michelangelo had wanted to transfer them to the Capitoline Square. Intimates of the people of Rome for two thousand years, they gave the Quirinal the name of Monte Cavallo by which it was so long known, as the signs show in the old streets that lead to it.

The industry of Sixtus V was extraordinary: he wanted to turn the Colosseum into a kind of workers' housing project; he had the remains of the Septizonium demolished in order to use its materials; he filled the Forum with the rubbish left over from his innumerable enterprises. He insisted on the speedy execution of the hugest projects. What this meant was that he obtained the prompt completion of what had been begun by his predecessors. Such was the case for the Roman College and the Palace of Wisdom, the ancient pontifical university, whose unappealing exterior is wholly in the style of the period but whose courtyard is beautiful.

RELIGIOUS ARCHITECTURE UNDER SIXTUS V

Many churches bear the stamp of the construction work of Sixtus V: San Girolamo degli Schiavoni was completely rebuilt by him; Santa Maria della Scala was completed in Trastevere in 1592; Santa Maria in Traspontina received its façade, the richest of the Counter-Reformation, in 1587; the Chiesa Nuova (Santa Maria in Vallicella) was substantially furthered during his reign, under which work was completed on St. Mary of the Hills, on whose steps a French saint, Benoît Labre, was to lie in his last agony. In 1590 St. Agnes Outside the Walls received its great stair of forty-three steps, the walls of which are filled with inscriptions collected from the neighboring catacombs. Raphael had said that modern Rome was built almost entirely with the wreckage of ancient Rome. St. Agnes affords a further illustration of the indifference with which these ruins were handled; the steps of the stairs were simply bas-reliefs reversed without even a moment's glance to see what they portrayed.

Sixtus V made some changes in the church of San Spirito in Sassia, which had been begun by Paul III near the arch of San Spirito, one of the gates of the Citadel of Leo. His intervention at St. Sabina was less successful; he had twenty of the twenty-six windows walled, despite the golden light that they distributed throughout the whole interior. The church remained dim for three and a half centuries, until the restoration of 1936 gave it back its original state.

Many other churches were the beneficiaries of revisions and new decorations. Two churches particularly dear to Frenchmen were consecrated under Sixtus V or by him: Trinità dei Monti and St. Louis. Founded by King Charles VIII, Trinità dei Monti had been built slowly with the help of irregular contributions from the kings of France and a few generous Roman donors. It could not be completed until after the receipt of a large sum from Charles IX that made it possible to construct the elegant façade with two towers that is so striking when seen from the Corso. Sixtus V dedicated it in 1585 and made it easier of access by constructing at his own expense the great flight of steps that leads up to it (designed by Fontana) and cutting an ascending path from Piazza di Spagna that was the first stage of the present large stairway.

As for St. Louis, which is the national church and the religious center for French residents of Rome, it was not suitable for consecration (by François Cardinal de Joyeuse) until 1589, although Giulio Cardinal de' Medici had laid its first stone in 1518. In order to further the work it had been necessary to wait for the generous help of Catherine de' Medici. The noble façade in two orders by Giacomo della Porta is not without a certain heaviness. Its decoration is completed by the statues of Charlemagne, St. Louis, and the two canonized queens of France, St. Clotilde and St. Jeanne de Valois. Its interior, of three naves without a transept, remained extremely austere until it was decorated with frescoes by Domenico Zampieri, known as Domenichino; paintings by Caravaggio (Michelangelo Amerighi); and the *Assumption* by Bassano* that brought the color of Venice to the main altar. The chapels are filled with tombs and memorial monuments. It is an exhibition "frozen into a cemetery of the great shades of our royal past." The chapel dedicated to St. Louis enjoys the rather rare property of having been built from the designs of a woman architect, Plantella Bricci.

Sixtus V completed his religious architectural work by adding to Santa Maria Maggiore the Sistine chapel destined to receive his tomb as well as that of Pius V. This chapel alone is a veritable church, with its own chapels, its sacristy, and its confessional. It includes the shrine of the manger that Fontana moved as a whole from its original site in a basement, using one of those ingenious mechanisms of which he had the secret. All the decoration, from the sumptuous tabernacle supported by four angels to the monumental tombs of the popes, is directed to the exaltation of pontifical majesty. But the polychromy of the marble had no splendor, the statues are stiff, the caryatids are frozen, the paintings are mediocre. This period was decidedly short of great artists.

CITY PLANNING UNDER SIXTUS V

At least there was no lack of good city planners, and Sixtus V did not condemn them to unemployment. Great municipal projects were undertaken throughout the city, one of the most important being the construction of the great Via Felice, which is still one of the finest streets in Rome; it is now called Via Sistina. The pope had conceived the ambitious project of establishing communications among the major basilicas and all the quarters by means of broad streets. Although he executed it only in part, he made Rome the best intraconnected city of its time. His finest achieve-

---

* Apparently Jacopo Bassano (Giacomo da Ponte): three generations of this family produced six painters.—Translator.

ment in this domain was the Four Fountains square in the new Quirinal quarter. It is a right-angled intersection of four new absolutely straight streets, linking Porta Pia and the three obelisks of the Quirinal, Trinità dei Monti, and Santa Maria Maggiore with a system of beautiful symmetrical vistas. The corners of the square are softened by being decorated with four beautiful fountains, themselves adorned with niches and statues. It has been well said that this crossroads is a summary of Rome.

The greatest city-planning conception of Sixtus V was to bring back to life the hills of Rome, too long depopulated because they were without water. For that matter, the whole city was short of water, for only one aqueduct was operational, that of the Acqua Vergine. Resolved, as we know, to rival the ancient Caesars, "Sixtus V devoted himself, like them, to the conquest of nature and undertook to build gigantic aqueducts to bring the city the water that it needed. 'So that these hills, made glorious in the earliest Christian age by the sacred basilicas,' he said, 'and endowed with health-giving air, a delightful site, and a pleasant view, can be places of residence again.' " Hence he brought water to Rome over a distance of fifteen miles from Colonna, in the Alban Hills, and baptized it with the name that he had borne before becoming pope, Acqua Felice. The price was eighteen months of work and sixty thousand Roman crowns. This was when that monumental fountain of Moses was constructed at the corner of Piazza San Bernardo, showing the patriarch in the act of striking the rock and bringing forth water. This fountain is cited as an example of the disasters that can befall untalented imitators under Michelangelo's influence. Size became bombast here, and this Moses, a caricature of that in San Pietro in Vincoli, certainly earned the criticisms that were hurled at its unhappy creator, Prospero da Brescia, who died, it is said, of grief. Of the twenty-seven fountains erected under Sixtus V, only one is truly graceful and beautiful, that of the Turtles in Piazza Mattei: it depicts four handsome bronze boys pushing turtles into a higher basin. One feels that one is watching a silent dance, a ballet step. How can one believe that this charming group was the creation of Giacomo della Porta, especially when not far away, in the square of the Ara Coeli, there is another fountain by him that is static and heavy? In actuality, all the credit for the Turtle fountain should go to the sculptor, Landini: delightfully Florentine, the work is reminiscent of Benvenuto Cellini.

During the Second World War this fountain suffered a singular misadventure. It had been disassembled for storage outside the danger area. After the war, its component parts were miraculously discovered in second-hand shops, where they had arrived no one knew how. A popular belief had it that the fountain was built in a single night, in romantic circumstances. A young lord, betrothed to an heiress of the Mattei family, had been rejected by her parents when his own family suffered financial reverses. Having come to bid his beloved farewell, he asked her to look out her window at the farewell gift that he was giving her. The girl thereupon saw in the square the delightful fountain that had not been there the day before. This munificence restored the lover's credit and the wedding was duly celebrated. This fountain is in fact in front of one of the five Mattei palaces built at various periods and joined in a vast architectonic whole, somewhat decayed today from its antique splendor. The *cortile* preserves only a few statues and some ancient vestiges set in the building as high as the fourth story. This is all that survives of the famous Mattei collections whose marvels were so much admired by great personages visiting Rome.

More than 4.25 million cubic feet of water per day fertilized the hills, especially the Pincio and the Quirinal. New buildings were begun at once, stimulated by special inducements. In the whole city the only sight was masons at their tasks. The population was rising so swiftly that foreigners had difficulty mingling with the older inhabitants. The whole Christian world believed that anything was possible in Rome, that there was nothing "that was beyond the hopes and the entreaties of everyone." Every immigrant could have taken for application to himself the answer given by Cardinal Cossa, when he was asked why he was going to Rome, that "he wanted to become pope." Fortified by the recent examples of the two most recently elevated pontiffs, "everyone believed himself capable of everything and expected everything." The transformations of the Roman court justified this revival of ambitions. In fact Sixtus V had created a myriad of new positions: treasurers of the datary,* of the prefecture, of the prisons; twenty-four chief clerkships; two hundred knighthoods; papal notaries in vast numbers. Having found the papal cash drawers empty, he had chosen this means of filling them.

But his enterprises were extremely costly, and, in order to keep pace with them, he had to order substantial increases in the taxes on persons

---

* The datary was a division of the Vatican chancellory that processed prior decisions made by the pope outside the Consistory (special graces, dispensations, etc.).— Translator.

and property. Such measures are never popular. The reaction exploded on the Holy Father's death (August 27, 1590). Immediately his good works, his skillful political leadership, and the glory that he had gained for Rome were forgotten; all that was remembered was the cost and the strictness of his rule. It was even charged that he had made an agreement with the devil, and the populace brutally overturned the statues that had been erected to him. This was when it was decided that statues would no longer be erected to popes during their lifetimes. This tide of posthumous reproach had no echo in France, where Sixtus V had become very popular after he had reproved the excesses of the League* and refused to join the enemies of Henri de Navarre. The Béarnais held him in high regard. "He was a great pope," he said when he heard of his death; "God grant that his successor be like him."

TASSO / HENRI IV AND THE CENCIS

This prayer of Henri de Navarre was not granted, and the weak rule of the first three successors to Sixtus V soon imperiled all his achievements. Bandits regained mastery over the Roman countryside, insecurity led to hunger, wheat grew expensive and then disappeared. A kind of bread was confected out of beans and leguminous vegetables, but even this could be rationed only very meagerly. Famine reigned even in rural areas, and, as usual, an epidemic followed. One would like to believe that Cicarelli exaggerated when he stated that it caused the deaths of sixteen thousand persons in 1591 alone. The fact remains that Rome's population dropped substantially, as much through the effects of the "plague" as by reason of the exodus to which it led. Clement VIII managed to restore an almost normal situation through measures that, however, aroused bitter resistance. According to custom, the Romans' ill humors were vented in the sarcasms of Pasquino, and the marble satirist's virulence so deeply offended the pope that he had a committee of cardinals formally sentence the statue to be shattered and cast into the Tiber. It was saved by Tasso, who wisely counseled the preservation of the sole opposition outlet:

* The League, also known as the Holy League, was a Catholic confederation founded by the Duc de Guise in 1576 to defend the Catholic faith against the Calvinists, overthrow Henri III, and place the Guises on the French throne. Henri IV recognized that his renunciation of Calvinism would put an end to the League.— Translator.

"Leave Pasquino on his pedestal," he said, "for, if you threw him into the Tiber, his dust would spawn a thousand frogs whose croaking day and night would deafen you."

It was three years later, in 1595, just when the pope was preparing to crown him on the Capitoline, that the unfortunate poet who had paid with a wandering and often miserable life for his glory and his prodigious infatuation died in the monastery of Sant'Onofrio on the Janiculum, leaving Italy the treasure of his genius. Visitors can see the cell in which he died, the wretched stone under which he rests, the oak at whose base he loved to sit. This garden of Sant'Onofrio has been called one of the most delightful places in the world. It offers an incomparable view over the city and the nearby mountains. It is an enthralling spectacle that justifies the awed comment of Chateaubriand, carved on the outer wall of the monastery's exquisite church.

It was under this same pontificate that the reconciliation between Henri IV and the church was celebrated. On September 17, 1595, Clement VIII opened wide the gates of St. Peter's to Messieurs d'Ossat and Duperron, future cardinals who had come to present the solemn profession of Catholic faith of the king of France; to celebrate the event, the pope ordered the erection of a column topped by a cross near Santa Maria Maggiore. The exigencies of traffic subsequently compelled the Roman authorities to move it to the right side of the basilica. The cross crowns a pink marble column that reproduces the shaft of a cannon, round which is carved: *In hoc signo vinces.* This ambiguous inscription has given rise to considerable commentary; the skeptical say that one cannot quite tell whether the arm of victory is the cross or in fact the cannon.

The recantation of Henri IV is portrayed in detail in a bas-relief on the tomb of Leo XI in St. Peter's. It was he who, while still a cardinal, had received the king's profession of faith at St.-Denis.

The memory of Henri IV is also strong in St. John Lateran, but his bronze statue, which one sees when one leaves the cathedral by the Sixtus portal, was erected only in 1609 by the chapter of the basilica in memory of the king's having given it the abbey of Clairac in the diocese of Agen. This contribution also earned the donor the title of "first canon of the Lateran," which he passed on to his successors. The Romans were much amused during the French Revolution by the thought that the one and indivisible republic held a canonry at the Lateran. The presidents of the successive French Republics have retained the honor, and their ambassadors in Rome have preserved the habit of attending, every December 13—St. Lucy's day and the birthday of Henri IV—the solemn mass that is celebrated in the basilica *pro felice statu Gallicae nationis* (for the blessed state of the Gallic nation). On this occasion the three celebrants wear the same vestments that were worn for the nuptial mass of Louis XV and Maria Leczinska, and the floor of the chancel is covered with the carpet from the study of Napoleon I.

In 1599 all Rome was aroused by the tragedy of Beatrice Cenci, whose agony has never ceased providing material for a host of popular songs, explanatory accounts, and dramatic works. Beatrice was the daughter of Francesco Cenci, a man sunk in all the vices, the head of a very ancient Roman family whose palace still stands on the height formed by the ruins of the theater of Balbus. The savage aspect of the Cencis' house is in perfect accord with the drama that made their name famous; it has a look of mystery and prison. The choked little square at its entrance still preserves inscriptions and traces of altars that are the family's genealogical chart in stone: it was descended from Crescentius Centius, a son of Empress Theodora of Byzantium, who arrogated to himself the titles of patrician and consul in the tenth century and who boasted of descent from a Roman *gens*. It might be observed in passing that the great Roman families often claimed descent from some illustrious figure of ancient Rome.

In order to purge herself of the outrage of incest, it is said, Beatrice had her unnatural father murdered with the help of her mother and her brother. All three were to die on the scaffold of Ponte Sant'Angelo at the express decision of the pope and in spite of the whole city's entreaties. Their execution was accompanied by horrible circumstances well adapted to impress the popular imagination and re-echo in it for generations. The youngest Cenci, a boy of fifteen, was found innocent, but he was dragged to the execution "by way of example"; he was drenched with the blood of his mother and sister, while the executioner butchered his elder brother between the women's corpses. Guido Reni has painted a portrait of Beatrice Cenci in her prison that is one of the most beautiful works in the Barberini gallery. It shows the girl with the modest and almost childlike features of a nymph in an eclogue. But is this really Beatrice? There is reason to doubt it.

The Cencis' property was confiscated. Later, Paul V bestowed a large part of it on his nephews, and thus one of the doomed family's estates became Villa Borghese. The insurance building erected in 1906 opposite Palazzo Venezia, in the Ghibelline style, occupies the site of a palace that belonged to the Cenci family.

The unrest that had brought on the harsh measures of Clement VIII had quite disappeared when, three months later, the jubilee of 1600 opened, bringing more than three million pilgrims to the apostles' tombs. The merchants made fortunes, the papal treasury was filled, and above all the power and the glory of the papacy were displayed like a triumph. As if the better to establish them, Giordano Bruno, the Dominican who had broken his vows and briefly been a Calvinist and a pantheist, was solemnly burned to death in Campo dei Fiori. Two hundred eighty-seven years later the new masters of Rome, in mockery of the Holy See, erected a statue to him as a champion of freedom.

THE BIRTH OF A NEW ARISTOCRACY

"The spiritual power that resorted so harshly to the temporal arm labored more actively than ever to gather in its share of temporal goods" (Bertaux). This was the reign of nepotism. The disease had a long history. Its regrettable effects had been seen in the times of the della Roveres and the Borgias. But Julius II had condemned it, like Sixtus V, who, it must be said, had not assumed this admirable position until after he had made a cardinal of his thirteen-year-old nephew. Still, thus far the popes had shown a relative moderation. Starting with Clement VIII, nepotism was to flourish openly and give society a new structure that was to set the tone and the rhythm for Roman society for two centuries. The popes began bestowing high church offices and church property on their relatives. And this kind of behavior excited neither criticism nor reproof. Everyone conceded that "it would not be right for a pope's relative to find himself in restricted circumstances when the pontiff died." The application of this rule led the popes to make their nephews cardinals without regard to their aptitudes or their characters. But a cardinal's dignity could not pass by inheritance; it could still be said that a pope's nephew died twice, once on his own and once through his uncle. In order to eliminate this serious embarrassment, the popes were to make their loved ones hereditary Roman princes, always being sure to reinforce the titles with substantial properties that would stay in the family.

These were the bases on which a new aristocracy arose that might be called "papal." Each pope was to leave behind him a swarm of princes: after the Farneses and the Aldobrandinis there came the Borgheses, the Ludovisis, the Barberinis, the Pamphilis, the Odescalchis to fill Rome's heraldic rolls. Clement VIII lavished titles and money on his five Aldobrandini nephews: to one of them, Pietro, he gave sixty thousand crowns in benefices in a single year. Paul V, who succeeded him in 1605 after the brief reign of Leo XI, was a Borghese; he made one of his nephews his prime minister (chief cardinal), turned over the papal treasury to the others, and assured his family of the eminent position that it still holds. The path had been marked: few popes were to stray from it for two centuries.

But one must do the new aristocrats the justice of admitting that "they nobly gave Rome what they took from the church." They were to imitate the princes of the Renaissance and the rich patricians of antiquity. They led ostentatious lives, they gave splendid parties; thanks to them the carnival would be restored to its best days. Staggering under the gifts of generous uncles, they were never to be lax in adding to the donors' renown by founding hospitals and convents, building palaces and churches that they would deck with pictures and sculptures. They practiced an intelligent and fecund patronage of the arts. Artists flocked from all parts of Italy to take service with them; they were to offer employment to artisans of every craft. The providence of the merchants, they were to fill Rome with activity and with the prosperity that flows from it.

THE BOLOGNA SCHOOL

The mediocre artists of the sixteenth century had just been succeeded by a new generation that was to renew painting. It was dominated by a few great names—Caravaggio, the Carracci brothers, Guido Reni, and Domenichino. Caravaggio was a Lombard whose naturalistic art, dark and violent, invested sacred painting with a rough and popular humanity. With him, it has been said, any religious scene is degraded. The tragic power of this painting, and its sincerity, made a dramatic contrast to the propaganda productions of the Counter-Reformation.

Trained in Bologna and more eclectic, the three Carracci brothers brought Rome a knowledgeable and easy art, "well made," it has been said, "to provide a background to amorous parties and princely plots." Certainly they inspired the art of Versailles. We have already met Annibale Carracci in Palazzo Farnese.

Guido Reni was to be the decorator of the great palaces of this period. As for Domenichino, also a Bolognese, his stirring, virile work, which can be admired without reservation in the frescoes of Sant'Andrea della Valle, attained its peak in the *Communication of St. Jerome,* painted in 1614 for a small church and finally found worthy to hang in the Vatican beside Raphael's *Transfiguration,* whose equal in merit, as Nicolas Poussin said, it undoubtedly is.

The Bolognese painters left a body of work of which it has been said that it alone would be enough to make the glory of Rome. But art was to grow pallid after them, and, over the next two centuries, the churches of Rome were to acquire hardly any decoration that was not tainted with propaganda and preciosity. The painting of baroque ceilings and domes was to be no more than a brilliant decoration "inseparable from the architecture of whose fantasies it was the continuation."

CHAPTER 25

THE BEGINNINGS OF THE BAROQUE

THE FAÇADE OF ST. PETER'S AND THE PAULINE CHAPEL

Before the baroque began, the monumental era of Sixtus V was to be continued splendidly under Paul V. But the creations of his pontificate departed from the severity that prevailed in the time of the Counter-Reformation. Their inspiration was freer and sought more sustained effects; the marble facings were gayer; stucco acquired a growing place. Art was making great strides toward the baroque, which was soon to establish itself as the master. This interval was not unrelated to the contemporary political evolution: Catholicism had triumphed in France, Protestantism was pulling back into central Europe, and the great crisis of the church seemed to have ended.

The transition to the baroque was to show itself first in the architecture and decoration of the basilica of St. Peter's. Once the dome had been completed, the other work had been neglected. Paul V ordered its active resumption and entrusted its direction to Carlo Maderna. What still remained standing of the old nave and the original *atrium* was demolished; when the question of going farther arose, it became clear that Michelangelo's Greek-cross design no longer suited the present state of Christendom. The religious ideal of the Council of Trent having triumphed with the papacy, the church could not desert the tradition of its

307

first basilicas in the shrine that it proposed to construct in the heart of Catholicism. The design reverted to the Latin cross, which had already been emphasized by the architect of the Gesù. Maderna therefore lengthened the nave with three bays and widened it in proportion, as a result upsetting its harmony. For the exterior he retained Michelangelo's design in erecting the façade and the attic story, decorated with statues. But he placed them much farther forward of the nave than the Florentine master had intended. It is because of this unfortunate shift that the dome disappears from sight when it is approached from the square. If the original plan had been retained, the dome would have been visible from the square as in Paris the dome of the Invalides is seen from the Esplanade. Maderna's façade sets up a screen, and this is certainly the most serious flaw in the edifice.

Paul V, however, was not restrained in his pride in it, and his name is displayed there in huge letters. He did not live long enough to consecrate the basilica; this was to be the task of Urban VIII in 1626. Nevertheless the project was virtually completed when Paul V died. After so many changes it no longer bore any resemblance to "the fantastic and classic Babel" that Bramante had imagined. Just as it stood, it was to serve as the official model for all the churches that were to be built in great number in Rome and throughout Christendom. Not only its architectural conception but its interior decoration was to be followed. It was already beginning to be invaded by marble and stucco, in evidence of a growing trend toward luxuriousness. It was Paul V who appointed the central nave as the site for the venerable statue of St. Peter seated, probably the work of Arnolfo di Cambio, which the Middle Ages had revered as the protector of the city. Its bronze foot had already been worn by the kisses of millions and millions of the faithful.

The new taste for richness was confirmed again in the abundance and color of the architectonic decorations of the Pauline chapel of Santa Maria Maggiore. Pursuing the beginning made by Sixtus V, Paul V had this chapel built to house his tomb and that of Clement VIII. Its arrangements imitated those of the Sistine chapel, but, revealing the evolution that had taken place, its polychromy is more brilliant and richer, and the shaping of the statues is more supple; there is a hint of the advent of the age of Bernini. It was also in imitation of Sixtus V that Paul V, mingling the sacred and the profane, transferred to the square of Santa Maria Maggiore, as a pedestal for a statue of the Virgin, the great column of Parian marble that was still in Constantine's basilica.

SANT'ANDREA DELLA VALLE AND THE CHURCHES OF THE TIME OF PAUL V

Of the many churches built during the pontificate of Paul V, the most grandiose is undoubtedly Sant'Andrea della Valle, the work of Maderna. Its high dome is the largest in Rome next to that of St. Peter's, and its façade is one of the best of the seventeenth century. Its design as prepared by Maderna already showed the architectural conceptions that, elaborated forty-five years later by Carlo Rainaldi, were to make it a typically baroque work: columns give rhythm to the façade and enliven it with their breaks. The interior ornamentation is of great richness: there are two bronze candelabra that are regarded as the most beautiful in Rome; twelve columns of an extremely rare marble, *la lumachella;* admirable paintings by Domenichino—the four Evangelists in the pendentives of the dome, and the Virtues in the persons of highly attractive ladies. The fresco on the dome, by Lanfranco, was the first to be "actually conceived in terms of this special type of surface." Sant'Andrea della Valle stands on the site of an ancient and very much venerated shrine that marked the place where, according to tradition, St. Sebastian was thrown into the sewer after his martyrdom in Campo dei Fiori. An inscription carved in a niche recalls the action of the virtuous and mysterious "Lucina," who retrieved the martyr's body by night and had it placed in a catacomb.

At the end of the little square to the left of the church there is a very worn statue of a man solemnly draped in his toga. The Romans called it Abate Luigi (Abbot Louis) and ascribed a great perspicacity to it as one of Rome's speaking statues; it often debated with Pasquino, Signora Lucrezia, and Marforio.

Two other products of this period were St. James of the Incurables, an interesting composition by Maderna that may have inspired Francesco Borromini's Sant'Agnese in Agone, and San Carlo di Catinari, which is in the shape of a Greek cross surmounted by a magnificent dome. The main altar is embellished with four ancient columns in red porphyry; so some of these must still have remained intact at the end of the sixteenth century. Let us also list Santa Maria della Vittoria and take the opportunity to recall its curious history. Some poor Carmelite brothers owned a vineyard near Diocletian's baths, where they hoped to build a church: they began in 1605 to dig its foundations, relying on Providence to assume the charge of providing them with the money required for continuing the work. However unreasonable it seemed, this touching hope was not long in being fulfilled. In the hole that they had dug, the good monks found a splendid Greek statue of a hermaphrodite. Wisely deeming this sculpture inappropriate to the adornment of a church, they thought that they might gain some profit from it by offering it to Scipione Cardinal Borghese, as renowned for his generosity as for his passion for ancient art. Struck with wonder at the hermaphrodite, the cardinal immediately packed it off to the villa that he was building on the Pincio to house his collections. The statue is now in the Louvre, but Rome has two copies of it: one in the Museum of the Baths, the other in the Borghese gallery. In this instance the cardinal did not belie the reputation for magnificence that had given him the epithet of "the delight of Rome." He assumed the financing of the greater part of the work on the church, which still bears his family's arms. It is this church that contains Bernini's most celebrated work, St. Theresa being transfixed by an angel with rays of divine love. It has so troubled the critics' dreams that one may wonder whether they would have been equally upset by the Borghese hermaphrodite.

We gladly omit from the list of churches built under Paul V that of San Nicola de Tolentino, which is of only mediocre interest, as well as those that were not finished until later, such as Sant'Andrea delle Fratte or St. Charles in the Corso. On the other hand such a list would have to include the churches that were partly rebuilt or that acquired additions of some importance: almost fifty of these have been catalogued. The size of this figure is explained by the obligation that the pope had imposed on his cardinals: to restore at their own expense the churches of which they were the titulars. Without embarking on too protracted an inventory, let us note that Santa Maria Maggiore was enriched with a baptistry and the tomb of the Congolese ambassador, Nigrita; that Santa Susanna (on Piazza San Bernardo), restored so many times since the fifth century, acquired a beautiful façade by Maderna: the national church of the Americans, it is one of the oldest shrines in Rome, since it is the successor of a chapel that is supposed to have been built in 290 in honor of Susanna, niece of Pope St. Caius. Sought in marriage by Diocletian's son, she was beheaded on the emperor's order because she refused a marriage in violation of her faith. Curiously, this church had already been rebuilt in the sixteenth century at the expense of a Roman laundress, Camilla Peretti. Let there be no surprise that a person of such modest condition had access to such great means: Camilla Peretti was the sister of Sixtus V. In Santa Susanna even more than in Sant'Andrea della Valle, Maderna demonstrated his character as a precursor of the baroque. Here for the first time the architectural precepts of the Counter-Reformation were violated: relief and movement give life to what was immobile. Columns rise out of the façade; still encased in the wall, they foreshadow the baroque façades in which truly independent columns would allow the light to play among their alternated capitals.

The church of St. Gregory the Great (at the foot of the Caelian Hill), an old structure from the twelfth century built on foundations dating from the imperial epoch, was also rebuilt under Paul V. It houses most disparate objects: the very ancient madonna who spoke to the saint, and the tomb of the courtesan Imperia. Above the exterior arches the Borghese eagle spreads its wings; for once more it was Scipione, the cardinal, who caused this harmonious façade to be built. It was also he who, in 1614, had the basilica of St. Sebastian in Via Appia reduced to its present size on plans by Flaminio Ponzio, while Domenichino designed the splendid paneled ceiling of Santa Maria Trasteverina.

COUNTER-REFORMATION PALACES

The palaces built in great number during the period of the Counter-Reformation shared only to a much lesser degree in the evolution of architecture. While the sacred structures were advancing in great strides toward that new form of art that was to be the baroque, the palaces remained like those of the preceding centuries: sober and sturdy, devoid of fantasy, certainly less profane in appearance than their contemporaries, the churches. The walls were bare: even the decorative caprices of Palazzo Sciara or Palazzo Massimo, whose vogue had been brief, had been abandoned. Only the openings had become wider, in particular the gates, in order to admit carriages. The buildings were usually crowned with cornices, generally in imitation of that of Palazzo Farnese. The palaces of this period seem to have been designed less for comfort than for show. But they do not hint at a brilliant life, elegant festivities, or ingenious diversions. Some, like Palazzo Ruspoli (formerly Gaetani), on the Corso, have the severe aspect of the Florentine palaces. Martino Longhi the Younger gave this palace an unusual staircase, each of whose hundred steps is formed of a single block of marble ten feet wide. Queen Hortense lived in this beautiful house with her two children, one of whom was to become Emperor Napoleon III. The Ruspoli restaurant, which was the ultimate to nineteenth-century Romans, was established in the magnificent halls that looked out on a garden planted with orange trees.

The most characteristic palace of the period is the one that was begun by Pope Paul V near Via di Ripetta while he was still Cardinal Borghese. It still bears his name. It is the famous *cembalo di Roma* (clavichord of Rome): it has indeed the outer shape of a concert piano, while within there is a huge square court that represents what is picturesque in the composition. But the two stories of paired columns, the gay fountain called "the bath of Venus," the large open loggia on the charming terrace were all the achievements of a later time. Its general architecture, sober and impressive, is all that dates from the Counter-Reformation.

At the same time, the pope's nephew, Scipione Borghese, built an extremely huge palace, between court and garden, on the Quirinal, near Villa Colonna; it was later to become the property of Mazarin,* and, many times remodeled since then, it is now known as Palazzo Rospigliosi. Here again the severity of the façades is belied by the interior decoration, especially that of the casino, which recalls the Farnesina; Guido Reni's famous fresco, *Aurora,* whose rounded arms hold roses that she scatters, is painted on the ceiling of the gallery.

Many other princely palaces were to be built during this period: one of the largest is Palazzo Lancellotti, which Maderna erected and in which, at the end, Domenichino collaborated no longer as a painter but in the capacity of architect. The Corso quarter, which was beginning to be the center of fashionable life, was filled with luxurious residences. There Rainaldi built Palazzo Veroski, which was to become the headquarters of the Credito Italiano, and Giacomo della Porta designed Palazzo Chigi, long the seat of the Ministry of Foreign Affairs. The exterior offers the customary severity of the buildings of the time, but the courtyard, remodeled fifty years later, once more emphasizes in contrast the relaxation brought by the baroque.

COUNTER-REFORMATION VILLAS: VILLA MEDICI AND VILLA BORGHESE

In the days of the Renaissance, the villas of the financiers and the higher prelates had begun to girdle Rome with the flowered belt of their gardens.

---

* Born Giulio Mazarini in Italy, Cardinal Mazarin was a seventeenth-century French statesman who had begun his career in the papal army and moved into diplomacy.—Translator.

The Counter-Reformation was not to halt this trend—far from it; beyond Aurelian's Wall and occasionally even quite far out in the country there were to be a prodigious number of resort residences, whose destiny was to give rise to a new style. Released from the contemporary sobriety, their elegant lines would afford picturesque profiles. Above all, the architects were to concentrate on incorporating them into the landscapes that provided their frames. This concern was to produce polychrome decorations: walls were to be adorned with mosaics and ancient bas-reliefs, often of very high quality. The most characteristic example of this style is to be found in the first of these villas to be built, constructed by Cardinal Montepulciano on the Pincio not far from the former gardens of Lucullus. Bought in 1600 by a Medici cardinal, it bears his family's name. The Academy of France was to be established there in 1803. In the meantime it had served as a prison for the most illustrious victims of the Inquisition. This was the occasion of Galileo's enforced visit there. After a visit to the room in which he had lived, Edmond About* exclaimed: "I wish every martyr to truth could have such a cell!"

The severe outer façade of Villa Medici gives no hint of the grace of the inner façade that looks over the gardens and, though it shows no originality of conception, derives its charm from the bas-reliefs and the fragments of antique sculpture with which it is, so to speak, embroidered, even more than Palazzo Spada. The poet Kotzebue† said that it resembled "a pretty woman in splendid attire, sparkling with diamonds, about to leave for the opera." A beautiful park adorned with statues and a *bosco* (woods) of untamed charm add to the attractions of this residence. From its terraces there is a panorama that cannot be surpassed by the most celebrated "views" in Rome. Facing the city, admirably framed in evergreen oaks, the famous fountain so often depicted by painters murmurs.

Villa Celimontana (or Mattei), whose entrance opens on Piazza della Navicella, houses the Roman Geographical Society. Its park is a kind of paradise: areas of light and shadow were never distributed with such rare felicity. White statues make bright intervals against the high walls of shrubbery. Palm trees and cypresses are mirrored in the sleepy pools. An Egyptian obelisk taken from the shrine of Isis Capitolina rises in a clearing. From the terrace one can see the Baths of Caracalla: Hubert Robert and Fragonard often gazed out over the balustrade.

---

* Nineteenth-century French novelist and member of the Académie Française.— Translator.

† August von Kotzebue, a late eighteenth-century German poet and dramatist.— Translator.

Villa Aldobrandini, erected at the end of the sixteenth century on top of a group of Roman houses of the imperial period, is also a marvel. Its hanging garden, in which marble statues stand in rows beneath the pines, overlooks Piazza Magnanapoli. General François de Miollis made this his headquarters when he was governor of Rome under Napoleon I. Scipione Borghese wanted to have a villa, and he wanted it to be the most beautiful of all: it has retained its rank. In fact, Villa Borghese on the Pincio enhances the beauty of its setting with an inestimable artistic treasure, largely taken from the palace of Paul V and considerably enriched by later contributions that have made it one of the finest museums in Rome. Pauline Bonaparte lived there after her marriage to Camillo Borghese in 1803; she still greets its visitors, in a half-nude statue with a Greek headdress by Antonio Canova. Since 1902 the villa's collections, purchased by the Italian state, have been open to the public, like the sumptuous gardens that surround it. The splendid foliage, the great number of fountains, the statues, and the ancient groups that adorn the paths make this patrician residence and its lordly park one of the most characteristic places in Rome.

As in the times of Augustus, the outskirts of Rome began again to fill with luxurious dwellings. Paul V had bought, repaired, and beautified Villa Mondragone in Frascati, where Gregory XIII had signed the proclamation of the calendar reform. Paul's nephew, Scipione, had made haste to build an equally luxurious villa nearby. In fifty years Frascati had been covered by a wave of princely residences where high prelates, ambassadors, and bankers furnished lordly hospitality to their friends. This graceful hill had become fashionable again, quite as much as it had been in the time of Cicero and Crassus. This is enough to show that, in spite of the austere tastes of the era, the aristocracy had not quite given up the pleasures of Renaissance living.

THE COUNTER-REFORMATION'S LAST CREATIONS / THE
PAULINE FOUNTAIN / ST. IGNATIUS / THE COLLEGE
FOR THE PROPAGATION OF THE FAITH

The last Counter-Reformation popes, moreover, were to depart more and more from the harsh rules that had dominated the previous period. Great municipal constructions were prosecuted by Paul V: a great number of houses were demolished in order to make way for new streets.

Beautiful structures rose almost everywhere. In imitation of Sixtus V, the Borghese pope brought back to Rome a source of water that had been unused for centuries. Trajan's aqueduct, restored to service, led to the monumental Pauline fountain on the Janiculum. Six oriental granite columns supported its upper story; a huge marble bowl caught the enormous volume of its water. It is one of the most beautiful fountains in Rome, a veritable water tower with tumultuous liquid masses like those of the Fontana di Trevi.

Its materials were taken from Nerva's Forum, for Paul V did not boggle at using the ancient remains that still survived. Constantine's baths, which had thus far been relatively spared in recognition of that emperor's services to the church, were razed from top to bottom and the materials were used for new construction. When the pope removed from the basilica of Maxentius the column that he installed on the square before Santa Maria Maggiore, the basilica's vault collapsed and there was not a tremor of regret. A significant detail: among the privileges conferred by Paul V on the members of his family, who were great builders like himself, he included that "of not being disturbed by any demolition."

Paul V was succeeded in 1621 by Gregory XV, an old man with good intentions but much weakened by age, who bore the weight of the tiara only two years. His pontificate was made glorious, however, by the active part taken in its business by his young nephew, Alessandro Ludovisi, whom he had made a cardinal. Although he affected the manners of a dilettante diligent in attendance at gatherings of poets, this young man demonstrated a great firmness of mind in the service of the church: nepotism did not always have the evil results that are attributed to it. A former pupil of the Jesuits, Ludovisi accelerated the canonization of Ignatius Loyola and, to celebrate the event, he built the church of St. Ignatius, which represents the complete culmination of the works of the Counter-Reformation. The baroque era was to give it a magnificence rivaling that of the Gesù.

It was also Cardinal Ludovisi's personal intervention that was responsible for the foundation of the College for the Propagation of the Faith, whence Catholic proselytization would radiate over the face of the earth. The church had regained a great part of the lost ground, and now it was regrouping for the conquest of new empires; it was not long before there would be a monastery of the Virgin in Peking and a host of schools in India, Japan, and America. Cardinal Ludovisi began the construction of the huge seat of this college at Piazza di Spagna. Irreverent as always, de

Brosses said that this was where the missionaries were fattened for the cannibals' dinners. It is difficult to believe that its façade was the work of Bernini, so alien is it to the work that this artist, who was then starting his career, was very soon to produce. In contrast, Borromini was already manifesting the full flight of his imagination in the part of the building on Via di Propaganda that he designed.

For his own use Cardinal Ludovisi improved the most grandiose of the patrician residences, for which Le Nôtre designed the gardens. It has completely vanished, a victim of the city planners of the late nineteenth century, who never hesitated, in order to create new quarters and occasionally merely to grieve the pope, to massacre trees and sacrifice the noblest gardens of Rome.

The Counter-Reformation had been a period of retreat and severity; the church was bandaging its wounds, the papacy was preparing for its further expansion. Once danger had passed, austerity was to be swiftly repudiated. The baroque arrived to "frolic" in all the arts and enliven Roman life with new pleasures.

PART FIVE

BAROQUE ROME

SEVENTEENTH AND

EIGHTEENTH

CENTURIES

CHAPTER 26

ARTISTIC LIFE

BAROQUE ART

The names of Borromini and Bernini mark the emergence of a new style destined for a very great development, the Roman baroque. Since the end of the eighteenth century it had been inching its way into art, progressively launching its trends that were to express the conqueror's part that the victorious papacy henceforth envisaged for the Eternal City. In its new splendor the pilgrims were to read the victory of the church over heresy. And that victory had to be extended to the borders of the world, establishing its foundations not only on repentance and recollection but even more on the magnificence of the spectacle afforded to all by the capital of Christendom. Everything was to be concerted to show the faithful, so to speak, a reflection of eternal blessedness. Henceforth the work of artists would be turned in this direction by the popes, and it was in the spirit of a crusade that the artistic revolution that was to transform the city's aspect was to be carried out.

It was about 1625 when the baroque concluded its period of groping and trial. For almost two centuries it was to inspire everything that would be done in the realm of the arts in Rome. Torrential in its fecundity, "in spite of the wealth and the variety of the earlier contributions, it shaped the physiognomy of the city in preponderant fashion" (*Itinéraires romains*).

One cannot walk twenty feet in Rome without encountering its mobile façades, its theatrical churches, its exuberant fountains. Everything bears its stamp. It so strongly sets the tone of the urban landscape that, "like it or not," as Maurice Denis* said, it constituted "Rome's style."

These are those, especially in France, who deplore the fact. In truth, an apparent incompatibility of character has long produced misunderstandings between the French classic genius and the audacities of the baroque. This is the observation of Victor L. Tapié in his recent very knowledgeable study, *Baroque et classicisme,* from which we have largely borrowed. The baroque strove more to arouse emotion than to satisfy logic, and on that account it has been invested with a character of weakness and femininity, a tendency to disorder, against which classicism supposedly reacted. Obviously the absolute monarchy of Louis XIV looked elsewhere for its effects, and it is understandable that the "great century" of France should have diverted its artists from an esthetic doctrine in which sentiment and imagery occupied a rank regarded as excessive and in which it saw only "grimaces, contortions, and false pretenses." Having completely overcome these prejudices, our age is capable of sympathizing with the ideal that was incarnated by the baroque, with "the world of which it was the formal expression." Today we can admire its brilliant aspects, admit the sincerity of its enthusiasms, acknowledge that by exalting the imagination it saved world art from the danger of overly severe disciplines, even if these be classic. The movement, the splendor, the luxuriance of its shapes no longer inspire in us that sensation of uprootedness that our fathers experienced. There are aspects of the baroque that can still surprise us, but they no longer shock us, they no longer move us to mockery. What is left of the political and social system that gave birth to our classic art? But the church still lives, and St. Peter's in Rome remains the meeting place of the vast Christian family. Yet, within virtually a half century of each other, St. Peter's and Versailles were born of a single epoch and a single Europe. "Between classicism and the baroque," Tapié wrote, "would there not always exist common sources and concealed affinities? Would these not always be two expressions of a single civilization, or, to be still more exact, two styles that satisfied, perhaps, different sensibilities but that equally express the spirit of a single society?"

We have felt it fitting to repeat these views here in order to help the

---

* A French religious painter of the nineteenth and twentieth centuries.—Translator.

Frenchman who visits Rome* not to erect "any irreducible barrier between the work that he contemplates and his own fashion of imagining and feeling." For Pierre Gaxotte,† classicism and the baroque, which coexist in certain works and which developed together, are not even two opposite forms of imagination: "Classicism," he said, "is a contained, controlled imagination: the baroque is an imagination that escapes, that breaks free, that enjoys itself. When imagination wanes, classicism declines into boredom and the baroque into technique."

THE BARBERINIS, THEIR WORK AND THEIR PALACE

In the seventeenth century the enrichment of a pope's relatives and their entrance into the ranks of the Roman nobility were sanctified by custom. Under Urban VIII the Aldobrandinis, the Borgheses, the Ludovisis were to be joined by the Barberinis, who had poured in from Florence at news of their unce's election, "flying," a chronicler said, "like a swarm of those bees that they bear on their escutcheon to suck the honey of the church." It is not without good reason that this family and its head are regarded as having been particularly greedy; their faces are still red at Pasquino's epigrams. The most famous is still extant: *"Quod non fecerunt Barbari, fecerunt Barberini* (What the Barbarians did not do, the Barberinis did)." There were many others, from one that represented the church covered with the Barberinis' bees and complaining that they had stung it even to its entrails, to another that alluded to the demolition of the Colosseum: "Urban undressed Flavius to clothe St. Peter." For the sake of justice it must be admitted that, if the apostolic treasury was emptied under Urban VIII, it was chiefly because this pope undertook to restore the military power of the Holy See. He fortified Castello Sant'Angelo, extended the Vatican's walls, surrounded the Quirinal gardens with a strong enclosure, established an arms factory in Tivoli, and set up an arsenal beneath the Vatican library.

These military preparations were all the more onerous for the pontifical treasury because they were carried on at the same time as the increasing

* The assistance would seem to be equally valuable to the traveler shaped by the traditions of Anglo-Saxon culture.—Translator.

† A twentieth-century French historical author, member of the Académie Française.—Translator.

religious construction projects. Urban VIII loved the arts, and his nephews comported themselves like princes. It was their efforts or at any rate their initiatives that were responsible for several reconstructions: the church of St. Urban, which dated from the second century, on Via Caffarella, which leads out of Via Appia just beyond the chapel of Quo Vadis; San Sebastiano in Palatino, which stood in the Borgheses' vineyard on the Palatine; and San Salvatore in Lauro, in Via dei Vecchiarelli. The church of St. Bibiana, near the modern Via Giolitti, was rebuilt in 1625 by Bernini, who enriched it with the beautiful statue of the saint that is on the main altar. It contains the old red marble column to which St. Bibiana was bound for her cruel flogging under Julian the Apostate; the urn beneath the altar that contains the remains of the saint, her sister, and their mother, martyred with her, was the largest block of Oriental alabaster that existed in Rome until the khedive of Egypt sent Gregory XVI the four columns that flank the central gate of St. Paul Beyond the Walls.

The basilica of Saints Cosmas and Damian (in Via dei Fori Imperiali) was the sole example of a heathen temple converted into a Christian church before the Byzantine epoch. In the sixth century Pope Felix IV had built this shrine out of two ancient structures: the so-called Templum Sacrae Urbis (temple of the Holy City) had become the vestibule, while the side walls of the temple of the Penates constituted the body of the basilica. Finding that the subsoil made the church too damp, Urban VIII had it raised almost twenty feet, with the result that the esthetic effect was altered and, above all, some parts of its beautiful mosaic were sacrificed. During the soil soundings that were taken in connection with this project, workmen discovered the twenty-six tables that together constitute the famous plan of Rome (*Forma Urbis*) that is now in the Capitoline Museum.

The complex dedicated to St. Luke and St. Martina, near the arch of Septimius Severus and the ancient Senate, was rebuilt from floor to roof in 1640. The crypt hollowed into the substructure of the Secretarium Senatus contains sixteen columns taken from that old edifice. The beautiful façade is the first, still tentative attempt made to give life to architectural masses by shaping them in a convex movement. The underground chapel, where St. Martina's body lies, has the rather rare distinction of having been built at the expense (he had bequeathed 100,000 crowns for the purpose) of the artist who had drawn its plans, Pietro da Cortona, whose tomb is at the foot of the stairway leading to the lower church.

The modern visitor to Rome's churches and convents encounters the generous hand of the Barberinis at every step. They built a great number of churches, and beautified many others, often in a splendid style, such as St. Agatha of the Goths and San Lorenzo in Damaso, which they enriched with many gilded stucco figures and precious marbles. They rebuilt the monasteries of St. Bartholomew and the Minerva, and they founded the convent of the Holy Incarnation, where two nuns of their family instituted the order of St. Theresa. They built colleges (the Nardini and the Ruccioli) and created charitable institutions. The specialist in this field was the pope's brother, Antonio, the old cardinal of Sant'Onofrio. He was distinguished from the other members of the family by a moving humility: after having devoted his life and his fortune to the construction of convents, he ordered that he be buried with this simple epitaph: *"Hic jacet pulvis, cinis, et nihil* (Here lie dust, ashes, and nothing)." It is this austere Capuchin to whom we owe a very singular monument: the materials for its construction were the bones of members of his order. This is the ossuary of Santa Maria della Concezione, near Piazza Barberini: the skulls and the thigh bones of four thousand Franciscans make gruesome arabesques in it. In order to compensate for the sinister element of this decoration, the cardinal had also given his church Guido Reni's painting of Lucifer's defeat by the archangel Michael. The painter endowed the fallen demon with the face of that Cardinal Pamphili who twenty years later would be Pope Innocent X. Harshly criticized for this tasteless joke, Reni justified it by saying: "I painted the angel from imagination, because I have never seen him; as for the devil, I have met him occasionally and I showed him as he looked to me."

Antonio Cardinal Barberini's brother and nephews were undoubtedly less retiring than he. Aside from the fact that they never neglected to place their coat of arms on the pediment of every building that they had merely, and occasionally summarily, restored, they built themselves magnificent residences in order to display the splendor of their mode of living. The example was set by the pope. He had begun his palace in 1625, while he was still only a cardinal, and he had entrusted its execution to Maderna, who had exhausted his last energies on it, insisting on being carried on to the scaffolding even in his last illness. He was succeeded in the work by Borromini and then by Bernini, both of whom altered the design in several respects, notably through the addition of the curious elliptical-shaped stairway that leads to the beautiful rooms of the National Gallery of Painting. Few princes of Europe could pride themselves on owning so sumptuous a home. Its library contained eighty thousand volumes and ten thousand manuscripts; its huge drawing rooms displayed the largest collection of paintings in Rome: it already included the portraits of Beatrice Cenci and La Fornarina.

Palazzo Barberini is composed of a central core flanked by wings at right angles, like the great suburban villas. This was justified by the fact that the Four Fountains quarter was still only sparsely populated at that time; a great open space spread before the palace, giving it a kind of court of honor suitable for the presentation of spectacles. Immense gardens peopled with antique statues covered the site of the ancient Circus of Flora.

Today the palace looks out on the beautiful Barberini Square adorned with two fountains by Bernini. The Fountain of the Bees, a skillful flattery of the reigning pope's family, is witty and charming; as for the Triton Fountain, it is impossible not to yield to its ingenuity, its movement, and its somewhat clowning grace. Stendhal admired it considerably and he managed to impart this taste to the rather prim Parisian women who traveled with him in 1828. "These ladies," he said, "though they are good Frenchwomen, felt that it was better than the fountain of Grenelle." Its theme is unusual: four dolphins, whose gaping mouths are on a level with the water in the basin, support a huge shell with their turned-up tails; in the middle, a Triton flexes his muscles to blow into a conch, from which the water rushes with such force that it falls back in a mist into the basin. The two fountains collaborate with the tasteful structures round them to give this quarter a style that is precisely what was the model for the city's physiognomy in the baroque period.

THE CANOPY OF ST. PETER'S / THE ARRANGEMENT OF THE PILLARS

As we have seen, few buildings were erected then in which Bernini did not have a hand. Although he was still quite young (he was born in Naples in 1598), Giovanni Lorenzo Bernini—Cavaliere Bernini—had already given much evidence of a talent that was considered the more prodigious in view of his age. He was still only an adolescent when Paul V said of him: "I flatter myself that he will become the Michelangelo of his time." Urban VIII made him his sculptor, his architect, and his personal adviser on art. "Undoubtedly you are happy to see Maffeo Barberini pope," he said to him, "but Maffeo reckons himself even more fortunate to have Bernini living during his reign." Professing such admiration for the artist, the pope naturally did not leave his talents unoccupied; that is why Bernini's audacities can be seen in all his undertakings, and especially in that for which he won his greatest renown, the canopy of St. Peter's.

The huge dais, almost ninety feet high, was erected beneath the dome after nine years of preparation and labor. It excited general admiration: it was praised for the felicity of its proportions, the luxury of its gilding, and above all its height, which was greater than that of many a palace and many an obelisk. In later years it was to be above all its great height that was to be criticized in the canopy, the conception of which was attacked on many grounds. What some called fertility of imagination was to others only foolhardy fantasy. The spiral columns are still variously appraised. But to reproach Bernini for having sought as a matter of principle to escape once more from the straight line is to forget that he had taken as his model the ancient columns that had surrounded the altar in the first basilica and that were supposed to be relics of the temple of Jerusalem. In the other "fantasies" of the enterprise, neo-classic critics professed to see nothing more than the patterns of an upholsterer. "Valances and drapes," Bertaux wrote, "are contorted as if a whirlwind blowing through the arches had shaken the fretted bronze. Angels do balancing acts at the corners of the enormous contraption, which culminates in a crown out of a bad play." For those who admire the baroque, nothing could be more disturbing than such incomprehension. They believe, with Tapié, that, in the composition of the canopy as in the decoration of the pillars of St. Peter's, Bernini "achieved for the Catholic world of his time what the builders of the medieval cathedrals had accomplished for theirs."

Having thus set side by side the opposing views that Bernini still arouses, we shall now limit ourselves to pointing out the range of his work and the circumstances of its flowering. The bronze that was used for the casting of the columns of the canopy came from the portico of the Pantheon; it was this startling salvage that produced Pasquino's famous pun. But it is doubtful whether in the seventeenth century anything was left of the bronze facings of the Pantheon after the successive depredations of the Barbarians, the Eastern emperors, and the Renaissance popes. Undoubtedly Urban VIII had to be satisfied to supply Bernini's gigantic molds with the masses of bronze that were under the portico and, since they were neither decorated nor even visible, had no merit apart from their antiquity. In such case, far from vitiating the character of the edifice, the pope would simply, in the words of his defenders, "have made a monument out of what was not one." In any case a genuine masterpiece did emerge from that daring transmutation of the metal.

Let us return to St. Peter's. This was not to be the last time that Bernini's hand would appear there, for it seems that the artist devoted his entire career to composing the magnificent stage for liturgical pomps that Bramante's and Michelangelo's austere creation was, as if by magic, to become. The opulence of the canopy made a strange contrast to the austerity of the rest of the building; two doctrines, two styles were thus set in unpleasant conflict. In order to accomplish a transition between them, Bernini undertook to remedy the bareness of Bramante's enormous pillars, accentuated even more by Michelangelo. He turned them into reliquaries: at the bottom, a large statue was placed in a great niche, while a "display case" was erected at a higher level, from the balcony of which the holy images and the relics were shown to the faithful. Thus enlivened, the pillars so thoroughly lost their aspect of massiveness that it is quite amazing to learn that the church of St. Charles at the Four Fountains has exactly the same area as each of them. (A whim of Borromini gave this charming shrine the dimensions and the shape of Bramante's pillars.) One must resort to comparisons of this kind in order to arrive at an exact understanding of the dimensions of St. Peter's. Without lingering over the basilica's measurements, let us note this one detail that offers some idea of them: the interior of the golden ball from which the cross soars to surmount the dome can easily accommodate fifteen persons!

While Bernini's work was being carried out in St. Peter's, a crack appeared in the skylight of the dome, and everyone hastened to ascribe it to the hollows that the architect had cut into the pillars. There was a little war of speaking statues, pamphlets, and satirical songs. Bernini's passing fall into disfavor was to arise out of this incident and also from the unfortunate bell tower that, at the pope's request, he built above the façade of the basilica. Topped with the papal arms and the statues of four doctors of the Latin church, this tower with its two stories of loggie, though certainly elegant, committed the fault of adding to the architectural whole a factitious element that enhanced neither the façade nor the dome. It was said, too, that it endangered the solidity of the building, a pretext that was utilized for its demolition when Urban VIII died. It was fated that Bernini should have problems with bell towers, for again in 1882 it was necessary to raze those that he had built in 1634 on the façade of the Pantheon and that were sufficiently described for the history of art by their nickname: "Bernini's donkey ears."

VARIOUS WORKS BY BORROMINI

It would be quite unjust to overlook the part that was played in the flowering of the arts at that time by a man who for a brief interval was to supplant Bernini in the pope's favor, after having long been his collaborator and then his unsuccessful competitor. This was Borromini, who perhaps advanced the conquests of the baroque and the daring of its techniques even farther than Bernini. It has been said that he was a pure acrobat who performed his feats of strength in the open. Without falling back on superfluities of marble and gold, his work carried to its full height, "through the qualities of the fantastic and the marvelous inherent in the curved line and rippling movement," that inner festival, that climate of Paradise that was the essential character of the new style.

Borromini's gifts, his bravura and his unprecedented grace blazed out in the picturesque chapel of St. Ives that he built at the back of the courtyard of the Sapienza, the old papal university. The clever play of curves is an enchantment, like the exuberant fantasy of the spiral skylight. The Philippine chapel, next to the Chiesa Nuova, which was intended for sacred concerts, is a veritable hymn to joy, from its façade with its contrasting lines to the illusion in perpective of its central bay.

Borromini's most successful work was the church of St. Charles of the Four Fountains, which we have already mentioned because of the originality of its design. A small convent church, it is perhaps the most nearly perfect product of the baroque, and in any event a masterpiece of contemplative grace: "Sixteen Corinthian columns develop the elliptical nave in their sinuous course from the entrance to the rounded chancel and fill it with a movement and a rhythm devoid of violence like that of a beating heart" (Tapié). Borromini was perhaps somewhat less felicitous with Sant'Andrea delle Fratte, where he seems to have made special efforts to accumulate curiosities and caprices; the strange dome of this church, half cupola and half bell tower, is nonetheless one of the most fascinating curiosities of the whole baroque.

When Cardinal Pamphili acceded to the throne of St. Peter under the name of Innocent X, one of his first acts was to oust Bernini and to replace him with Borromini. Ambitious and authoritarian, the new pope was eager to associate his memory with the embellishment of his capital, but by adopting new avenues. Hence he turned away from St. Peter's in order to restore the former luster of the Lateran. The approach of the jubilee of 1650 gave him the opportunity to decorate it in the style of the time. The credit for this transformation went to Borromini. Under Clement VIII the basilica had become an elaborate hall for celebrations. Borromini was careful not to add bits of eloquence to the superfluities that had made this "a basilica of gold" and that were already out of harmony with the sturdiness of the structure. The charming decorations that he placed in the lateral naves are modest and move the observer to contemplation. As for the high fluted pilasters with which he faced the pillars, and the huge statues of the apostles in colored marbles that he placed in the niches, they attest to his praiseworthy concern for restoring the harmony of the building. This undertaking, however, resulted in a defeat that demonstrates the limitations of the baroque: superimposed, in the basilica of St. Peter's, on the art of the Renaissance, it seems to carry that art further; added to a much older architectural style like that of the Lateran, it contributes only a painful discord.

THE CHURCH OF SANT'AGNESE IN AGONE AND THE PIAZZA NAVONE

Borromini was to be more successful when, no longer obliged to adapt himself to an existing framework, he could give free rein to his imagination. He was to find the opportunity to do so in the reconstruction of the church of Sant'Agnese in Agone on Piazza Navone, next to the Pamphilis' palace, which Rainaldi was then building and for which the church was in effect to serve as the chapel. The interior decoration of this church is extremely rich, and it is for that very reason far remote from Borromini's esthetic. What is properly his here is the very individual design of the church and especially the façade, one of the most beautiful in Rome with its very elegant concave outline. It curves inward between two graceful bell towers that are like a reminder of those that would have risen above St. Peter's if Maderna's design had been followed in the matter. The whole is at once majestic and restrained, simple and ingenious.

It is impossible to give credence to the fable that pretends that Bernini demonstrated his disapproval of Borromini's work by designing the fountain that stands before the church. Each of the rivers of marble that surround the artificial rock, supposedly, expressed his doubts or his disgust. One is afraid that the bell towers of the church may fall into the square, another calls the obelisk to witness for the ugliness of the building, the third turns away its head in order not to see; the fourth evidences revulsion and even disgust. These absurdities are very easily disposed of by the fact that the fountain was built before the church was rebuilt. In actual fact, the rivers' gesticulations, their dramatic or affected postures express nothing, apart from their allegorical meanings, except the sculptor's imagination, in which at times affectation and intemperance were mingled with passion. In addition, Bernini was so far from finding serious fault with Borromini's creation that he drew great inspiration from it when he built Sant'Andrea on the Quirinal. A secret rivalry may have existed between the two artists, but nothing gives any ground for the belief that it took the rude forms that have been ascribed to it.

The fact remains, however, that these two men were of completely opposite temperaments and characters. Bernini had gained great renown even before he had emerged from adolescence. He found his natural element in work and success, creating the industry of a beehive round him. Bubbling with life, he loved women and parties: he was a voluptuary, although the climate of the loftiest spirituality was "accessible and often familiar" to him. Borromini was quite different; he had started life in Milan as a simple cutter of marble, and he was very reserved, given to the environment of cloisters and monks, a lover of contemplation. These tendencies had not prevented him from breaking, even more emphatically than Bernini, with rules and logic, occasionally even with common sense. This proclivity might have driven him into the absurd and the extravagant if he had not preserved in his fantasies a profound sincerity and a very pure poetry.

Bernini had always known how to make fountains share in the decoration of a square; his are never isolated creations. Let us not leave the Fountain of the Rivers without pointing out that its theatrical aspect cannot overshadow either its bold conception or its perfect suitability to the purpose for which it was intended. The aim was in fact the adornment of the center of Piazza Navone, and Bernini's group, surmounted by his obelisk, fufilled this purpose like a miracle. It is in no way dwarfed by the towers of Sant'Agnese, and it does not clash with them. It harmonizes perfectly with the buildings that surround Domitian's ancient circus. It is a complete success, which very felicitously complements the pleasant Moro fountain (also by Bernini), in the center of which an Ethiopian wrestles with a dolphin in a setting of masks and Tritons. The Neptune fountain, which completes this setting, dates only from 1878.

These three fountains recall the original purpose of the ancient Circo Agonale, which was intended for nautical games. Its tradition was revived, furthermore, in the time of Pope Clement X. The square would be flooded every Saturday and Sunday in August. This improvised port became the scene of tourneys and historical re-enactments, after which the great gentlemen's carriages mingled with the boats. It had become a fashion to cross this lake by carriage, the horses floundering in water up to their chests, each man trying to splash the others: there were always amusing episodes and no one ever grew angry. An orchestra on a platform gave the scene a musical background. Crowded round the sides of the square, the poor got what they could from the amusements. The last occasion on which Piazza Navone was flooded for a nautical circus was August 15, 1810, the birthday of Emperor Napoleon I.

The square and the quarter that encloses it are the most flavorful vestige of seventeenth-century Rome. All round the square there is a tangle of streets that have preserved their old names (del Leone, del Pavone, della Gatta, della Maschera Dorata, della Stella, dell'Amore Divino, del Giglio, delle Cinque Lune—Lion, Peacock, Cat, Golden Mask, Star, Divine Love, Lily, Five Moons). Decaying palaces in each of them provide a stately setting for the life of the people.

Let us linger a moment over this charming Piazza Navone to point out that the Fountain of the Rivers was the occasion of Bernini's return to favor with the Pamphili pope. This was the time of another episode in the alleged war between the two great architects of the age. Borromini, it was said, was deeply hurt by the fact that his rival, through the backing of Prince Ludovisi and as the result of a competition from which at first he had been barred, had obtained the commission to design a fountain for the square. He thought that Bernini would commit some error that would make a fool of him, and he made no secret of these charitable hopes. "Water will never reach that fountain," he said. This threat, coming from so knowledgeable a man, threw a certain fear into the Cavaliere, who wanted to know more about it and arranged, through one of his pupils—at the cost of no one could guess what favors—the subornation of a woman (a servant or more intimate associate of his rival). Pressing the master with questions, she received for answer this cryptic sally: "Tell me: could you breathe if you had no mouth?" From this Bernini perceived that he had indeed forgotten to provide for "breathers" in the pipelines that would bring the water to his fountain. This omission rectified, the water leaped in triumph on the day of the fountain's inauguration, to the applause of the crowd, and Borromini suffered a cruel disappointment, to which many have attributed his fateful decision—which he did not make until much later—to run his sword through his body. Bernini's success convinced the pope that he had been wrong to entertain suspicions about the greatest artist of his time on the strength of gossip and criticisms based on ulterior motivations. "With this wonderful spectacle," Innocent X said to him, "you have added ten more years to my life." And very soon afterward all his offices and privileges were restored.

To finish—regretfully—with Piazza Navone, let us add at least that in 1650 the pope had Rainaldi build his family palace there, next to the reconstructed Sant'Agnese. In this house he established his collection of antique statues and paintings by Guercino (Giovanni Francesco Barbieri) and the Cavaliere d'Arpino (Giuseppe Cesari); Pietro da Cortona had decorated the vast gallery with scenes taken from the *Aeneid*. It was this Palazzo Pamphili to which later the pope's sister-in-law would retire—that Olympia Maidalchini who had acquired so evil a mastery over him. Her name was the occasion for a much-favored pun: *olim pia* (formerly pious). She lived in the Vatican like a sovereign, maintaining her own personal court; ambassadors went to pay their respects to her. Her presumptuousness did great harm to the apostolic dignity. The bust of her by Alessandro Algardi is most revealing of this scheming woman. It is in Villa Doria Pamphili, which Prince Camillo, the pope's nephew, built in the same period behind the Janiculum.

BERNINI AT ST. PETER'S / THE DECORATION

Restored to grace, Cavaliere Bernini was to resume his interrupted work on St. Peter's and never again to desert it until his death. For forty years, and under the reigns of six popes, his industry and that of his pupils were to be unceasingly employed from the square to the end of the apse. Bernini was directly responsible for the presentation and the decoration of the basilica as we see it today. It was he who gave the huge nave "its jewelry of brilliant colors and sharp relief, its facings of purple and yellow marbles brightened with inlays, its holy-water fonts surrounded with nests of chubby Cupids, its gigantic saints that overflow their niches, its enormous angels that march in perilous attitudes above its arches" (Bertaux).

It all began with the highly ingenious arrangement of the lateral naves that accentuate the impression of the building's depth and heighten its sumptuousness. It was under Alexander VII, who had succeeded Innocent X, that Bernini resolved the difficult problem of the decoration of the back of the church. The pope wished it to recall Peter's memory and to offer to the veneration of the faithful, "as the symbol of doctrinal authority," the throne of ivory-encrusted wood on which the apostle had sat and that had always been part of the treasure of the church. But the canopy was already there, and its presence, like the dimensions themselves of the apse, called for a monument of colossal proportions. Hence Bernini conceived the remarkable composition that blended lightness and gigantism and harmoniously combined disparate elements and individual scenes in a dramatic unity. On the lower level, an event out of earthly life: the fathers of the church support the throne of St. Peter encased in a huge reliquary. On the upper level, a vision of heaven: a host of angels and seraphim glides in a mysterious light and, in the rays of heavenly glory, the Holy Ghost covers the apostle's throne with its wings while all the enemies of the church assail it in vain. The miracle of this daring composition is that everything in it seems to be in motion: the statues walk, the angels' tunics "palpitate with amazing life." What the spectator sees, it has been observed, is a scene, rather than a monument to be contemplated. It can certainly be argued that this is a theatrical technique, and thus one can from this point of view renew the old battle betwen the classic and the baroque. But this does not prevent the work from justifying all the comparisons that have been made between Bernini and Michelangelo. What is more, here the baroque finds its complete justification; it renders, Tapié wrote, "to the teaching of the church the most orthodox homage that has ever been paid by a Christian artist."

While this prodigious monument was in the process of creation, the decoration of the vaults, the pillars, and the dome was being finished in a blaze of fireworks. The resources that the theme offered to artists had been augmented by the revival of mosaic. The school of mosaic artists that had come into being in the Vatican and that still exists had undertaken new studies. If it had restricted itself to taking its inspiration from the great mosaics of the past, it would have given St. Peter's only a decoration in little harmony with the most sumptuous of the baroque churches. It had the good sense to turn toward the imitation of painting, executing completely faithful copies in freshened colors and protected from any deterioration. They can still be seen on the walls, reproduced on the scale of the setting: the *Transfiguration* of Raphael was enlarged four times. Well varnished, glowing, they contribute to the splendor and the radiance that have so often been criticized in St. Peter's.

For the effect of the spectacular is so consistently striven for in the basilica, and richness is displayed there in such fashion, that the result can be shocking to spirits devoted principally to the idea of poverty and penitence. But it was by other ways that the popes of that time sought the glory of God and the triumph of His church. One can regard the decoration of St. Peter's as overdone; one can argue that it has too much gilt, too many bronzes, too much porphyry. The fact remains that all these rhetorical statues, all these altars overflowing with festoons and astragals, all this operatic apparatus are framed in a singularly majestic setting. If the basilica were only a theater, one would still have to admit that it was the most impressive in the world. In reality there is no hint of theater there—not the precious marbles, not the striking tones of the mosaics, not the gold that gleams everywhere. Luxury and splendor are made magnificent by their very excess. As it stands, this magnificent forum of Catholicism seems a huge tabernacle that inspires a sudden reverence. And, when one is inside it, one feels that one is in not only a place of faith but a place of intelligence; its space, it has been said, seems to have been distributed as in a well-made world.

Furthermore, whoever finds that the luxuriousness of St. Peter's intrudes on his spiritual recollection can, if he wishes, turn his back on the debauch of ornamentation and recapture his zeal in front of Michelangelo's *Pietà*, hidden in a side chapel before the humble pulpit of Christ's first vicar, or else at that moving statue of St. Peter for which it was long believed that an anonymous sculptor of the fifth century had melted down an image of Jupiter Capitolinus; but very recent chemical analyses have shown that it is made of the same bronze as the known works of Arnolfo di Cambio.

THE COLONNADE OF ST. PETER'S

On August 25, 1661, the first stone was laid for the colonnade of St. Peter's, which was to cost 850,000 Roman crowns and to be regarded as the most magnificent creation that had emerged in Rome since the emperors. Bernini had looked at the square that lies in front of the basilica as a kind of court of honor. It is embraced in a vast elliptical decoration composed of a gallery of four rows of columns separated by three aisles. In the architect's mind the church ought to be isolated from the city in order to emphasize its exceptional character as the final stage of a pilgrimage. It should remain hidden to the visitor until the very moment when he penetrates among the columns, themselves so arranged as to enhance the impressions of discovery. Bernini's plan was not wholly followed: the little arch of triumph that he had proposed was not built at the point where the colonnade is interrupted. The creation of Via della Conciliazione, in spite of the new improvements in it, attenuates the effect of surprise and wonder that Bernini had intended to arouse in the pilgrims. At least, however, it has the advantage of making the colonnade seem to open before us in a stirring gesture of welcome. In any event the theatrical point of view retains its rights; here its influence is apparent everywhere, in the poses of the statues that adorn the balustrades as in the sloping plane of the esplanade, in the intelligent design of the galleries as in the curious arrangement of the columns that preserves an unvarying relation in their thickness and their intervals. The little white marble circles fixed in the pavement on either side of the obelisk indicate the exact center of the circumference described by each hemicycle. The stripes that run from these points to the periphery are laid with such rigorous precision that, when one stands on one of the circles, one sees only one row of columns instead of four.

The grandiose harmony of this whole emphasizes Bernini's architectural mastery. His exact feeling for perspective enabled him even to correct his predecessors' errors. It is the colonnade that makes the church appear less wide and more lofty, and that conceals the lack of invention and the coldness of the shapes in Maderna's façade.

Framed in the colonnade, St. Peter's Square is itself a masterpiece of balance. "Our Louvre," Taine said, "and the Place de la Concorde, in comparison, are only stage settings for an opera. The Egyptian obelisk and the two fountains adorn the site without taking away anything of its majesty." These fountains, whose brilliant aquatic pyramids rise forty-five feet to fall back in spray into huge basins made from a single block of Oriental granite, are so magnificent that, when Christina of Sweden arrived in Rome after her dramatic conversion, she thought that they were playing in order to pay a personal tribute to her. She expressed her thanks to the pope, who, it is reported, undeceived her "with a fine frankness."

At the same time when he was leaving his mark so forcefully on the basilica and its approaches, Bernini was endowing the Vatican palace with two creations in his own manner. He completed the ceremonial apartments with a state hall, the Ducal Hall, which opens into the Royal Hall, and, in order to provide access to it, he built the Royal Stair (Scala Regia), which is always used by ambassadors and sovereigns. Here he achieved the masterpiece of an architecture that accomplished grandeur by artifice. Between the old fifteenth-century walls he had available only a narrow passage. He was able to give his staircase a monumental aspect by an optical illusion comparable to Borromini's in Palazzo Spada: an ingenious arrangement of rows of columns and the insertion of a brightly lighted landing that leaves the upper part of the stairs in a penumbra give the Scala Regia the fullness and the solemnity that the paucity of available space seemed to have made impossible.

SANTA TERESA AND THE STATUES ON THE PONTE SANT'ANGELO

In the Vatican Bernini worked not only as a decorator and an architect but also as a sculptor. Everywhere he employed the principles of the baroque, even in funeral settings. Here again Bernini created a school; henceforth funeral sculpture was to devote itself to the exaltation of the virtues of the deceased in scenes of dramatic intensity. The mausoleum became a complex architectonic composition, adorned with sorrowing figures, charged with allegories and symbols, filled with movement and feeling.

A genius of passion, Bernini invested religious sculpture with the ardors of his own temperament. He was not made to express the humility, the renunciation, the simplicity of Christian death; but the wound of divine love found a disturbing interpreter in him. Some of his feminine saints are shaken by such breathless emotion that a few critics have even discovered a kind of profanation in them. In the church of San Francesco a Ripa, in Trastevere, where Blessed Luisa Albertoni is shown dying in her robe of the Order of St. Clare, God's love seems to have entered the death chamber like a tempest. As for Santa Teresa, so completely in her place in the church of Santa Maria della Vittoria, "more gilded than the opera lobby," she is recognized today as one of the peaks of Christian sculpture. But how many controversies she has incited over three centuries! De Brosses—a poor judge, in actuality—felt nothing at the sight of her but bedroom memories, and many others too have reacted only with profane emotions. ("No novel," Taine wrote, "was ever so charming and so tender.") That is because this work, like all the other creations of the baroque, can be understood only if one transposes it to the spirituality of the time that gave birth to it. In this ecstasy of love and suffering at the threshold of death, the zeal of those days saw no hint of sensuality.

The angels carved by Bernini are not so bold as the youth who transfixes Santa Teresa with the arrow of divine love. It is a long way from him to the rather affected grace of the angels carrying the instruments of the Passion who adorn Ponte Sant'Angelo. It is true that these angels never knew the touch of the master's chisel; they merely came from the studio that he directed with a hand that had lost much of its firmness to old age. Nevertheless, these statues aroused the unbounded admiration of Pope Clement IX, who found them too beautiful to be left exposed to the weather: he had two of them placed in the church of Sant'Andrea delle Fratte, that church whose belfry and dome were a caprice of Borromini's.

Having become narrative, the sculpture of this period professed to interpret the soul by detailing "the agitations by which it is shaken." At Bernini's instigation, or in imitation of him, statuary burst into gesticulation that was intended to be poetic but that did not always attain its goal. "There are no more figures in repose. They are always about to rise, to run, to bless, to battle, to dance, to take wing. The wind is lost in their clothes." Only one artist of this time was able to remain moving and simple: he was Stefano Maderna, the brother of the architect of St. Peter's, who created for the church of Santa Cecilia in Trastevere the statue of the melodious martyr lying on her side, her knees bent, "her soft neck riven by the sword, her face pressed against the earth." This was no artistic fantasy. The martyred young patrician's tomb had been opened for the canonical identification—she had been killed under the Antonines—and her body had been found almost intact in the position in which Maderna portrayed it.

THE CONTEMPORARIES OF BERNINI AND BORROMINI

Leaders of the army of the baroque, Borromini and Bernini unquestionably dominated their epoch. But around them, and often associated with their work, an army of artists produced their own works. Such was notably the case of Pietro da Cortona, who has left us, in addition to his celebrated frescoes of Palazzo Barberini and the Chiesa Nuova, splendid evidences of his architectural talent: "the beautiful concave façade of St. Luke and St. Martina in the Forum, the noble arrangement of Santa Maria della Pace with its little columned portico in front of a convex fa-çade, the two galleries of columns that form the *atrium* of Santa Maria in Via Lata on the Corso" (Tapié). As for Carlo Rainaldi, his fame was so great that Louis XIV asked him, as he had also asked Bernini, to design the Louvre. He was responsible for the twin churches of Piazza del Popolo, Santa Maria dei Miracoli and Santa Maria in Monte Santo (one noted for its piety, the other for its symmetry). When Santa Maria in Campitelli was rebuilt in fulfillment of a vow after the plague epidemic of 1656, he made it a church of most advanced baroque style. It became the shrine of a madonna that had been much revered earlier in the ancient church of Santa Maria in Portico, which owed its name to the proximity of Octavia's portico and its prosperity to its position on the route of the pontifical processions to the Lateran. Its clerics swung their censers as the pope passed, and for this service they received a compensation that aroused considerable envy. In 1665 Carlo Rainaldi also completed the façade of Sant'Andrea della Valle, which Maderna had left unfinished. Very freely interpreting his predecessor's designs, Rainaldi made it one of the most beautiful façades of baroque Rome, correcting the slight asymmetry of Maderna's design by giving the pediment an angel that spreads one of his great wings as if to support a threatened wall. Some have chosen to interpret this as an attempt to ridicule Maderna's work, which did in fact produce a certain feeling of unbalance.

Also in competition with Bernini, Algardi has left us admirable marble altars and a collection of architectural achievements whose finest flower has recently been plucked: the façade of St. Ignatius, now credited to its rightful designer, Father Orazio Grassi. But Algardi still has the glory of having created Villa Doria Pamphili and its casino.

Among other seventeenth-century architects of great renown we should also mention Martino Longhi the Younger, who built the church of Saints Vincent and Anastasius in 1650 for Mazarin at the corner of Piazza di Trevi. It was the great cardinal's homage to the city where he had got his start. It is of interest essentially for its façade, with its accumulation of intervals and columns in fluted clusters. The upper cartouche carries the cardinal's arms; the bust above the portal is supposed to be that of his niece, Maria Mancini, made famous by the sad story of her romance with Louis XIV. This church was the repository for the entrails of the dead popes of the Quirinal, which were removed before their embalming.

Another fashionable architect was a Fontana. There had always been an artist of this illustrious name in Rome ever since Julius III had summoned Prospero Fontana from Bologna to become the painter of his palace; Prospero's daughter, Lavinia, was the painter of Gregory XIII. Giovanni Fontana, a native of Como, had worked at St. Peter's and, with Maderna, built the Pauline fountain. Domenico, "the brother of the preceding," as the reference books put it, had erected the obelisk in St. Peter's Square and built the papal palace on the Quirinal. The Fontana who was living in Rome during the great period of the baroque was called Carlo. He was responsible for the Grimani and Bolognetti palaces, the church of San Michele a Ripagrande, and the mausoleum of Queen Christina in St. Peter's.

His most personal work was the church of La Maddalena, completed only after his death. Fontana had the skill to give this church of modest size majestic proportions by means of a fine optical effect derived from techniques as imaginative as they were scientific.

THE INVASION OF ROME BY THE BAROQUE

With the seventeenth century Rome was invaded by the regal luxury of the popes. The great pontifical families built fortunes in short order. In order to make this speedy enrichment palatable to the people, crumbs of it were allowed to filter down in various forms, most often in that of the sumptuous decoration of churches, which were at once houses of God and houses of the people. Side by side with the popes, the cardinals, and the Roman princes, the monastic orders and the merchants' guilds built churches and chapels in the prevailing taste.

In addition to those that we have already mentioned, there were, above all, the reconstructions of the ancient edifices. The most important was that of the church of the Holy Apostles, which went on from 1701 to 1724 and left nothing of the Renaissance monument standing except the portico with the eagle from Trajan's Forum and the two red granite lions that flanked the door of the medieval church. The interior sought to imitate St. Peter's, but already it hinted at the weakness of the baroque in its decadence. Let us also mention Santa Maria in Campo di Marte, which replaced a very old Greek monastery and which is dedicated to the Syrian rite; San Lorenzo in Lucina, rebuilt on a twelfth-century basilica, which contains the monument to Poussin erected by Chateaubriand; St. Joseph of the Carpenters, built above the Mamertine Prison; St. Anthony of the Portuguese; St. Charles in the Corso; the church of the Holy Stigmata; Trinità degli Spagnoli; San Marcello; San Silvestro in Capite; St. James of the Incurables; Santa Maria in Trivio; Jesus and Mary; and Holy Name of Mary, which was built by a Frenchman, Derizet. There were also St. Catherine of Siena at Magnanapoli, Saints Domenick and Sixtus (a dependency of the Angelicum, the Dominican university), Santa Maria della Vittoria, whose design, on a reduced scale, reproduced the Gesù and Sant'Andrea della Valle; and St. Isidore, which spreads graceful garlands of stone across its gilded façade. In these churches, which are listed here without any special order and very incompletely, baroque art occasionally reached a kind of paroxysm. All of them reveal a fanatical striving for brilliance and theatrical effect. Religion must be pleasant, lovely ladies must not be bored at mass: hence they were offered, for their devotions, a setting that was an extension of what they had in their palaces. There were lady's-bower churches and there were little-theater churches. And this atmosphere of a religion of the rich was to conquer the poor quite as much. Popular imagination was to be aroused at the spectacle of gilded stucco, of spiral columns, of festoons, of the vast population of gilded figures beneath luminous ceilings that hinted at paradise.

Of the four hundred churches of the Rome of that period, few escaped the influences of the baroque. That is why a visit to Rome leaves the impression that that style had enjoyed a universal reign there. Whether built a week before or ten centuries before, the majority of the churches were clothed in the seventeenth and eighteenth century with marble in the manner of the time, peopled with languorous angels and chubby cherubs. Everywhere the new decoration was plastered on the ancient carcasses.

This practice robbed many churches of their original characters, to such a point, in fact, as to make us forget the spirit that had dictated their construction. Who, seeing the Gesù so gleaming in its precious jewels as to be the most ostentatious of all examples of the baroque, could even imagine that in the beginning it was most austere and reflected all that was harshest in the spirit of the communities of the Counter-Reformation? And what in Santa Maria in Via Lata, so resplendent in its jasper, its bronzes, its gildings, speaks to us of the humble diaconate improvised on the room in the Saepta Julia in which St. Paul had waited for the hour of his martyrdom? As for St. Ignatius, it was during the sixteen years of its construction that its somewhat cold majesty was rectified by the audacities of the baroque architects. All its walls gleam with gilded bronzes and precious marbles. The vault that portrays the apotheosis of its patron saint is the most amazing achievement of perspective to be seen anywhere. Father Pozzo makes the visitor feel "that a world is in flight above his head," Gaxotte wrote.

Santa Cecilia with its overgraceful musical decoration, the Chiesa Nuova, Santa Maria in Trivio, Santa Maria della Scala, St. Nicholas of Lorraine, and hundreds of other churches provide instances of similar transformations.

The most significant, perhaps, is that of Santa Maria dell'Orto. Let us summarize its history, though there is nothing exceptional in it. Santa Maria del Giardino (in Via Anicia, in Trastevere) had been built inside the area of the ancient gardens of Caesar, on the site of a very old temple of Fortune (Fors Fortuna) in whose ruins a statue of the Virgin had been discovered in the fifteenth century. Michelangelo may have drawn the plans for the church, which were modified by Giulio Romano, and construction was begun chiefly with contributions from the neighboring merchants. It was a structure of pure Renaissance style, with a broad and sober façade; the interior, with three naves separated by slender rectangular pillars, was very restrained and perfect in its proportions. It is now very different. The façade was remodeled by Martino Longhi the Younger, who decorated it with a series of little obelisks; the interior was given an exuberant ornamentation. The vaults are covered with an abundance of gilded stucco that evokes "the joyous prodigality of the Roman summer." The guilds of the gardeners, the pork butchers, and the other food purveyors whose church this was had their merchandise portrayed in it. Each has its tombs, which are adorned not with lordly arms but with the symbols of trades: a rooster for the poultry dealers, artichokes for the vegetable sellers. The arches and the pillars are covered with a wealth of vegetables and fruits in gilded stucco, creating a delightful effect. This display of naturalism, at once casual and luxurious, is altogether enjoyable. It is also highly expressive of baroque sensibility. In all the churches—as numerous as they are—in which it manifests itself, there are the same audacities of form, the same propensity for the theatrical, the same taste for the picturesque and the colorful.

SANT'ANDREA OF THE QUIRINAL AND ST. MARY OF THE ANGELS

It was not that the artists of this time did not know how to rein their impulsiveness when they had to deal with matters that would have been ill suited to the fantasy that the baroque carried with it. Rome and its surroundings possess remarkable examples of that honorable acceptance of the necessities imposed by the purpose of a creation or by the environment that surrounded it. Let us remember that it was Cavaliere Bernini himself who gave the outer fortifications of Castello Sant'Angelo the appearance that we see today. He intruded no inappropriate fantasy or emphasis, while at the same time he gave this military architecture beauty and a style. Near the popes' summer residence in Castel Gandolfo he built an austere, silent little church, St. Thomas of Villanova, in complete harmony with the severe palace of which it is, so to speak, the dependent. Not far away, in Ariccia, he built St. Mary of the Assumption, which is quite simple with its low colonnade, devoid of gold or lavish decoration. It was not at all untouched by theatrical techniques, for the church is very cleverly presented in a gallery as if in a jewel case. The master never lost his concern with the alliance of decoration and architecture; but he had the art of making the one or the other predominate as the occasion required.

He offered new proof of this in Sant'Andrea on the Quirinal, erected in 1658 for the Jesuits' novitiate. Everything here is simple and sophisticated at the same time: the composition is perfectly suited to its functional requirements. Its mission would be not the accommodation of large crowds of worshipers but the service of young clerics entering it singly to meditate or to officiate. The arrangement of the sanctuary assures the privacy of their comings and goings: numerous side chapels make it possible to hold several services at the same time. As for the decoration, it is perhaps Bernini's greatest success: he himself, for that matter, was aware of this, and, though generally he was a harsh judge of his own work, he took great satisfaction in this structure. Its effects, however, are achieved more through subtleties than through contrasts, and the decoration remains serene in spite of its splendor. The charming *farandole* of angels who come together "in a smiling assemblage" is perhaps the most graceful production in baroque art. It has been said that, "if a source were to be sought for the Louis XV style of France, one need look no farther than the gilded apse of the ogival vault of Sant'Andrea."

But it must be admitted that not all the alterations of churches were successful, and especially that the masters of the baroque often displayed too much disregard of their most illustrious predecessors. St. Mary of the Angels affords the most grievous example of this. The shameful treatment that was given to it in 1749 by a presumptuous young architect named Luigi Vanvitelli deserves to be ranked with the worst acts of vandalism. Michelangelo had created this church, at the end of his life, out of the Tepidarium of Diocletian's baths. He had found eight enormous granite columns still erect there, supporting great semicircular arches; tremendously thick walls bore an immense dome. Utilizing this magnificent setting without changing anything in it, he had given Rome one of its most beautiful shrines. Vanvitelli changed all that: he walled up Michelangelo's chapels, he changed the direction of the naves, he closed the magnificent entrance and replaced it with the low door of a village church ("*come si andasse giù in una grotta*," the Romans said: "as if one were going down into a cave"). The result of this tinkering was the destruction of the church's harmony; in an effort to restore it, Vanvitelli added eight columns of painted masonry—which support nothing—to those that Diocletian's architects had erected to carry the arches.

THE BAROQUE IN ST. JOHN LATERAN AND SANTA MARIA MAGGIORE

The two ancient basilicas of St. John Lateran and Santa Maria Maggiore did not escape the baroque. We have mentioned Borromini's unsuccessful attempts to graft the new style on the interior of the Lateran. In 1735 Pope Clement XII (Corsini) had a million crowns to spend; it was suggested to him that he improve the Tiber quays, but he preferred to enrich his cathedral. Therefore he added the Corsini chapel, one of the richest in Rome, in which the baroque burgeoned in its most sophisticated and most graceful effects. Alessandro Galilei, commissioned to remodel the main façade, incorporated into the pediment a fragment of a medieval mosaic showing the Holy Savior, and he crowned the edifice with statues of Jesus and the apostles, whose stone robes are filled with a tempest; they seem "to be making speeches to the clouds."

Bernini had conceived extraordinary changes for Santa Maria Maggiore, but his ambitious plans were dropped for lack of funds. It was Benedict XIV who restored the basilica and gave it the appearance that it still preserves. Ferdinando Fuga was responsible for its main façade, burdened with balusters, pediments, and statues, which Taine said resembled "the front of a town hall." But the baroque restorations did not rob the interior of the church of its "antique idea": two rows of Ionic columns support the ample horizontal vault: "it is as if one were in a Greek temple."

On the whole, Santa Maria Maggiore is the Roman monument in which the marks of the centuries are best mingled and harmonized: an Egyptian obelisk guards the apse, and before the altar stands the only marble column that survives from Constantine's basilica. A marvel of the Renaissance, the church has a romanesque belfry; its interior colonnade is a beautiful specimen of the antique; the mosaics in the apse are Byzantine; the porphyry and the jasper and the gold of the chapels recall the great popes. The memories of ancient days and the labor of modern times are harmonized in what has been called a symphony of centuries.

PALACES OF THE BAROQUE PERIOD

Many palaces were built in Rome during the baroque period. The popes, whose reigns were short, showed the greatest haste to establish their families in ostentatious palaces peopled with armies of servitors and dependents. This luxuriousness of the papal nephews rallied round the pontifical institution those who were dazzled by it and those who hoped to live on it. Hence edifices were required that created an impression of opulence. Baroque art was a miraculous fulfillment of this wish; it was to decorate the princely palaces in the same spirit as the churches, while at the same time showing much more restraint. Perhaps the laity was less in love with novelties than the cardinals. In any case, the architects were afraid to reject systematically, at least as far as external appearance was concerned, the great models of the Renaissance.

The Monte Citorio palace is a characteristic example of the resistance put up by the Maecenases and the public to architectural innovations. It was the Ludovisi family for whom Bernini began in 1650 to erect the palace in which the Chamber of Deputies has met since 1871. As it appeared after its completion by Fontana in 1690 and the substantial enlargements that were later made, it is very far from the plans drawn by

Bernini. Making use of the artificial plateau formed in the area by the accumulated rubbish of medieval buildings, Bernini wanted to seat the structure on a gigantic pile of rock. This idea was very close to his heart. When he went to France in 1665 (to be at once honored and misunderstood), he was to propose that Louis XIV build the colonnade of the Louvre on a foundation of the same type. The Monte Citorio project, however, was much bolder, or, to put it more accurately, much more extravagant. Some idea of the extent of its fantasy may be derived from the fact that Bernini specified the use of the pillars of Trajan and Antoninus, the transfer of which would not have been easy. Bernini was to renounce these great plans, only with the utmost regret, however, and barely a trace of them remains in the substructure of Monte Citorio.

In 1734 an architect named Valvassori was able, without exciting the antagonisms that had paralyzed Bernini, to adorn the Corso with the façade of Palazzo Doria, which is typically baroque and even, according to some, something more, since it is described, though inaccurately, as "the finest specimen of the rococo style to be found in Rome." It should be regarded only as the extreme interpretation of Borromini's models, as this was preached by the successors of Father Pozzo, whose influence we shall presently have occasion to discuss. The present Palazzo Doria, one of the magnificences of Rome, is a combination of three palaces built in different periods and put together by the Pamphili family. It has an austere façade on Via del Plebiscito and, on the square of the Roman College, a splendid court attributed to Bramante. Its cellars enclose (like those of the neighboring church, Santa Maria in Via Lata) substantial remnants of the Saepta Julia, and its picture gallery (open to the public) prides itself on the possession of the masterpiece of portraiture of all time, Velásquez' painting of Innocent X Pamphili.

While Palazzo Madama, the present seat of the Senate after having been the Medicis' residence in the sixteenth century, acquired in the eighteenth century its beautiful façade, very free in the detail of its ornamentation, with a pretty frieze and the picturesque crown of its chimneys, Palazzo Pamphili in Piazza Navone has a most sober exterior, as does the Consulta, built on the Quirinal in 1734, whose upper parts alone are enlivened by rather brisk movement. All the fantasy of Palazzo Altieri, near the Gesù, resides in its *cortile*. Palazzi Giustiniani and Falconieri, which reveal some interesting boldnesses, owe their best parts to Borromini; the graceful loggia of Palazzo Falconieri along the Tiber (Lungotevere dei

Tebaldi) is indeed one of his most resounding successes. Cardinal Fesch, uncle of Emperor Napoleon I, housed his famous collection of objects of art there.

Three other palaces of this period have French associations. It was in Palazzo Salviati, on the Corso, that Louis XIV established the Academy of France; the building was later the residence of Louis Bonaparte after he had put aside his crown as king of Holland. Palazzo Simonetti, also on the Corso and now the head office of the Banco di Roma, was long the residence of the French ambassadors. In its drawing rooms that open out of the magnificent staircase *a lumaca,** Cardinal de Bernis gave the showy receptions that staggered Rome in the eighteenth century and that were in no way surpassed by those of his successor, Chateaubriand, no matter what the latter said. Built into the wall of this palace is the Facchino (the Porter), one of the most popular fountains in Rome. A corpulent man wearing the typical porter's cap and shirt holds in his arms a barrel from whose bung a stream of water falls into a basin. The populace has attributed this to Michelangelo, but that is manifestly ridiculous. Others have professed to see in it a caricature of Martin Luther, but this is no more likely. Still others contend that it represents one Rizzo, who had the finest reputation for drunkenness of all the Roman porters; it is said that his intemperance caused the infernal powers to condemn him to spend eternity as a water merchant. In reality the figure is merely one of those decorative elements produced more or less in quantity, and there are replicas of it elsewhere in the city.

In the Bonaparte palace, which is at the corner of the Corso and Piazza Venezia, Napoleon's mother, Letizia Ramolino (Signora Letizia, as the Romans familiarly called her), spent the last eighteen years of her life. After her family's misfortunes she lived as a recluse, her chief pleasure being the spectacle of the street. In order that she might see without being seen, a little green loggia whose shutters were always closed was built for her; anachronistic and charming, it can still be seen on the second story of the palace. After she became blind, about 1830, she clung to her observatory nonetheless, making her reader-companion describe the sights that she could no longer see. She died on February 2, 1836; Joseph Méry, † who had gone to the palace to pay his respect to the deceased, observed the startling

---

* Literally, "with snails." Lumachella, of which the staircase was built, is a type of limestone in which the shells of snails are often found in profusion.—Translator.

† A nineteenth-century French political and satirical writer.—Translator.

contrast that he saw while in the death chamber, encompassing at the same time the Capitoline tower and the motionless face of the French Caesar's mother.

We cannot conclude this very imcomplete review without mentioning Palazzo Colonna, perhaps the most characteristic of this period. The eighteenth-century reconstruction of the ancient fortress built by Martin V utilized all its antique elements and respected all its treasures, notably the great gallery that had been opened in 1572 to honor the glorious deeds of Marco Antonio Colonna in the victory of Lepanto: it was Jules Hardouin-Mansart's inspiration for his architecture of Versailles. But everything was replaced in a new arrangement and oriented toward a grandiose showiness. The contrast between the two styles is also very obvious in the Florence Palace; in Palazzo Chigi, whose court was completely redone in the new style; and in Palazzo Odescalchi, which, built by Maderna opposite the church of the Holy Apostles, was rebuilt by Bernini.

The Roman palaces of that era were made neither for comfort nor for discreet luxury, but for show. Their balconies thrust forward "as if to issue proclamations," their halls of state took up almost all their area; it is amazing to see how little room was reserved in these vast structures for private life. What a difference from the "little apartments" so highly prized in France at the same time, and from the delicate striving for intimacy by the architects of Louis XIV!

VILLAS OF THE BAROQUE PERIOD

Villas mushroomed in the seventeenth and eighteenth centuries, like the palaces of which they were the mandatory complement. Since custom forbade that they should be dedicated exclusively to rural relaxation, parties and receptions were continual in them. Furthermore, it was customary to open their gardens to the public. Therefore the princely villas, like the palaces, were conceived as sumptuous settings.

Even more than those of the Renaissance the baroque villas accentuate this character of ostentation. Nature by itself is almost invisible in them; stone and marble, manipulated in a hundred ways, reigned there as if to justify Fontana's witticism: "Nature was created in order to provide architecture with a place in which to display its greatest beauties." The gardens matched the architectural taste of the time: no straight lines. There were only arabesques: all the floral embroideries were inspired by ornamental motivations. It was indeed baroque art "applied to plants." Villas were to become so numerous in the eighteenth century that they would make a girdle of flowers for the city. A traveler from Lyons said that they were "enchanted places, true earthly paradises." Speculation in land has destroyed the greater number of them; among the gardens that survive, three claim attention: those of the Borgheses, already described; those of the Pamphilis; and those of the Albanis.

Villa Doria Pamphili unfolds its lovely harmonies to the west of Rome, behind the Janiculum, on the site of Galba's ancient gardens. It was along its flowered slopes, with their nymph grottoes and their little waterfalls, that the French troops made their last attack in 1849. Many of them fell there. Their names appear on their marble gravestones, accompanied with strange epitaphs in which the stonecutters of Trastevere reveal their ignorance of French spelling. The villa served twice as staff headquarters: first to the Roman republicans and then to the French general staff. The military have little regard for sites: the fountains were damaged, the bas-reliefs and the statues were mutilated. Time, too, has changed the appearance of the villa: the umbrella pines have grown, and they are famous now for their tremendous height. This is the tree, "always dark beneath a blazing sun and always motionless in spite of all the winds," that gives Rome its aristocratic beauty. Standing alone before a house, it ennobles the building. In groves, as at Villa Pamphili, "each contributes its part of magnificence, and the sum is dizzying" (André Maurel).

The gardens of the Quirinal palace date from the same time: there are giant shrubs trimmed into walls and hedges, among which the water courses indulge in all kinds of delightful fantasies.

The villa built by Alessandro Cardinal Albani near Porta Salaria has more lawns and flowerbeds than big trees, and the purely architectural design of the gardens leaves virtually nothing to nature. They are indeed floral drawing rooms. Strangely, the buildings are much more restrained than the gardens. This does not prevent the casino from being charming, full of unexpected details. The *"caffè"* opposite is the most exquisite type of those light structures where one does not linger long but that are ideal for a small refection or a brief rest.

Villa Albani is enriched with splendid bas-reliefs and beautiful antique figures, mere remnants of the cardinal's huge collection, which was regarded then as the richest museum of antiquities anywhere in Europe. Its reputation was so well known to Napoleon I's scouts that they stripped the Albani gardens of more than three hundred rare pieces for shipment to

Paris. Not all were restored in 1815. It was in this villa that Rome's surrender to the Piedmontese was signed in September, 1870.

SQUARES: THE ROTONDA, THE MINERVA, ST. IGNATIUS, THE QUIRINAL, SPAIN

If baroque Rome is the Rome of theatrical churches, gaudy palaces, gardens jeweled in marble, and extravagant fountains, it is also the Rome of picturesque squares where the fraternization of the grandiose and the familiar recreates for our enjoyment the good nature that filled the old papal citadel. The variously pastel tints of the *intonaco* (pebbled plaster) of their houses gives them that warm ocher light, running over sometimes into orange, that is the first of the revelations of Rome for the newcomer. There is hardly any that does not have for neighbors a church, a palace, and a fountain grouped "like musicians playing a concert" (these three, Abel Bonnard said, perform the symphony of Rome). The proximity of the great palaces and the beautiful churches does not prevent the squares from holding on to their market stalls, their artisans, their popular character, and their scent of the past.

Without going back again to Piazza Navone, which we have so often mentioned, let us briefly consider some of those charming squares where the stroller comes out into bright sunlight after having prowled the cool, dark streets of the old quarters. The most characteristic is undoubtedly that Piazza della Rotonda that lies before the Pantheon. It was in sorry condition in the seventeenth century when Pope Alexander VII undertook to give it the pleasant aspect that it has retained. He began by ridding the temple's portico of the hawkers and stalls that encumbered it. Two columns were missing; they were replaced by two granite pillars taken from Agrippa's baths that had long been lying in front of the church of St. Louis of the French. Rubbish of all sorts, accumulated through the centuries, had raised the ground level so high that the Pantheon seemed half-buried. The pope had it dug out and then had the square leveled—a task that was not easy. In the process the workmen discovered one of the basalt lions that in antiquity had marked the start of the staircase to the temple, as well as the magnificent porphyry urn—no one knew how it had got there—that is now in the Corsini chapel in St. John Lateran. In the center of the square, Longhi's beautiful fountain was adorned with one of the three obelisks that had been discovered in the foundations of the

Roman College. Surrounded by modest houses washed in a warm ocher, one of which bears an artless image of the madonna, this Piazza della Rotonda with its elegant fountain and the solemn façade of the Pantheon recreates for us the most expressive vision of old papal Rome. The neighboring streets are full of picturesqueness: they mark the boundaries of Agrippa's baths, where well-fed cats bask in the shadow of the old walls or atop the broken columns. These are the posterity of those cats that a prudent city government had assigned, before the construction of the Tiber quays, to the extermination of the rats that flocked into the Pantheon in search of safety when the river flooded. The cats have maintained their domicile in the ruins that surround the Pantheon, and they are tenderly cared for by a society of Roman ladies who come every day to bring them food. They live in a very closed colony: woe to the alien cat who would show any inclination to share their quiet and their meals.

No less flavorful is Piazza della Minerva, quite close, in the center of which Bernini erected in 1667 the second of the three obelisks from the foundations of the Roman College (the third stands before the central railway station, called the Baths). Since this monolith is not very high, the architect amused himself by setting it on the back of a placid elephant to which the Romans have given an irreverent nickname: they call it *il pulcino della Minerva* (the Minerva's chicken). An elliptical inscription by Urban VIII calls on the observer to note this proof that the mark of a sturdy mind is its support of a solid wisdom. This "chicken" that the Romans teased, which is one of the rare comic notes in their city, was almost taken away from them in 1946 by American soldiers looking for "souvenirs." A Dodge truck pulled up at the square one morning and disgorged a gang of workmen in khaki uniforms who began to disassemble the monument in preparation for its transatlantic journey. A neighboring porter fortunately gave the alarm, and the highly disappointed clandestine fatigue party was compelled to withdraw.

A fine example of artistic achievement is the very curious Square of St. Ignatius, where, opposite the church, there is a group of houses in the shape of Louis XV chests of drawers, one fitted into another, and separated by streets so skillfully laid out that at no point is the general line broken. The whole thing would seem a parody if it were not so perfectly done. A scenic decoration was desired, and it was so well achieved that one expects to see the classic characters of Italian comedy come out of the houses. The little streets that run into the square seem to be the wings of an unreal stage. One is called Via del Burro. It is no use opening the

Italian dictionary to find the origin of the name, which has nothing to do with butter: this was where, under the Napoleonic occupation, the French set up their *bureaux* (offices). The theatrical illusion is so successful in this square that it forcefully enlarges a very small area. Marvelously adapting to the picturesque quarter that surrounds it, it is a delightful spot.

It might be thought surprising that the creator of this setting, a certain Reguzzini, produced nothing else worthy of interest; for his church of the Madonna of Divine Love is extremely mediocre, and the altar of St. Francis that he built in Santa Maria in Ara Coeli evoked such sharp criticism that he was completely discredited. Here is the explanation of the mystery: Reguzzini had got his start as a furniture maker, and, when he turned his back on his first trade, he lost all his talent.

Rome's streets and squares owe much to Pope Clement XII (1730-40). It was during his reign that they were paved, *con il nuovo metodo* (with the new method), which consisted of small square flint blocks. This pope also gave the Quirinal square its final shape. He had the pontifical stables built there, as well as the splendid façade of the Consulta palace. The square was also surrounded on three sides by harmoniously designed large structures. On the fourth side Clement put the long balustrade from which one can see the center of the city and, above it in the distance, the dome of St. Peter's. This is the best place from which to take in that thrilling color of Rome that is the color of a lion's skin. The great central monument that already included the Dioscuri was enriched by Pius VI fifty years later with the obelisk taken from the tomb of Augustus. Pius VII was to arrange the whole into a fountain, adding the great granite basin that had served as a trough in the Forum. Thus we see what a composite this famous group is: four popes collaborated in it, using ancient pieces of very different origins, in order to achieve a coherent whole. It could be taken as a symbol of the Roman genius, so marvelously adept at fusing the diverse elements of its conquests into an original whole.

The great stairway that rises from Piazza di Spagna to Trinità dei Monti was built in 1725. Until then the only access to the French church was provided by a dirt path. The monumental stair was erected through a bequest by the French ambassador, Etienne Gouffier. The architect, Francesco de Sanctis, gave its landings and its railings an elliptical design that recalls the colonnade of St. Peter's. The cascade of its 137 steps encompasses in its course two cantilevered terraces. Its graceful gesture is an invitation to descend into the city. Florists have their stalls at the foot of the steps, which, for certain holidays, are completely hidden under an iridescent carpet of flowers. The staircase has belonged to France since Louis XV, and Rome is only its tenant, paying an infinitesimal token rent. At its foot is the Barcaccia fountain, sometimes attributed to Bernini but actually the work of his father, Pietro Bernini. It is a little boat in a basin flush with the ground, and it recalls a memorable event: in 1624 the waters of the Tiber rose to the foot of the Pincio, and Piazza di Spagna could be crossed by boat.

As one goes up the stairs toward Trinità dei Monti, the façade of the church diminishes; the church seems cut in two by the small obelisk in front of its entrance. This monolith is very ancient, for it once adorned the gardens of Sallust. There is nothing Egyptian about it, however, in spite of the hieroglyphs with which it is decorated; it is only a Roman imitation. Pius VI crowned it with a *fleur-de-lys,* a star, and an iron cross. It marks the ultimate point of the monumental ascent at the end of which the visitor finds all Rome at his feet. The amazing transparency of the air gives their full worth to the successive levels, to the bristling spikes of the towers, the belfries, the domes. "It is like a mirage," Ferdinand Bach wrote. "So many picturesque effects at once within a single radius make one think of those composite landscapes beloved of the eighteenth-century painters. They found that reality never afforded them enough dramatic effects. So they were forever adding their own. But here what more could they do? It is a magnificent backdrop for an opera setting. And yet it is really this, the city of Rome."

With the staircase by de Sanctis, Piazza di Spagna had its last improvement. We see it today as it really was in 1725. "The discrepancies of the centuries fuse there in a baroque unity that is indeed the fundamental tone of the city" (*Itinéraires*).

THE FONTANA DI TREVI

Its fountains are the eternal youth of Rome. There is not another city in the world where this luxury has been carried so far: they are works of art as well as of utility. And they are everywhere—at street corners, in public squares, in the shadows of villas, in cloisters, even in the humblest courtyards. They are so many that de Brosses complained that the sound of their waters disturbed his sleep.

The Roman passion for fountains no doubt descends from Agrippa. At the end of the empire there were thirteen hundred, which Vitiges cut off in one swoop by severing the aqueducts. They were to be silent for nine centuries before they would be brought back to life. When the Renaissance popes set out to rouse the city from its long lethargy, they could imagine no better overture to the resurrection than to give it back its waters.

Since then it has been a point of honor for each pope to select a site for a new stream of water or an array of plumed sprays. Fountains have been designed in an infinite variety of forms, but always with an exquisite concern for their harmony with their surroundings. The fountains of Rome owe their charm quite as much to their close relations with their surroundings as to their artistic quality in itself. Let us consider especially those of St. Peter's Square or Piazza Farnese; it is their complete harmony with the architectural setting that provides their background and produces a great part of their beauty.

The finest example of this exact harmony with site is undoubtedly the marble fountain in front of Villa Medici. "The builder," Maurice Paléologue* wrote, "had access only to a thin, barely trickling stream of water. On the other hand, the site assigned to him dominated one of the most majestic panoramas in Rome. Under these unfavorable conditions, however, he created an exquisite object through the ingenuity with which he was able to combine the curves of the basin, the frame of the foliage, the perspective of the distances, and even the reflections of the sky in the undulating surface of the water."

Fountain art was to be a triumph for the baroque. The exuberance of its ornamentation is a happy visual echo of the tumult of the water. The joyous vigor and the ingenuous boldness of the artists of this period were exalted by the open air. Each of them gave some corner of Rome one of those fountains that are so gay that they seem to have come out of fairy tales. Bernini's heroic-comic dash was in its element in the creation of the fantastic animals and the demigods that preside over the play of the water. We have seen his joyous Triton rise before Palazzo Barberini, his picturesque Moro in Piazza Navone, and that amazing Fountain of the Rivers that has been compared with a carnival float that has stopped in front of Sant'Agnese. In this field Bernini had rivals, notably Bizzacheri, who

---

* A nineteenth- and twentieth-century French diplomat (at one time ambassador in Rome) and author, member of the Académie Française.—Translator.

decorated Piazza della Bocca della Verità with the pretty fountain whose bowl is supported by two Silenuses.

Without lingering over descriptions of the innumerable fountains of this period, let us limit our discussion to their most characteristic representative, which has become the most popular and the most visited monument in Rome, that Fontana di Trevi that is a place of pilgrimage for the whole world's tourists. No one—however brief his stay might have to be—would forget to visit it and to throw into it over his shoulder the coins that will earn him the inestimable privilege of not dying before he has seen Rome again. This ingenuous belief is only a popular distortion of an older custom: when the fountain was still only the structure with three outlets that Alberti had built in the fifteenth century, young girls would bring their betrotheds there to drink its water if the young men had to leave Rome; they then would break the glass and feel certain that the men would return, whatever the hazards of their journeys. This practice was connected with the legends that had attributed all kinds of magic virtues to the Aqua Virgo since remote antiquity.

It is indeed the Aqua Virgo that flows from the Fontana di Trevi, and the story of its discovery in the time of Augustus is written in the bas-reliefs of the monument. Roman soldiers, having lost their way in the countryside during a search for water that could supply Agrippa's baths, encountered a girl eight miles out of Rome: she told them of a nearby spring whose water was plentiful and pure. Agrippa having been told of this discovery, which had hardly been difficult for his prospectors, work was begun to bring the water to the Field of Mars; it was called "the virgin's water" as a tribute to the girl who had pointed it out. This water, which is the best in Rome and is reputed to cure divers diseases, reaches the city, where it supplies a whole quarter, through the same conduits— repaired by Nicholas V and Sixtus IV—that carried it almost twenty centuries ago. The Aqua Virgo aqueduct was in fact the only one that escaped destruction by the Barbarians, because it runs underground. It had simply become clogged. It enters Rome by way of the Pincio, which, in part, it penetrates at a great depth.

Erected in 1762 by belated disciples of Bernini who were inspired by the master's designs, the Fontana di Trevi employs a whole façade of Palazzo Poli for its scenic effects. Neptune is portrayed in it standing in a chariot drawn by sea horses as it leaves his palace, decorated with a sumptuous row of Corinthian columns. Statues, bas-reliefs, and commemorative inscriptions complement the remarkably animated mythological picture. It is the apogee of the baroque, but it is also an astonishing exaltation of water. "The play of its waters is marvelous in its abundance and its variety." They surge from every part of it in a dazzling mysterious beauty and with such music that Mme. de Staël could say that, when the waters stopped their play, it was as if a great silence had fallen on Rome.

That there is much bombast in all this cannot be denied, but in Rome all bombast is pleasant, and this more than any other. It is also possible that the Neptune, the Nereids, the Tritons, and the sea horses are not worth much; that does not prevent the combination of them from being alive and superb. The Fontana di Trevi is certainly theatrical; its dripping groups, its cascades, its great basin are a veritable operatic tableau when one comes upon them from the dark streets that surround them. Except that this tableau is a mythology at play, a poem in marble and emerald, a brilliant evocation of "the joy of living that illuminated old papal Rome." None of this can be understood from maps or photographs; everything must be seen in the soft air of Rome, and only then does it have its real worth, for "an unexpected harmony comes into being among the white statues, the blue-green water scintillating with golden sparks of sunlight, and the great azure of the air" (Charles de Nouy).

Let us not leave the fountain without mention of a curious episode during its construction. A barber who had his shop on the ground floor of Palazzo Castellani, at the side of the square, was regaling his customers with extremely harsh criticisms of the labors being performed at his door. Word of his acid jests reached the architect, Niccolò Salvi, who demanded more moderation of his caustic opponent: "Mind your own business," the architect told the barber. "But it is precisely my business," the barber retorted, "because all day long I see your horror reflected in my mirror." "Then," Salvi said, "I shall see to it that you do not see it." Thereupon he equipped the balustrade that surrounds the fountain with that strange travertine urn that Romans have baptized the *asso di coppe* (ace of hearts) because of its resemblance to a card in the Tarot pack. No relation, however remote, can be found between the urn and the mythological subject of the fountain, for it is nothing but a much enlarged replica of the soap jar that was the barber's shop sign. But it is so placed that it appears alone in the mirror and completely blocks out the fountain that the barber found so distressing. Whoever finds this story unlikely can easily verify it by going to be shaved by the barber's successor, still in the same place; he will find himself face to face with the ace of hearts, staring solitary, huge, and mocking at him from the mirror.

FROM BAROQUE TO ROCOCO

Baroque reigned in a universal fashion over the whole Roman eighteenth century and a large part of the next century. The style of an age and the reflection of an epoch, it was also, so to speak, the culmination and the full flower of the atavistic tendencies of a people and a race. It was the most Roman manifestation of Roman art, and, in a word, a kind of Roman classicism. No one could argue that the invasion of the baroque had only good results, any more than one could blame the great creators for the clumsy imitations that they inspired and the flaws in taste that they engendered.

Let us remark first of all that, through a distortion that is common to all styles, what has been most imitated in the baroque has not always been its best works. If one limits oneself to Bernini, whose influence was predominant, one should not lose sight of the fact that that universal and prodigiously productive artist devoted himself to innumerable minor activities of which nothing remains to us today but which nevertheless fed the general inspiration of artists and their concern with imitation. Bernini was not only an architect and a sculptor; he painted more than two hundred pictures, only one of which has come down to us, preserved in the Vatican's mosaic studio. He also drew innumerable caricatures, of which some very curious examples are in the print section of the Galleria Nazionale. The moving spirit in every celebration, he also designed floats and platforms, as well as lighting themes and fireworks displays. It was these passing fantasies that were taken by his imitators as the model for their tastes, quite as much as his works of much higher quality. Introduced to baroque art by his excesses, many second-rate artists naturally clung most to its somewhat tinselly aspect and its artifices. As for his apparent facility, that suited a time in which, as much by inclination as by necessity, there was a haste to accomplish. Michelangelo, everyone knew, had labored for years on the ceiling of the Sistine Chapel, and Leonardo da Vinci had left works unfinished because of his insistence on perfection. In the baroque age, artists were in a hurry to deliver their paintings or their sculptures, architects rushed through their designs and were equally hasty in their execution. This was because the patrons who commissioned the works, having spent their lives in scaling the social heights, had little time remaining in which to leave behind them the resounding reputations on which they had focused all their desires. The cardinals who ordered the decoration of their churches expected to enjoy the rewards of their generosity without delay; if they commissioned their tombs, they wanted to see them before they entered them.

In this prevailing feverishness, artists resorted to the quickest and the easiest. That is the reason for the proliferation of so many hasty works in which expressionism and the magic of effects were striven for in excesses of form. The great creators were cognizant that they "proclaimed doctrinal truth to the world and spoke in the name of the pontiffs"; their rhetorical fullness sprang from this. All too often their imitators merely yielded to a fashion, and the baselessness of their doctrines is apparent in their lack of the conviction of a master.

Creative fecundity diminished perceptibly in the eighteenth century, whose strictly Roman contributions were to be of minimal importance. The majority of European countries and even of Italian cities had their own clearly characterized versions of the *settecento;* France, in particular, moved from the sustained majesty of the Louis XIV style to the charming involutions of the rococo. Rome did not experience this evolution, from which it was precluded by its own temperament. Until the neo-classic reaction it was to remain faithful to the baroque, a baroque that sometimes moderated its decorations and lightened its lines, sometimes soared off into a return to Borromini and linear efforts at fantasy.

This return has created confusion: the epithet of *rococo* has been summarily attached to eighteenth-century Roman works that show exaggeratedly swollen façades, or planes in which curves and ovals are somewhat excessively intertwined. This is an abuse of vocabulary. It may be said that the rococo succeeded the baroque, of which it is only a deviation, but this statement is justified only if things are viewed in a very general fashion without any regard to local peculiarities. In the form in which it triumphed in central Europe in particular, the rococo can be explained by the many Slavic and Germanic influences that Roman art completely escaped. In Rome, an ecclesiastical state, commissions came chiefly from the church and the clergy. It was impossible for the rococo to impose its strivings for affected graces and its very free femininity on a society that, no doubt, was no more virtuous than any other but whose choices were still guided by a certain theological conformism.

That is the reason why there are virtually no rococo works in Rome. Those to which the label has been given derived from a belated return to Borromini and to the principles that had given his art its novelty. In reaction against the domestication of the baroque, the Jesuit Father Pozzo achieved amazing decorative effects in the two churches of his order early in the eighteenth century. In the Gesù he extended the architecture by means of a *trompe-l'oeil:* in the inner dome of the apse, he provided the miracles of St. Ignatius with the theater of a vision of the sky. On the saint's altar he placed the reredos whose columns and globe of lapis lazuli give the whole an extraordinary richness. Carrying his daring in the matter of perspective even further in St. Ignatius, he accomplished that painting of the vault that we have already mentioned and that makes all its lines converge on a point established in the center of the church.

At most one might associate some details of the church of the Maddalena with the rococo esthetic, the indented treatment of its façade, the "exacerbated" style of the *cantoria* chancel above its organ platform. But the whole is irresistibly reminiscent of Borromini, and it repeats a number of effects for which he strove especially: the conception of the oblong nave with its undulant wall is clearly derived from St. Charles of the Four Fountains, and, if the overabundance of ornamentation occasionally gives it an air of the gratuitous, it must be recognized as only the excess that often marked the twilight of the baroque. As it stands, however, this decoration gives the church a very strong charm, like an old drawing room.

A rococo character has also been ascribed to the loggia added in 1711 to the Zuccari house. It is much more evocative of the architecture of a summer house of the Farnese period. What is more, it is a French creation executed for Marie-Louise de Gonzague, that lady of Nevers who, having been queen of Poland, went to end her days in the shadow of Trinità dei Monti. If one wishes to see a genuinely rococo work, one must look for it in Santa Maria della Scala, in Trastevere: it is the magnificent organ that dominated the entrance door of the church. But it came from Spain, the gift of the Infante Louis de Bourbon.

Sometimes, furthermore, in this period of the baroque's quest for the luxuriance of its origins, it so restrained itself that it almost repudiated itself. The finest example of this return to humility is afforded by the church of the Priory of Malta on the Aventine, the creation of the most impetuous artist of his time, the Venetian Giambattista Piranesi. Everyone knows the engravings by this poet of Rome. It has been said that, next to his, Hubert Robert's ruins seem soft and soluble. Toward the end of his life he was given the opportunity to translate his inspired artistic dreams into brick and marble. The result was this church of St. Mary of the Priory, which, though richly ornamented, is still sober and moderate in its lines, far indeed from hinting at the daring of the master engraver.

His style is fortunately unimpaired in the arrangement of the site, which is like a living print. A rare pearl is pricelessly encased in this setting: through the keyhole of the entrance door, the dome of St. Peter's can be seen with striking sharpness. All of Piranesi is in the neighboring little square, which he decorated with obelisks and trophies, and shaded with cypresses. A rather conventional opera background, no doubt, but "knightly and gallant," and rightly made to evoke the shade of "the artist of so many ruins adorned with foliage."

CHAPTER 27

SUMMARY OF PAPAL ROME

GOVERNMENT

The age in which the "carnival" of the baroque wound its saraband through Rome was the best period of papal Rome, the most serene, the most indulgent, and, in sum, the happiest.

Next to the Kingdom of the Two Sicilies, the Holy See's temporal realm was the largest in Italy: St. Peter's flag flew from the banks of the Tiber to the borders of the Republic of Venice. The Sacred College, under the pope's authority, was the real sovereign. Two papal ministers, the treasurer and the secretary of state, whose powers were much intertwined and who were traditionally rivals, ran the government. But they acted only as representatives of the congregations, which were grand councils of a kind, among which the cardinals were distributed and on which all matters both temporal and spiritual depended.

Rome and its territory enjoyed a separate administration: this was under the charge of a high prelate, the governor, who dealt directly with the pope and in a sense was his third minister: minister of Rome. His powers embraced those of a director general, a prefect of police, and a chief judge. But he was still subject to the supervision of those of the congregations (*Consulta* and *Buon Governo*) whose jurisdiction was internal administration. Since their respective powers were determined only by an incongruous mesh of traditions and privileges, the congregations and the governor were constantly at odds. The resultant instability was aggravated by personal rivalries among prelates and by the competition among the various bodies under their direction. A foreign diplomat summed up the entire situation when he said: "Here everyone commands and no one obeys, and yet things somehow go on." In effect, the army of functionaries of minor degree took advantage of their betters' disputes to impose their own arbitrary decisions. Countless departments were clogged with thirty thousand of these officials. This plethora had a long ancestry, but even so it had been immeasurably augmented through nepotism, each papacy having created new offices to satisfy its dependents.

All these functionaries wore the ecclesiastical habit, even though they had not necessarily been ordained. Every young man who aspired to high position "dressed like a priest," and in this he was imitating very many laymen who wore the clerical cloth though they made no other pretension to clerical status. "An apothecary with a wife and children who did not dress like a priest ran the risk of losing the trade of the cardinal, his neighbor." But the apothecary would not climb the stairway of the ecclesiastical hierarchy. He would not, however, endure the hobbles of some fresh beginner who had put on the black robes in order to become a paper pusher for one of the congregations. But, if he knew his way about, even a little, he could be found, in his violet garment, in the troop of *monsignori*, a numerous species lacking the episcopal character that custom attaches in France to this title. Our man might even—still without having become a priest—become a cardinal. It was a matter of gifts and influence, with this one peculiarity, that genuine piety—which purified ambition—was still a powerful means of advancement. But nothing stood in the way of a *monsignore* who, somewhere along his road, decided to exchange his title for the hand of an heiress. What was essential for success was to wear the ecclesiastical robe from the very outset. It was not uncommon to see a wet nurse giving suck to some six-month-old Carmelite or Franciscan. When young Casanova, glowing with the pride of his fine presence, entered Rome to launch his career in seduction and adventurism, the holy priest to whom he turned for counsel advised him: "I hope that, when you take your letter to Cardinal Acquaviva, you will dress like a humble priest and not in those fine clothes, which are not calculated to attract luck." That evening, when he dined, Casanova was the only man at the table without the clerical collar. "In Rome," he observed, "every man is a priest, or wants to look like one." In short, since no one was forbidden the uniform, everyone who wanted to be respected wore it.

High positions were held by cardinals—great lords backed by great fortunes, with butlers, secretaries, and footmen in abundance. They surrounded themselves with splendor everywhere, in their palaces as in the street, where they traveled in handsome red carriages behind superb horses. Great honors were paid to them. They were the ornament of the papal court, which was quite as formalistic as Versailles; a minutely detailed code governed precedence. This rigid protocol was all the more surprising in that the sovereign pontiff was exposed in his private dealings to a whole host of the great but also to more or less polished servants of the lowest rank. Most of them, indeed, styled themselves fellow townsmen of the pope or distant cousins of some authentic servant. Cardinals and great lords also tolerated the invasion of their palaces by strangers who were there for nothing but their own ends. It was not customary to resist these encroachments. Behavior ignored social barriers. It was common for a servant to proffer his own snuffbox to a cardinal, who took a pinch from it as a matter of course. Servants joined in their masters' conversations, and there were lackeys with the gift of discourse whose lengthy dissertations held an audience of prelates. Such extreme and spontaneous familiarity is certainly touching. It also reveals the pleasant anarchy of the papal state.

SOCIAL STRUCTURE

Five great families, involved since the Middle Ages in political struggles, constituted the unchallenged elite of Roman aristocracy. The first rank was the fief of the Colonnas and the Orsinis; behind them came the Savellis, the Contis, and the Gaetanis. Many popes had come out of these ancient houses, which had continually striven to exert their weight in the decisions of the conclaves from the time when popes had been made by princes.

Now the tables had been turned by the entrenchment of nepotism, and it was the popes who made princes of their nephews. None since Sixtus V had breached this tradition, and thus the Roman nobility's ranks had been swollen successively by the Aldobrandinis, the Borgheses, the Ludovisis, the Barberinis, the Pamphilis, the Chigis, the Rospigliosis, the Altieris. All were fantastically wealthy princes, their divers uncles having been careful to furnish them with money and benefices as well as honors. The newer lords had bestirred themselves to contract alliances with the old houses of feudal origin whose incomes had often declined. The fusion of fame and fortune had given rise to a brilliant aristocracy. Its members lived like feudal barons, dispensing justice in a whole quarter in which they were responsible for the police protection and the maintenance of the streets (for nepotism had given rise to paternalism). Each of them had in effect his own court, complete with master of protocol, managers, and deputies, and a veritable population of courtiers in gold-decked garments followed in his train wherever he moved.

A third class, of less well-appointed nobles whose incomes had been the victims of various financial manipulations, had regilded their arms through profitable alliances with the families of cardinals. For these high prelates emulated, to the advantage of their loved ones, the nepotism of their superior.

What was lacking in papal Rome was that middle class that was in the process of becoming the most living force in the majority of European states. The middle class had neither fortune nor freedom, and the liberal professions occupied a subordinate position.

A very justly condemned judicial system kept judges and lawyers in a most obscure corner. The average judge who had the power to send a man to the galleys for five years would have been unable to survive if he had had to become bookkeeper to a ghetto merchant. Though he have an eloquence greater than Cicero's, a lawyer could never achieve renown because all proceedings were in writing. He had to be satisfied with very miserable fees and augment his income through the emoluments derived from some one of those rich families that wanted a man of the law in their employ.

Physicians would have died of starvation if they had not been the dependents of some great house. They competed with the pharmacists, to whose customers they offered cut-rate services. They were followers of Dr. Purgon:* "virtually all their patients were purged for breakfast and bled for dinner." When a patient died, his decease was invariably ascribed to his doctor's ignorance. If he recovered, it was the madonna who got the thanks.

Merchants rarely attained great wealth, in spite of substantial margins

* The ignorant and pettifogging physician in Molière's *Malade imaginaire* (*The Imaginary Invalid*).—Translator.

of profit. These were deeply slashed by brokerage commissions: claimants of all kinds surged up from everywhere to seize each his share. Let us add that, being naturally lazy, the shopkeeper made no great efforts: "I have what you are looking for," one of them told a customer, "but come back tomorrow: it's too high."

However mediocre their rank, the burghers of Rome did not sin by any excess of modesty. They loved to make a show, to wear jewelry, and above all to visit the taverns in order to show the world that they were spending money. There were indeed a considerable number of authentic ecclesiastics in Rome, really too many not to have a certain amount of chaff among the wheat. There were 95 parishes, 250 churches served by chaplains, 23 seminaries, and 45 convents housing several thousand monks.

THE PEOPLE

In the shadow of the aristocratic families, and subsisting more or less directly on subsidies from them, the mass of the people kept alive without bowing beneath the yoke of burdensome tasks. Rome of that day bore so little resemblance to a swarming beehive that no one has challenged the picture of it drawn by de Brosses: "Imagine a population in which one-third consists of priests, one-third consists of people who barely work at all, and one-third consists of people who do absolutely nothing." Sismondi,* in his own way, offered this description of the Eternal City's rather paradoxical situation: "In Rome everyone wears the priest's *soutane,* the servant's livery, or the beggar's rags."

Rome in the eighteenth century was in fact an amazing city. Situated beside a navigable river, populated by 180,000 persons, it had neither trade nor industry. In the midst of a fertile countryside, its agriculture was so impoverished that the basic foods required to sustain life had to be brought from great distances. In actuality the city lived on the huge income that the Holy See derived from the Christian world.

It was not that the population was totally idle, as the jests of so many travelers deceived by appearances would imply. The number of churches and palaces that were built at that time gives the lie to extreme statements. Scaffoldings swarmed with masons, painters, stucco mixers, iron workers

* Jean-Charles-Léonard Simonde, who added "de Sismondi," was a Swiss economist and historian (1773–1842) specializing in Italy, and one of the major early theoreticians of socialism.—Translator.

trained in difficult trades. The city was spotted with artisans' workshops whose proprietors were perhaps somewhat disorganized, but were skilled, industrious, and inventive. We owe them a great number of technical advances and some important inventions, such as the methods for backing paintings with new canvas, which have thwarted the ruin of so many precious works. The humble workman who invented these methods knew absolutely nothing of painting, and therefore there was talk of traffic with the demon. He escaped trial for sorcery only by claiming to have had his secret from St. Joseph, to whom he had given alms "in the guise of a poor man." Artisans took pride in their crafts to such a degree that they all claimed to be artists: artists in shoemaking, artists in blacksmithing, artists in locksmithing, artists in barbering. In the end the word *artist* was so cheapened that the most incompetent copyist of pictures refused to have anything to do with it. "I am not an artist," he would say. "I am a professor."

These "artists," however, made up only a very small minority of the Roman people. A horde of others stayed alive without any regular employment, living miserably but certainly not interested in work as a means of improving their precarious lot. For in Rome more than anywhere else in the world the people believed in the proverb that said: *"Chi si contenta gode* (He who is satisfied enjoys)." Everyone hoped for a better tomorrow, but it was expected to arrive through the will of God rather than the effort of men. A whole class of parasites who were half confidence men ate at the tables of the great and paid the bill with flattery. These practitioners were known as "the knights of the teeth." Knights of industry and gallant ladies prospered. Whoever felt himself unendowed for high endeavor could always manage to earn something without undue subjection to arduous labors. The custom of the *buona mano* (the Roman term for tipping) was universal, and any pretext sufficed for a request for money.

The only street lighting was candles placed beneath images of the madonna: so a little money could be made by acquiring a lantern and guiding hesitant pedestrians; opening a door, announcing a visitor, kindly giving up one's seat at a ceremony were other ways of earning tips. Good speakers set themselves up as preachers in the porches or the alcoves of the churches; when they had finished their sermons, they passed the hat. In a country where the greatest good was the least activity possible, begging was enough to stave off starvation, for the "good hand" was everywhere.

A slight deformity or a pitiful appearance naturally encouraged its owner to adopt mendicancy as a career. It was a lucrative profession, encouraged as an evangelical institution and, for this reason, protected by the popes' police. There were companies of beggars in front of all the palaces, on the steps of all the churches, playing cards but interrupting the game whenever anyone passed. The 137 steps of the staircase of Trinità dei Monti were considered a particularly rich hunting ground, because the quarter was always filled with a mass of generous and exploitable foreigners. Those Romans who were not servants, handymen, or beggars simply did nothing. This was the final third of the population as catalogued by de Brosses, and he was not merely jesting. This third third, if one may say so, was indeed a very large third.

This host of loafers subsisted to the best of its abilities on Rome's inexhaustible charity. Rome was the city of help; the clerical government justified its presence there by its extensive practice of charity. It would have been impossible for even the poorest to die of hunger; succor for every suffering was assured. A welfare commission headed by a cardinal distributed cash allotments of staggering proportions to the poor. In periods of shortages, the public treasury paid for the milling of grain that it imported, and bread was distributed gratis. The popes maintained workshops in which the poor and the infirm were paid wages for crossing and uncrossing their arms at the command of a cardinal. Charitable institutions were innumerable: modern Rome, Voltaire said, had as many of them as ancient Rome had arches of triumph. Nowhere were hospitals so amply available to all. Papal Rome's zeal for charity was of such militance that two brotherhoods, that of the Holy Apostles and that of the Divine Mercy, had assumed the task of seeking out the poor and the wretched in order to take care of their needs. Another order (Prayer and Death) took charge of their funerals: under its banner, princes and cardinals, candles in their hands and sacks over their heads, followed the coffins to the graves. The brotherhood *della Pietà dei Carcerati* (of Charity for Prisoners) visited the jails; that of St. Ives provided lawyers without charge, and that of St. John the Baptist prepared those under sentence of death for a Christian end.

This huge network of official benevolence was complemented by the very broad charitable works of the great families and the monasteries. There were hundreds of doors in Rome at which one had only to present oneself in order to be helped. Nowhere was bread refused to a beggar. In a country based on such a system, only fools worked.

That did not mean that the poor led lives of any great comfort; they were packed into worse than wretched lodgings, in which the sole furniture was often a single bed for a whole family—a condition that is not unknown in our own epoch, so proud of its progress. The lowest class was not unhappy, however, for it lived above all on hope and illusion. Even the most insignificant knew a cardinal's or a prince's servant, who brought them occasional help, and above all they hoped for more, and more regularly. Every conclave created new chances, every promotion to the Sacred College gave rise to new hopes; and the lottery kept everyone's spirits high. In one form or another everyone was waiting for the favor of heaven. It was this fantasy that prevented the disparities of condition from arousing hatred in the least fortunate. Everyone was pleased that there were rich men, so that the poor would have benefactors.

Let us further point out that, whatever may be said to the contrary, the population of Rome was the freest in all Europe. The popes gave wide scope to the old spirit of criticism; satires appeared so freely on Pasquino's pedestal that they seemed to be a state institution. The supposed debates of the speaking statues were repeated in many taverns where "the vinegar of opposition" was distilled. In Piazza Navone, an open forum for any who chose to speak, the guitar players delighted in slipping a satire among their couplets. The puppeteers were overtly contemptuous of the government before audiences in which there was no lack of men of the church.

As for the Inquisition, about which the French philosophers made so much noise, in Rome it was nothing but a bogey. De Brosses stands surety for that. "It must not be thought," he wrote, "that the Holy Office is as devilish as it is black: I have not heard of a single instance of anyone's having been subjected to the Inquisition or harshly treated." In a word, everyone lived as he liked in a city where the pope reigned like a father.

The greatest charm of Roman life was the cordiality of human relations. There was no arrogance in the great, no inferiority complex in the humble. All classes mingled in a patriarchal conglomerate. Nobles, prelates, burghers, and proletarians "spoke to one another in a tone of gay familiarity of which it is hard to find another example." That familiarity had a thousand turns: the Capuchins, always equipped with red umbrellas and huge baskets from which to supply the needs of poor households; "the laundry hanging from the windows of the Vatican, the palaces of the great open to the servants' country cousins, the snuffbox casually offered by a cardinal to a poor friar, the jokes traded by a prince and an artisan, the fishmongers installed without permission in the porch of a palace, down to the characteristic medley of a lordly mansion, sinister taverns, richly gilded churches, and filthy shacks in the same little street" (Madelin).*

All this was possible, and in a certain style, only because priests, noblemen, artisans, and beggars alike were keenly aware of their membership in the same family: the Romans of Rome. It was a title of which all of them were proud, with a feeling of national pride that reached back over centuries and was expressed in the ancient phrase *"Civis sum Romanus"* (I am a Roman citizen), which is still used, sometimes for astonishing purposes. "Let me through, I'm a Roman citizen," a man will say to a group of foreigners. A bookbinder and a grocer, discussing their problems, will conclude the subject: "With all of it, we're Romans, the leaders of the world." Nothing has surprised them, a traveler has observed, since the rape of the Sabines. In all honesty they genuinely believe that they themselves once conquered the universe and gave it their king. The humblest Roman has not the slightest doubt of a primacy that seems so natural to him that he makes no effort to support it. This pride is always accompanied with great tolerance toward the foreigner; not only is he neither insulted nor mocked, but he is welcomed everywhere with a cordiality that compels affection. It is a detail most characteristic of Rome that it is the only city in which the Jews were never stoned. The Romans' subtlety of mind has always kept them from excesses.

These mental attitudes are enough to explain why this childish, parasitical, flippant, vain, and undisciplined people lived happily under a despotic paternal government that was protective and, above all, indulgent.

FESTIVALS

The Romans have always enjoyed a good time. The old phrase *panem et circenses* (bread and circuses), quite adequately states their basic aspirations. Under the papal government, the bread was distributed at the gates of presbyteries and convents; the games of the circuses were replaced by religious ceremonials and public holidays. In eighteenth-century Rome there were 150 holidays in the year, including Sundays, but without taking into account parish celebrations and those that arose out of special occasions.

---

* Louis Madelin, who died in 1956, was a French historian, member of the Académie Française.—Translator.

The splendor of the celebrations gave the baroque decoration of the churches its full meaning. The tone of the ceremonies has been reported for us by a French traveler of the time, Dupaty. "I went," he wrote, "to hear the opera of Vespers and to see the illumination of the evening service." These are wholly proper terms for the great solemnities. In churches adorned with tapestries and hangings, illuminated by "wells of fire," carpeted with foliage, the whole office was celebrated in music; people strolled about, greeted one another loudly, chatted, laughed, crowded round the musicians. Nothing that struck the eye or the ear evoked the sanctity of the place. Silence and contemplation arrived only with the elevation of the Host. Huge crowds followed every procession. The great basilicas were the theaters of magnificent ceremonies at which the pope on his *sedia* (chair) glided above three hundred multicolored prelates, operetta soldiers, and gentlemen in heraldic costumes. When on great occasions the sovereign pontiff traversed his capital, the splendor of his procession exceeded that of the Medicis. As for the governor of Rome, he moved only to the sound of trumpets and surrounded by halberdiers. At every opportunity there were fireworks displays. It is reported that the pope budgeted fifteen thousand pounds a year to this aspect of popular rejoicing. But one wonders how he got away so cheaply when one learns that one cluster in the fireworks display at Castello Sant'Angelo on the night of June 28 and 29, the feasts of St. Peter and St. Paul, included five thousand rockets.

Illuminations were also very highly esteemed. Sometimes they lighted a church, sometimes they brightened a whole quarter, and occasionally the entire city. Those of the basilica of St. Peter's, which were planned by Michelangelo, were grandiose: a small army of specialists set the whole edifice alight in a few instants. And these splendors were surpassed at Castello Sant'Angelo; it was a fairy tale in light, whose theme was changed every year. No prince, ambassador, cardinal, or banker gave a party without illuminating his palace and its outbuildings. These parties, to which the population flocked for its share, were sumptuous. Those given by Cardinal de Bernis when he was French ambassador in Rome would have earned him the reputation of a madman if he had staged them in Paris. The creation of a cardinal was celebrated with public rejoicings. His palace was decorated and illuminated, as was the whole quarter round it. At the gates, orchestras played and ices were distributed. For every important event Castello Sant'Angelo was dressed in a dazzling robe of banners.

The carnival period unleashed a universal merrymaking. Its start was announced by the bells of the Capitoline, which rang only on that occasion and to announce the death of a pope. Then pleasure was the ruler of the street: the crowd poured out in an overwhelming confusion of class and rank; men and women in comic costumes traded jests and candies, and the mobile kitchens that dispensed fried fish were taken by storm.

Everyone joined in the almond battles that raged in the Corso: people on the sidewalks, people in carriages, lovely ladies in their windows, girls rushing out of the shops; but a strict code governed the targets of their missiles. Only people in masks could hurl their candies at everyone; the others could attack only those who were masked; servants were supposed not to attack one another. Every day of the carnival period ended with horse races that excited the whole city. The riderless horses, their manes flying in the wind, were started at Piazza del Popolo and they did not stop until they reached Piazza Venezia, where a banner marked the finish line. It was a miracle that their chaotic rush through the narrow aisle left for them by the spectators did not cause more injuries. When the Angelus sounded, everyone stopped whatever he was doing, knelt in the street and recited the *Ave Maria*. On the last night of the carnival everyone carried a lighted candle and did his best to extinguish his neighbor's.

A city of contrast, Rome forgot its carnival follies to celebrate moving festivals, such as the blessing of the lambs at St. Agnes Beyond the Walls. On January 21 the abbot of the chapter blessed two lambs placed on the altar, and they were at once turned over to the canons of the Lateran. Cared for in a nuns' convent, they were served at Easter on the pontifical table. Their wool was made into the *pallium,* that once exclusive vestment of the pope that reminded him of his obligation to carry the strayed lambs on his shoulders, after the example of the Good Shepherd.

Another picturesque ceremony, on January 18, brought the entire four-footed population of Rome together in front of Santa Maria Maggiore to receive benediction in the name of St. Anthony: bulls, cows, horses, mules, and donkeys appeared in great numbers, decked with ribbons and flowers. A priest in stole and surplice gave each the holy water. The owner thanked him with a cheese or some other product of his farm. All Rome flocked to this observance.

POLICE AND COURTS

In contrast to the country roads, always infested with bandits in spite of the popes' consistent efforts, the streets of Rome were relatively safe. One could walk through them, even at night, without running the risk of being robbed. It was not that the police were so active, but the Romans of those days held theft in low esteem: the crowd would set out with incredible ferocity after a man who had stolen a handkerchief. On the other hand, it openly protected killers, who were quite numerous. Murders occurred by the dozen every day: there were eighteen thousand during the pontificate of Paul V, arising for the most part out of unpremeditated quarrels in taverns and the very peculiar customs of the lower classes, among whom a knife was generally used rather than a fist. Most police reports ended with the same sentence: "The criminal escaped by fleeing." This flight was very often assisted by those who had witnessed the crime, and their sentiments were generally on the side of the criminal. The popular exclamation *povero cristiano,* a traveler reported, was applied not to the man stretched out on the ground in his own blood but to the man who had put him there. In a word, it never entered anyone's mind to help the police. *Lo sbirro* (the cop) was regarded as a thoroughly vile being; the worst insult that one could hurl at an enemy was "son of a cop." With the crowd's protection, the criminal had no difficulty in finding a place of asylum. For everything was an asylum: churches, convents, the quarter where an ambassador lived, a cardinal's house. "The criminal who manages to catch hold of a monk's robe is safe, and it will do the police no good to beg the *fraticello* (little friar) to make him let go." The banks of the Tiber also represented an inviolable asylum, lest the criminal throw himself into the water. The worst thing possible was that a man should die without confession: hence all pursuit halted if the quarry threatened suicide.

Those murderers who were caught and sentenced to death were the objects of general commiseration: everyone asked anxiously whether they had gone to confession. Once reassurance on the question had been given, everyone turned out for the execution. The year's best criminals were held back for the carnival period: in order to make clear the recreational character of the performance, the executioners wore clown costumes and told dirty jokes to their victims as they disposed of them. If there were no death sentences pending, there were always public floggings, which were very numerous and quite well attended, especially when the criminal was a courtesan whose offense had consisted of appearing masked in public. The flogger was permanently assigned to a point close to the Corso, where he waited for volunteer assistants to round up offenders for him.

Civil justice was in no better case; the delays of procedure, the venality of the judges, and the inextricable chaos of the nondescript rules that governed litigation made justice totally impotent. There were seventy-two avenues of appeal from any judgment. As for obtaining execution of a judgment won after years of bitter struggle, it was hardly worth contemplating, so vast was the arsenal of delaying tactics.

THE LOTTERY

Games of chance have always been the great passion of the Romans. Diligently played in all periods, in all circles, and in an infinite variety of combinations, under Clement XII in the first third of the eighteenth century they had become a national institution in the shape of the great Roman lottery. The *lotto* at once penetrated the customs and, it has been said, "the blood of a people that lived chiefly on imagination and hope." The lottery was drawn every Saturday, and long before that day patricians and plebeians alike laid siege to the windows where the tickets were sold. The great preoccupation of Romans of both sexes was the quest for a good number and, above all, the composition of the best wager, the tern. One could bet on a random draw, on the first number drawn, or a combination, but the tern was the favorite. There were ninety numbers, of which, for a tern, the bettor could choose three; if they appeared in the same order among the five that were drawn each week, the return was more than five thousand to one. The choice of a tern was never left to chance: everyone had his own rule, and spent all his energies on cabalistic systems to make it work. Some relied on dreams, which were translatable into numbers through the use of the dream book. "Every occurrence, good or bad, lost its real meaning in its use as a sign." Anyone who had chanced to see a drowned man chose the number 88 without hesitation. The combination of 18–28–48 was virtually obligatory for a family in which a child had been stricken by fever. Those disappointed in love relied on 90; they used it as the basis for a tern whose other elements were the betrayer's age and the date of the rupture.

The crow of a rooster, the bark of a dog, an unaccustomed noise in the house or the street were viewed as hints from heaven; hunches were based even on murders, or the number of teeth still in the head of the man executed the day before. Once the tern had been decided on, the bettor made novenas for its success. People climbed the stairs of the Ara Coeli to seek the intercession of the *sacro bambino* (holy child). This was an infant Jesus carved out of olive wood, whose face had miraculously acquired colors. Sumptuously adorned, it was always on display at the Ara Coeli among the innumerable letters that were sent to it every day by the faithful throughout the world. It goes without saying that everyone sent word of his numbers to the madonna, who was regarded as the greatest power in heaven. In the familiar dealings that the Romans carried on with God and his saints, they found it natural to interest the heavenly host in their affairs. Sometimes priests were offered large sums if they would put the three numbers of a tern under the holy ciborium during the celebration of the mass. The day of the drawing brought the inevitable disappointments, of course, but hope was philosophically postponed for a week and the delinquent tern was never blamed. "My tern did not come out," an unlucky gambler would say, "but it doesn't matter, it's a good tern." Edmond About, observing the Roman gamblers a century later—there had been hardly any change in their attitudes—said: "I really think that, by looking numbers in the face, they, like Pythagoras, see all sorts of things in them that are not there."

THE *CICISBEO*

The center of the pleasures of carnival, the Corso was at all times of the year the elegant promenade of Rome. It was proper for a lady to be seen there every day in the company of her *cavaliere servente*. For every woman had one—the shopkeeper and the hairdresser just the same as the lady of highest station. "They would rather go hungry than be without a *cavaliere servente*," Father Chiari wrote. This fashion of the *cicisbeo*, which was to extend into the whole of Italy and find its greatest development in Venice, had been brought to Rome from Spain by the gentlemen who had come with the Spanish popes. It was to persist into the early years of the nineteenth century. It was so characteristic a part of the customs of the time that it should be dealt with in some detail.

Marriage in the nobility and the comfortable middle class was almost always a matter of practicality in which inclination had no part. Little time was needed, as a rule, for the spouses to become strangers to each other, especially since marital fidelity was a virtue that was, if not absolutely unknown, certainly out of fashion. In anticipation of the inevitable rupture, efforts began on the wedding day to find a suitable *cicisbeo* for the bride and to make certain that the two parties would be compatible.

Generally of the husband's age and class, he was often a relative or a penniless friend, occasionally too a man from whom some financial assistance was expected. This gallant fellow, who derived from the old days of chivalry, was supposed to wait upon his lady meticulously, to pay court to her at church, to entertain her in town, to offer her his arm everywhere, to whisper into her ear at parties (the derivation of *cicisbeo* is occasionally linked to *bisbiglio,* a whisper). The *cavaliere servente,* or gentleman in attendance, overwhelmed his partner with delicate attentions and little gallantries: he filled her life with pleasant manners, he gave her advice, he defended her against herself and others, he spared her worry, "he kept her in good humor," and he amused her. He accompanied her like her shadow, from her rising in the morning, at which he was often present, to her going to bed. It was only then that the husband resumed his rights, for the practice of twin beds had not yet been introduced into the manners of marriage.

Intimacies and half surrenders were the prerogatives of the *cicisbeo.* Did he ask for more than this amorous friendship? It was taken for granted in society that he did not. The *cavaliere servente* was the essence of the gallant suitor. No husband made a fool of himself by being jealous of him. And anyone who argued that "fire and straw cannot be put together without flames" succeeded only in acquiring the reputation of having a coarse mind, incapable of appreciating the charm of half-tones. De Brosses was one of those skeptics: he said that the *cicisbeo* married a woman "ten times as much as her husband."

The practice was not expressly condemned by the church. It was openly carried on in the best society. It was not unusual for the right to have a *cavaliere servente* to be stipulated in the marriage contract.

It goes without saying that the tolerance of the church did not extend to infringements of conjugal vows; a special sermon in Holy Week, delivered behind closed doors to a congregation of married women, warned the ladies against such a sin. Ladies in their very best went to hear this sermon in the church on Piazza Sciarra (it has since disappeared). When they came out, they were awaited by their coachmen and footmen, smiling at their contrite mien and determined to observe the effect of the moral lecture. It was invariable: the ladies' scruples were very soon assuaged: they were frightened for a week, and then they began again.

The fact remains, however, that the general indulgence engendered a dangerous relaxation of morals; love was viewed as a hazard that one could not control and that conferred special rights. A mother would say of her daughter: "She doesn't eat, she doesn't sleep: she's in love," just as if she were saying: "She has a cold." A great lady barred her door to all visitors, who were informed that she was *inamorata* (in love). Adultery flourished in the most flagrant manner: the most open promiscuity did no damage to a woman's reputation.

RELIGION

At bottom the Roman religion had once more become what it had often been for many before the Reformation: a convenient religion that was satisfied with the admission of sin (do as you like and then come and tell us about it). A good confession at Easter wiped out everything. When young Casanova arrived in Rome he remarked that there was no other Catholic city where a man was less restricted in matters of religion. The Romans, he said, "are like the workers in the tobacco shop who are allowed to take as much as they like without paying." There was no element of hypocrisy: they were profoundly religious, but they did not belong to that race of northern puritans who will not go for a walk on Sunday lest they offend God. Their genius led them to live comfortably. They were convinced that all the saints in paradise were busy watching over the smallest details of their lives. For the general affairs of life, they took this supernatural protection for granted, and in serious situations they expressly applied for it. Writing to the saints was a common practice: St. Louis of Gonzaga, who was supposed to be glad to endorse all petitions, received a great amount of mail. When there was serious illness, the rich made sure of having the actual presence of the *bambino* from Ara Coeli at their bedsides. Two priests brought the miraculous statue in its splendid carriage, and it remained in the house, at so much per day, until the patient was either cured or dead.

But the mass of popular devotion went to Mary, Mother of God, and it flowed out in a great flood of tenderness, *con amore*. The seventy-four churches—without counting the private chapels—that were dedicated to the Virgin were not enough to exhaust the fervor of the people. The madonna was everywhere, in palaces and shacks, at street corners, on the poorest houses as well as on the richest palaces. It was in courtyards, in hallways of houses, and even in stables and barns. It adorned the shops and the *trattorie*. "There was no trade, enterprise, or industry that did not protect itself with an image of Mary." Belief in her omnipotence and her infinite goodness was such that her aid was besought in every circumstance of life. She was begged to cure the ill and to further honorable plans, but also to satisfy dishonorable desires and the most preposterous caprices.

At the foot of each of the innumerable images of the madonna that Roman piety erected at corners and on houses there was a continuously burning light, whether *lampioncino* (lantern) or *moccolo* (little candle). This was the only illumination in the streets. When innovators called for *l'illuminazione pubblica* (public illumination) of the public streets, their proposals were branded sacrilegious: only the lights of the madonnas ought to shine in the Roman night. That was why Rome was to be one of the last cities in Europe to have public lighting. At the very least one should let the Romans have the benefit of this pious scruple: we shall have occasion to see that they clung to the darkness of their streets for other, less honorable reasons.

THE ELYSIAN FIELDS OF EUROPE

The Rome of the popes was a delightful abode. A traveler who had appreciated it at its true worth wrote: "One would have to be unlucky by nature not to find satisfaction in the thousand varieties of this city."

If literature had turned toward the road of decadence, music was experiencing a splendid revival: this art was to become for Rome in the eighteenth century what painting had been in the fifteenth. Every day had its quota of concerts in churches and palaces. In addition there were four opera houses for the delight of melomaniacs, who were extremely numerous and knowledgeable in all classes of society. Listening to music, besides, was not the only pleasure to be had in the theater. At once stock exchanges, chambers of commerce, and drawing rooms, they served chiefly as meeting places. The great ladies' boxes, always leased by the year, were annexes of their drawing rooms; their admirers went to visit them in the theater. Men discussed business or politics. Friends had supper together. In the body of the hall, the lower classes had picnics. As for the actors and singers, their profession was under no shadow; they were received in the most exacting society, even the *castrati,* "who charmed delicate ears and touched sensitive hearts." The ecclesiastical decencies barred female stage parts to everyone except these young boys "for whom diabolical tinkers had found a way of making their voices fluted." A French traveler observed: "Their hips, rumps, bosoms, and necks are rounded and plump. It would be very easy to take them for girls. It is said that at times, indeed, the country people carry this mistake to the end."

In spite of the relaxation of morals, Rome had indeed become the city of religion, that home of the Christian religion of which Paul V had dreamed. His successors had enhanced the splendor of the ritual and caused churches to spring up a few paces apart. Multiplied solely for the bedazzlement of the pilgrim, in the eighteenth century they took on "the air of resting places permanently established along the route of a procession." The city owes its modern fascination in large part to the work of the baroque.

This marvelous city filled with treasures of every kind attracted foreigners from every part of the world—famous personages, obscure travelers, artists completing their apprenticeships in Roman studios, ordinary citizens in love with beauty, priests flocking to the bosom of the Holy Mother. How many of them were to settle forever in that Rome to which they had gone only for a short visit! Entering it as sightseers, they recognized that they were in their own country, that they could not or would not leave it again. Such in particular was the case of a French nobleman, Séroux d'Agincourt, known to bibliophiles throughout the world as the compiler of the famous edition of La Fontaine's *Fables* called the *Fermiers Généraux* (Farmers General). Under Louis XV he had made a large fortune as a tax farmer. Enchanted by the Eternal City during a journey that he had intended to be a swift one, d'Agincourt never left it. He became a successful archeologist and died in 1814. It was he who had Poussin's bust placed in the Pantheon; he himself lies in the church of St. Louis of the French.

Many other great men were to establish themselves in Rome. No other city in Europe offered them a more entrancing residence or more refined modes of living. "You must recognize," de Brosses wrote, "that people are never to be believed when they tell you that they are going to leave Rome. Life is so good there, so pleasant, and there is so much to see and see again that one never finishes." Even those who merely passed through the city experienced a kind of dazzlement, and took home with them the fond nostalgia of which Goethe spoke. Mozart himself felt this, even though he was so small when he arrived in Rome in 1770 that he had to be lifted up so that he could kiss St. Peter's foot.

Great French artists have lived so long in Rome and left such masterly works there that they belong to the city's history quite as much as Michelangelo and Raphael. It was Pierre Legros, who carried on Bernini's work, who was to be proclaimed "the finest sculptor in Italy." Before him, Claude Lorrain lived sixty years in Rome and painted its ideal image. He is buried at St. Louis of the French. It was Poussin of whom it was said that no other painter had learned the lessons of Rome so completely as he. They worked side by side on the Pincio, in the neighborhood of Trinità dei Monti, and, having become true Romans, they were never able to tear themselves away from the panorama that they saw from their hill.

How many other great artists have gone to Rome and left their mark there, from Velásquez to Jean-Antoine Houdon, who was a student at the Academy of France when he carved the huge *St. Bruno* of St. Mary of the Angels. In those days Rome was the Mecca of all Europe's artists, whose work "completed its Italianization by becoming Roman." No synthesis of the diverse components of mankind's heritage was more inspiring then than that whose image was provided by Rome. In actuality, the Holy See had begun to lose force under the pressure of the ideas of the philosophers. The archeological vogue that sprang up was a poor mask for the inability to sire original works. A certain artistic stagnation was burdening a city that was beginning to lose its recognition of the value of its message. But the admirable envelope remained, with its unmatchable worth as a teacher and an example.

Rome had become, as it were, the Elysian Fields of Europe, and its old customs attracted as many visitors as did its old stones. It was the asylum of dethroned kings, the refuge of artists and poets. Everyone could grow comfortably there according to his own tastes. "Money did not weigh on life," Abel Bonnard wrote. The scholars browsed peacefully on the knowledge accumulated in the enormous libraries; the talkers, in the restaurants, perorated over their ices; the devout clustered round the saints; the ambitious moved forward with impatient slowness toward the hat or the miter that fascinated their desires; the Colosseum, draped in foliage, posed for the artists; one could love God because one was in Rome and women because one was in Italy. Foreigners grafted their national characters on the calm incuriosity of a people whom nothing surprised. One went to Rome to live "above the present." In the triumph of its light, Rome spread over everyone that warming good nature that is to be found in no other place in the world. The popes set the example. Never had they been so liberal, so familiar, so refined. They undertook no reforms, lest they disturb the good folk settled into their abuses. *"Fa dolce! sono pastore dei popoli,"* one of them said to the painter who was doing his portrait—"Go gently! I am the pastor of the peoples." The most charming of these popes was undoubtedly the incomparable Benedict XIV (1740–58): free in his speech, exemplary in his behavior, always kind and tolerant. It was to him that Voltaire dedicated his *Mahomet;* it was from him that Montesquieu obtained permission to "eat meat" during Lent. His indulgent philosophy is illustrated in an anecdote: "One day an excited monk presented himself and announced with certainty the unimaginable agonies that the birth of Antichrist was about to loose on the church. 'How old is this Antichrist?' the pope asked. The monk, without interrupting his lamentations, replied that he was three years old. 'Well,' the pope sighed with relief, 'in that case it is my successor's problem.'" This characteristic undoubtedly explains the growing weakness of the papacy that was to emerge soon afterward into broad daylight, but it accurately defines the tone of Roman life on the eve of the fatal tempests of the French Revolution.

PART SIX

THE FINAL CENTURY OF PAPAL ROME

1770-1870

CHAPTER 28

THE BEGINNING OF THE HOLY SEE'S PROBLEMS

THE NEO-CLASSIC REACTION

During the eighteenth century the Holy See had grown progressively weaker under the philosophical influences coming out of France. The rise of the new ideas had been opposed only with pitiful barriers by popes overly concerned with peaceful conciliation; those who had made some gesture of resistance, like Clement XIII, had not known how to choose their battlegrounds and had resorted to inadequate weapons. The suppression of the Jesuits, which the courts of Paris and Madrid had wrested from Clement XIV in 1773, marked the definitive abasement of the papacy. Discussing the matter in a letter to Frederick of Prussia, d'Alembert* drew this judicious lesson from it: "This treaty is like that between the wolf and the sheep, the first stipulation of which was that the sheep should surrender their dogs." Rome's history had not prepared it for an accommodation with materialism or with a spiritualism lacking in consistency. But the papacy's misfortunes had extinguished its vital flame. A deplorable inferiority complex was to cause it to submit without a move to the revolutionary spoliations. In the field of the arts, it was to follow,

---

* Jean Le Rond d'Alembert, eighteenth-century French author, philosopher, and mathematician, was one of the founders of the *Encyclopédie* and permanent secretary of the Académie Française.—Translator.

without conviction, trends that had originated elsewhere and that were to bring it only insipidity and banality.

The paradox of this time was the fact that the city again became the center of the artistic world in the framework of that modernity whose principles remained profoundly alien to it. It was in the last third of the eighteenth century that the neo-classic reaction began. Born of a displacement of the old humanism, it found its sustenance and its apparent justification in the recent excavation of Herculaneum and Pompeii, which revived ancient life. A marvelous discovery, a hundred times more astounding than those that brought on the Renaissance! It was to stimulate artists to take antiquity as the subject of their studies and the theme of their creations. But it was not in the excavations of Vesuvius that they would seek their inspiration: only the cabinet makers and the bronze workers would derive from there that Pompeian style that was to influence those of Louis XVI and the Empire. In the other arts, the discovery of Pompeii was to have no effect other than the initiation of a fashion that would spread quickly. And it was Rome, with its accumulated collections, its rows of columns, and its massive ruins, that would still be its inspiration, for all that each day brought new discoveries of the first rank. In 1765 the famous dove mosaic from Hadrian's villa was presented to the Capitoline Museum; in 1774 the Vatican collections were enriched by the statues of the nine muses and the seven sages of Greece brought to light by the searches at Tivoli. It was because of its archeological fortune that Rome was again to become the goddess of the world of the mind. The Brandenburger Winckelmann* summed up the tendencies of neo-classicism in a famous sentence: "The only way to become great and, if possible, inimitable is the study of the ancients." Now antiquity for everyone meant Rome, Rome alone, in which all ancient art, even that of Greece, was epitomized. Goethe, entering the Eternal City in 1786, found his adopted country there: "I am just beginning to live," he said. Fragonard, Hubert Robert, and perhaps David and Ingres too could have said the same thing.

It was in Rome that all the artists of Italy and Europe would gather to work, excited by an ardor quite as burning as that of the first humanists. They were to create there that intellectual ferment from which European classicism would arise. The new school—this new religion, it might be called—in which the prestige of ideas outranked that of the arts, had its theoreticians and its pontiffs; they met in the magnificent villa that

---

* Johann Joachim Winckelmann, an eighteenth-century archeologist, was the first to examine the monuments of antiquity with scientific method.—Translator.

Cardinal Albani had just built near Porta Pinciana and in which he lived surrounded by artists like one of Leo X's prelates, in a veritable museum of antiquities. It is in this Palazzo Albani that one can see the so-called Parnassus ceiling that Raphael Mengs painted in order to make it the manifesto of the neo-classic esthetic. His skillful and cold composition did indeed faithfully state the spirit of the new school, but it fixed its boundaries inexorably. This third renaissance was to be pale and frigid, incapable of creating a fruitful artistic life. Taking the opposite direction to the baroque, without succeeding in replacing it, it sank finally into imitation of the ancients and of the sixteenth-century masters.

More brilliant in its theoreticians than in its artists, the new school left us no very characteristic architectural works. All that deserve mention as typical are the façades of Sant'Andrea delle Fratte, San Pantaleone, and especially Palazzo Braschi, built about 1790 between Piazza Navone and Piazza S. Pantaleone on the site of the palace that Sangallo had erected for the Duchesse de la Trémouille, born an Orsini. (It is now the Roman Museum.) The whole is cold and without character. It offers a series of variations on ancient themes—the Torlonia boudoir, the Etruscan room, and a great inner staircase whose arches, richly decorated with arabesques, are supported by sixteen magnificent Oriental granite columns from Agrippina's gardens.

The reaction produced by the influence of the antique mode affected sculpture in particular. Scorning Houdon, who was, however, a complete master and who left to it as his apprentice work the *St. Bruno* in St. Mary of the Angels (he would speak, Clement XIV said, if he were not restrained by the rule of his order), Rome fell in love with a sculptor from Treviso, Antonio Canova. If posterity accepted the validity of judgments made by fashion, Italy would have in him the greatest sculptor in her history. He was carried to the heights even with his first work, the tomb of Clement XIV in the church of the Holy Apostles. With the second, the theatrical mausoleum of Clement XIII in St. Peter's, he was ranked above Michelangelo. His funeral monument for the Stuarts made him a kind of god of the arts.

For two centuries sculpture had offered the spectacle of the souls of painters expressing themselves with the chisel. With the new school sculpture became plastic again, and modeled shapes "without telling fables or composing dramas." It is enough to compare Canova's first works, pure of line, but rigid, with Bernini's tumultuous mausoleums to see that baroque had been repudiated. But the least that can be said of the art that replaced it is that it did not have baroque's movement, or its dash, or its trembling life, or its overflowing virility.

For his contemporaries Canova symbolized the purity of the antique. Today we feel above all the frigidity of this sculpture from which life seems to have fled. It is said that his masterpiece is the famous work in the Borgheses' casino in which the lady of the house is presented in a pose that is intended to be immodest and provocative. But one finds oneself moved to address to this beautiful undressed person no homage "other than the respectful." Canova's famous work, Abel Bonnard wrote, seems to have preserved Pauline Bonaparte's beauty for eternity in a glacier.

Every epoch expresses itself in its art. The flowering of the baroque and the magic of its effects represented the proud triumph of religion and the papacy. The chills of the neo-classic mark Rome's artistic exhaustion in the period when new ideas were creating tragic difficulties for the Holy See. It is significant that the most moving of Canova's marbles, the statue of Pius VI kneeling before St. Peter's Confession, should be that of the pontiff whom the Revolution was to drive out of Rome.

THE ROMAN REPUBLIC

When the first revolutionary storms broke out over France, Rome paid no attention to them. From the highest clergy to the lowest plebeians, the public regarded the leaders' aspirations as the absurdities of visionaries. In other words, no one feared lest they spread. Much more attention was given to the trial of Cagliostro,* who had thwarted justice in Paris only to be clapped into the irons of the Inquisition. The smell of sulphur that enveloped the notorious adventurer was the prime topic of every conversation; there was no end to speculation on his traffic with the devil. There was also much talk of the great undertaking of Pius VI for the draining of the Pontine marshes, the remodeling of the sacristy of St. Peter's, and the construction of Palazzo Braschi, which was to perpetuate his family's name. The Revolution might break out in France, the peasants might burn the *châteaux,* the Parisians might take the Bastille, the Convention might try Louis XVI—all those things were nothing but the eccentricities of a nation that had momentarily lost its way.

The tragedy was that, having got rid of the nobility and the king, this

* Giuseppe Balsamo, known as Alessandro Conte di Cagliostro, was an Italian physician and charlatan, freemason, and expert in the occult.—Translator.

Revolution found the priests in its path, struck them hard, and inflicted wounds on the church that were felt not only by the Holy See but by the whole Roman population. The people were suddenly inflamed by shouts of "Long live the pope!" and "Long live religion!" A deplorable incident on January 13, 1793, loosed the wrath of the Convention. Two of its emissaries, Basseville and Flotte, sent to Rome to present demands to the pope, adopted provocative attitudes; they strutted about wearing the republican cockade in their hats; they had the portraits of cardinals and popes removed from the reception rooms of the Academy of France and replaced with those of the most savage republicans in history. "The eyes of the *Trasteverini* were shot with blood." On January 13, riding with their wives on the Corso in a carriage decorated with the tricolor, the two French representatives were attacked with "a deluge of stones." Fleeing with their wives into the house of a banker, Moulte, behind Palazzo Chigi, they were followed by the mob, and Basseville was slashed with a razor by a barber; he died the next day. The event was celebrated in Rome as a glorious episode; there was no poet who did not produce his ode or his sonnet on it, no musician who did not make it into a cantata. An inscription on the Corso, not far from the scene of the murder, gave thanks for it to the madonna.

The Convention ordered the generals of its army of Italy to exact a stunning vengeance. For three years this threat remained platonic, the requirements of the military situation having created obstacles to its execution. During this interval the Romans felt free to multiply their insults to the government of France, while the pope showed the most resolute antagonism to it, castigating it for the execution of Louis XVI and giving asylum to the royal princesses and the most active figures in the emigration. When General Bonaparte took command of the French armies, their advance became lightning-like; they threatened Rome, and Pope Pius VI had no choice but to yield to force, buying peace with the most enormous sacrifices in the treaty of Tolentino, which cost the Holy See twenty-one million crowns and a huge quantity of pictures and objects of art. In order to meet the terms of this treaty, the Roman sanctuaries were stripped: the gold of the chalices and the statues of the museums, "the imperishable proofs of old Italian glory," crossed the Alps.

The peace concluded at Tolentino in 1796, however, was only a false peace. Republican France wanted to overthrow the government of the pope. In his proclamation of Milan, Bonaparte had very explicitly stated his aims; the French, friends of all peoples and more especially of the descendants of Brutus and Scipio, were going to restore the Capitol, give it back, with honor, the statues of the heroes who had made it famous, and awaken the Roman people, debased by many centuries of slavery. The Directory itself explained the strategy of conquest: "It will be your task," it wrote to its representative in Rome, "to assist the good intentions of those who believe that it is time to put an end to the reign of the popes." There could be no clearer expression of orders to organize a revolt. But these instructions had no effect: only a few depraved characters were willing to play at revolution, either out of resentment or in hope of gain.

French blood had to flow once more on the stones of *la vecchia Roma* to bring matters to a head. In December, 1797, an insurrection broke out among the papal troops. Joseph Bonaparte, the Directory's ambassador, attempted to intervene, and one of his young generals, Duphot, fell with a bullet in his heart on the steps of Palazzo Corsini. Berthier, who commanded the army of Italy, was ordered to march on Rome and avenge the affront to French honor. On February 10, 1798, he occupied Monte Mario and Castello Sant'Angelo and deposed Pope Pius VI, who, removed by force to Valence, was to die there in the following year.

If the French press of the time was to be believed, Rome was inflamed with a revolutionary delirium; the people supposedly planted the liberty pole in the Forum, topped with the Phrygian cap, and the seven hills re-echoed with the cry of freedom "that they had not heard for four centuries." It was a beautiful thing, the *Moniteur* said in Paris, to see a great people forever quench the lightnings of the Vatican with the same hands that re-erected the altars of Freedom on the Capitoline (14 Nivôse, Year VII).*

Reality did not support these paeans of victory. The popular movement "organized" by the French, on Berthier's own admission, was so far from unanimous and spontaneous that it was difficult to find petitioners for the republic. The French general at once granted the freedom of Rome to the handful of provocateurs who were alone in requesting it. Thereupon Berthier made his solemn entrance to the sound of trumpets. At the Capitol, which he ascended as a conqueror, and before the gilded horse of Marcus Aurelius, decorated with the French colors, he accepted a wreath of laurel and delivered one of those bombastic speeches of which the French Revolution had the secret.

Then Rome experienced all the buffoonery of freedom "with all the

* This date in the French Revolution's calendar corresponds to January 3, 1799.— Translator.

stale *bric-à-brac* of the civic celebrations of the Year II"; altars to the fatherland, liberty trees, republican processions—nothing was omitted. Beribboned busts of Cato, Mucius Scaevola, and Brutus presided at every observance. Romans took part in these trumperies only as mockers or hecklers: the actors were the French themselves, or the "friends of France," Lombards and Neapolitans hired for the part.

The pope having been exiled and the cardinals having been scattered, the French, as the masters of Rome, established a new state on the ruins of the pontifical power. They did not strain their imaginations: the Roman constitution of 1789 was only a pallid copy of the Directory's. Rome had consuls, tribunes, and senators in togas who spent their time in quarrels as despicable as their wives' squabbles over the bedrooms of the Quirinal and the Vatican. Adopting the example of their colleagues in Paris, they fomented plots against one another without interrupting their incessant and pitiful debauches "of wine and women." Under the cover of empty institutions, French generals and commissars exercised a collective dicta-torship that presented every characteristic of anarchy. There were five commanders in chief, always at odds; three or four appointees battled for every post of any importance in a torrent of insults. Every one of the dignitaries of this singular republic was surrounded "by an escort of courtiers, whores, Jews, and men who would do anything, swept up from the whole of Italy." The only industry of this flock of crows was the pillage of Rome, to which the Jacobin government abandoned itself with a hideous shamelessness, oscillating among spoliative laws, semi-official sei-zures, and outright confiscations, which were the preferred procedure. "Men cloaked with public office enter the richest houses and, with no further formality, carry off everything that they find." Who said this? French officers who met in the Pantheon to condemn the brigandage of their leaders.

The Directory itself did not overlook its share of the loot. One of its agents, the former oratorian father, Daunou, was ordered to ship to Paris five hundred cases filled with treasures stolen from churches and museums. He was asked even to send Trajan's column, but he refused, alleging the costly nature of such an undertaking. Palaces, churches, sacristies, middle-class houses were the targets of systematic depredations. Paul-Louis Courier, who served in the army of Italy, has left us a picture of Rome bled white by the exactions of his brothers in arms. But even his inventory of the tragedies of Rome does not mention what was the cruelest of all to its inhabitants: the scorn of their most respectable traditions, the persecution of their religion, the blasphemies uttered from every platform. The Romans showed great charity in giving this odious system the name of "republic to laugh at." It is certainly no page of glory in our Revolution. Napoleon was to find it very difficult to wipe out its memory, ten years later, through the austere probity of his agents. The Roman Republic was to collapse when the French, defeated in northern Italy, abandoned Rome to Neapolitan occupation, which unleashed the appalling reaction whose climate is so well represented in the story of Tosca.

THE FIRST EXCAVATIONS IN THE FORUM

As successor to Pope Pius VI, dead in exile "with the dignity of a bishop and the resignation of a saint," the conclave of Venice chose the bishop of Imola, who took the name of Pius VII. His entrance into Rome was triumphal, as much because it renewed the true papal tradition, so tragically interrupted two years earlier, as because it put an end to the Neapolitan occupation, which had been almost unbearable to the Romans.

At the same time, law and order were restored to France under Bonaparte's powerful dictatorship. Having conquered Italy in one day at Marengo, the first consul wanted, in his own phrase, to "live well" with the pope, whose backing was indispensable to his plans for monarchical restoration. Resolved to restore the altars in France and the Holy See in Rome, Bonaparte proposed a concordat, and, in his typically military briskness, gave the pope three days to accept its provisions. This showed little knowledge of papal diplomacy's habits: the seventeen articles of the concordat were debated for a year. Putting aside the Curia's resistances in order to save the ship of St. Peter's, in 1801 Pius VII signed the religious treaty, for which he was bitterly reproached by the Roman clergy. Under the protection of the concordat, the pope could restore order to his government and the administration of his capital.

The Republic had instituted fanatical economic planning and strict regulation of farm prices, the sharpest result of which was to discourage production and induce famine. The pope replaced this paralyzing system with that of the freedom that makes possible the growth of agriculture and commerce. Work having been stimulated and prosperity having been restored, Rome enjoyed "a sweet peace" that was enhanced by a revival of the fine arts. Scattered by the Revolution, painters and sculptors returned to their studios, while the musical tradition of the eighteenth century came back to life.

It was in this period that the first attempts were made to clear the Forum. Thrown back into its original condition and once more become a cattle market, the seat of Rome's ancient grandeur was nothing but a square choked with wild grass and surrounded by mediocre churches and ruined monuments more than half buried. A few columns and broken arches barely thrust above the ground. The whole of antiquity lay buried under thirty feet of rubble. Poussin, Lorrain, and Piranesi have left us pictures of that melancholy wasteland, eminently suited, as Gaston Boissier wrote, "for the visits of men who contemplate the frailty of human grandeurs and the vicissitudes of fate." The triumphal arches of Constantine and Septimius Severus were the first beneficiaries of the efforts of Pius VII. They were so well entombed that pedestrians could walk on top of sculptures that are now high above the ground: they were isolated from the rubble that surrounded them, and this endeavor led to the discovery of the Umbilicus Romae, a cylindrical monument dating from the third century that represented the center of the city and the Empire. Excavations on the site of the Basilica Julia brought to light the marble paving and the stairs that led to Via Sacra. The walls of the Colosseum were shored up by an overbold buttress. But political events, which were going to send Pius VII out of Rome, interrupted these labors before they could be really profitable to a study of the topography of the Forum.

CHAPTER 29

ROME AND NAPOLEON I

THE FRENCH OCCUPATION

In the years that followed the concordat, Napoleon constantly expressed his respect for the papacy. Asked by one of his ambassadors how Pius VII should be dealt with, he replied: "As if he had 200,000 men." The pope, for his part, crossed the Alps to preside at the coronation of the new Caesar. After the proclamation of the Empire, Napoleon's statements were no longer reassuring: had he not spoken of making the archbishopric of Paris a new Vatican? This threat had not been elaborated, but it had revived the hatred for revolutionary France that had never been altogether extinguished in the Sacred College. Rome, which until then had been neutral territory, became the hotbed of plots against the emperor: it was in Rome that Mme. de Staël conspired in comfort with Kotzebue. And she was not alone.

Napoleon's ambitions increased in direct proportion to the number of crowns that fell at his feet. The master of northern Italy, he could no longer tolerate the interruption of his communications by the Roman state. He asserted that the pope was no longer worthy to protect what Charlemagne had given to his predecessors for the good of Christendom "because he allowed it to benefit the English heretics." Ordered to restrict himself to the nonspeaking part of an imperial prefect, Pius VII retorted sharply that Napoleon had been crowned and consecrated as emperor of

390

the French and not of Rome. This kind of polemic is rarely beneficial to the weaker of the parties. On February 2, 1808, a French force of six thousand men commanded by General Miollis forced its way into Rome through Porta del Popolo and occupied the city and Castello Sant'Angelo.

The military occupation was the first symptom of annexation. The emperor had planned this move in order that the transition from one rule to another could be accomplished "without being noticed." It was a futile maneuver. It was very quickly remarked that, of the two authorities that shared Rome, "the one more obeyed was the power that had neither bayonets nor cannon." The dissolved pontifical police force was clandestinely reorganized: monks ran through the city carrying orders from the Quirinal. The pope dictated and organized the resistance. His sufferings angered consciences; the pious monk, Louis Madelin said, "now held the whole of Rome in his feeble hands as no pope had ever held it." This view was entirely corroborated by General Lefebvre, who wrote: "The pope's authority has never been more absolute than it is today." In fact, a single word from him prevented the establishment of the civil guard that the military authority was attempting to activate. The French were powerless to stop the flood of posters and placards that covered the city with the vilest insults against the "impious usurpers." They began even to fear a popular rising, which would have made their position highly critical. When Miollis wanted to have the papal secretary of state arrested, his energetic emissary, Paca, was brutally thrown out by the pope in person. Driven into a series of retreats by Pius VII's forcefulness, Miollis tried in vain to recoover some prestige through his efforts at "fusion," which turned against him. His celebration of the emperor's birthday on August 15, 1808, was a total failure.

The carnival of 1809 afforded the opportunity for a new test of strength. The pope expressly forbade Romans to take any part in the traditional amusements. We know how important a place was held in their lives by parades, masquerades, the flower and candy battles in the Corso: it was obvious that their abstention would demonstrate the authority of the head of the church. Miollis wanted to compel the people to entertainment. He had platforms built under the supervision of his police, and arenas sanded by his dragoons; he forced the costume sellers to open their shops; he requisitioned horses for the carrousel; he ordered buildings decorated. It was all fruitless. The shops remained closed, the Corso was empty, and behind their windows the Romans snickered at the spectacle of the French dragoons maintaining order in a desert. Only the Borgheses attended a reception given by Miollis and thronged with French officers: "Since the old princess was now seventy-five, it was a pitiful affair for dashing captains who had been dreaming of splendid balls and voluptuous seductions." Three cruel epigrams of Pasquino underlined the lesson of this humiliating setback. One said: *"L'orso e non l'uomo balla col bastone* (Bears, not men, dance to a stick)"; another declared that tears but not laughter can be compelled by force *("si piange ma non si canta per forza")*; the third said: *"Vi è stata la corsa e chi ha vinto? Il papa* (There was a race and who won? The pope)." The pope won another race a short time later, on his birthday, March 21. To the stunned shock of the occupier, all Rome was illuminated in honor of the Holy Father.

Since the French army's position was deteriorating from day to day, the emperor resolved to dispossess the pope from the government of his states. On June 10, 1809, the cannon of Castello Sant'Angelo announced to the Eternal City that it was no longer the capital of the universe but only an imperial citadel. Pope Pius VII fired back at once with a bull of excommunication "against the author and the executors of innovations that afflict the church." He had to wait only a few days more for the inevitable violence that he anticipated. On July 6 he was seized by General Radet and forced into exile after having given the city of Rome his solemn blessing from the terrace of the Quirinal.

THE CONSULTA

The rule of the Consulta was the first step in Rome's rise to the function that was Napoleon's secret plan for the city: capital of an empire. A Latin, he turned instinctively to the metropolis of the Latin races: Roman memories were virtually the substance of his spirit. He wished to be the successor of Augustus and Charlemagne. In the delirium of his death agony, he was to envisage himself entering the Eternal City in triumph. His imperial intentions, however, were accompanied by a touching sentimental attachment. More than Paris, Rome was the city beloved of Napoleon. It was, as they say, in his blood. It might be put this way: Napoleon loved Rome as a bride desired for years; he was a violent and clumsy lover to her, a jealous lover, but a genuine and generous lover. For all that, he was still a disappointed lover. He was never to enter his mystic capital, because he refused to do so until he could appear as its accepted and unchallenged master without having to kneel on the block of porphyry where popes placed crowns on emperors' foreheads. The snows of Russia "were to cover with their shroud the sun-drenched dream of the Latin emperor." But, before that disaster, he was to exhaust his thirst for Rome in good works of all kinds without succeeding in his seduction. Disappointed by his failures, he was to turn too late to the technique of force, with no result other than that of angering, without overcoming, a people that he sincerely loved, but that he loved too much and badly, and of whom, in the bargain, he always had a false conception.

Before its official annexation to the Empire, Rome was given first a special status, and was governed by an Extraordinary Council—the Consulta—composed of five French officials and headed by Miollis. The emperor had given this Consulta the task of abolishing government by priests and preparing the Roman states to receive the imperial constitution on January 1, 1810. In fact the Consulta survived a year longer than had been anticipated; but, hampered in its work and divided within itself, it did not afford much progress to the "Gallicization" that was the thankless goal of its mission. It was principally an enterprise of liquidation and destruction, often without thought. Immediately after the *coup d'état* it ran into an unforeseen obstacle. Before going into exile, the pope had forbidden his subjects to accept or retain employment under the usurping government, and the little sheet that contained this watchword enjoyed more credit among the Romans than the huge placard that detailed the dazzling promises of the French emperor. From the cardinals who directed courts and departments to the humblest of messengers, everyone at once resigned his post. The street cleaners turned in their brooms "with the dignity of Roman senators." These gaps could be filled only by vagabonds; the French had to hire thieves and make policemen of them. The government of the city, turned over to incompetent servants and often to very dishonest ones, fell into a dangerous disorganization.

The Consulta launched an attack on the Inquisition in order to destroy it, and it was extremely amazed to find in the target premises none of the torture chambers and tools that it was reputed to use so consistently and so cruelly. Napoleon had simplistic notions of Rome; he believed that the Roman population was oppressed by Torquemada's legions, and he had pledged himself to its liberation with the cry of "Down with the stake!" Now it was a long time since anyone had been burned at the stake. The emperor committed another error of the same character when he ordered the opening of the ghetto, which he imagined as the prison of an oppressed race. But the Jews had never been mistreated in Rome,* and they had never encountered the unjustified hostility of the Romans until precisely that moment when the French took it upon themselves to liberate them from their supposed slavery. Another great mistake was transferring the Vatican's secret archives to Paris: it was expected that they would furnish proofs of the misdeeds of the papacy, but they revealed only the record of its good works.

In order to flood what to Napoleon was that "cavern of obscurantism" called Rome with the illumination of France, the Consulta hastily adopted a mass of measures dealing with all public and private activities. These ranged from the substitution of the Napoleonic Code for all the old laws to the reform of hospitals and the reorganization of the Academies. Everything was changed: the postal service, the courts, the prisons, the customs regulations. Rome was equipped with fire pumps. Other ordinances strove at the same time to codify morals; there was even an effort to eliminate the *lotto*. While some of these reforms might seem futile or absurd, others were obviously valuable. But all aroused the same contemptuous resistance in the Roman people. They were not dazzled by the French style; it was repugnant to freedom and it rejected the benefits of civilization. The installation of street lighting was regarded as a profanation. Until this time, as we know, the little votive lights of the madonnas were all the illumination that the streets possessed. Carriages were driven without lanterns, and, if some fearful burgher carried one in especially dark areas, he was supposed to shield it whenever he approached anyone; the cry of *"Volti la lanterna* (turn away your light)" was common and what it meant was: "Don't interfere with what I am doing." To de Brosses these lovers of darkness were only "shameful prelates who preferred secrecy for the performance of their charities to their neighbors." This is an indication of his prejudiced irreverence. In reality the state of mind and the habits of the time were such that Romans held the inviolability of their darkness to be as sacred as the inviolability of their homes. Any invasion of this nocturnal privacy assumed in their minds the aspect of a police investigation, and that was odious even to those who had no

---

* But see the author's description of the "Jews' races" in the carnivals, p. 277, and of the pope's re-imposition of the ghetto in the nineteenth century, p. 410.— Translator.

thought of making the best of the conveniences of darkness. A law of nature plunged the earth into obscurity daily. Any profane illumination that disturbed the night was considered sacrilege.

All the French reforms encountered resistances of the same type. It really seemed that, even more than Napoleon's agents had thought, the Romans had been "debased by the ecclesiastical government." The emperor was not gentle in letting the Consulta know of his dissatisfaction. In order to return to the master's good graces, it increased its demands on the Roman people, doing everything possible to overcome the defiance. But every time it ran up against the immobility of the crowd, at all other times so warm. Even the lavish celebration of December 2, 1809, left the Romans like ice. Yet this was a great date, a double anniversary: the coronation and the battle of Austerlitz. In 1809, when the Empire was at its peak, the celebration had a special splendor everywhere. Everywhere except in Rome, although the government spent itself in its efforts to organize balls, parties, illuminations, and fireworks.

ANNEXATION

Eager to "finish this business of Rome," Napoleon decided at the beginning of 1810 to relieve the Consulta of its mandate and to make the Roman state an integral part of the Empire. Rome then became the chief city of one of the 130 French departments. In fact, it was proclaimed the second city of the Empire; a high dignitary would hold imperial court there, and the emperor's eldest son would have the title of king of Rome. French emperors would be crowned in St. Peter's within the first ten years of their accession. This new status accorded to their city was not to change the Romans' attitude, which was always dictated by the pope's stubborn resistance in his exile.

And yet the men whom the emperor's confidence had established in Rome had good intentions. They set up a government that might in a way be called Athenian. General Miollis, who had headed the Consulta, remained as the emperor's representative to the Senatus Consultus of 1810, and therefore as the leading figure in Rome. He had fixed his residence and his court in the former Villa Aldobrandini, now known as Villa Miollis al Quirinale, which he had decorated with four hundred paintings by master artists, chosen with considerable taste: Caravaggio and Tintoretto were the neighbors of Holbein, Teniers, and Philippe de Champaigne* in this surprising gallery.

As a matter of fact, Miollis was a lover of the arts and, in his own way, himself an artist; an admirer of Virgil, he was not afraid to attempt poetry. The versifiers who were so numerous in Rome at that time regarded him as their colleague. He was so much their friend that the villa became the center of the city's intellectual life. The Academy of the Arches held its meetings there; it was open to French officials who wished to submit their own lyric or light compositions. These minds nourished on classic eloquence and literature were intoxicated by the air of Rome, whose charm is so difficult to elude. St. Luke's Academy and the Lincei, erected by Miollis as conservatories, stimulated an outburst of a whole literature that was at once adolescent and senile and did little to enrich Roman letters. Miollis was a Maecenas of the most generous kind to all the arts: he fostered even music, to which his master, Napoleon, nursed a stubborn aversion. Sculptors and painters were given very important commissions: their work derived from the period that considered Canova a god. In matters of painting, Miollis had for a time as his adviser "Monsieur Ingres." The painter had set up his studio in the church of Trinità dei Monti, which the French revolutionaries had reduced to a hovel. A self-portrait shows him, almost unnoticeable in front of one of his huge canvases, his violin within easy reach. For now and then he interrupted his work "to put a bit of vinegar into the echoes of Trinità dei Monti."

A tremendous favorite with women, though he was more than fifty years old, took little care of his person, and wore a most disfiguring scar, Miollis was much better at charming than at forcing, and he always tried to soften the imperial rigors. In these efforts he was aided by the happy collaboration of the prefect of Rome, Comte de Tournon. Tournon was a gentleman by character as well as by birth, young (thirty), enthusiastic, industrious, sanguine. This charming man with the elegant manners was to win the sympathies of the Roman nobility; for a time it seemed that his supple hand might caress the clergy into docility and his cordiality might melt the hostility of the people. What brought Tournon this passing prestige was his warm and genuine love for Rome. Every page of his

* David Teniers the Elder and the Younger (father and son) were Flemish painters of the sixteenth and seventeenth centuries; de Champaigne, a seventeenth-century Fleming, became one of the outstanding French classic painters.—Translator.

letters to his family told of his wonder, and his dream "of being fortunate enough to sow a few seeds of prosperity in this poetic soil." Everything in Rome charmed him and touched him: "its beautiful language, worthy to be sung by sirens," its gentle air, its people "slandered all over Europe."

Such sentiments moved the Romans all the more because the young prefect displayed the most delightful zeal in translating them into concrete actions. Unfortunately it happened that imperial policy took an aggressive turn that aroused opposition in Rome, without, it is true, much violence, but that resistance was consistently to harden. Rome would not accept conscription, or the closing of the convents, or the proscription of the priests, or the Empire's fiscal exactions. Innumerable difficulties were to be created by these measures. Tournon was to exert every effort to remain aloof from political agitation in order to devote himself to the administration of "his city." Undoubtedly he, like Miollis, would have succeeded in winning over a number of the resistants if the brutal policy imposed by Paris had not periodically wiped out the meager gains achieved with infinite effort by these two well-intentioned men. Nevertheless their generous actions have left the real pride of a French contribution to the beauty of Rome. Their names are associated in the closest and, one might say, the most glorious fashion with the labors through which Napoleon I sought to leave his mark forever on a land that had seen the procession of all human grandeurs.

THE RESURRECTION OF THE FORUM

The resurrection of the Forum filled Napoleon with a remarkable exaltation. His solemn promise to complete the work was inscribed in the decree that united Rome to France: "The remains of the monuments erected by the Romans shall be maintained and preserved at the expense of our Treasury." The miserable state of the Forum transformed into a cow pasture particularly preoccupied the emperor: in "this sacrilegious profanation" he saw the symbol of the insolvency of the papacy, "the negligent mistress of the heritage of Caesar."

But Napoleon was far from an accurate assessment of the magnitude and the difficulties of the program that he had set himself. In the first year of his Roman rule, work had to be restricted to the excavation of the temple of Fortuna Virile and the charming round temple ascribed to Vesta, both of which were on the bank of the Tiber and had been sealed in by later constructions. The first stroke of a pick near the temple of Antoninus and Faustina aroused the neighbors' protests; the shifting of earth, they said, would bring on "miasmas that would infect them with the fevers"; in addition, they would suffer broken bones in the abysses dug at their doors. That was all that was needed to stop the work. It was then that the emperor decided to take a hand: on October 6, 1810, he assigned Tournon to supervise the labor and gave him substantial funds for it. Work was resumed at once and there was no further interruption in its industrious progress.

The first efforts were directed at the Tabularium, which was hidden by a huge mound of earth except for the capitals of three columns bearing an entablature on which it was barely possible to read eight letters of the word *restituerunt* (they will restore). Archeologists thought these were the ruins of the temple of Jupiter the Thunderer: they were the temple of Vespasian. The columns could be freed only at the cost of tremendous toil; since they were now supported only by the mass of earth round them, the substructures had first to be restored, at a depth of almost fifty feet, after the removal of the capitals, which, it was feared, might fall. In July, 1811, the columns of Vespasian's temple reared their majestic profiles against the sky and the venerable stones of the Tabularium emerged. This bold task was carried out by the architect Valadier, whom we have mentioned earlier and shall have frequent occasion to mention again. At the same time it became possible to identify the pillar of Phocas, which rose in solitude in the middle of the Forum and the origin of which had provoked bitter disputes among the archeologists. A few strokes with a pick were enough to resolve the mystery. A rather humiliating episode, which we have already described, and which gave the Romans an occasion for gloating.

Excavations were undertaken at the same time at various points in the Forum. The modern buildings that encumbered the ruins had been purchased from their owners, and deep trenches were dug at the bases of the monuments. The soil thus removed was transferred to distant spots, a precaution that had thus far been overlooked and for lack of which the existing cuts had soon been made useless by landslides. Care was also taken to reassure the neighbors that they were being protected against "the fevers" that frightened them more than ever.

The French administration wanted to "discover the old level of the Forum and finally uncover the bases of the monuments." This followed the ideas of Raphael, who, in a very curious letter addressed to Leo X, had proposed this same general excavation. In his *Etudes statistiques sur Rome* (*Statistical Studies on Rome*), Tournon expressly asserts that his staff had been inspired by this project. In 1811 the three columns of the temple of Castor and Pollux, cleared down to the base of the wall, emerged in their elegant purity. Excavation thus far, after having brought to light the great granite basin that is now at the foot of the Quirinal obelisk, had reached the stones of Via Sacra. This was a solemn moment, hailed in dithyrambs by the *Journal du Capitole* and the Parisian press. It was an excellent opportunity to liken Napoleon to the great conquerors of history and to pay tribute to him "for having restored to the light of Rome the road that they had trodden."

The clearing of Constantine's basilica (which at the time was believed to be the temple of Concord) was extremely difficult. The pile of rubble rose as high as the beginnings of the three great arches, and what open space there was had been walled in for use as a barn. After a year of work, the huge naves appeared in all their majesty, in one of the most impressive visions of ancient Rome. "This ruin has become an admirable thing," Tournon wrote on September 12, 1812.

The top of the Forum was crowded with nondescript structures that joined the arch of Titus to the church of Santa Francesca Romana, leaving only a passage intended to spare the Jews the humiliation of walking through the monument that celebrated the destruction of Jerusalem. Once all these buildings had been demolished, the arch of Titus stood clear, but nothing was done to restore it. Pius VII was to assume this task when he returned from his exile. The steps and the portico of the temple of Venus and Rome were also cleared. For a moment there was talk of sacrificing Santa Francesca Romana, which in the end was left untouched, not nearly so much because of the veneration in which it was held as because it contained the tomb of a French pope, Gregory XI, who had brought the Holy See back to Rome from Avignon.

THE COLOSSEUM / THE BATHS OF TITUS / TRAJAN'S FORUM

The work of reinforcement in the Colosseum that Pius VII had had to abandon was resumed, and at the same time its heavinesses and awkwardnesses were corrected. The inside of the monument had been disfigured, and the arena had been choked with the rubbish accumulated for centuries; the galleries were blocked, the steps were covered under several yards of dirt. Almost everything was cleaned, to the great distaste of lovers of the picturesque, who mourned the disordered vegetation that had invaded the whole structure.

Excavations were resumed in the baths of Titus and the ruins of Nero's House of Gold on which they had been built. It was there that in the sixteenth century the *Laocoön* group had been unearthed, and there was again hope of some fabulous discovery. The best that could be found was a mediocre statue of Pluto. In his feverish insistence on finding the traces of "his august predecessors," Napoleon had ordered excavations in the gardens of the Palatine, which were slumbering beneath the roses of the Farnese garden. The shortness of his reign thwarted that ambitious design.

Trajan's column was of very special interest to the French, who had copied it already in the design of the Grand Army column. Pius VI had excavated it in a shabby manner. Napoleon wanted the whole forum that had surrounded it to be cleared; the site was now occupied by convents and the two churches of the Bakers' Guild, Holy Name of Mary and Our Lady of Loreto. The fate of the convents was promptly settled by confiscation, but, when work was about to begin on the churches, it was found that Holy Name of Mary had been built by the royal house of Austria. Since its destruction might offend the royal court in Vienna, the emperor's great project was revised downward. Basilica Ulpia, however, was entirely cleared. This was a large basilica with five naves, supported by four rows of columns running between two opposing apses and falling back at a right angle on another row of columns. Altogether there were 108 interior columns. Napoleon's excavations made it possible to identify their emplacements and to reproduce the exact plan of the structure on the site. This remarkable undertaking was unfortunately flawed by an error that was revealed by later excavations. Tournon's archeologists believed that all the columns in the basilica were of the same character and the same size. On this premise, they had built identical bases on which they had set columns without regard to where they had originated. It is now known that the corner columns were of greater diameter and that only those of the lateral naves were of onion marble. The columns of the central nave, higher and thicker, were of granite from the island of Elba, which Napoleon's assistants had deemed unsuitable for so splendid a basilica. This error—perfectly pardonable when one thinks of the uncertainties that still hovered over the monuments of antiquity—should not prevent us from rendering to the scholars of those days the tribute of admiration that their work deserves, without at the same time exaggerating the scientific importance of their labors. The Napoleonic excavations were only a succession of soundings, and they posed more problems than they solved. The knowledge that was gained from them was so incomplete that it left an unlimited field for the archeologists' disputes. The whole nineteenth century was to be devoted to dissipating this confusion. But the way had been opened to the great movement that was to give back to the Eternal City its distant history.

"THE EMBELLISHMENTS OF ROME"

The excavations had provided full-time employment for twelve hundred workers for four years. At the same time the French administration had busied itself with what a decree had called "the embellishments of Rome." It was Napoleon's intention to eclipse Augustus, Julius II, Leo X, and Sixtus V. It is our good fortune, however, that the emperor's architectural pruritus was contained by the twin lacks of money and time. One shudders at the thought of what Rome would have become with the execution of the uncountable projects that filled the offices of Miollis and Tournon.

The largest was the construction of the gigantic palace—or, rather, the gigantic collection of palaces—in which the emperor would establish himself when he had accomplished "the great historic deed"—that is, when he had been crowned in St. Peter's and received in triumph at the Capitol. Rome as the capital of his empire would have given the most powerful sovereign in the universe, in the most glorious of backgrounds, a residence more fabulous than Nero's. Taking the Capitol as its center, the imperial palace would have extended from Piazza Colonna to the Colosseum: Palazzo Venezia was to have been its administrative department, the church of the Ara Coeli its chapel, and the Forum its inner courtyard.

This project having quickly been discarded as too costly, the planners fell back on the Quirinal: the old pontifical dwelling was to be enlarged to an absurd degree, including the Consulta and the Datary, all the monasteries that crowded the neighborhood, and even as far as the Barberini gardens. In anticipation of the realization of a plan so grandiose that it was called "capable of reviving in all Italy the enthusiasm of the age of Augustus," work was limited to a few modifications and to the decoration of the palace walls with academic paintings of wholly sycophantic inspiration. This debauch of official art entitles one to measure one's regret that the miraculous designs for the imperial palace could not be realized. One may also reflect that it is preferable that the basilica of St. Peter's escaped the transformations that French architects dreamed of making in it; they did not recoil at the idea of rectifying the work of Bramante and Michelangelo, correcting the audacities of Bernini, demolishing Maderna's façade. There was considerable presumptuousness in this; fortunately, all that was actually done was minuscule repairs that have left no sign.

When they departed, the French were to leave a vast accumulation of projects unpursued. Miollis and Tournon had not cleared the Pantheon; the Fontana di Trevi was still running in too small a square, and the "galleys" were not anchoring at the foot of the Aventine. Nevertheless the emperor's "good works" would have been enough to do honor to several pontificates. In justice it must be said that the imperial eagle would have to crown many creations that were entirely Napoleon's. Rome is indebted to him for its splendid cemetery, Campo Verano behind San Lorenzo fuori le Mura, for markets, for hospitals, for workhouses. How many palaces were restored with French money, from the Quirinal to the Chancellery that became the Palace of Justice, from the Capitol to Monte Citorio and the Colosseum! How many streets were carved out, broadened, straightened, how many green oases were created in the city, how much foliage came to adorn the stones of the ruins! The French planted many trees all along Rome's great arteries and in the gardens. There had been hardly any before their arrival; the Romans took very little interest in planting them, no doubt because they did not like them (they plant only obelisks, Canova told Napoleon). The French are very fond of trees, like all the northern peoples, Stendhal observed: they do not need the shade twenty times in a year, but they cling to this taste "out of the instinct of that race of men born in forests." And on April 1, 1812, the *Journal de Rome* said that "France does not intend, perhaps, to leave in marble the city that she found in brick; she plans to leave in flowers a Rome that she found in fallow, and to plant lawns where the sparse grass fed the flocks of the convents."

The most beautiful imperial achievement in this sphere was the development of the Pincio. It was conceived, executed, and accomplished by France alone, and at her cost alone. And yet this French achievement has the grace that is peculiar to things Roman, that matchless mixture of nobility and simplicity imbued with a light and tender melancholy. On the flank of the hill where the gardens of Lucullus stretched, the charming terraced walk unfolds its flowered slopes. From the great balcony a splendid setting of foliage and stone dominates the dazzling panorama of the city; the glowing Roman twilight drenches it in that warm light that made an artist say that, in order to paint such a landscape, "one needs a palette full of gold." The delightful gardens, which blend with those of Villa Medici, were laid out by Valadier. Broken by lawns and paths of rose laurels, adorned with statues, fountains, and little lakes, they are jeweled with the most beautiful umbrella pines in the world. Louis Madelin said that the Pincio gardens were an integral part of Rome and that it is difficult to believe that they became so only relatively recently, and through foreigners. In fact, Pius VII was to return from exile just in time to impress the seal of his arms on this French achievement. Roman chauvinists were to lose no time, however, in the composition of pompous inscriptions in marble to ascribe all the other accomplishments of the imperial government to the pope.

ROMAN LIFE UNDER IMPERIAL RULE

Unable to compel the population of Rome, the Empire sought to seduce it. Miollis and Tournon applied themselves to this endeavor with all the more zeal because it was in complete accord with their own aptitudes and tastes. As we have said, their good will was only poorly rewarded. The mass of the people never gave in. Not once could they succeed in arousing its enthusiasm. When Rome celebrated Napoleon's wedding to Marie-Louise, the French thought that they found indications that the people enjoyed the concerts and the bonfires, and that the nobility had sulked less than usual at the receptions at the Capitol; and they flattered themselves that this indication would be the prelude to a broader acceptance. Nothing of the sort followed, and the birth of the king of Rome was to be a sharp challenge to the progress that was supposed to have been observed.

But the forthcoming arrival of Caesar's son in the world had been abundantly utilized for propaganda purposes. By dint of saying it to the Romans often enough, the French agents had persuaded themselves that the heir to the empire would be greeted like the Messiah. Nevertheless his birth, announced on March 25, 1811, by the Quirinal cannon and the bells of three hundred churches, aroused neither enthusiasm nor even curiosity. Norvins had an interesting explanation for this apathy: "The Romans," he wrote on April 10, "are not demonstrative." And, since the official celebrations were held "without joy or trouble,"—that is, in the midst of the dreariest indifference—this same Norvins was to conclude, on a note of disenchantment, that "the public spirit is not inclined to celebrations" and that in Rome there was no "electricity." It was hardly worth the trouble of having lighted so many candles, burned so much gunpowder, and expended so much imagination, to say nothing of the creation of the flattering allegorical ballet in which the new Romulus was handed over to Rome, whose personification for the occasion was the very beautiful Pauline Bonaparte.

As for the *Te Deum* sung for the first time in St. Peter's, it was miserable, the basilica's singers having gone on strike under the leadership of their conductor, the most illustrious *maestro*, Nicola Zingarelli. There was a sparse audience aside from the official world and soldiers assigned to attend so that the naves would not be altogether empty. The balls were similarly disastrous. Of the two thousand guests invited to the Capitol, fewer than four hundred made brief appearances. The ball in the Quirinal gardens, illuminated *a giorno* (like daylight) with an orchestra in every bush, brought a rush of cards of refusal "like a plague of grasshoppers." In short, Rome refused to be amused except at carnival time. The French were to rack their brains to give these traditional celebrations their character of a universal rejoicing bringing the people and the patricians together in a common pleasure. But, while the carnival became more splendid and more noisy with every year, this was chiefly because that fulfilled a deep need in the people, a pull of nature that could be resisted only with difficulty. Besides, the carnival was in no way regarded as a French festival, so one could take part in it without giving up one's political opposition, even if the oppressor was paying the musicians and the illuminators. In any event, once again the maskers would toss their confetti at the beautiful ladies whose flowered carriages cut their furrows through the decorated streets. *Lazzi* and laughter would mingle as before. And it was to become acceptable even that the French should add the reinforcement of their liveliness to the rejoicings. They were to take part in great numbers, and officers of high rank were not to be behindhand "in assaulting mysterious masked ladies with gallant speech" (from a letter of Tournon to his family). During Lent, the Romans were as assiduous in attendance in the huge naves of the basilicas as they had been before the usurpers' arrival, delighting in those "voices made angelic by means that were anything but human." After all, they felt, sacred concerts were in the Roman tradition, and the French had nothing to do with them. Nonetheless it was the French who were paying for the singers and the candles.

Similarly, it was acceptable to go to the theater, making oneself the excuse that this was an exclusively Roman business. The excuse was poor, given the fact that it was the French administration that hired the actors—who were excellent—and paid them. Certain great ladies had no illusions on this score, and they refused to renew the leases on their boxes. But Miollis' agents made them listen to reason, and all of good society allowed itself to be persuaded; behind it, the burghers and the artisans trooped into the theaters in greater number than ever. Light plays were given in the Clementino theater, more substantial comedies in the Valle, dramas in the Argentina. The populace thronged the puppet shows in the Pallacorda.

Nevertheless the people had not, as they say, "learned a thing or two." It took what pleasure was going, but it was still on guard as far as the French were concerned. This was not always true among the patricians, who have always been the least tractable element in Roman society. Intransigent in the field of politics, Rome had increasingly abandoned itself to the usurpers in the social sphere. At first the lovely ladies entered the official drawing rooms "like victims dragged to be sacrificed." For a long time they remained aloof, but the love of pleasure that was so natural to them finally conquered. In the end they surrendered "to the sound of violins." How could they have resisted the waltz, that new dance that the French had introduced in Rome, or that other immeasurably seductive innovation, champagne? At official parties, which were bathed in truly royal splendor, everything was conducive to pleasure and to flirtation. Romances flourished. The merger of Rome and Paris that Napoleon had so ardently desired "acquired a character of intimacy that the emperor himself had not dared to anticipate."

If the men of the upper class seemed to surrender in their turn, it was because in some cases they hoped to obtain privileges; but the majority were motivated by the fear of incurring the masters' wrath. The people could stand firm in their bitterness without any great danger. Resistance is more dangerous for the prominent; they know very well that it is at the top that lightning strikes, and they have no vocation to martyrdom. Furthermore, the fine flower of the Roman nobility flocked into the official drawing rooms because there was no longer any risk of being face to face with the French alone. Rome had in fact become the crossroads of Europe. A composite society had come into being. Rome in 1813 had fifteen thousand foreigners. Theirs was a brilliant society, for one could meet, in addition to old Séroux d'Agincourt, who was always present, St. Vallier, Mme. de Custine, Chateaubriand's friend; Paul-Louis Courier, and Mme. Récamier, who had her own salon in Palazzo Fiano without the faintest notion that beneath her feet lay the finest remnant of Roman antiquity, the Ara Pacis of Augustus. A tall young man whom absolutely no one knew had a brief love affair with a singer, Camilla: he was Lamartine. Shudders accompanied the glances directed at a man who had sentenced the king of France to death: he was Vicomte Paul de Barras.

THE END OF THE "COMEDY"

If the French government could flatter itself in the setting of this cosmopolis that it had won over at least a part of the Roman aristocracy, its campaign of seduction had completely collapsed with respect to the other social classes.

Every year the priests had grown in their hatred of the excommunicated persecutor—a prudent hatred, without manifestations, but continuously impregnating minds. The middle class was still profoundly opposed to French rule, and its venomous gossip did its best to foment popular discontent. As for the people, while they agreed to enjoy the carnival, they had repudiated nothing of their hatred, and conscription, which sent their sons off to be killed for a cause that was not theirs, sharpened resentments that were fed on the misery of daily life. For the workshops had closed, and the stagnation of agriculture was complete. There was one epidemic after another. The exile of the cardinals and the closing of the convents had taken the bread out of the mouths of the vast horde of idlers whom the old order had accustomed to a life of parasitism. Official benefactions were far more parsimonious than those of the church. Men died of hunger as they watched the French burn good English merchandise—clothing and food—that had been illegally smuggled in and then seized by the government. "People in rags sat on the steps of palaces where the nobility, in harlequin and goddess dress, danced with the oppressor and ate his ices" (Madelin).

Hope of liberation was born with the invasion of Russia. The Muscovite, the whispers said, would cut off Bonaparte's head. The government replied to these rumors with spectacular celebrations of the victory: the Moskowa, the entrance to Moscow. But the *Te Deum* was sung in empty churches; solemn parades were greeted with shrugs. The drawing rooms were deserted, and a vast silence spread over Rome. In vain the authorities tried to draw red herrings, issued more and more optimistic announcements, increased the demonstrations of prestige. Rome was like ice, awaiting the collapse that it now took for granted and knew to be near. It could not be kept in ignorance of the defeat in Russia or the breakdowns in the imperial machinery. When "the end of the comedy" seemed to be at hand, insubordination appeared: payment of taxes was evaded, conscripts refused to obey, seditious posters were put up, Tournon's announcements were torn down.

The concordat of January 25, 1813, forced out of the pope, who was to delay only briefly in repudiating it, was regarded as a capitulation by the emperor. The Holy Father's return was awaited. A host of priests who had lived in hiding or abandoned their robes emerged. The prefect of Rome wrote to his family: "The people has abandoned itself again to its hopes."

On December 18 the last resort of a government with its back to the wall made its first appearance in Rome, at Piazza del Popolo: the guillotine, or, as the Romans called it, *"il nuovo edificio* (the new building)." It was too late; the sinister apparatus no longer frightened anyone, least of all the bands of robbers who were now operating at the gates of Rome and whose activity had acquired an insurrectionary character. In January, 1814, the English advanced to a point within ten hours of the Capitol, and their agents were already flooding Trastevere with propaganda leaflets. Rome was without defenses. Murat, king of the Two Sicilies, having joined Austria and England in the coalition that was to bring down the empire, found the time opportune for the annexation of the papal states to his kingdom. Tournon was one of the first to leave Rome. Miollis withdrew to Castello Sant'Angelo, but he was driven out by famine.

French domination had ended. Murat's lasted only a few months. Napoleon's rage exploded at the thought of this traitor prancing through "his beloved Rome," and reigning at the Capitol. He preferred to return Rome, as he put it, to "the degrading rule of the church." So he sent back to Rome the old monk who, without the help of men, had conquered him by his firm resistance.

Pius VII arrived at Porta del Popolo on May 24, 1814. At his entrance Rome was illuminated as no city had ever been: the shabbiest huts of the smallest alleys had their lamps. Rome had already forgot its Napoleonic experience when, thirteen months later, it got the bulletin that announced the disaster of Waterloo. This startling document is preserved in the Napoleon Museum in the house on Lungotevere in which Conte Primoli, who was related to the Bonaparte family, assembled a priceless collection of mementos of the imperial era.

DRAWING THE BALANCE

Napoleon had ruled Rome for five years with scarcely any result other than acquiring the reputation of being Antichrist in a city for which he had all the weaknesses of a lover. He had failed with it because, in his acute desire to seduce it, he had become its brutal oppressor. Yet he had sent men of great talent to woo it; Rome had consistently rejected and denigrated the work that they had carried on with love. As firm against seduction as against compulsion, Rome had remained unshakably papal in heart and mind.

Nevertheless, despised on their arrival and unpopular as long as they remained, the French were to leave Rome with their heads high and to leave behind them a memory that has never ceased to grow greater. No one was to be touched when they left. At no time were they to be the targets of the anathemas and the threats that had accompanied their sorry predecessors of the Year VII. Pasquino himself was somewhat to mute his satiric edge in judging them. Except for the stupid tirades of a few irresponsibles, it seemed, from the city's moderation in its supreme moment and from its silence, that Rome was offering to these men of good faith the tribute that is the due of unfortunate courage. In spite of prejudices and antagonisms, public opinion recognized that Miollis had comported himself as a soldier full of rectitude and profound goodness, that Tournon had been a gracious and decent administrator. Their collaborators had shown proof of surprising qualities: after an era in which one could get nothing from a public official without bribing his mistress or his confessor, they had proved honest and conscientious. Loving Rome like their own country, they had done more for the city in five years than other governments had done in a century. Although they had been able to carry through only part of their master's tremendous projects, they were leaving behind them restored monuments, new streets, beautified areas. And they had brought ancient Rome back to life.

That is why the shadow of Napoleon I always hovers over Rome, in spite of his faults and his failure. It was not in vain that, as he had promised to do, he inundated the beloved city with "the benefits of civilization." Many of his innovations have survived, however little they might have conformed to the old Roman spirit. "Having known the felicity of managing Caesar's property for a moment, he had the tremendous virtue of managing it better than any of the provinces that destiny put into his hands." That is Louis Madelin's appraisal of his work, in a masterly book from which we have barely departed and from which we have borrowed much. What is more, if Napoleon had no other claim to its gratitude, Rome would be obliged to forgive him much because, to his last breath, in spite of scorn and rebuffs, he was consumed for Rome's sake with one of those "loves of the mind" from which one never recovers.

CHAPTER 30

THE ROMAN RESTORATION

ROME RETURNS TO ITS TRADITIONS

In his exile Pius VII had proved the strength of his spirit. As a prelude to the work of reconstruction that he was about to undertake, he practiced forgiveness of sins and forgetting of offenses. When Roman noblemen came to him to apologize for having compromised themselves with the usurper, he replied: "And We? Do you suppose then that We have no fault with which to reproach Ourselves?" Thus in large measure he prevented the revenges and the reprisals that are usually the currency of restorations.

As was natural, the policy of Pius VII tended toward the reconstitution of the old order that the French occupation had overthrown. But the old pontiff was able to guard against a short-sighted spirit of reaction. On many points, instead of making a flat reversion to the errors of the past, he was content to adjust to the new situation created by the innovations of the French: thus, instead of abolishing the Napoleonic Code, he limited himself to giving it "the Roman collar." Nevertheless, papal Rome returned to its former structure: the Inquisition was re-established, the Society of Jesus regained its privileges, the Jews who had scattered throughout the city were sent back to the ghetto.

The pope was especially concerned that the reaction should be accomplished in men's minds; he strove to give back to the Roman people their habits of the past and the savor of their former life. Every square acquired a platform from which priests preached the return to tradition. In order to draw crowds to these open-air missions, indulgences were promised to whoever attended. Often the Holy Father appeared at them in great pomp. He also increased the blessings of the multitudes from his window, receiving endless ovations. Great celebrations were organized by the papal secretary of state, Cardinal Consalvi, who had a very acute sense of decorum and was a master at creating an atmosphere of pleasure in the city. Hence his popularity was tremendous: he was called the Siren of Rome.

The celebrations of Cardinal Consalvi were matched by those that the senator of Rome lavished on his subjects. Prince Corsini gave this office a special luster. He was one of the rare Roman patricians who had managed to hide their precious gold and silver from the revolutionary looters. He gave the people festivals worthy of the Renaissance. Fireworks displays, illuminations of the whole Capitoline Hill, abundant refreshments, generous distributions of ices—nothing was missing. A magnificent party drew a thousand guests to the Capitol; the bronze wolf, the symbol of Rome's permanence, was in the center of the honor guests' table. The square had been sumptuously decorated. On another brilliant occasion, the two basalt lions in the square of the Ara Coeli disgorged wine for two days. Another time, two fountains in the Forum were turned to the same use. The throng refreshed itself so thoroughly at these miraculous fountains that the papal *sbirri* had to disperse it with bull whips.

These indications make it clear that Rome had returned to its old traditions. The way of life that had been so pleasant before the French came to disturb it was completely re-established. The sponge was passed over an unpleasant page of history, and the French occupation and even the pope's exile were forgot. The inscriptions that commemorated the good works of Napoleonic France had vanished. There was talk even of abolishing street lighting because Miollis had initiated it. On the other hand, the *fleur-de-lys* had blossomed again on French properties. An inscription placed in the church of St. Louis of the French promised indulgences to anyone who would pray for the king of France. The convent of Trinità dei Monti still has its historical gallery of French mementos: there is no sign of Napoleon I, as if he had never existed.

THE MUSEUMS / THE FORUM EXCAVATIONS / THE VATICAN GALLERY

One of the measures promulgated by Pius VII on his return from exile was to order the filling up of the excavations that Tournon's engineers had made in the Colosseum in order to clear the steps, the *vomitoria,* and the corridors. This move was regarded as a condemnation of the French archeological researches, and the whole world's "antiquarians" were grieved by it. In reality, all that interested the Holy Father was the restoration of the Stations of the Cross that had existed in the amphitheater for centuries and that had been damaged by the excavations. Pius VII was so little opposed to the discovery of Roman ruins that he himself had opened the way to excavations during the first part of his pontificate. And without further delay he was to continue the work of the French with interest and even with enthusiasm. On his orders, Cardinal Consalvi had estimates prepared for the general clearing of the Forum; a plan was published that set a timetable for the work. It was begun by "cleaning up" the projects already begun, which the precipitateness of their departure had caused the French to abandon in great disorder. It was then that the great granite basin that Comte de Tournon had uncovered was moved to the Quirinal square.

The first excavations by Pius VII led to very important discoveries. The unearthing of the left-side stairway and the wall that supports the three columns of the temple that was believed to be that of Jupiter Stator showed that it was in fact the temple of Castor. In a nearby area the discovery of round foundations led to the identification of the temple of Vesta. Excavations in the temple of Concord similarly revealed its name, which until then had not been certain. Other discoveries included the stairway of Constantine's basilica, fragments of six red porphyry columns, parts of the gigantic statue of Domitian; Via Sacra was cleared at several points and the temple of Saturn was completely dug out.

An international association of archeologists offered to assume all the costs of the labors, but Pope Pius VII refused because he wanted the enterprise to preserve its specifically Roman character. But he did not discourage individual investigations, and the French ambassador, Duc de Blacas, was able to conduct several in the Forum: in the temple of Castor he identified and traced the substructure that supported the temple's *cella* and the three columns unearthed during imperial rule.

Among the most important restorations ordered by Pius VII that of the arch of Titus must be listed; it was carried out by Valadier, and it gave rise to many disputes among the learned. Some argued that Valadier had demonstrated taste and skill beyond all praise and had restored its severe grace and the original harmony of its lines. Others found the incorporation of apocryphal elements into the original an inexpiable profanation. Listen to the vehemence of J.-J. Ampère: "What is there to be said of the 'restoration' of the arch of Titus? We know that the Jews shrink from passing under this arch, the triumphal monument to the capture of Jerusalem; I felt almost the same repugnance. To the curses that they address to the emperor who built it I add my own against the architect who restored it. What a profanation it all is!"

Pius VII did not restrict himself to unearthing the monuments of ancient Rome. He was also responsible for restoring order to the Roman museums and for their considerable enrichment. In the Capitoline Museum there are hardly any other signs of his generosity than the marble slab that celebrates it. In effect, he confined his efforts in this museum to transferring to it the busts of the famous men of Italy that had accumulated in the Pantheon. The pope's labors were directed chiefly to the Vatican, where he established the Chiaramonti Museum, which occupies part of Bramante's gallery, and the Braccio Nuovo (New Wing), for which the large gallery was built—more than two hundred feet long and about thirty feet wide—that divide the Belvedere courtyard. It is in this gallery that enchanted Stendhal (he said of its architect that he was the last man of talent in Rome) that one can see, not far from the famous *Nile* (from which so many ancient and modern statues of rivers are derived), the admirable statue of Augustus that is the most beautiful speciment of great official Roman art.

In addition, Pius VII assembled a great number of Egyptian and Greek antiquities in the octagon of the Belvedere, and it was he who was responsible for the creation of the Vatican's picture gallery. Until then the popes had had no picture collection of their own. Rome's painting museums were its churches, which had been partly despoiled of their masterpieces for the benefit of France under the Directory and the Empire. When these canvases returned from Paris after the Napoleonic disasters, Pius VII added them to the Vatican collection. This was its origin; today it houses works of secondary interest among the paintings of the greatest masters of every age. Pierre de Nolhac* said that the finest

* Nineteenth- and twentieth-century art historian and curator of Versailles.— Translator.

work of art that is to be seen there is not hung among so many famous paintings: it must be admired from the balcony placed on the axis of St. Peter's: "the dome of the basilica surges out of the pines, under the guard of the cypresses, in the splendid setting of the gardens. It is a unique vision of harmony and peace."

While Pius VII's work in city development is important, some of his achievements are not unanimously appreciated. He found that some people were grieved enough to complain of the damage done to the ancient physiognomy of the city by the renovation of the Corso into a broad and almost straight avenue. In order to attain this result, it had been necessary to sacrifice an old section of picturesque stalls, and a few crumbling shacks to which certain associations were attached. The old lovers of Rome did not gladly suffer these minor mutilations, just as they had not liked the clearing of the Forum and the "unintelligent" excavations that, according to them, robbed the ruins of their poetry. They would have preferred to keep their city whole, to preserve the superannuated charm of its abandoned quarters, its deserted monuments. Such tastes are certainly respectable, and even, in some ways, they can be shared; but city planners' work would become impossible if they had to respect them blindly. Certainly Pope Pius VII cannot be ranked with the iconoclasts or the vandals. There were to be others who would give the purists more serious cause to weep than he.

PIAZZA DEL POPOLO / THE ROMAN PEOPLE'S CLOCK

In any case, the completion of the Pincio promenade and the beautification of its gardens brought the pope only compliments, as did the final renovation of Piazza del Popolo. Valadier gave the square its definitive form, achieving one of the finest compositions in Rome. The gate that leads into the great road to the north had been set into the ancient rampart by Vignola and enriched by Bernini for the entrance of Christina of Sweden. The church of Santa Maria del Popolo had been built in the second century on the presumed site of Nero's tomb, and the Egyptian obelisk had been erected under Sixtus V. The two churches of Santa Maria in Montesanto and Santa Maria dei Miracoli that frame the entrance to the Corso "in eminently scenic fashion" are of the baroque period. Valadier succeeded in a marvelous and delightful amalgamation of so many disparate elements. He surrounded the huge square with two hemicycles decorated with fountains, sphinxes, and statues. Thus made elliptical, and crowned on one side by the greenery and the foliage of the Pincio, Piazza del Popolo acquired a unity in which the styles of all the ages, from the Egyptian to the baroque, agree and harmonize. The architect's virtuosity assuredly had a great deal to do with the result, but it is no denigration of his talent to recall once again Rome's remarkable capacity to fuse all the centuries in its magic crucible.

Another project carried out under Pius VII had an especially fortunate result, out of all proportion to the extreme modesty of the effort that it required. The triangle formed by the stairways of the Ara Coeli and the Capitoline were still cluttered with wooden shacks and all kinds of rubbish. Pius VII cleared all this away in 1818, and this simple mainte-nance measure opened an entirely new vista on the double peak. The church and the Capitol, which had seemed to be separated, were now joined in a whole made more majestic by the divergence of their accesses.

We should not leave the church of the Ara Coeli without pointing out that Pius VII—undoubtedly to the consternation of the champions of the picturesque—relieved it of its famous clock of the Roman people, which had governed municipal life. It had existed since 1412, placed on the left of the entrance door, above the round window. Although it had been put into the care of a winder whose assignment was hereditary, it had stopped running in 1705 and resisted the best efforts of all the specialists. Its replacement had to be accepted as inevitable, and a new clock occupied the place in the middle of the façade that can still be seen. It had cost the municipal officials three hundred crowns. Unfortunately, the clock balked almost immediately. After a series of repairs, its replacement too was deemed inevitable. But it had been observed that in every city of Italy the campanile of the town hall was adorned with a clock. As a sacrifice to this fashion, the new clock of the Roman people was installed in the bell tower of the Capitol. Thus the façade of the Ara Coeli was deprived of the only decoration that remained to it. Still unfinished, it preserves the church's appearance of "an ancestress in a homespun dress," an appearance that is given the lie in magnificent fashion by the interior richness of the struc-ture. With its frescoes by Pinturicchio, its Cosmati ambos, its admirable tombs, one of which is by Donatello, its twenty-two antique columns in blue marble from the temple of Juno Moneta, Santa Maria in Ara Coeli is in fact one of the richest churches in Rome.

Finally, in 1822 Pius VII erected on the Pincio the slender obelisk that

Emperor Hadrian had placed on the tomb of his favorite, Antinoüs; it had been discovered in the sixteenth century near Porta Maggiore. While the Roman population was grieving over the serious illness that was to prove fatal to the pope a month later, a terrible catastrophe befell the most ancient basilica of Christendom: St. Paul Beyond the Walls was completely destroyed by fire on July 16, 1823. The basilica had no ceiling: above their heads the faithful could see the huge girders of cedar of Lebanon that supported the roof. It was this heavy wood, dried out by the centuries, that was ignited by burning coals falling from the small portable stove being used by a workman repairing the roof. The fire was discovered in the middle of the night; the monks entrusted with the care of the church had left their convent in order to escape the summer heat; the fire brigade arrived too late. By daylight all that was left of the venerable edifice was a heap of smoking ruins. Pius VII had been abbot of St. Paul and he had always retained a tender predilection for this basilica; out of kindness, he was allowed to die in ignorance of the cataclysm. Curiously, the destruction of the basilica allayed a fear that had arisen: the great nave was ringed by the long procession of portraits of all the popes since St. Leo in the fifth century. In some cases these were the only original portraits in existence. By the time of the fire there was no room left for the portrait of Pius VII's successor, and this was regarded as an omen of the early end of the Holy See.

Another superstition worried the Romans. A proverb said: *Non videbis annos Petri* (You will not see Peter's years). It owed its origin to the fact that no pope since St. Peter had occupied the papal throne for twenty-five years. If such a thing should occur, it was thought, Rome would be totally and immediately destroyed. Whether this was actually so might have been demonstrated if Pius VII had lived until March 14, 1825. That was why there was not too much sorrow at his death, which occurred many months before the fateful date.

ANOTHER INTERVAL OF AUSTERITY

The liberal policy of Pius VII had made it possible for a certain revolutionary spirit to grow. There had been political assassinations during his reign: *carbonarismo*,* originating in Naples, had penetrated the

---

* The *carbonari* (literally, charcoal burners) were a secret political society that owed its name to the fact that originally it held its meetings in the woods: its major objectives were the triumph of liberal political ideas and the unification of Italy.—Translator.

Papal States and poisoned the civil service, the nobility, and even the clergy. Disturbed by the progress of this new spirit, the conclave of 1823 wanted to choose a pope who would react vigorously against sects. Its selection was an aged, ailing prelate ("You are electing a corpse," he told his colleagues), amazingly old; but he was to devote an equally remarkable energy to the service of reactionary ideas, so that he would be accused of having spent the six years of his pontificate in steering the ship of St. Peter's against the tide of the age.

The great goal of Leo XII was to make Rome once again the city of religion that it had been in its glorious past. He believed that the growth of piety should be accompanied by a forceful reform of morals, which, it should hardly be necessary to say, was not to everyone's taste. From the start of his reign, the pope incurred the violent discontent of his subjects by forbidding them all traffic with cafés and restaurants, which were just the things that they particularly enjoyed. Under various names there was a great variety of them in Rome. Luxurious establishments were favored by the elite: the best known was the Veneziano, at the corner of Piazza Sciarra where the savings bank is now. It was the meeting place of Rome's wits, and the most splendidly attired ladies did not scorn to go there for their ices. The Ricco, on the Corso, was the scene of endless card games interspersed with knowledgeable discussions on the finer points of archeology and history. The artists and men of letters who live near Piazza di Spagna or Via del Babbuino preferred the Greco, in Via Condotti, which still exists. Its back room, called "the omnibus" because it was so narrow, preserves the effigies of the most assiduous of its old customers, and it is watched over by eminent men to whom its tradition is dear and who see to it that it does not become a shop or a beauty parlor. Aside from these elegant resorts, a host of taverns provided their clients with those light, aromatic wines of the Castelli Romani, which, we have been assured by Horace and Seneca, do not intoxicate. The Romans had an age-old habit of spending long hours in these establishments, where they found the best occupation of the leisure that their city's social structure afforded them with such inexhaustible generosity.

It is easy to understand the consternation of the good folk when the ordinance of March 24, 1824, forbade them these places of delight. Henceforth the tavern owners could communicate with their customers only through a narrow barred aperture. "He who wished to drink could do so only outside and on his feet." Holes were cut into the doors, which were permanently closed, so that the papal police could see to the strict observance of the edict. The penalty for violation, furthermore, was extremely high: three months at hard labor. It should not be necessary to report that Pasquino and colleagues had a few sarcasms to deliver on the subject of these offensive restrictions. Indifferent to criticism, the pope furthered his moral reform with a series of draconian police regulations; in 1824 a butcher was sent to prison for having sold meat on a Friday. Another was similarly punished "for having raised his voice to a theater porter." Severe corporal punishment was provided for "taking another's seat" at a spectacle. The most trivial offenses were tried *ex inquisitione:* that is, under the procedures of the Inquisition, which had never been so much discussed. And penalties were inflicted at once. There was a permanent scaffold in Piazza Navone. But let the tender-hearted be of good cheer: it was used only for flogging. One innovation by Leo XII was especially unpopular among the young: anyone who followed a young girl too closely was thrown into prison and could be freed only if he married the "victim"; she was brought to him by a priest in his liturgical vestments, accompanied by volunteer witnesses, usually laughing. The wedding was held without delay, and the vows were exchanged through the bars of the cell. The parties to this forced marriage then left the prison amid the jokes of all present.

The pope's reforming zeal led him to prohibit the waltz, which he considered obscene. The governor of Rome, who was ordered to enforce the pontifical decision, wanted to know exactly what this hellish dance was. His secretaries kindly showed him. They were sober men: Don Bartolomeo Capranica was a holy monk, and his colleague was better known as the translator of Petrarch's Latin epistles than as a libertine. It is not known whether they were able completely to instruct their master. In any event, Monsignor Marco y Catalan, auditor of the Rota, governor of Rome, and a Spaniard to boot, could never believe that this was the dance that had so scandalized the pope. The ban on the waltz had another amusing effect. At the great ball in the Argentina, which was the primary target of the interdict, the orchestra played only the quadrille and the Piedmontese *monferrina,* a country dance, but throughout the evening the guests insisted on dancing nothing but the waltz despite the inconvenient rhythms. All Rome was laughing.

But, to tell the truth, Leo XII occasionally fared better with his crusade. He succeeded in purging the Roman countryside of the bandits who had infested it since the French occupation and on whom the magnanimity of Pius VII had had no effect. Leo XII employed the technique of strength. His troops captured several hundred robbers, whom they executed after summary trials. Intimidated by this, the others returned to the path of righteousness. It was high time, for the success of the jubilee of 1825, which would soon begin, was already threatened by the plague of brigandage. In former times pilgrims never hesitated to brave the dangers of the roads: those of the nineteenth century were less courageous, or less strongly upheld by their faith. Now, having no longer to fear armed attack, they flocked in great numbers to earn their indulgences; for one year Rome was "the great establishment of spiritual exercises" that the pope wished it to be. All that was to be seen in the city was processions; all that was to be heard was sermons, canticles, and homilies. The theaters were closed; profane street spectacles and all social gatherings were forbidden.

The lovers of pleasure had got no benefit from the rule of austerity that the pope had imposed on them. To them the end of the jubilee was an opportunity to throw off its constraints. They exerted every effort to restore to their city—in spite of the objections of Leo XII—the carefree atmosphere that under Pius VII had made it the meeting place of exiled princes, artists, and *dilettanti* from the whole of Europe. In short order a whole generation of young cosmopolitans—poets, writers, artists—flocked to Rome as to an inexhaustible source of inspiration. Rome became, as Byron called it, "the city of the soul." The theaters flourished: it was the great age of marionette shows, in a carriage house belonging to Palazzo Fiano. Roman high society and the Eternal City's illustrious guests thronged the drawing rooms of the old palaces. Chateaubriand, when he became France's ambassador in 1828, made sure of the embassy's participation in this brilliant world of fashion.

The pope was too busy putting down and undermining the conspiracies of the "liberal sects" to have time to combat the trend toward liberation that was growing day by day in his states in spite of all his homilies. Rome, in truth, seemed completely indifferent to the complots against papal rule that endlessly succeeded one another. It must be pointed out that there were very few *carbonari* in the urban population, which had little liking for revolutionary ideas and was highly devoted to the pope's government. That does not mean that Romans approved all its decisions; the speaking statues had never been more acerb in their satires. They were reinforced by a marionette character, Cassandro, whom Rome had adopted as its spokesman and who shouted the most impertinent sallies from his little stage.

By sheer bad luck, Leo XII died in February, 1829, at the height of the carnival, and all festivities were canceled; Romans were thoroughly angry at this pope, who had never been popular. The speaking statues vented their ill humor. "You have played three low tricks on us, Holy Father," one of them said. "You accepted the papacy, you lived too long, and you died during the carnival and must be mourned." Although his illness had been a long one, the pope's death, as custom dictated, was attributed to his doctor. "On February 10," a speaking statue said, "a remarkable phenomenon occurred: a terrible lion was killed by an ass."

The excavations that the previous pope had begun were vigorously furthered by Leo XII. He had Valadier prepare a new plan, much more ambitious than that of Pius VII, that combined Tournon's projects; they called for nothing less than the total clearing and the complete exploration of the whole area lying between the Capitoline and the Colosseum. The pope launched numerous projects that led to interesting discoveries. The podium of the temple of Concord was completely cleared, as well as Constantine's basilica. The old ground level between the arch of Septimius Severus and the temple of Concord was brought to light; many inscriptions on the Basilica Julia were discovered. If not all the undertakings were carried out with great speed, it was because a new and important one was engaging the attention of the pope's architects: the rebuilding of the basilica of St. Paul. A papal bull had called for the collaboration of the whole of Christendom, and money had poured in from everywhere in the world. King Charles X of France had sent a private contribution of sixty thousand francs.

Leo XII's successor, Pius VIII, reigned only twenty months. He was a mild, inoffensive man, rather torpid. The story of his papacy was summed up by Pasquino: "Those who wish to inform themselves on the eighth Pius should be told that life went on as if he had not existed." He took one step, however, that was enough to earn him the people's thanks: he repealed his predecessor's edict on the sale of beverages, and Romans joyfully found their way back to the taverns. Another event of his reign was the earthquake that shook Rome in 1830. The ball above the dome of St. Peter's rocked back and forth so frighteningly that a Spanish monk who was inside it died of fright. This incident made the whole population of Rome tremble at the thought that the city's most beautiful monument could be shattered by one of those tremors that occurred so often.

THE RISE OF LIBERAL OPPOSITION

Under the long reign of Gregory XVI (1831–46) liberal ideas were to make huge strides throughout the peninsula. The pope, who disliked political problems, never gave any attention to this intellectual ferment. As for the Roman population, it took no interest in it whatever, and so we are relieved of the necessity of discussing its development. Conspiracies were already beginning within Rome, however, but these were still limited to a few patrician palaces. The people were so alien to the questions that were being discussed in secret that it did not understand the reasons why shots had been exchanged in the café in Piazza Colonna, claiming as their sole victim Prince Piombino's porter, who was watching the excitement. The whole aim was simply the overthrow of the papal government, and the instigator of the plot was Prince Louis-Napoleon Bonaparte himself, who was ostensibly living quietly in Palazzo Ruspoli with his mother, Queen Hortense. Romans were far more interested at that time in the new Apollo theater, which was just beginning its career. An incident that occurred there might have opened their eyes. During a performance of an opera called *The Arabs in Gaul,* the audience burst out in frantic applause when the baritone, Lalli, eloquently delivered these two lines:

> *Beneath the steel of vengeance*
> *The evil sect will have to fall.*

It was not the artist's talent that was being applauded. The liberal clan had read a political meaning into the words; the evil sect from which vengeance was to be exacted was the Roman Curia. Other indications of the same character went completely unnoticed by the good folk.

It could be stirred by nothing less than the great epidemic of 1837, which interrupted the "perpetual carnival" that life in Rome had become at that period. Many persons died of cholera in spite of sanitary precautions. No better effect was obtained from processions, public prayers, and novenas. In addition, a few poor devils suspected of spreading the epidemic "by diabolical means" were torn to pieces.

His mind resolutely oriented toward the past, the pope was as hostile to material progress as he was to social change. Everywhere in Europe a new means of transportation, the railroad, was being developed. Gregory XVI considered it an invention of the devil, and he took great pains to save his states from it.

On the other hand, he was deeply devoted to furthering scholarship and archeology. It was during his pontificate that the letters of Marcus Aurelius, the history of Dionysius Halicarnassensis, several of Cicero's orations, and many other ancient texts were discovered. The learned prelate whom the pope had appointed to head the Vatican library (he knew fifty languages) found the method that made it possible to read palimpsests. More Roman antiquities were being rescued from obscurity. At Porta Maggiore the archeologists unearthed the monument of the Aqua Claudia, which stood like a majestic arch of triumph. It was also the time of the discovery of the famous mausoleum of Eurysaces, which showed that the bakers' methods had changed hardly at all since the last years of the Republic. The reign of Gregory XVI was marked, too, by the methodical exploration of the catacombs and the creation of the Lateran museum. The Vatican museums were enriched with Etruscan and Egyptian antiquities. The excavations in the Forum were accelerated after the pope's dismissal of his chamberlain, who had not devoted all the requisite zeal to their execution. The Basilica Julia was uncovered; so was the street that ran from Caesar's temple to the Argiletum; for the first time the topography of the Forum could be physically re-established. Archeologists hailed these undertakings, and drawing-room conversations never tired of the ancient inscriptions and customs: Stendhal said that no one could take part who did not know the eighteen ways in which sculptors dressed Minerva's hair.

Sound regulations for the excavations enabled the government to control the passion for searches that had taken possession of all circles. It was forbidden to remove anything that was found; the pontifical state gave itself first option in cases of sale, whether the object was a large piece, a small artifact, or the site of an ancient structure; it was thus that the Baths of Caracalla, in particular, became a papal property.

Gregory XVI was so concerned for ancient monuments that he even had them cleaned. This innovation infuriated the stubborn champions of the poetry of ruins. Once again Ampère made himself their spokesman when he told the restorers: "The Englishman who said: 'The Colosseum will be a fine thing when it is finished' should be satisfied now: it is like new."

Work having been energetically carried forward on the reconstruction of St. Paul Beyond the Walls, the transverse nave of the basilica was consecrated in 1840.

CHATEAUBRIAND AND STENDHAL IN ROME / AMPÈRE

After the death of Gregory XVI in 1846, Rome was to acquire a new physiognomy from the French revolution and occupation and the birth of a liberal Italy. Before we leave this period of Roman life in which customs and morals derived wholly from the social and political order maintained by the government of the popes, we should like to evoke the memories of two French visitors who knew and loved the city of that time, Chateaubriand and Stendhal. Both were in love with Rome, though they were lovers of very opposite kinds, the one solemn, always bored, the friend of the dead, more at home among phantoms than among men, and the other enthusiastic, a lover of music and dancing, always ironic and paradoxical.

Having first gone to Rome in 1803 as an embassy secretary, Chateaubriand was to return twenty years later as ambassador, and each of his short stays held an important place in his life. Two tombs commemorate them. At St. Louis of the French, the illustrious viscount, who did not want his name carved on his own sepulcher, wrote it in large letters on the tomb of his frail and tender friend, Pauline de Beaumont. He did the same thing on the flat gravestone that he erected for Nicolas Poussin in the church of San Lorenzo in Lucina. And there is so little modesty in the epitaphs that each of them seems a tribute that he was paying to himself. There are memories of the melancholy René everywhere in Rome: in the Colosseum, where one evening he went with the dying Pauline de Beaumont; at Sant'Onofrio, his favorite place, where he wanted to be buried; at Villa Medici, where he would go to sit with the young French artists; in that Palazzo Simonetti on the Corso where, as a splendid and improvident *grand seigneur,* he was determined to eclipse the memory of Cardinal de Bernis, who had so brilliantly represented Louis XIV there. For him every ruin was conducive to grave and melancholy meditations. In quest of traces of the past, he himself dug up his property of Terra Vergata in that Roman Campagna that inspired him to such beautiful funeral songs.

Stendhal too is to be found in all the great places of Rome, but his walks most often took him into the network of twisting streets in the old quarters whose kaleidoscopes and contradictions and contrasts he loved. Stendhal spent much time in Rome, especially during the period when he was the French consul in the little town of Civitavecchia, which bored him immeasurably. A long list has been made of the houses in which he lived; it goes from official palaces (he stayed in the Quirinal in 1811) to the humblest inns. In 1816 he was in Via di Pietra, a few steps from the stock exchange, in the house of a certain Signora Giacinta who rented him a very suitable room for two francs. In 1823 he was in the Cesaris' house, then in that of a pharmacist near San Lorenzo in Lucina. In 1827 he lived on the Pincio in a hotel that he recommended thus: "You must sacrifice eighty francs and have a beautiful view of Rome for two months: you will have something to remember all your life." Later he was to rent quarters from the "late Cardinal Lante's" mistress near Palazzo Gaetani, in Via delle Botteghe Oscure. He was to be one of the first customers of the Minerva hotel, which a Frenchman, Joseph Sauve, established in Palazzo Conti and which is still one of the most pleasant in Rome. His last Roman residence was at Via Condotti, 48, where a pair of boots was stolen from him.

It would be unjust not to include here something about another Frenchman, J.-J. Ampère, the historian, who loved Rome so much that he became a foreigner to his own country. He had gone to Rome with Mme. Récamier, and Stendhal had been his first guide. "As a result of living in Rome," Sainte-Beuve wrote, "and of possessing it in its antiquities, in its ruins, he felt completely at home in it and, in his thoughts, he lived in it in all its epochs." He wrote an invaluable *Histoire romaine à Rome* (*Roman History in Rome*). Those who criticized him for the length of this work were told that "one does not leave Rome at will, and he had too much enjoyment in living there, in such good company, to be in any hurry to leave." Ampère more than anyone else was enchanted with the delights of that life, "lazy and busy, tranquil and varied, quiet without boredom and full without fatigue, that one leads in Rome and only in Rome." He admitted that it was possible not to enjoy Rome, but that anyone who had enjoyed it for a while would always enjoy it more and would not be able to leave it. It is common knowledge, indeed, that it is only after weeks and months that one learns the secrets of Rome's harmony and begins to be impregnated with the charm that emanates from it. Pope Gregory XVI always expressed this sentiment to foreigners who came to take leave of him on their departure from Rome. He said *addio* to those whose stay in the city had been short; but to those who had lingered long he said *arrivederci*.

ROMAN MANNERS AND MORALS

To describe Roman life as Chateaubriand and Stendhal knew it would be to repeat what we have been able to observe of it in the eighteenth century. After the agony of the French Revolution and the Empire, the pontiffs had dedicated themselves to the restoration of the old order, and they had completely succeeded in it. The form of government was what it had been before the storm; the social structure was identical. In manners and morals there were no differences other than those very minimal ones that the inevitable changes of fashion had imposed on a profoundly traditionalist people with very little taste for innovations. But the lower classes had fallen in love with a new festival season that was very quickly to become a time of indulgence comparable to the carnival. A remote descendant of the Bacchanalia, the grape harvest of October was devoted to rural pleasures. Every day the populace went out into the country, packed into rustic vehicles and singing on the road. Then there were picnics: the older merrymakers drank the new wine while the younger generation danced the *saltarella* to the music of improvised orchestras. In the evening the crowd flocked to Villa Pamphili and Villa Borghese, where dances were held on the lawns. Loyal to the immutable Roman tradition, ladies of the highest degree mingled with the throngs of Trasteverini.

These feasts of heathen aspect, however, did not seduce Romans from their religious solemnities. The wind of impiety from French "philosophical" ideas had blown away and left no trace in men's minds. The liturgy was still as faithfully followed, the processions drew the same crowds of spectators. Indeed, the abstinences of Lent were observed with greater devotion: women wore black dresses and abstained from having flowers at their bosoms; "girls in love economized on their glances." Everyone went to confession, even, we are told, the confessors.

This ardor of repentance did not deter Romans from expressing their satiric minds against the hierarchy. Gregory XVI, whom nature had unhappily equipped with an almost monstrous nasal appendage, was constantly caricatured and sung about. He himself had a lively sense of humor: he was said to have had a particular fondness for tripping his cardinals so that they would fall into the Vatican pools. The busiest arena of political satire was the marionette theater in Palazzo Fiano, where the pillars of society were harshly dealt with. There was no prior censorship; the director was merely thrown into prison when his actors had spoken too strongly. In consequence, this gentleman had learned to supply ample wine to the spy sent to keep an ear on him.

As before, there was the most intimate simplicity in relations with men of the church. In a country where the government's finger was in everything and everyone was primarily concerned with evading the established rules, they were logical and obliging intermediaries. Accustomed for centuries to enter all the houses and take a hand in family matters, the priests had acquired the habit of paying special attention only to the political opinions that they heard. But they completely ignored the superstitions that were spreading among the people and that often led to dangerous divagations. There were even some parishioners who criticized Jesus Christ for having waited thirty years to be baptized in the Jordan. Strange interpretations of episodes in the Gospels were current: the fact that Christ had driven the moneychangers out of the temple was taken to mean that Jesus would forgive any sin except the profanation of a church. The madonna was always regarded as the most powerful resident of heaven. There was not a square, not a street corner without an image of her. The neighbors kept candles and lamps burning before it; at night it was rare that there was not a group at prayer beneath it.

Throughout December the Roman night was troubled with the sound of the bagpipes that were serenading the street-corner madonnas. These were played by the *pifferari*, the pipers, peasants clad in sheepskins who came down from the mountains of the Abruzzi to perform this pious office. They were richly rewarded by the population; the Roman who did not have a novena said for the *pifferari* before the nearest madonna was looked at harshly by his neighbors and his parish priest. The novenas enabled every bagpiper to go back to his village with enough money to feed his family for six months. As for his benefactors, they simply lost a month's sleep. They were lucky if they were not thanked for their generosity with uncomplimentary verses about themselves and, especially, their wives; for the *pifferari* were not averse to seasoning their melancholy chants with a joke or two.

The piety of those days sometimes took a touching turn; at night, when the little bells of the last sacrament were heard in the street, everyone got out of bed and put a lamp in his window: closer and closer God's passage was illumined. Popular devotion turned to the saints for help in matters in which each had his own jurisdiction: San Rocco was the protector against the plague and St. Emidius was the guardian against earthquakes; St. Bibiana cured headaches, St. Blasius cured throat ailments, S. Andrea

Avellino prevented attacks of apoplexy, St. Anne helped women in labor. Side by side with the great liturgical ceremonies there were strange heathen usages. Vendors of fried fish decorated their stalls on St. Joseph's day. As the Easter rejoicing drew near, there were lard statues of Moses outside the pork butchers' shops and butter madonnas in grottoes of salami. On New Year's Day an exhibition of edibles transformed the great stair of the Ara Coeli into a vast sideboard loaded with everything that could make people greedy. On Easter Day there was great ingestion of *zuppa inglese* (literally, English soup; actually, what the British call trifle) to the glory of the Holy Church. St. Catherine's day was celebrated with the lighting of the first fires in the houses. Throughout Christmas week, the smallest children were allowed to preach in front of the *bambino* of the Ara Coeli. It was neither Infant Jesus nor St. Nicholas who brought them their toys on Twelfth Night: it was *La Befana,* a kind of gift fairy, who had no connection with any religious notion, even though her name also means Epiphany.

It would seem that holidays were celebrated in the intimacy of the family more than had been the case in the previous century. Family life had unquestionably become closer. The institution of the *cavaliere servente* was no more than a memory among the upper classes; in the rest of society marriage was once more a serious matter. The enforced marriages imposed by Pope Leo XII had changed the behavior of the young, who now did not go beyond a kind of very innocent flirtation. What was called *fare all'amore* was a complex ritual of furtive glances and clandestine little presents. Mothers watched their daughters like hawks, for the boys, "less out of considerations of morality than out of the possessive instinct," would marry only virgins. The status of spinsterhood, which was much despised, was very early arrived at, even before "putting the cap on St. Catherine," which in the French idiom means "reaching the age of twenty-five unmarried." If it did happen that a seducer took advantage of a too-trusting girl with false promises, this was an affront that had to be avenged in blood by the entire male contingent of her family. The use of the knife was still a very much honored custom. It was employed in situations in which the Frenchman would be satisfied to use a fist or a lawyer. "Not to take vengeance by murder," a traveler said, "is in certain cases like being slapped in Paris without doing something about it."

The custom of the dowry, which was general, made marriages easier. Every year, as we have seen, the pope gave dowries to twelve hundred girls of good conduct. In each lottery drawing the five winning numbers bore the names of penniless girls, each of whom received a dowry of fifty Roman crowns. All the orders distributed dowries; the municipality and the convents followed the example. If there were some priestly doings behind a wedding—and this was often the case—the girl could be sure of dozens of crowns to ease her road to marriage.

This was only one of the aspects of the Roman benefactions that continued to support a whole population of idlers. The nobility still felt an obligation to perform works of charity; rank and tradition forbade any haggling on this point. Every year the city government distributed three hundred thousand crowns in doles; the orders and the monasteries were generous; the Holy See poured a river of gold into the charitable institutions. In this city where the highest good was to do as little as possible, asking sufficed to keep one alive. Every street corner had its public scribes busily writing out entreaties, "hat on head, umbrella beside them, and stone holding down their paper." These entreaties were addressed to the palaces of the rich, but burghers and workers too were beset and besought from every side. All, rich and poor, obeyed the precept of charity according to their means. "Ostentation," Edmond About observed, "may have something to do with the practice of so expensive a virtue, but the natural goodness of the people plays its part."

Whatever the motivations, the result of this system of benevolences was the existence of a large number of people in Rome who had neither incomes nor trades. Abstention from work had preserved its ancient dignity. Stendhal reported that he had incredible difficulty in finding a barber who would shave him every morning. "Work," he remarked, "is a thing that is so much against nature for a true Roman that he must have extremely exigent reasons for inconveniencing himself every day." This unconcern, moreover, led to strange habitudes. Nothing is more illustrative of this than the distribution of mail at that time. The addressee was supposed to give the postman a *baiocco,* a small copper coin, for each letter that he brought. Therefore this civil servant would simply take a table in a tavern, spread the mail on it, and let anyone who wished take what he wished, provided only that he leave the *baiocco* and that everything be claimed quickly. In other words, anyone could take any letter that appealed to him: it never occurred to the postman to ask whether he was indeed the addressee.

There were many other curious twists in the customs of the time. Without lingering over their picturesque catalogue, we shall limit ourselves to mentioning—because of the light that it throws on the religion of the Romans and on the frivolity of their violent and demonstrative souls—the curious usages invoked for the obsequies of princes or dignitaries. When one of them died, his body, in ceremonial vestments, was placed under a canopy and surrounded by a constellation of candles. Whoever cared to do so passed before the bier to pay his respects or to satisfy his curiosity. As for the relatives, they had all fled the house at the first sign of the threat of death, for the dying "had the evil eye." The deceased was attended, therefore, only by hired mourners. In the stately procession that carried him to the grave there were neither kin nor friends. The various religious orders supplied bereaved in variable quantities dependent on the standing of the deceased. They were joined by his servants, his carriages, his horses, and, if he had any, his dogs, "if they felt like going," as a malicious observer put it.

Roman life had hardly altered its tone or its pace since the pontificate of Benedict XIV. The Holy Father and the cardinals ruled with fatherly mildness over a people that was their property. Princes and noblemen were handled with special care; there were a host of minor jobs to occupy the middle class. The *popolino* (the "lower classes") was treated kindly, helped, entertained. In return for this it was subjugated to its masters, and its respect for social inequalities was genuine and deep. In a word, the papal states were governed pleasantly "by gentle, courteous men whose education, cloth, and faith predisposed them to indulgence."

CHAPTER 31

THE STORMY YEARS

THE SIEGE OF ROME (1849)

An organization so strong as to have withstood the thrust of the revolutionary spirit was to be swept away by the vast aspiration to national unity that was penetrating every part of the peninsula. Among all the events that were to lead to the unification of all the Italian states under a common banner, we shall confine ourselves to those whose theater was Rome.

In 1846 the election of Pius IX, who was to occupy St. Peter's throne for thirty-two years—and thus to give the lie to the sinister predictions that menaced reigns that were too long—was hailed by Romans with delirious enthusiasm. Never had a pope been so acclaimed. He seemed to be the champion of that new order whose advent was assured by an irresistible tide. In fact, Pius IX amnestied political prisoners and authorized the publication of liberal newspapers (until then there had been only one newspaper in Rome, *Il Diario di Roma,* an official sheet of the utmost wretchedness) and the establishment of political clubs; the effect of all these measures was to bring out into daylight the demands of the "sects" that had until then been clandestine. Each concession to modern ideas was followed by new demands.

The Parisian revolution of February, 1848, abruptly loosed on all Europe the storm that had been threatening for so long. Agitators, most of them foreigners in Rome, provoked artificial sentiments. Rome resorted to more illuminations, a greater flood of processions in the streets. But the pope had to accept the assistance of a cabinet in which the lay element was predominant; parliamentary government was instituted in the Papal States. It was in vain that Pius IX sought to dam the revolutionary tide by calling Conte Pellegrino Rossi to the leadership of the government; the assassination of his minister compelled him to flee to Gaeta. Anarchy took over in Rome, where a junta organized the election of a constituent assembly. This election was nothing but a sham. The most cynical pressures had been exerted on voters in order to impose a democratic system on a population that did not want it. It was given to understand that "the friends of tyranny" would reveal themselves by refusing to go to the polls and that they would be sentenced to prison. Orchestras were set up near the voting places, and music lovers were immediately assaulted by vote recruiters, whose arguments took the form of very explicit threats. Except for the poor devils who were dragged to the polls by fraud or duress, the majority of the voters were composed of the paid hirelings of the revolutionary demonstrations. The disorder of the voting lists made it possible for them to vote as often as they liked in various polling places.

The fraudulently elected constituent assembly hastily proclaimed the Republic in February, 1849. The scenes of 1798 were re-enacted: the Phrygian cap was placed once more atop the obelisk in Piazza del Popolo; liberty trees were planted, innumerable orations were delivered, there were parades in the streets to the sound of revolutionary songs. Scenes out of the carnival flaunted their indecent parodies even in the churches. The pursuit of priests and monks began; murders multiplied. Still conservative and faithful to the church, the Roman people disapproved of the republican movement, but the people were no longer the masters of their own destiny: patriots pouring in from all the Italian states, with Giuseppe Garibaldi among them, inflamed public opinion with their stormy demonstrations. The international rabble that revolutions always attract kept up a sustained but counterfeit excitement. A host of publications established for the purpose fanned the demagogic flames.

At the height of the agitation, a French army commanded by General Oudinot disembarked at Civitavecchia. Louis-Napoleon, prince-president, had decided on armed intervention with the dual purpose of eliminating Austria from the resolution of the Italian problem and of rescuing the Holy See from the impious faction that was imposing its revolutionary despotism on Rome. The French troops reached the outskirts of Rome on

April 30, 1849, but they could not dislodge Garibaldi's militia from Villa Pamphili, to which it had retreated. This setback induced the government in Paris to seek a compromise with the republican authorities. But the work of its emissary, Ferdinand de Lesseps, an engineer suddenly turned diplomat, was counteracted by Oudinot, who intended to compel a strictly military solution. Matters rapidly approached a point at which a siege of Rome seemed the sole possible course.

The city prepared to endure it amid indescribable confusion and agitation. The assembly was holding a permanent debate on the best possible constitution—utterly laughable at that moment. The volunteers who had flocked to the defense of freedom were running the city, hunting down the priests, who, hardly eager to offer themselves to sacrifice, had for the most part changed their clothes. Palaces and wealthy houses were sacked, confessionals were torn out of the churches to become fuel for bonfires, and the cardinals' carriages were seized for use in barricades. Only the pretence that the pope's carriage was the state coach of the *bambino* of Ara Coeli saved it. As for the adversaries of the Republic, who constituted the vast majority of the Roman people, they did everything possible to make themselves inconspicuous. Some, as a cover, took part in the demonstrations and parades, whose violence they endeavored to restrain; all provided refuge for the priests; some established secret communications with the French command and spied out the strength of the city's defenses for it. The Roman garrison had a strength of some twenty thousand men, most of them foreigners of the most varied origins. It included a number of students, more impassioned by Italian unity than by democratic ideology; its main force lay in Garibaldi's legion, ill equipped but disciplined and courageous under the command of a fearless leader always dressed in a large white *pancho* that served as a rallying point, like Henri IV's plume in another era.

Hostilities began on June 3, 1849, with a general battle in which much heroism was expended on both sides. Four times the Italians vainly tried to dislodge Oudinot's forces from their positions; the battle raged within Villa Pamphili. Among many others, the new Italy honored the charming poet Mameli and the Dandolo brothers, all Venetians "with magnanimous hearts"; Nino Boxio, Garibaldi's close companion, and the young and attractive Morosini—all of them fell in this bitter fighting. For Rome's defenses had to be battered down one by one, during a thirty-six-day struggle that was made the more difficult by the courage of the defenders and the determination of the French command to avoid destruction.

While Garibaldi was leaving the Eternal City with the remnants of his heroic army, the French entered it, on July 3. All power was then consolidated in the hands of the military authority, pending the pope's return. In effect the French officially restored the papal government, abolished the Republic, closed the political clubs, and prohibited political newspapers and organizations.

FRENCH OCCUPATION AND THE PALATINE EXCAVATIONS

Pius IX did not return to Rome until the excitement seemed totally extinguished. Thrilling popular demonstrations welcomed him on his arrival on April 12, 1850. French troops provided a guard of honor from the Lateran to St. Peter's, and their presence was a wound in the hearts of those Romans who had supported Garibaldi. Discontent increased when the sovereign pontiff went to visit the French wounded in the hospitals and to bless the French graves at Villa Pamphili; some critics professed to see in these acts "an insult to the defenders of the Republic." Inscriptions appeared on the doors of several churches: "Priests, the martyrs' blood cries out for vengeance." This ill temper could not have serious consequences. French forces were to be kept in Rome for twenty years without any notable incidents attributable to the occupation. Remaining in its very vast majority faithful to its pontiffs, the Roman population could feel only sympathy for those pontiffs' protectors. The French expeditionary corps became highly popular, and members of all ranks were treated as friends. The cardinals and the chapters of the basilicas in rotation gave magnificent banquets for the members of the general staff; the nobility and the upper middle class opened their drawing rooms wide to French officers; at the tables of the Caffè Moro ladies and gentlemen of the middle class could be seen enjoying their sherbets in the company of the "charming conquerors." As for the people, their natural good humor resulted in very cordial friendship with the soldiery. The attitude to the officers was a mixture of familiarity and respect: an officer was addressed as *Eccellenza,* but this was immediately followed by the intimate rather than the formal second person.

There were still, of course, some reservations, by which the ill will of the republicans sought to profit. But only very rarely was the shadow of a threat cast over the Romans' affability and helpfulness. And then they themselves meted out prompt justice to anyone who made an uncomplimentary remark. If a strolling singer began to bawl out a song offensive to the French, the crowd assumed the duty of escorting him to the nearest policeman. Reciprocal courtesy always governed the relations between Romans and Frenchmen: congenial exchanges of every kind were the order of the day. It was in imitation of French ways, in particular, that the Roman aristocrats—who had always been riveted to their carriages— adopted a taste for strolling through the tree-shaded Pincio. On the other hand, the French could never surrender to the Roman habit of the siesta during the hotter hours of the day. This was the period that gave rise to the Roman adage to the effect that "only dogs and Frenchmen walk in Piazza di Spagna in the heat of the day."

The services that the French performed for the pontifical government were on the whole highly appreciated: they organized its police force and built its little army from scratch. Above all, they kept it safe from political storms. In a much different sphere, Rome is the debtor of the French occupation for the transformations of the Palatine. Following the example of his great predecessor, Napoleon III, who had a passion for Roman history, took a great interest in the resurrection of ruins. Until then the Palatine's imperial palaces had been overlooked by the archeologists' investigations. The methodical excavations launched by Napoleon III and paid for by him (he had bought the Farnese gardens) uncovered entire rooms and a tremendous number of ornaments, frescoes, and statues. They marked the start of the improvements that have made the Palatine a great garden of commingled stones and flowers.

CITY PLANNING UNDER PIUS IX / THE CATACOMBS OF ST. AGNES AND THE RECONSTRUCTION OF THE BASILICA OF ST. PAUL

Under French protection, the paternal government of Pius IX did much to assuage the unhappy memories of the anguish of the revolution. A merry pontiff whose good humor was proverbial, he enjoyed gossip and wit, and he liked to take part in the life of his people. He would stroll through the streets of Rome without escort and casually enter an artist's studio or a modest artisan's workshop. If on the way, Fernand Hayward said, he met "a priest carrying the last sacrament in procession to a sick man's bedside, he left his carriage, took a lighted candle from the nearest hand, and followed bareheaded into the dying man's room." His ease of manner was so great that he could be approached without formality. Yet he knew how to defend himself against unwelcome requests. Besieged by a group of old women with lamentations over a rise in the price of olive oil, he told them off: "Tongue is high too—your tongues, old gossips."

He gave great attention to the excavations that were going on in almost all parts of Rome. It was during his pontificate that archeologists discovered the catacombs of St. Agnes, where on April 12, 1855, during his first visit there, he was almost killed. A plank gave way beneath him and everyone was plunged to the bottom of the crypt in a confusion of rubble and dust. No one was hurt; even the pope's vestments were undamaged. There was great haste to proclaim a miracle and offer a *triduum* (three-day service) of acts of grace. In gratitude to St. Agnes, Pius IX ordered the restoration of the monastery and the church, where a fresco depicts the accident.

Modern progress was introduced into the Eternal City under Pius IX in the double guise of its two most notable achievements: railways and street lighting. Until his last breath Gregory XVI had denounced the railway as the demon's work; in one stroke his successor authorized the construction of four lines in his states, and work was begun on the central station in Rome. In 1854 gas lamps were installed on the major arteries by an English company. At the same time, the Monti quarter was cleaned and provided with sanitation, and a large street was cut through to join the upper city with the lower city. It bore the Holy Father's name (Via Pia) until it was made the present Via Nazionale. A bold plan called for the digging of a tunnel under the Quirinal at the very point where it was to be executed much later.

In 1854 Pius IX consecrated the great basilica of St. Paul Beyond the Walls, which had finally been completed after thirty years of arduous labors. All that had escaped the fire was a few tombs, parts of the triumphal arch, and the pontifical altar, the work of Arnolfo di Cambio. Even the great bronze gate had disappeared with the ancient mosaics and the single set of portraits of the popes. The whole structure had had to be rebuilt as a new edifice. In 1854 the basilica looked as it does today. Its five tremendous naves and the forest of Corinthian columns created "a thrilling effect of space, of calm, and of majesty"; but the ostentatious luxury lavished everywhere without true nobility accentuates the impression of coldness in a creation of which it has been said—not without considerable exaggeration—that it looks more like a railway station than a temple.

In the same year as the consecration of St. Paul, Pius IX erected the column of the Immaculate Conception in Piazza di Spagna, copied from the one that Pius V had placed before Santa Maria Maggiore. This was the last monument of note that was to be erected in his capital by a pope.

SOCIAL CHANGES

Restored as a center of international life that was a magnet for the illustrious, the artists, and the writers of all Europe, Rome had recovered its carefree air. The social structure, however, had been modified in several respects. The great dignitaries of the church had lost some of their influence in the government; in most of the congregations, even in that of the Holy Office, high positions were held by mere laymen. The result was a certain financial constriction for the higher clergy. The nobility had suffered in the political upheavals; many of its members, compelled to emigrate, had found their palaces sacked and their assets scattered when they returned. The heavy taxes that the municipality had had to impose in order to remedy the damage of a calamitous past had borne heavily on the patriciate. The more opulent the princes had been in the past, the more they had been affected by the disasters of the times. Hence the great palaces that had been witness to so many prodigalities now seemed abandoned. Their ruined owners limited themselves to a few rooms on the upper floors. Solitude had invaded the huge state drawing rooms; the vast courts where horses had once pranced were deserted: grass grew among the paving stones. The Roman aristocracy of this time, Taine said, was like "a lizard nestled in the armor of an antediluvian crocodile, his ancestor; the crocodile was beautiful, but he was dead."

Many of the ruined noblemen still strove to put up an appearance: some borrowed servants, wearing livery that did not fit them, to ride behind their carriages; others had to rent vehicles for their daily rides down the Corso, which were still a sacred ritual. The expedients adopted in those days by great names in order to keep alive have occasionally left unexpected traces. When the Marchese di Lepri could no longer pay his cook, he granted him the right to set up a small food shop in the courtyard of the marchese's palace in Via Condotti, and this soon became a *trattoria* that gained a reputation—La Lepre, which competed with La Rosetta in the Pantheon square, Il Buco in Piazza delle Coppelle, and even "the inn of the three thieves," so called because it had three owners. The big sign of La Lepre is still there; it shows an eagle in pursuit of a fleeing hare; this is the Lepri family's coat of arms.

There was a great contrast between the huge deserted palaces and the charming new or remodeled houses in the elegant quarters near Piazza di Spagna and the Pincio. Practical in size, pretty and glowing, these houses in Via Sistina, Via Condotti, or Via del Babbuino were the setting for a life that was at once comfortable and pleasant. Who lived in them? A new class of minor nobility and rich burghers, both of which groups tended more and more to unite. The minor nobility had suffered less than its superiors in the torments: in addition it had absorbed what was left of what were called "the country merchants." Rome, which had previously had neither commerce nor industry, had possessed a prosperous agriculture ever since the disappearance of banditry and the draining of the marshes had made it possible to exploit the plains that surrounded the city. Intelligent men who came out of the rural *plebs* had risen to wealth through farming. Having bought the properties of the great families in distress, they had often purchased their ancestors at the same time when, as Edmond About said, it pleased them "to be descended from Livy's heroes rather than Cato's slaves." In this way or through honest marriage, they had given the middle nobility a transfusion of new blood, at the same time bringing it closer to the upper middle class. That group, from its side, had found in the liberalization of customs the opportunity for a similar rise. The progressive accession of laymen to power had placed many middle-class men in important offices. Having become judges, consistorial lawyers, or high officials, they had come to represent a new class, the *generone*, in contrast to the *generetto*, which consisted of the less socially acceptable and less rich middle class. The *generone* was a typically Roman group, deeply imbued with its brand-new tradition; completely faithful to the pope, this class was to be infinitely slow in accepting the Savoy monarchy. And yet it was from its ranks that in the end the best servitors of the new Italy would emerge.

The situation of the lower middle class, the artisans, and the shopkeepers had changed hardly at all and was still quite unstable. Physicians were still searching for unwilling patients; the minor lay employees of the government existed very miserably in spite of the extremely low cost of living.

As for the proletariat, nothing had changed in its habits and its customs.

Still greedy for spectacles and processions, it did a "magnificent business" with the benevolent institutions with which Rome swarmed more than ever. The census of 1871 was to show that, in a population of 200,000, there were 70,000 perfectly healthy adults who did nothing. Thus it was clear that the proportion of idlers had not much changed from the one-third of the population estimated by de Brosses. Another traveler, Taine, has given us a psychological portrait of the Romans of this period that makes them exactly like their compatriots of a century before, feature for feature: "They are skilled at dawdling, chatting, being satisfied with the little that they have, enjoying a good cool salad, savoring a glass of very pure water drunk in a good light. In addition they have a basic good humor; they believe that one must spend one's time pleasurably, that useless anger is stupid, that sorrow is a disease; their temperament thrusts toward joy like a plant toward the sun."

THE END OF THE TEMPORAL POWER

While Roman life remained calm and peaceful under Pius IX, the political situation was growing constantly worse. The old dream of unification was threatening the temporal power. The Roman problem had come into existence. In vain the Curia was to entrust to General Lamoricière, the hero of Constantine, the command of the army that it had improvised, whose largest unit, composed of French legitimists, was that battalion of papal Zouaves whom the Romans insisted on calling *i soavi* (the soft). This elite force was garrisoned in the ancient Pretorian Camp, which, in an interesting reversal, was now occupied by unpaid volunteers who had come to defend the pope. This handful of young French royalists, despite its heroism, was defeated in 1860 when it attempted to oppose the Piedmontese troops marching on Naples. Thereafter the Holy See lost ten of its provinces, and the kingdom of Italy gained them. This kingdom already existed *de facto,* and Victor Emmanuel I was its sovereign. All that was left in issue was whether he would receive Rome as his capital with the pope's consent. Pius IX held out with all his strength against pressures and plots, but the disaster of Sedan robbed him of his last support. The French expeditionary corps had sailed from Civitavecchia on August 4. Victor Emmanuel took advantage of the reverses of the French to send against Rome an army to which the papal troops offered only brief resistance. On September 21, 1870, after a four-hour artillery bombardment, General Cadorna's *bersaglieri* opened a breach in the Aurelian Wall near Porta Pia and entered Rome. Through that breach the soul of the ecclesiastical and patrician citadel fled forever. The idea of a nation had made such rapid strides that the Romans greeted the Piedmontese as victors. In the plebiscite of October 2, only 46 voters refused their consent to the unification of Italy. The affirmative votes totaled 40,785. The Holy Father alone remained to protest against the sacrilegious blow of which he was the victim. The temporal power of the popes was dead, and henceforth the history of Rome would be commingled with that of the kingdom of which it became the capital.

The bombardment of Porta Pia had damaged the statues of St. Agnes and St. Alexander, which Pius IX had placed there in order to make the gate into an arch of triumph dedicated to these saints. Removed to the marble workshop of the basilica of St. Paul, the statues lay in oblivion there for sixty years; they were not to return to their niches until July 21, 1929.

CHAPTER 32

MODERN ROME

THE CAPITAL OF ITALY

On September 20, 1870, the papacy lost Rome. The popes were to seal themselves into the Vatican, calling themselves prisoners there; conscious of their mission to all peoples, they would refuse to accept the government of any one of them.

The city then had 240,000 inhabitants. In spite of the great projects that had been undertaken in the old papal citadel since Sixtus V, and although it was adorned with a huge number of churches, palaces, and monumental fountains, it could meet neither the needs nor the aspirations of a modern capital. There were too many sordid quarters; too many dark little alleys still had a cutthroat air; "the millennial and venerable filth" of *Roma sporca* (dirty Rome) was scattered over too many unsanitary areas. In order to modernize its new capital, the royal government was to devote itself to huge works of city planning, without hesitation at the sacrifices that radical changes require. It would be impossible, of course, to contend that all the projects that were supposed to contribute to the health and prosperity of modern Rome were successful. Some demolitions of gardens and green areas, in the beginning, were executed only out of hatred against Pius IX. Torn down and burned in 1897, the picturesque ghetto vanished, and the local color of Trastevere, disemboweled and shrunken, is hardly more than a memory. It must be conceded, however, that in general these public works were carried out with good judgment and the resolve to keep the inevitable mutilations to the minimum.

New quarters were constructed, one in the old Prati di Castello, between the Vatican and Piazza del Popolo, and the other on the Esquiline, round the station and Santa Maria Maggiore. It is quite true that their broad, airy streets have been cut through princely gardens that were the admiration of travelers and artists. Many have been broken into smaller plots, and Villa Ludovisi has vanished completely with its palace and its casino, the last echo of the Renaissance, its park and its cypress woods, one of the city's lungs and its most graceful jewel. Every friend of Rome wept at its disappearance. But, since an aristocratic quarter had to be built, it could not have been better placed than in these ancient gardens of Sallust. The construction of the Tiber quays has caused—to no good end—the disappearance of the curious port of Ripetta and its marble stairway, of which Piranesi made such beautiful drawings. This project also mutilated the Farnesina's gardens, whose little laurel woods no longer are reflected in the river; it destroyed the quiet shaded road at the foot of Villa Madama, the classic promenade of the cardinals. Encased now between two identical walls, the Tiber lost the little beaches that alternated with the graceful houses fronting on the water. One of the great beauties of Rome is gone. But it was essential and urgent to save the riverside quarters from periodic floods, some of which, like that of 1870, caused veritable disasters. Could people be left to drown so that others might still have the pleasure of strolling where Raphael and Leo X had walked?

In order to build streets that would meet the needs of modern traffic, it was necessary to tear down many houses in the very heart of the city, but no one touched a palace or a church, or any structure that offered real esthetic or historical interest. The sinuosities of Corso Vittorio Emanuele testify to the determination to respect the monuments of the past. The street bends to the left in order to avoid the Chancellery Palace, then to the right for Palazzo Massimo and Palazzo Vidoni; it makes a sharp turn to accommodate Palazzo Strozzi. When two important buildings stand face to face, like Palazzo Altieri and the lateral façade of the Gesù, or Palazzo Venezia and Palazzo Doria, there is no hesitation in doubling the street back on itself to the point of strangulation.

In order to scale the cliff of the Quirinal, it would have been possible to cut into the hill at the cost of a few palaces and a few churches. But the planners rejected this easy way; they graded the Viminal and, on the steepest slope, they built a winding road that turns on itself twice in order to respect the ancient edifices. It was the same spirit of regard for the past that governed the planning of Via Cavour, which runs through the ancient Suburra, and of Via del Tritone, which became the major business street in Rome. The problem that was created by the insurmountable obstacle of the Quirinal was resolved by the great white tunnel that runs beneath the gardens of the palace. The courses of the Archeological Promenade and the great circular boulevards at the bottom of the old hills respect what deserved to be preserved.

Who would deny that, in spite of precautions, the majesty and the charm of papal Rome have been impaired? Such misfortunes are the law of life, and this was not the first time that Rome had seen the accomplishment of "one of those metamorphoses that signal the opening of new eras." At least, the approved sacrifices have had their compensations in the discoveries to which they have led. Emile Bertaux contended that the creation of new streets was as valuable to the study of ancient topography as any official excavations directed by scholars could have been. It is a fact that Rome's archeological riches have been singularly enhanced during the period of modern improvement of the ancient city. The bed of the Tiber has not yielded the sheets of gold with which, according to a legend of the Middle Ages, it was paved, or the seven-branched candlestick, or the spoils of the temple of Jerusalem. But it has disgorged a great treasure of coins, carved inscriptions, instruments, and statues. On the bank, in front of the Farnesina, an elegant summer house of the early imperial period was found, with its stuccoes and its paintings, finer than those in Livia's villa. The tunnel through the Quirinal led to the discovery of works of art as precious as the marbles unearthed during the Renaissance, and in such great number that they filled the whole new museum in the palace of the conservators. Every day brought ancient ruins, sculptures, mosaics, bas-reliefs out of the ground. Idlers used to divert themselves by going to watch the excavations. While it is only fair to give the Roman city administration credit for the care with which everything was handled, it is entitled to no glory for its discoveries, since one has only to dig anywhere in Rome in order to find important relics. The city is built on five or six layers of ages, and no one can say that there is not a statue or a temple beneath his feet. We have mentioned the fortuitous discovery of temples of the republican era at Largo Argentina and of the Ara Pacis of Augustus beneath Palazzo Fiano. It was because of a defect in the Rome-Naples railway that in 1917 the Pythagorean basilica of Porta Maggiore was discovered. Even today, when a house is torn down, one can never be sure that it can be rebuilt, because there may be treasures in its foundations.

The new Rome established residence in the monuments taken from the pope: the Quirinal became the royal palace, the Montecitorio palace was remodeled to house the Chamber of Deputies, the Senate occupied Villa Madama. But the young Italian state soon wanted new monuments, and, in the wind of glory then blowing, it gave them colossal dimensions and bombastic shapes. It is well known that to seek to behave with modesty and discretion in Rome is to invite the accusation of cheapness, but this fact could not excuse so many structures whose mass affords no impression of grandeur. The largest, the Palace of Justice, rivals even that of Brussels for thickness and heaviness. Bad taste was general in Europe at that time.

It is not forbidden to extend this opinion to the cyclopean monument that modern Italy has dedicated to her unification. More than 250 feet high, and invincibly new in appearance (its stone rebels at patina), the Vittoriano irreparably blocks the view of the Forum and the Capitoline. It is totally unsuited to its setting, and whatever is said out of politeness about the pride and the majesty of its lines does not convince the Romans. They are not proud of this "petrified pastry," which they also call "the typewriter"; some regret that Mussolini died too soon to demolish it. He indicated his intention of doing so, it is said, whenever he confronted its vulgar mass from the little pink balcony of Palazzo Venezia that was the tribune for his harangues. Many parts of this enormous heap of stones and sculptures are indeed remarkably bad. So audacious an undertaking would have required the genius of Michelangelo. Nineteenth-century Rome did not have a Michelangelo, or even a Bernini.

Nevertheless the House of Savoy has left some respectable monuments—the beautiful Esedra fountain, whose background is the ruins of Diocletian's baths, and also the monumental statue of Garibaldi that stands on the Janiculum looking out over the sublime panorama of the city. It is approached along the green paths of the Passeggiata Margherita; a marble lighthouse presented by Italians in America watches over the monument in honor of Italian unity.

If Rome in this period produced only monuments that testified more to its ambition that to its genius, it had at least the good fortune to enrich its museums substantially. Heir to the invaluable collections accumulated by the popes, it was able to augment them with those of the Roman princes who had been ruined by the fever for building and speculation. There had been a surge of construction as if overnight Rome were going to have a population of a million, all with money. Therefore, the huge apartment houses built at great expense and standing empty of tenants quickly lost their value. Goethe said that, "of all the disasters that have afflicted humanity, none has given posterity so much pleasure as the destruction of Pompeii." The same remark might be applied to the financial catastrophe that gave the public access to a great number of works of art whose owners were compelled to sell them. The royal government assumed the pre-emptive right that had been invented by the popes; this was how the marbles of Villa Ludovisi found their way into the Museum of the Baths and Villa Borghese was transformed into the National Gallery.

The Borgheses had needed only a few years to amass the huge fortune that bought their way into Napoleon's family. They destroyed it in a few days in an attempt at multiplying their income tenfold through dangerous speculations. The king of Italy bought their collections and their villa at a good price and presented them to the city of Rome. The Pincio promenade, which until then could be circumnavigated in ten minutes, became the incomparable creation that was to be extended farther by later works. Art and nature are commingled there to give Rome its most magical site. The broad paths and the little lanes wind through an admirable setting of rose laurels and umbrella pines. The variety of light effects, the great number of fountains, the ancient groups, and the ornamental structures give the vista softness and nobility at the same time. The busts of great men of ancient and modern times that are set along the walks make the Pincio the true Pantheon of Rome, even though here and there, as one skeptical visitor observed, one encounters "a few obscure or premature divinities." As a pendant to the Pincio promenade the city government has provided the vast *belvedere* on the Janiculum that joins the shadows of Villa Corsini and Villa Lanti.

These projects were undertaken at the same time as the exploration of the ancient places. The stones of the Palatine were laid bare; the Caesars' palaces raised their skeletal profiles against the sky; but the diggings destroyed the jewelry of flowered terraces with which the ingenious art of the Renaissance had clothed the hill.

As for the Forum, in 1884 it could be considered to have been completely dug out, and thereafter the excavations could be concentrated on reaching greater depths. As it lies before the visitor today, it is a miraculous garden. There one still feels the power of Rome and its poetry; one has the feeling of participation in its grandeur.

There is little to be said of the religious architecture of the new era, for it was to be expected that the kings of Italy would hardly rely on churches to perpetuate their glory. Roman tradition, however, was not interrupted under their reign, which saw the erection of a number of churches without any great originality (St. Joseph, St. Joachim, St. Vincent de Paul, St. Anthony, S. Alfonso dei Liguori, Santa Maria Liberatrice, etc.). The only one with an important historical association is the church of the Holy Cross, which Pius X commissioned in 1913 to celebrate the sixteen hundredth anniversary of Constantine's victory over Maxentius.

ROME TODAY

Under the impetus of the authoritarian government that was established in 1922, Rome experienced profound upheavals that made it the most modern capital in Europe. Many of the streets of old Rome became broad boulevards planted with trees; huge buildings were constructed almost everywhere; the University City attained grandiose proportions. The tremendous Foro Italico provided stadia and sports fields for the young. Oases of greenery and tranquility were provided in the promenade. The great highway to Ostia accomplished—overland, it is true—the old Roman dream of linking Rome to the sea. In many places modern apartment houses replaced crumbling old dwellings. Overflowing out of the heart of the city, they mounted an assault on the surrounding hills: broad streets were laid out on the mystic Aventine; Monteverde, covered with tall white houses, no longer deserves its name.

Without going into detail, let us note only that, while in some places these changes have resulted in the disappearance of worthwhile relics, they have more often accentuated the historic riches of the Eternal City. Many antique remnants, freed from the superimpositions of centuries, have been restored to their former greatness and their poetry. The mausoleum of Augustus, the theater of Marcellus, Castello Sant'Angelo, the Conti tower, disencumbered of their old neighbors, have been made accessible by broad roads. The Circus Maximus, cleared of the rubble that had cluttered it for centuries, has been restored to us in its ancient form.

Via del Mare connects the Capitoline Square with the theater of Marcellus. Via dei Trionfi (now Via S. Gregorio), a reconstruction of the road traveled by the triumphal *imperatores,* runs along the Palatine to reach Constantine's Arch and continues by way of the archeological promenade in the direction of the Alban Hills. A great straight avenue traverses the ancient imperial forums from Piazza Venezia to the Colosseum, so that in a single glance one can see all the places that were witnesses to the greatest history of Rome. The ancient Roman Forum is once again the heart of the city. This Via dell'Impero (as it was called at first), the masterpiece of Fascist city planning, is truly worthy of the imperial tradition. From Piazza Venezia to the Colosseum the intense rhythm of life pulses among green areas and the solemn surroundings of the great remnants of the past. Let us emphasize that now, through a kind of dictate of public conscience, these great achievements are supposed to have sprung of themselves out of the earth. At the very most, it is permissible to remark that this phenomenon of spontaneous generation occurred "during the 1930's."

But Benito Mussolini's name is splashed more than a hundred times on the great marble obelisk that he raised to his own glory and that dominates the Olympic stadium. It is only from Carrara, but just like its Egyptian ancestors it had to wait months for a favorable change in the current before it could be moved up the Tiber. In 1937 the Duce was to repeat the action of the emperors when, near the Circus Maximus, he erected the obelisk of Aksum, the holy city of Ethiopia.

The queen of imperial roads, Via Appia Antica, has been carefully safeguarded against all attempts at modernization. Protected by a *zona di rispetto,* flanked with cypresses and tombs thousands of years old, it has preserved all its melancholy nobility. The Roman *campagna* no longer bears any resemblance at all to the countryside in which Chateaubriand walked with his disenchanted memories and Poussin found his land-scapes. Cultivated and irrigated, brought to life by engineers, the broad plain has lost "that air of uselessness that made it so majestic." At the same time, while the outskirts of other capitals "have fallen to the country cottage and the tiny garden," the Roman *campagna* has kept enough of its antique pride so that the traveler responds with emotion to its solemn serenity. If he enters Rome by Via Appia or Via Aurelia, he has still the feeling "that the city is rising for him from the grave in which it lay."

The Roman problem, left pending ever since Cadorna's troops had occupied the city in 1870, was resolved in 1929 by the Lateran treaty that guaranteed the sovereign pontiff's independence from the international point of view and recognized him as the ruler of the Vatican State. This state covers fewer than one hundred and ten acres but, in addition to the Vatican, it includes the Lateran basilica and palace, the basilicas of Santa Maria Maggiore and St. Paul Beyond the Walls, and the palaces housing the Chancellery and the Congregation for the Propagation of the Faith. Outside Rome—and enjoying the same extraterritorial status as the Vatican—the popes have the great estate of Castel Gandolfo, which has been their summer residence since Urban VIII. For two hundred years the popes had embellished the pontifical villa built by Maderna. They had given it up in 1870 when they made themselves the prisoners of the Vatican. The Lateran agreements brought them back to it. Its restoration has made it one of the most splendid mansions in Italy. The beautiful arrangement of its gardens stretches out against a setting that is unique in the world, embracing, from the lake of Albano to the most distant hills, the Roman countryside and the Eternal City.

The French cemetery on Monte Mario, the highest of the hills on the outskirts of Rome, recalls the memory of the Second World War, which did little damage to the Eternal City's monuments. When the storm had passed, the young Italian Republic set enthusiastically to work on the beautification and modernization of its capital without departing from the tradition that for twenty centuries has led the Roman genius always to link the past and the present. Rome's population today is larger than it was at the height of the Empire. But it is remarkable that only one-seventh of its two million inhabitants lives within Aurelian's Wall. The development of the peripheral quarters has saved *la vecchia Roma* from the intrusions of modernism. Rome has preserved its provincial manners; in spite of its hugeness it has remained a charming little city. It seems that everyone knows everyone in its kaleidoscopic streets. And it would be most unjust not to mention the contribution that is made to this intimacy by the kindliness of its inhabitants. This people of Romans of Rome, as full of contrasts as its history, has perhaps not virtues alone. But it is a spontaneous people, good-natured, without guile. Granted that Romans love showy demonstrations and have every intention of magnifying every incident to a drama or turning it into a comedy. But, in spite of this surface exuberance, this people remains "simple in its joys and patient in its sufferings." A congenial and cordial people, it truly deserves our fraternal friendship.

Having come to the end of our overspeedy walk through the streets of Rome and the centuries of its history, we do not propose to dictate to the reader what teaching he shall derive from his visit: everyone sees Rome in his own fashion and draws his own lesson. One impression, however, is universal in every mind that is not stupid or vulgar: it is the magic that invades us in the company of Rome. This charm of Rome, this perfume of Rome that no one can forget if he has once known them, are of course beyond definition, and no alchemy could ever duplicate them. At the very most one can try to isolate the least mysterious elements.

Is Rome the most beautiful city in the world? The question is open. But it is certainly the city whose disappearance would make the greatest vacuum. It is the synthesis of the world, the pivot on which it has turned for twenty centuries. The ancient world and the modern world fill its streets with the evidences of its universality. St. Peter's statue crowns Trajan's column and the archangel St. Michael stands atop Hadrian's tomb. The Christian cross glows on the Egyptian obelisks. The "eternal walls" of which Pliny spoke are mingled with the labors of the latest centuries, the palaces are built with the stones of the temples, and the churches are peopled with "the grand army of conquered columns." The miracle of Rome is the fusion of its ancient ruins and its modern magnificences in a unique whole, as if the city were a higher entity that dominates all epochs and combines them for its own glory.

In this synthesis of civilization, everything speaks without dissonance to the spirit: life and art are not discrete domains here; one moves incessantly from the one to the other, and subjects for meditation succeed one another constantly. Every step that one takes in Rome broadens the horizon of one's intelligence. Quite apart from everything in the Holy City that exalts the soul of the believer, Rome adds stature to every man who contemplates it or studies it; petty thoughts are impossible in the shadow of the hills that have given birth to the laws of the universe. That was already known to a French visitor of the seventeenth century, J.-L. Guez de Balzac.* "It is certain," he wrote in 1621, "that I never go up to the Palatine or the Capitoline without a change in my spirit, and that there I am always filled with thoughts quite different from my usual ones. This air fills me with something great and generous that I did not at all have before." Those who do not aspire to such lofty transcendencies find

---

* A philosophical and religious writer who made great contributions to the growth of classical French prose.—Translator.

forgetfulness of cares and hurts in the lofty Roman softness. "Other cities," Gaston Boissier wrote, "make us satisfied only with themselves; Rome enjoys the unique privilege of making us satisfied at the same time with itself and with ourselves." And the hero of *Tempo di Roma* tells us that, "even when I dragged my weariness there, the city opened itself to me like a legible book of which I had only to turn the pages in order that my sorrow vanish."

It is quite sure that no place better removes us from the concerns of active life, inspires us more to a sensitive reverie that gives birth to that tranquil felicity of which Stendhal said that, when he was steeped in it, if he should be told that he had just been made king of the world, he would not bother to rise even to take possession of a throne.

The price of this intoxication is the nostalgia that is always in the luggage of everyone leaving Rome who has felt its charm, at once smiling and melancholy. Its deep and mysterious harmonies, its colorful vistas changing with the hours of the day, its streets where ideas swirl as in a sieve, the thousand curiosities aroused by thirty centuries of history, and "that kind of friendship, as if with persons, that Rome alone can give us for places and things"—as soon as we leave them, we miss them with a regret that time will not diminish. When Goethe left Rome, where he had found the great illumination of his life, he shivered at the fear of never seeing it again. Indeed, he was always thereafter to be intoxicated by that sadness: "I have not spent a single wholly happy day," he wrote in his old age, "since I crossed Ponte Molle on my way home."

All of us in the same circumstances, according to the measure of our minds, feel Goethe's sentiments. But, when we have set out on "the road to our country and the burden of our obligations," we no longer feel condemned to the lamentations of exile until the end of our days. It needs only a few hours in an airplane for us to return to the source of so many joys of the spirit and to learn again the great lesson of assuagement and balance that rises out of the stones of the Universal City.

Arrivederci, Roma!

INDEX

Jugurtha, 36
Julian the Apostate, 126, 127
Julius II, Pope, 148, 228–245, 248, 250, 255; tomb of, 234–235, 244, 273
Julius III, Pope, 277–278, 284, 338
Jupiter, temple of, 13–15, 23, 52, 58, 80, 398
Justin II, Emperor, 132
Justinian, 140
Juvenal, 23, 34, 52, 72, 99

Keats, John, 67
Kotzebue, August von, 313

Lacordaire, Jean-Baptiste Henri, 41 n.
Ladislas of Naples, King, 185
Lamartine, Alphonse de, 406
Landini, 299
Lanfranco, 309
lapis Niger, 6
Last Judgment (Michelangelo), 165, 206, 241, 267, 270–271, 273–274, 282
Lateran Concordat, 87
Lateran Palace, 98, 203, 293–296; see also Sancta Sanctorum
Latin Confederation, 5, 15
Latins, 4–5, 11
Latium, 9, 13, 16
Law of the Twelve Tables, 19
League, see Holy League
Legros, Pierre, 286, 377
Le Nôtre, André, 275, 316
Leo I, Pope, 136
Leo III, Pope, 153, 156
Leo IV, Pope, 155
Leo X, Pope, 157, 230, 233, 246–259, 260, 262, 266, 383, 398
Leo XI, Pope, 305
Leo XII, Pope, 417–420, 427
Leo XIII, Pope, 225
Lepidus, 47
Liberus, Pope, 128
Livia's House, 6, 63, 66–67
Livy, 4, 64
Lombards, 146, 152

Longhi (the Younger), Martino, 311, 337, 340, 348
Louis XI, King, 195
Louis XII, King, 219, 228
Louis XIV, King, 105, 320, 337, 338, 344, 345, 346, 423
Louis XV, King, 303, 342, 351
Louis XVI, King, 382, 384–385
Louis of Hungary, 180
Loyola, Ignatius (St. Ignatius), 282, 315
Lucius II, Pope, 120
Lucullus, 38, 60, 112
Ludovisi, Cardinal, 315–316
Ludovisi, family of, 330, 343, 361
Lupercal, cave of, 6
Luther, Martin, 236, 259, 265

Macellum, 25
Macellum Magnum, 75
Machiavelli, 228
Madelin, Louis, 367
Maderna, Carlo, 164, 307–308, 309–311, 312, 323, 328, 334, 337, 447
Maderna, Stefano, 336, 346
Madonna del Parto, 204
Maecenas, 64
Magna Graecia, 32
Magna Mater, temple of, 7, 30, 70
Malade imaginaire, le, 362 n.
Mamurra, 62
Mamertine Prison, 23–24, 77
Mantegna, Andrea, 215–216
Marcellus, 57
Marcellus, Pope, 119
Marcellus, theater of, 44, 56–57, 111, 445
Marcus Aurelius, 97–98, 112, 129, 422
Marius, 36, 39, 45, 61, 111
Mars Ultor, temple of, 51–52
Martial, 75, 87, 100
Martin I, Pope, 145
Martin V, Pope, 185, 189–190, 346
Masaccio, 31
Matella Fulvia, 39
Mauclair, Camille, 163–164
Maxentius, 118–119, 124–125, 131, 177
Maximilian, Emperor, 228

THE ARMS OF THE POPES
from 1389 *to* 1968

TOMACELLI	MIGLIORATI			
1389 — 1404 BONIFACE IX	1404 — 1406 INNOCENT VII			

CORRER	FILARGO	COSSA	COLONNA	CONDULMER
1406 — 1409 GREGORY XII	1409 — 1410 ALEXANDER V	1410 — 1415 JOHN XXIII	1417 — 1431 MARTIN V	1431 — 1447 EUGENE IV

CIBO				MEDICI
1484 — 1492 INNOCENT VIII	1492 — 1503 ALEXANDER VI	1503 — 1503 PIUS III	1503 — 1513 JULIUS II	1513 — 1521 LEO X

CARAFA	MEDICI	GHISLIERI	BONCOMPAGNI	PERETTI
1555 — 1559 PAUL IV	1559 — 1565 PIUS IV	1566 — 1572 PIUS V	1572 — 1585 GREGORY XIII	1585 — 1590 SIXTUS V

BORGHESE	LUDOVISI	BARBERINI	PAMPHILI	CHIGI
1605 — 1621 PAUL V	1621 — 1623 GREGORY XV	1623 — 1644 URBAN VIII	1644 — 1655 INNOCENT X	1655 — 1667 ALEXANDER VII

ALBANI	CONTI	ORSINI	CORSINI	LAMBERTINI
1700 — 1721 CLEMENT XI	1721 — 1724 INNOCENT XIII	1724 — 1730 BENEDICT XIII	1730 — 1740 CLEMENT XII	1740 — 1758 BENEDICT XIV

CASTIGLIONI	CAPPELLARI	MASTAI-FERRETTI	PECCI	SARTO
1829 — 1830 PIUS VIII	1831 — 1846 GREGORY XVI	1846 — 1878 PIUS IX	1878 — 1903 LEO XIII	1903 — 1914 PIUS X

DATE DUE

NOV 8